ENGLAND AND GERMANY

1740—1914

ENGLAND AND GERMANY

1740—1914

BY

BERNADOTTE EVERLY SCHMITT

New York · HOWARD FERTIG · 1967

First published in 1916 by Princeton University Press

HOWARD FERTIG, INC. EDITION 1967
Published by arrangement with the author

Library of Congress Catalog Card Number: 67-24596

PRINTED IN THE UNITED STATES OF AMERICA
BY NOBLE OFFSET PRINTERS, INC.

TO

THE MEMORY OF

MY FATHER AND MOTHER

PREFACE TO THE 1967 EDITION

It is certainly a high compliment to one's first book to have it reprinted fifty years after its first publication. When I wrote it, very few documents were available, and I had to depend on newspapers and periodicals. Today, thousands of documents and innumerable memoirs are available, most of which I have read, and while there are passages in the book one might have revised in the light of these materials, I think that the arguments I used and the conclusions I arrived at in 1916 are still valid.

October 1966   B. E. S.

PREFACE

THIS book is not entirely a product of the Great War. The Anglo-German problem first came under my notice some years ago, when I was an undergraduate at Oxford. A beneficiary of the Rhodes Trust, I was imbued with the idea of Anglo-Saxon solidarity, to promote which Cecil Rhodes founded the scholarships which bear his name. But, instead of harmony, I found discord. Some of my Oxford friends were members of the British Navy League, and from them I learned that the German navy was regarded as a menace to England's traditional supremacy of the seas. When I travelled in Germany I encountered considerable animosity to England in several places, and I saw little banks, in the shape of war-ships, which tempted patriotic Germans to make contributions for the propaganda of the German Navy League. At every turn one was made conscious of this rivalry between two kindred nations, each of which professed to fear the aggressive intentions of the other. The most contradictory statements were heard, and the stranger was at a loss to comprehend them.

In time, as I studied the problem, I collected a quantity of material from different sources and of varying value: this book is the result. I have used very sparingly the voluminous literature which has appeared since the war began, except, of course, the official documents published by the belligerent governments. Nearly all of the evidence upon which my conclusions are based was in my hands before August, 1914; indeed, the first six chapters, and the eighth, were practically written by that date, although they have since been rewritten. I have tried to present the subject of Anglo-German relations from a historical point of view, and if I have taken sides it is because the available evidence seemed to warrant certain conclusions. The book has been delayed by the severe pressure of private affairs, but the lapse of time has not essentially modified the opinions formulated before I began to write.

Several of the chapters treat of topics that have been discussed already in greater detail by other writers, but their inclusion seemed warranted in a synthetic treatment of my subject. I am well aware of the difficulty of writing a history of recent diplomatic affairs, for few documents are available, but the main course of events is not in doubt. The archives will throw fresh light upon the motives of statesmen and their reactions in definite crises; they may even disclose fresh facts; but, until they are opened, it is perhaps worth while to attempt to digest the enormous amount of unofficial evidence already obtainable.

My best thanks are due to my colleagues, Professors Samuel Ball Platner, Henry E. Bourne, and Elbert J. Benton, who have read the manuscript and offered many valuable suggestions.

BERNADOTTE E. SCHMITT.

WESTERN RESERVE UNIVERSITY,
CLEVELAND, 30 September, 1915.

ERRATA

Page 15, line 19: "destruction" should read "seizure"

Page 19, line 26: "1883" should read "1882"

Page 22, line 12: "diamonds" should read "gold"

Page 29, lines 17 and 18: "the major portion" should read "a large portion"

Page 32, line 19: delete "misguided"

Page 39, line 9 from bottom: "always" should read "usually"

Page 61, line 5 from bottom: "spirit of the spirit" should read "effect of the military spirit"

Page 101, line 12 of text: "obtai ed" should read "obtained"

Page 103, last line of table "EXPORTS PER HEAD OF POPULATION" should read "3 8 10" and "2 8 9"

Page 108, line 7: "imports" should read "exports"

Page 141, line 6 from bottom: "now" should read "later"

Page 157, second footnote: ",1911" should read " (1911)"
fourth footnote, line 4: ",1902" ",1908" and ",1912" should read " (1902)" " (1908)" and " (1912)"
fourth footnote, line 5: ",1912" should read " (1912)"
fourth footnote, line 6: ",1914" should read "(1914)"

Page 159, second footnote, line 2: ",1903" should read " (1903)"

Page 161, first footnote: ",1914" should read " (1914)"

Page 164, line 25: "unctiousness" should read "unctuousness"

Page 165, line 14 from bottom: "genuine" should read "genius"

Page 197, first footnote, line 2: ",1902" should read " (1902)"

Page 206, first footnote, line 2: "Bülow's" should read "Bülow"

Page 207, line 11: "now" should read "later"

Page 218, line 11: "*négligéable*" should read "*négligeable*"

Page 233, line 6 from bottom: "desirable;" should read "desirable—"

Page 245, line 8: "who" should read "which"

Page 259, line 8 from bottom: "Russian" should read "British"

Page 279, line 8 from bottom: "Bagdad" should read "Bagdad line"

Page 303, line 19: "treaty" should read "negotiations"

Page 310, first footnote, line 2: "either from" should read "from either"

Page 322, line 3: "eight" should read "six"

Page 340, line 6: "long" should read "long,"

Page 353, bottom of page: "20 June, 1913" should be identified as footnote "3"

Page 379, line 9 from bottom: *"Kölnischer"* should read *"Kölnische"*

Page 380, line 5 from bottom of text: *"Kölnischer"* should read *"Kölnische"*

Page 395, line 18: "aimed not only" should read "not only aimed"

Page 452, first footnote, line 3: "requiring to demobilize against Austria as well as herself" should read "requiring Russia to demobilize against Austria as well as against herself"

Page 454, third footnote: "Semain" should read "Semaine"

Page 455, line 5: "imposition" should read "impossible position"

Page 461, line 6 from bottom of text: *"Kölnischer"* should read *"Kölnische"*
line 5 from bottom of text: *"Neuste"* should read *"Neueste"*

Page 462, line 13: *"Kölnischer"* should read *"Kölnische"*

Page 509, under Bérard, Victor: *"Guillaum"* should read *"Guillaume"*

Page 520, under Pourtalès, Count: "442" should read "441"

Page 524: "Zimmermann, Alfred" should read "Zimmermann, Artur"

CONTENTS

MAPS

ENGLAND AND GERMANY, 1740—1914

CHAPTER I

INTRODUCTION

"THE central fact in the international situation to-day is the antagonism between England and Germany." So ran the first sentence of the first article of the first number of the *Round Table* (November, 1910), a non-partisan journal of the politics of the British Empire. A French writer described this rivalry as "the essential fact which dominates the whole policy of our time, which thrusts itself into all events to embitter and warp them, and which is to be found at the bottom of all the political crises by whose succession Europe is periodically agitated."[1] In Germany "the English danger" was discussed in countless books and pamphlets, and the press of the world took up the cue. An American magazine published an article, entitled "Will England and Germany Fight?" in which the issues were represented as irreconcilable and the results fraught with incalculable consequences for the whole world.[2] In fact, no such spectacular international quarrel had been seen since the days of the great Napoleon; its existence was recognized by people to whom diplomacy is usually intangible; while the inhabitants of both England and Germany were subjected to enormous taxes on account of the colossal

[1] René Pinon, *L'Europe et l'Empire Ottoman*, p. xii.
[2] William Bayard Hale, *World's Work*, February, 1909.

I

armaments which both caused and were caused by the strained relations between their governments and the mutual distrust of the two peoples.

In a broad sense, the issue in the struggle has been the balance of power, which, in the words of Bishop Stubbs, the great English historian, "is the principle which gives unity to the political plot of modern European history." [1] For since the days of Cardinal Wolsey and Henry VIII, four hundred years ago, Great Britain has been the principal factor in the maintenance of a European equilibrium: her statesmen have consistently held that, in spite of the North Sea and the Channel, the "precious stone set in the silver sea" was not secure "against the envy of less happy lands" if a single Power achieved the ascendency of the Continent. To prevent this consummation England waged successful war against Philip II of Spain, Louis XIV, and Napoleon. And because in the early years of the twentieth century Germany bestrode the European continent like a colossus, it was inevitable that she should find ranged against herself the weight of British public opinion and the resources of British diplomacy. [2]

A generation ago, when Anglo-Russian rivalry dominated the European situation, it was the fashion to speak of the struggle between the elephant and the whale, and at first sight Anglo-German tension presents a similar aspect. The British Empire is a maritime confederacy, with far-flung battle lines protected by an enormous fleet; Germany is primarily a land power, whose strong right arm is the mighty army assembled within her European frontiers. But a closer inspection reveals a situation singularly remi-

[1] *Lectures on Medieval and Modern History*, p. 258.

[2] "No nation can maintain the mastery of the continent of Europe as long as a strong and independent England exists on its flank. A nation which strives for supremacy in Europe is bound to attack Great Britain earlier or later. All the rulers from Julius Cæsar to Napoleon, who have striven to become supreme in Europe, have made war upon Great Britain." (J. Ellis Barker, *Modern Germany*, p. 243, edition of 1912.)

niscent of the eighteenth century. In that period of European history Great Britain was repeatedly at war with France for the nominal purpose of preserving the balance of power in Europe, but the actual result of this policy was to make the island kingdom the leading commercial nation of the world, to secure for it the control of the seas in time of war, and to obtain the fairest colonies of France for the extension of her own empire. Similarly, in our own age England abandoned her former friendship for Germany when that Power deliberately challenged Britain's traditional supremacy of the seas, became her doughty competitor in the markets of the world, and expressed in no uncertain voice the opinion that Britain possessed far too many of the undeveloped regions of the world, and Germany far too few.

That England took up the challenge from across the North Sea was due, not to jealousy and envy of Germany, as has been so often asserted, but to the instinct of self-preservation; which, however, did not exclude the possibility of an accommodation between the two Powers and did not prevent repeated agreements for the delimitation of their respective ambitions. But in one matter England remained adamant. Drawing the food of its people and the raw materials for its factories from every corner of the globe, and dependent upon its export trade as the staff of life, the United Kingdom was irresistibly driven to maintain a supreme navy. And that was intolerable to Germany after she had ceased to be a congeries of petty states held together in a loose confederation and became in fact the leading nation of the Continent. Furthermore, by the application of science and patience to industrial problems, she developed an overseas trade second only to that of England. Germany therefore argued that she must possess a fleet sufficient to protect her expanding foreign commerce, lest it should exist on the mere sufferance of the

overwhelming British navy; in spite of the fact that every
stage in the development of her fleet was followed by still
larger additions to that of England.

The colonial situation provided a third element of discord. Colonies serve a nation in various ways. They
offer markets, which may be controlled by tariffs, for the
surplus products of national industry; they may, with
proper management and exploitation, supply the mother
country with raw materials for that industry; and under
favorable climatic conditions they afford opportunities for
settlement to those who do not find the circumstances of
life profitable or pleasant, but who wish to preserve their
own institutions and their native allegiance in a new land.
In the actual organization of the world, Germany possessed
almost no colonies suitable for settlement and few territories worthy of exploitation. The British Empire, on the
other hand, was spread over a quarter of the globe, em-
braced every kind of land, and might, if an imperial protective tariff were adopted, become a self-sufficing, economic entity from which German competition would be
excluded. France likewise possessed a magnificent colonial domain in Africa and Asia in which she did not welcome the German merchant and the German capitalist.
Germany must also expand overseas, unless she was to be
outdistanced in the economic struggle, which is the basis
of modern civilization.

It is further to be noted that as in the eighteenth century the British Empire was pieced together in a fit of
absence of mind as the result of British Continental policy,
so the maintenance of the balance of power has led to further increases of the empire in the latest age, increases
which were not counterbalanced by the acquisitions of Germany. For in the last quarter of the nineteenth century,
when Great Britain stood more or less aloof from Continental politics, she added Egypt, Burmah, large stretches

of Africa, and finally the Boer republics to her already vast possessions, not to speak of extending her influence in Afghanistan and the Persian Gulf; while Germany had to be content with the least desirable lands in Africa and a few islands in the Pacific. Germany therefore boldly demanded "a place in the sun." France she despised as a decadent and sterile nation whose colonies were an anomaly; Russia she patronized as an unorganized mass, powerless for either good or evil; Belgium and Holland she perhaps hoped to dispossess of their holdings in Africa and the Far East; but Britain she feared as the great obstacle to the realization of her ambitions. Not that Germany really desired to become mistress of certain British colonies; it is more probable that her appetite was to be satisfied by the annexation of North Africa. If France were deprived of this, the richest and most accessible part of her colonial empire, she would be seriously weakened as a European Power and her decline as a great nation sensibly accentuated. Germany, in turn, would become a Mediterranean Power, thus laying the foundation of a future supremacy in that sea when the final collapse of the Ottoman Empire should endow her with Asia Minor and Mesopotamia. But the German Government was under no illusions as to the attitude of Great Britain toward such a transaction, which would at once upset the balance of power and endanger the route to India, and it therefore became the great purpose of German diplomacy to prevent that *rapprochement* and friendship between England and France which the statesmen of those countries were bent on achieving. This is the key to that antagonism between England and Germany which finally led to war, and it is truly astonishing that, although Germany had learned, first in 1905 and again in 1911, that England was prepared to resist excessive demands upon France, the imperial chancellor should, on the eve of the war, have asked the British

Government to stand aside while Germany appropriated the French colonies.

Behind these rivalries of commerce, sea power, and colonies there loomed the challenge of culture. "Is the world to become English?" was a question frequently to be found in German discussions of international politics. The nineteenth century witnessed the expansion of the Anglo-Saxon over every continent, often by means highly questionable from an austere moral standard; more than a million Germans settled in lands whose civilization was essentially English and there preserved but few links with their fatherland; English promised more and more to become the world language, so far as that honor was reserved for a particular speech. For generations French culture had enjoyed a wide popularity outside France itself; and even backward Russia was represented in the Balkan peninsula and the vast expanses of Siberia, not to mention the remnants of Spanish influence from the Rio Grande to the Straits of Magellan. Was there no place for "the German idea in the world"? demanded a well-known Pan-German book of that title.[1] German philosophy long dominated the abstractions of men, the researches of German science were appropriated by all nations, the battles of Sadowa and Sedan were held to establish the superiority of German education, and German discipline and thoroughness were eagerly imitated by the more sluggish but ambitious nations. Whatever the precise territorial ambitions of Germany, she demanded that no obstacle be raised if she offered her national culture to a world that had shown itself receptive, and the fact that English influence actually dominated a large part of the non-European world was all the more an incentive for challenging it and for proving the equality of the German spirit.

In this connection the profound difference between Eng-

---

[1] Paul Rohrbach, *Der deutsche Gedanke in der Welt* (1912).

lish and German ideals must be recognized. It is doubtless true, as was often asserted by those who sought to
minimize the issues of the Anglo-German quarrel, that no
European nations are so near in blood, in mental and physical characteristics, and in the conditions of their economic
life as England and Germany. But the parallel can easily
be carried too far. For centuries Englishmen have stood
forth as the champions of individual liberty, have resented
the interference of the state in their private affairs; and,
while in recent years a newer ideal of social obligation and
the pressure of German competition have compelled them
more and more to adopt the corporate theory of life, the
national reluctance to discard traditions handed down from
generation to generation has been frequently observed. In
the mental development of such a people, the idea of com-
pulsion obviously can play, and actually has played, but a
minor rôle. In all the great crises of English history the
desire for an amicable settlement has ever been to the fore,
till the fondness for compromise, and the ability to effect
it, has become notorious. And in the nineteenth century
a genuine abhorrence of war was instilled into the hearts
of Englishmen by statesmen like John Bright and Richard
Cobden on the one hand and Lord Salisbury on the other,
whose teachings were reinforced by the colossal slaughter of
the Crimean War and the mismanagement of the struggle
in South Africa. The British Empire has, indeed, waged
many wars in the last hundred years, but the vanquished
have always been generously treated, and the cause of
human freedom has been immeasurably advanced by the
exploits of British arms.

In Germany, on the other hand, the state has long lorded
it over the individual. Prussia has become notorious for
regulation and bureaucracy, and her ideas have slowly
penetrated the other German states, where, it may be remarked, there were old traditions of governmental inter-

ference which the Prussian example has galvanized into renewed popularity. Nor can it be denied that the material prosperity of Germany has been quite as much the result of official guidance as of the zeal and capacity of its people. In fact, "efficiency," as we understand the term, has been forced upon the world by the precept and practise of Germany.

From the historical point of view, Germany was necessarily a military state. By sheer valor of arms the electors of Brandenburg extended their dominions and created the modern kingdom of Prussia, and the kings of Prussia by similar means accomplished the unification of Germany. It would be surprising if the German, who read in his history how for hundreds of years his fatherland was the parade-ground of foreign armies, did not believe that the new empire must rely upon its military strength alone and be able to resist any kind of attack. And the maintenance of peace for forty-three years, during which Germany ceased to be a mere geographical expression and became a Great Power, was for the German a convincing argument for military preparedness and a thoroughgoing concentration upon the problems of national defense.

But there is a sinister aspect to the picture. After 1870 there grew up, first in one, then in another, and ultimately in almost every European country, a suspicion and a fear that united Germany would one day attempt to repeat the exploits of Bismarck, and the reputation for aggressiveness thus acquired was the most potent factor in the formation of the coalition now in arms against her. Unfortunately for every one, Germany did little toward creating a different impression of her policy beyond proclaiming its peaceful character. Rather, she did not hesitate, on numerous occasions, to rattle the sabre, till she was persuaded that this was sufficient to enforce her will. Also, she regularly took advantage of every ruffle in the international situation to increase the strength of her army, and more lately to accelerate the construction of her fleet, with the avowed object of becoming the supreme power on both land and sea.[1] In other words, at a time when most nations were asking themselves if war were not out of date, and economically unprofitable, Germany was frankly proclaiming that force, and force alone, was worthy of consideration as the solvent of international difficulties.

It will doubtless long be a matter of controversy as to how far the religion of war was accepted by the German people, for the evidence published during the last generation is contradictory. They have been alternately portrayed, by competent observers, as rabid jingoes and as lovers of peace at any price. General Bernhardi declared that "the political power of our nation . . . is fettered externally by its love of peace,"[2] and his writing is so far removed from passion or prejudice that his deliberate statement must be considered sincere. On the other side, innumerable writers so freely propounded his doctrine of the duty to make war, albeit without his learning or candor, that a people like the Germans, who are accustomed to have their views on political questions compounded for them by specialists, must have been more or less poisoned by the constant asseveration that might is right. Either thesis can be proved to the satisfaction of one who sets out to do so. The opinion of the present writer is that, if the mass of the German people did not show positive enthusiasm for war as war, they did desire the fruits of war, and that they were less eager to restrain their military leaders than any nation in Europe. In this respect the thoroughly undemocratic character of their political institutions gave the military party an enormous advantage, monopolizing as it

---

[1] "I shall reorganize my navy so that it shall stand on the same level as my army"—which was the most powerful and formidable in the world. (William II, 1 January, 1900.)

[2] *Germany and the Next War*, p. 12.

did the high offices of state, and controlling with an iron
hand the press and the educational machine, which in other
countries create an independent political opinion. It is a
significant commentary upon the two countries that the
British Government went to war only after taking Parliament into its confidence, while the German Emperor first
declared war and then appealed to the country to present
a united front.

A general view of the situation reveals Germany as the
challenging nation. England would have been quite content to let things stand as they were. Mistress of the seas
for two hundred years and guarantor of the balance of
power in Europe, the mother of many daughter nations, and
in consequence of her position in the world rather inclined
to ignore the susceptibilities of other peoples, her complacency received a profound shock by the advent of a
Power that demanded recognition as an equal and strove
for the means to secure it. The dominant note of English
writing anent the controversy with Germany was that of
determination to keep the heritage of the past, of insistence
upon the status quo. To this point of view it was difficult,
not to say impossible, for Germany to accede. "There can
be no standing still or stopping for us, no permanent renunciation of national expansion: we have to choose between loss of rank among the imperial peoples and a
struggle for a place beside the Anglo-Saxons;"[1] in General Bernhardi's phrase, "world power or downfall!"[2] If
each power held to its course in all stubbornness, war was
indeed inevitable.[3]

The most tragic feature of the Great War, however, is

[1] Rohrbach, *Der deutsche Gedanke in der Welt*, p. 8.
[2] *Germany and the Next War*, chap. 5.
[3] Price Collier remarked that an autocratic, philosophical, and continental race
was pitted against a democratic, political, and insular one, and that never the twain
should meet. The only remedy, in his opinion, was for them to let each other severely alone. Unfortunately, in the conditions of the modern world no nation can
live without contact with all other nations. (*Germany and the Germans*, p. 565.)

that in the two years preceding it Anglo-German relations had "sensibly improved," to use the language of Sir Edward Grey, and that the British Government was willing "to promote some arrangement, to which Germany could be a party, by which she could be assured that no aggressive or hostile policy would be pursued against her or her allies by France, Russia, and [England], jointly or separately."[1]   Great Britain and Germany had co-operated during the Balkan Wars to restrain their friends or allies, and the peace of Europe had been preserved.   The long naval rivalry had been considerably appeased by Admiral von Tirpitz's acceptance of a sixteen-to-ten ratio in the construction of *Dreadnoughts;* on the very eve of the war a treaty had been drafted which established a harmony of views as regards the Baghdad railway and African colonial questions; the animosity between the peoples, so long an obstacle to official negotiations, had to a large extent burnt itself out.   A few years more and their sound common sense would, one likes to think, have convinced both Germans and Britons that, despite their rivalries in all parts of the globe, the world was large enough for them both.   The friendship of the two countries would have become a bulwark for the peace of the world, and British statesmanship might then have addressed itself to the most pressing of all international problems, the reconciliation of France and Germany; after which an alliance of the three Powers would have inaugurated a new era in the history of Europe and of mankind.

[1] Sir Edward Grey to Sir Edward Goschen, 30 July, 1914, *Great Britain and the European Crisis,* no. 101.

CHAPTER II

MODERN ENGLAND

IT will be readily admitted, even by those to whom the fact is unpalatable, that since the end of the Napoleonic wars England has been the dominant nation of the world, and that her participation in the Great War will probably be the decisive factor in its length, if not in its termination. Why should so commanding a position belong to a couple of islands whose population was less than that of France (until a few years ago), Germany, Austria-Hungary, or Russia? For none of these nations has accepted British hegemony as a law of the universe. The answer is to be found in the accidents of history and geography, with which must be reckoned certain traits of character that are the product of free institutions and a peculiar consciousness of national unity.

First of all, at the end of the eighteenth century a series of remarkable inventions, for which English genius must receive full credit, transformed England from an agricultural into an industrial country and vastly stimulated its already thriving commerce. By chance this revamping of the national life coincided with the French Revolution and the first Napoleonic Empire, a period during which the continent of Europe was devastated by a succession of wars and thereby prevented from imitating the new English system. Though England was an active and the most steadfast participant in the long struggle to crush Napoleon, her territory was not invaded, and her sea power enabled her at once to destroy the foreign trade of the Napoleonic states and to establish her own monopoly in the Americas and the Far East. When peace was signed in 1815, the United Kingdom had secured such a lead that in a hundred years no rival nation has overcome it. France was about half a century behind England in appropriating the new industrialism, Germany nearly seventy-five years, and Russia's development has begun in the last generation. If Great Britain is no longer the "workshop of the world," as the Cobdenites of the mid-Victorian period were pleased to call her, she is still the premier industrial state and the richest.

But wealth alone, in spite of its power, would not enable her to exercise such preponderant influence all over the world: that she owes to the empire which the seafaring instincts of her people have built up in the seven seas. Here the accident that Great Britain is an island assumes extraordinary interest. For centuries the sea has been the life of England, and the fact has penetrated deep into the national consciousness. Not, of course, that Englishmen have enjoyed any iron-clad monopoly of the maritime spirit. The fleets of Italian and Hanseatic cities in the Middle Ages, the argosies of Spain, and the merchantmen of Holland recall days when England was a self-sufficient island kingdom; and in our own time Greece, Norway, and Germany have again shown their flags in the waters familiar to their fathers. But in no people has the tradition of the sea and an appreciation of its importance for the national destiny been so permanent, so abiding, and so all-pervading as in the inhabitants of the British Isles. If the first discoverers were Portuguese or Spaniards or Italians, from the middle of the sixteenth century Englishmen were in the forefront of that movement which colonized the New World and brought the Far East into close relations with the markets of Europe. Colonial adventure and exploration came as second nature to a race bred to the sea and by virtue of liberal political institutions free to work out social and economic problems without the interference of a bureaucratic government. Moreover, from the first, the desire to find new markets for English goods never slackened. Until the eighteenth century woollen and linen goods were the chief articles of the export trade; after the industrial revolution, when the country was no longer able to subsist on its home-grown food-supply, and when the output of the huge manufacturing establishments far exceeded the domestic demand, it was imperative to find outlets abroad for the commodities which must pay for the imports of food. Thus English commerce made an empire necessary; the hardihood of her seamen and the weight of an enlightened public opinion permitted the government to pursue a policy which in the course of three centuries has brought a fifth of the globe and a quarter of its population under the rule of England and her daughter nations.

Other peoples have at times been inspired by the imperial ideal—Portugal, Spain, Holland, France—, but their adventures beyond the seas have ever been secondary to their purely European interests, and they lost their colonies because of European complications. Great Britain, as an island, was happily relieved of such embarrassments. Her territory inviolate through the might of her fleet, she could not, on the other hand, extend her boundaries by annexation or conquest, in spite of the innumerable wars to which she was a party lest some Continental nation should become dominant in Europe. But she invariably recouped herself by the acquisition of lands in America, Asia, or Africa, till in 1815 she alone of the Great Powers possessed a colonial empire worthy of the name. Thus her geographical situation and the political and economic genius of her people had secured for the United Kingdom an accumulation of wealth and a position in the world quite out of proportion to her own human and material resources.

To protect this empire and its commerce, to see that Britannia ruled the waves in time of war, has been the first duty of every British government in modern times. Charles I was able to collect ship money without consent of Parliament in order to renew the fleet which his father James had allowed to fall into decay. The Commonwealth stopped at nothing to secure naval supremacy in home waters and to show the British flag in the Mediterranean, and the one creditable achievement of Charles II was his insistence on naval efficiency. In 1689 began the intermittent duel with France, which lasted till 1815; when it was over, the fleets of France, Spain, and Holland had been swept from the seas, and the Congress of Vienna tacitly accepted the maritime supremacy of the state whose resources had enabled the Continental nations to drive Napoleon from Europe. British power was not always wisely used in the seventeenth and eighteenth centuries, for Holland fell a victim to its jealousy, and in 1807 Denmark had to witness the destruction of her fleet in the harbor of Copenhagen at a moment when she was at peace with England. Likewise the laws relating to capture at sea and the right of search in time of war, which are considered illiberal in many quarters, are based mainly on British practises in the Napoleonic struggle. But, whatever one may think of the mistress of the seas, her overwhelming ascendency throughout the nineteenth century is the most important fact in the development of her foreign and colonial policy.

Since 1815 Great Britain has utilized her position to marvellous advantage. At that date only the fringes of Canada, Australia, and Cape Colony had been touched; no settlement had been made in New Zealand. Africa was almost an unknown continent. In India, although the foundations of British power had been laid, the great work of regeneration and reform which has justified British domination was yet to be conceived. How little the possibilities of this splendid heritage were appreciated by the mass of Englishmen is the favorite theme of modern imperialists. For fifty years after the treaties of Vienna, by which Great Britain retained only such conquests as were necessary to control the route to India, the aphorism of Turgot, that colonies were only fruits which fell from the tree when they were ripe, commanded general assent. The grant of self-government to the Canadian and Australasian colonies was almost welcomed as the preliminary of independence, and the military authorities repudiated responsibility for their defense. Perhaps the mother country was too absorbed with the political and social problems born of the industrial revolution to consider the prospect of a Greater Britain beyond the seas; but the revolt of the thirteen American colonies was still fresh in men's minds and another rule of conduct was hard to imagine.

Gradually, however, the old tradition reasserted itself. The enormous increase of population, the expansion of industry under the free-trade system adopted in the 'forties, and the subsequent decline of agriculture in both Great Britain and Ireland kept before the country the problem of food and the necessity of foreign markets. For these reasons Canada and Australasia began to fill up with British emigrants and a policy of expansion was pursued in India; coaling-stations or points of strategic value were picked up here and there. The Crimean War was fought to prevent a Russian domination in the Near East, which was conceived to endanger the Mediterranean route to India. Finally, the genius of Benjamin Disraeli, Earl of Beaconsfield, whose rise from a Jewish obscurity to the leadership of the Conservative party and finally to the office of prime minister reveals one of the most spectacular careers of modern history, endowed Victorian England with the ideal of an empire which should be the greatest political and civilizing force in the world, provided that empire was conscious of its future and responded to the needs and aspirations of its myriad races and peoples.

Nor was the father of modern British imperialism content with fine phrases and lofty speeches. During his second premiership (1874–80) he inaugurated a policy the results and continuation of which provided British statesmen with perplexing problems for nearly thirty years. He bought the Suez Canal for England in 1875, and the following year began to interfere in the financial affairs of Egypt. To South Africa he sent as high commissioner a soldier-statesman who had a vision of the later Union and allowed a subordinate to annex the Transvaal Republic to the British Empire. In 1877 Queen Victoria was proclaimed Empress of India, an act which gave the people of that land a new sense of loyalty and made possible a spontaneous and unanimous rally of the Indian princes at the outbreak of the present war. Lord Beaconsfield next intervened in the Near East to secure a revision of the Treaty of San Stefano, which promised to make the Balkan peninsula a Russian protectorate, and when in revenge Russia turned to the Middle East and instigated the Ameer of Afghanistan to resist British pretensions, the challenge was taken up and war declared against the sturdy little country which, in 1839–42, had inflicted notable reverses on British arms.[1]

Lord Beaconsfield resigned office in 1880, and died the next year, before he could devise a satisfactory solution for any of the four great problems created by his diplomacy. The new ministry, under Mr. Gladstone, was bound to at-

[1] For this and succeeding paragraphs, reference may be made to Ernest Lémonon, *L'Europe et la Politique britannique*, 1882–1911, a detailed and impartial study which abounds in quotations from the press and the speeches of politicians; and to Alfred L. P. Dennis, "Tendencies in British Foreign Policy since Disraeli," in *Proceedings of the American Political Science Association* (1909), a brief but illuminating account of British policy in its broadest aspects.

tempt a settlement of some kind in each case, but, because it was not sympathetic with this imperial policy and was not gifted with the imagination of the Conservative leader, it managed to store up much trouble for the future while apparently extricating itself with fair success from difficulties not of its own making. How the splendidly conceived plans of Disraeli scored a posthumous victory will be seen in subsequent paragraphs, but for the moment something must be said of Gladstone's efforts to upset them.

(1) Many provisions of the "peace with honor" dictated at Berlin by Lord Beaconsfield (1878) had not been carried out, for it satisfied neither the Turks nor the Russians, the two most interested parties. With the help of Prince Bismarck, Lord Granville, whose work at the foreign office is still the subject of controversy, patched up a tolerable solution, but it involved the alienation of Turkey and the abandonment of that pro-Turkish policy which Lord Beaconsfield and many of his predecessors had considered essential for the checking of Russian designs. Yet Great Britain did not win Russian good will by this change of front, rather Anglo-Russian rivalry in Near Eastern politics was quite pronounced until the first years of the twentieth century.

(2) The campaign in Afghanistan had resulted badly for the invaders, who were saved from complete destruction only by the famous march of Lord (then Sir Frederick) Roberts to Kandahar. The position was so delicate that in 1881 the British troops were withdrawn and the Ameer was left free to intrigue with the Russians if he desired. The latter interpreted the evacuation as a sign of British weakness. Resuming their aggressive policy, they occupied Afghan territory at Pendjeh in 1885, and war was narrowly avoided by the conciliatory policy of the Gladstone government. Not till the new century was British influence fully and definitively asserted.

(3) In South Africa the annexation of 1877 had produced bitter resentment among the Transvaal farmers, and rebellion followed. The defeat of a British force at Majuba Hill (February, 1881) strengthened Mr. Gladstone's objections to an imperialistic policy, and the Convention of Pretoria, reinforced by the London Convention of 1884, recognized the independence of the Boer republics. But the last word had not been said, for the problem was closely bound up with Cape Colony and Natal and was not unconnected with the disposition of the surrounding African lands.

(4) In Egypt, where the Anglo-French control of finances was working badly, trouble was brewing. In 1882 Arabi Pasha, a colonel in the Egyptian army, organized a revolt, and there was a massacre of Europeans at Alexandria. The Turkish Government showing no disposition to rescue the Western Powers from their predicament (Egypt was an autonomous province of the Ottoman Empire), Great Britain decided to intervene. But, recognizing that since Bonaparte's expedition in 1798 France had cherished a strong sentimental interest in the Nile valley and that her financial claims were considerable, Lord Granville invited the Republic to join in the armed demonstration. France refused. If she believed that England would not act alone, she was mistaken. A British squadron bombarded Alexandria, and in 1883 Sir Garnet Wolseley overthrew the Khedive's army at the battle of Tel-el-Kebir, which was followed immediately by the "occupation" of Egypt. But for Great Britain as many problems were created as had been solved. Lord Granville had incautiously declared that the occupation would end when order had been restored, but various circumstances made a fulfilment of this promise impracticable. So the French Government, which was much piqued by the turn of events and bitterly regretted its own lukewarmness in the critical days of 1882,

was always able to call attention to this obligation of Great Britain, and in a variety of ways to add to the difficulties under which the British administration of Egypt labored for many years. This hostility and tension, originally local, rapidly envenomed the general relations of France and England, caused both countries much trouble, and permitted Germany to lord it over the Continent at will till the opening years of the twentieth century.

Thus Gladstonian diplomacy had secured for England the active opposition of both France and Russia, and had failed to ameliorate the situation inherited from the Beaconsfield government. This was the more unfortunate because the 'eighties and 'nineties witnessed a scramble on the part of the Great Powers for those regions of the world which were open to colonization or exploitation by European governments and peoples, viz., most of Africa, parts of Asia, and the islands of the Pacific. And so systematic and regular were the conflicts between Great Britain and the two powers of the Dual Alliance (finally consummated between 1891 and 1896) that Englishmen came to regard these countries as their natural and hereditary enemies, and some confidently predicted that one day the innumerable quarrels would be settled by the arbitrament of war, which, in fact, more than once loomed on the horizon.

The French occupation of Tunis, which was felt to prejudice British commercial interests; intrigues in Morocco; rivalries in the Congo and Niger basins and elsewhere in Africa, which culminated in the affair of Fashoda; the hostility of English missionaries to the French penetration of Madagascar; English fears that the French conquests in Tonkin and Siam would endanger the northeastern frontiers of India and affect British commercial supremacy in the Yangtze valley; disputes about the Newfoundland fisheries which dated back to the Seven Years' War; and the problem of New Caledonia and the New Hebrides in the Pacific—all these show the inflammable character of Anglo-French relations. Twice, in 1893 about a Siamese question, and in 1898, when Lord Kitchener compelled Major Marchand to retire from Fashoda, war seemed possible, if not inevitable. Any of these disputes could have been settled with a little good will on both sides. But when an English statesman (Joseph Chamberlain) dared advise France to "mend her manners," and when the French press daily warned its readers against the wiles of *perfide Albion*, each government delighted to administer "pinpricks"[1] to the policy of the other and left the direction of world policy to more sensible Powers.

With Russia Great Britain had much the same experience. Finding every move in the Balkans blocked by the policy of the British Government, Russia continued her advance in Central Asia, which brought her in time to the frontiers of Afghanistan and India itself. She acquired a preponderant position in Persia, and seemed likely to push on to the Persian Gulf, which for a century had been the special preserve of England. To the latter, who refused to admit Russia's need of an outlet on warm waters, these enterprises betokened but one aim, the invasion of India, an opinion concurred in by Doctor Arminius Vambéry, the famous orientalist of the University of Budapest. In the Far East the construction of the Siberian railway across Manchuria foreboded the disintegration of China, where British commercial interests were extensive—a fear accentuated by the intervention of France and Russia (with the help of Germany), after the Chino-Japanese War, to compel the surrender of Port Arthur by Japan, only that Russia might seize it for herself. Also, Russian intrigues in Tibet promised nothing good for the northern regions of

---

[1] The phrase was used by Sir Edmond Monson, British ambassador to France, in a public speech in Paris on 6 December, 1898, and caused great resentment. *Cf.* Sir Thomas Barclay, *Anglo-French Reminiscences*, 1876–1906, p. 157.

India. Kipling's phrase about "the bear that walks like a man" expressed accurately the opinion of the man in the street, who incidentally regarded Russian officialdom as synonymous with corruption, inefficiency, and oppression.

Here, then, was a situation full of danger for the British Empire if British policy were at any time to become intransigent. Fortunately for England, her rulers declined to push home the quarrel with either France or Russia, but reserved their attention for another problem.

Scarcely had the autonomy of the Boer republics been conceded when the discovery of diamonds brought prospectors and speculators by the thousand into the Transvaal. Mainly Englishmen, with a sprinkling of Americans, they chafed under the political system of President Krüger, who compelled them to pay heavy taxes but denied them any share in the government. On 1 January, 1896, Doctor Leander Starr Jameson and a band of raiders, operating from British territory, led an expedition against the Boer Government, only to be routed and captured. Instead of cutting the Gordian knot, they had tied it tighter, because Boer pride and British stubbornness were stimulated, and the inevitable war broke out in October, 1899.

Without discussing the merits of that struggle, it may be remarked that both races learned to respect each other, and came to see that only by co-operation could they preserve South Africa for the white race; also, that the war made possible that unification of the land which its enlightened statesmen had long desired. To Englishmen the war disclosed three very unpalatable facts. (1) It had cost £250,000,000 and more than 25,000 men, yet the grant of self-government to the conquered Boer states conceded the very points for which the war had been fought. (2) The efficiency of the British army was called in grave question, and there were rumors that all was not well with the fleet. (3) The war had revealed an astonishing and un-expected hatred of England, her institutions, and her policy all over the Continent. In France, Russia, Austria, and Germany, especially the last-named, the press had used the most abusive language and had gloated over each re-verse of British arms. It was known that more than one attempt had been made to organize a coalition against Britain, which would, at the very least, have prevented the prosecution of the war in South Africa and might have precipitated the collapse of the whole Empire.

It is often said that only a sledge-hammer blow will per-mit a new idea to penetrate an Englishman's consciousness. If so, the recurrent shocks of the Boer War were of great value, for they compelled the country to readjust its polit-ical spectacles. Men began to reject the old conception of imperialism, to see that "the appetite for domination belongs to an outworn phase of patriotism," to apply Mr. Balfour's description of German ambitions.[1] At last the Empire had territory enough, and if that Empire was not to follow the example of its Roman predecessor, which crumbled under the pressure of continuous warfare, its energies must be diverted to the arts of peace and civiliza-tion. The dominant idea encountered in responsible and serious writings of the last decade is that "peace is the greatest of British interests." Englishmen further realized that they could neither ignore the opinions of Continental peoples nor dictate to those nations their principles of conduct, an admission the more galling because for gen-erations past these islanders had judged other men by their own standards, and had, accordingly, either given Conti-nental complications a wide berth or interfered metic-ulously in the affairs of all nations. But for the future England could not shun Europe; on the other hand, her action must be circumspect, her attitude considerate of

[1] *England and Germany* (1912), p. 7.

the susceptibilities of those with whom she must live in
contact.

How deeply these new conceptions took root in the popular mind is seen in the failure of the Conservative party,
which had made the Boer War and was associated with
jingoistic tendencies, to recover power after the disastrous
elections of January, 1906. The rise of the Labor party,
the tone of the Liberal press, the flood of pacificist literature, the objurgations of Conservative politicians, and the
reluctance for war manifested between 23 July and 4 August,
1914, leave no doubt that the temper of twentieth-century
England was anything but bellicose. The United Kingdom
desired only to be left alone to enjoy the heritage of the
past and, if possible, to set an example to the more warlike
nations. Not that militarism was entirely disposed of.
Lord Salisbury's famous remark, "The living nations will
gradually encroach on the territory of the dying, and the
seeds and causes of conflict among civilized nations will
speedily appear,"[1] included the suggestion that England
should be prepared for any eventuality and afforded a
small but noisy party the chance to demand larger military and naval establishments. But the country was not
converted to the gospel of force. Ten years of agitation
for a conscript army made but little impression, and the
navy was allowed to fall below that two-power standard
adopted by the Naval Defense Act of 1889; it was becoming increasingly difficult to maintain a full or sufficient personnel on either establishment; and, as will be seen in a
later chapter, the government which declared war against
Germany resolutely endeavored to keep down the ever-
mounting expenditure on armaments.

Isolation being impossible, what should be the aim of
"a new departure" (Lord Lansdowne's phrase)—by what
policy could the British Government perform its duty as

[1] Albert Hall, London, 4 May, 1898.

a member of the European community and at the same time do justice to its position as the trustee of a vast empire? The diplomacy of Downing Street since the conclusion of the South African war would seem to have been dictated by five considerations: the taking of a definite side in the balance of Europe; the settlement of outstanding disputes with foreign nations; the reorganization of the military and naval forces of the crown against an attack on the United Kingdom or the Empire; the revival of the concert of Europe; and the development of international arbitration.[1] It will be convenient to treat these tendencies in reverse order.

International arbitration, if not of Anglo-Saxon origin, has been chiefly practised by that race.[2] It dates from 1794, "when England and the United States concluded an arbitration treaty to deal with questions arising under the peace treaty of 1783. . . . La Fontaine, the learned historian of the subject, estimates that from 1794 to 1900 there were actually 177 instances of this arbitrament, of which he assigns no less than 70 cases as shared in by Great Britain, 56 by the United States, and 26 by France, with other nations relatively nowhere." [3] For our present purpose, the landmark is the Anglo-French treaty of 1903, which, though it reserved from arbitration questions affecting the honor, independence, or vital interests of either country, was an important step in advance, in that it has been copied by practically all civilized nations. Great Britain has since negotiated similar treaties with thirteen different governments. It has gone further. In 1911 it signed with the United States, and its example was followed by France, a treaty by which any and all differences

---

[1] George Peel, *The Future of England*, pp. 152–153.
[2] For a discussion of the historical origins of international arbitration, see the notes to vol. V of John Bassett Moore, *International Arbitrations of the United States*.
[3] George Peel, *The Future of England*, p. 156.

arising between the two governments might ultimately be submitted to arbitration. Though the amendments of the United States Senate practically nullified this happy arrangement, so that the treaty was not ratified, the good will of Great Britain was demonstrated; so much so that she revised her alliance with Japan to prevent its application against a country with which either party had signed a treaty of general arbitration.

Once at least in the new century, thanks to the leadership of the British Government, the concert of Europe did yeoman service in the cause of European peace. The outbreak of the Balkan War, in October, 1912, threatened to set all Europe by the ears, for it had long been assumed that the liquidation of the Macedonian problem would bring various Great Powers into the arena. But at the first sign of tension Sir Edward Grey proposed a conference of the ambassadors in London; with their assistance he piloted Europe through the most dangerous crisis that had arisen in fifty years. He had tried to assemble a conference in the crisis of 1908–9, and in July, 1914, he made a vain effort in the same direction. Under his direction British policy was true to the teaching of Lord Salisbury, that the concert is "the embryo of the only possible structure of Europe which can save civilization from the desolating effects of a disastrous war."

With respect to British military policy, the details will be set forth in a subsequent chapter. Here it is sufficient to point out that the whole Empire felt the necessity of an adequate system of defense. Before the war all of the self-governing colonies instituted military training of some description and, with the exception of South Africa, began to create naval forces. So far from this imperial development being a danger, it promised to become more and more a guarantee of peace, for the British Government had undertaken the task of consolidating these scattered outposts of the Empire's power into an effective enterprise animated by a single ideal. But the price of this direction was the admission of the overseas dominions to the *arcana* of the foreign office,[1] and, given the diversity of British, *i. e.*, imperial, interests, given the increasing influence of the colonies over foreign policy, it was unthinkable that the Empire should be plunged into war did not the constituent parts thereof believe it necessary and just.

The policy of settling extra-European disputes had been begun long before the altered situation in Europe made a conciliatory attitude incumbent on the foreign and colonial offices. The success of this give-and-take policy and the wide range of British interests may be gauged from the one hundred treaties, conventions, protocols, agreements, and exchanges of notes to which the British Government was a party between 1882 and the conclusion of peace with the Boer republics twenty years later. France, Germany, Italy, Russia, Holland, Belgium, Portugal, Spain, Morocco, Ethiopia, Zanzibar, China, the United States, Mexico, Nicaragua, Venezuela, and Brazil make a formidable list of possible antagonists; to have made amicable and satisfactory arrangements with each and all of them is surely a record of which any government might be proud and to which it might point as evidence of its pacific policy. Between 1902 and the outbreak of the present war sixty-seven more agreements of a similar character were concluded with twenty-five governments.[2]

It is true that most of the disputes so adjusted were petty matters, but after 1902 the same principle was applied to the larger problems of the Empire and its relations to the Great Powers. The first step was to negotiate an

---

[1] This was done at the imperial conference of 1911, and helps to explain the readiness of the colonies to support the mother country in the present war.

[2] A partial list of these agreements is given in Professor Dennis's paper, *op. cit.*, p. 118. The *British and Foreign State Papers* do not at present extend beyond 1911; for the years 1911–14 the *Parliamentary Papers* must be consulted.

alliance with Japan, which consolidated Britain's position in the Far East, where the Russian designs on Manchuria were awakening deep suspicion. The same year the Hay-Pauncefote treaty with the United States guaranteed that British interests in the Panama Canal would be protected; while the renunciation of a clearly defined treaty right to share in the construction of that canal earned for England the friendship of the United States and proclaimed that British and American policies in the New World were harmonious. These two momentous bargains left Lord Lansdowne, who had become foreign secretary in November, 1900, a free hand to deal with the European situation.

The settlement of the Fashoda affair had cleaned the slate with France; M. Delcassé, the French foreign minister, was determined to achieve a reconciliation with England; and the accession of Edward VII, an ardent lover of France and a prime favorite of the Parisians, was not without bearing on the problem. The arbitration treaty of 1903 paved the way. Finally, on 8 April, 1904, there was signed in London a series of declarations which soon secured a world-wide fame under the name *entente cordiale*. By far the most important feature was the recognition by France of the British occupation of Egypt in return for a free hand in Morocco, so far as Great Britain was concerned. Other points referred to Newfoundland, the Niger region, Madagascar, Siam, and the New Hebrides; some secret articles, not published till November, 1911, elaborated the policy of the two governments with respect to Egypt and Morocco. Some of the disputes were of long standing—none involved grave questions of national existence, all were the source of much trouble to both governments and prevented them from presenting a united front in the tense situation developing in Europe. By a few strokes of the pen two eminently wise statesmen relieved their respective countries of much anxiety and set an example which proved profitable and contagious.

A change of government in England installed Sir Edward Grey at the foreign office in December, 1905; but he was pledged to follow the policy of his predecessor. Accordingly, an exchange of notes with Spain in May, 1907, for which the ground had been prepared by the marriage of King Alfonso to Princess Ena of Battenberg, bound the British and Spanish Governments to maintain the *status quo* in the Mediterranean and the eastern Atlantic. When Italy was brought into this system by an agreement with France, the Mediterranean, which is the highway of the British Empire, seemed permanently secure. With Egypt practically a British protectorate, and with Gibraltar, Malta, and Cyprus as naval bases, it was reasonable to suppose that the British fleet could guarantee the safe transit of the grain ships which brought from Russia the major portion of England's food-supply, and insure the free passage through the Suez Canal of the countless liners that bore the commerce of England and India.

In Asia, where the difficulties of the British Government had always been great, the situation had been cleared by the defeat of Russia at the hands of Japan, who in August, 1905, renewed and extended her alliance with Great Britain. There was no longer any danger of a break-up or partition of China, and the Indian frontier was secure, more especially as the Ameer of Afghanistan had at last accepted freely and fully the proffered friendship of the Indian government. "Scientific frontiers," which were the obsession of Lord Beaconsfield and predicated a "forward policy," were no longer necessary. It was therefore possible to negotiate with the Russian Government, which was struggling with revolution at home and saw its interests in the Balkans threatened by its inability to stem the Austro-German advance. Incidentally, St. Petersburg appreciated that warnings from London, in 1903, that Japan was in earnest as regards Manchuria had been given sincerely and in the true interests of Russia. In the circumstances of the hour an Anglo-Russian agreement was more than a *desideratum*, it was a necessity. By the convention of 31 August, 1907, which astonished the world even more than the *entente cordiale*, both governments agreed to refrain from intrigues in Tibet, which in the past had been profitable to neither. Afghanistan was declared to be under the protection of Great Britain. Persia was divided into three spheres of influence, one (Russian) in the north, one (British) along the Gulf of Oman, and the third, a neutral zone, lying between the other two. By a letter annexed to the convention, Russia recognized the predominance of Great Britain in the Persian Gulf. The bargain merely gave expression to existing facts, but it was worth while to remove all distrust by a frank explanation, and from the English point of view, as it was hoped, to secure a lever against any future move of Russia in those regions.

There remained two problems for a constructive British diplomacy to solve. The first, the future of the Near East, was not pressing. Established in the Nile valley, and protected on her flank by the young Balkan states, with which her influence was considerable, Great Britain could be indifferent to the expulsion of the Turk from Europe. At the same time she was willing to co-operate in any scheme of reform which would enable the Sick Man to retain Macedonia, for a forcible solution of that problem might precipitate a general European war, which it was the great aim of British policy to avoid.

The other task, however, was of appalling difficulty— British relations with Germany. With this Power there was no historical quarrel, for such disputes as had arisen in the last generation had been promptly settled. Until a few years previous there was a tradition of friendship; any differences belonged to the future rather than to the past. At scarcely any point throughout the world were the two countries in contact, yet their diplomacy was animated by opposing motives, and public opinion on both sides of the North Sea was becoming irritated, suspicious, threatening. And a solution of the enigma was the more imperative because Germany was unquestionably the dominant power of the Continent. Were she to assume an attitude frankly and unreservedly hostile to Great Britain, the latter might be called upon to stake her own and her empire's existence upon a gigantic struggle with the greatest military machine in the world.

The preoccupation of the British foreign office after the Boer War was, therefore, to arrange a *modus vivendi* with Germany. And precisely because the latter did not, until too late, as it will be the main thesis of this book to show, respond to the overtures of Great Britain, the resources of British diplomacy and the weight of British public opinion were thrown into the scale in favor of those Powers whose interests were also the object of German attack, lest Germany by subduing them should be free to concentrate her energies upon a still greater enemy. For this reason England supported France and Russia in the diplomatic bouts of the decade preceding the Great War. But it will be seen that she made repeated efforts to secure the friendship of Germany, and, in the opinion of the present writer, she declared war reluctantly and only because she was convinced that no permanent understanding was possible.

The new foreign policy of the British Government was accompanied by a new treatment of certain imperial problems. Speaking generally, there was a reversion to the *laissez-faire* traditions of the mid-Victorian period. Just as the Whig aristocracy, which controlled England from the Reform Act of 1832 to the Reform Act of 1867, had extended

self-government to such colonies as were ready for full
blown parliamentary institutions, so the Liberal government, which held office from 1905 to 1915, was quite disposed to make large concessions to the national aspirations
of the non-English peoples of the Empire.   In some cases
the concessions were granted under pressure, but they
were made, and once made were loyally respected.

In 1899 England went to war with the Boer republics
of South Africa for reasons that, to say the least, are open
to criticism; in course of time she defeated them and took
away their independence.   Four years after the treaty of
peace was signed, the government of Sir Henry Campbell-
Bannerman had the courage to grant complete self-government to the late enemies of the crown, even at the risk of
placing the English element in South Africa at the mercy
of the Dutch majority.   What has been the answer?   The
reconciliation of British and Boer and, in this supreme crisis
of the Empire's history, unswerving loyalty and devotion
except on the part of a few misguided irreconcilables.   The
capture of German Southwest Africa by an Anglo-Boer
force, led by General Botha, is surely one of the most dramatic episodes of modern history, illustrating at once the
antithesis between freedom and force and the conclusive
superiority of the former.

In India and Egypt England has governed by force, and
although her rule has been one of tolerance, not of oppression, it has been to some extent resented by the educated
classes and the champions of nationality.   In keeping with
the spirit of the age, Lord Morley, as secretary of state for
India, and Lord Kitchener, as British representative in
Egypt, made reforms which have introduced those oriental
lands to the privileges of self-government, and have shown
that the ideal of liberty still rules, as it has made, the British Empire.   Hence that spontaneous and unanimous offer
of their lives and their substance from the seven hundred

princes of India, who might have seized the golden opportunity to sever the imperial connection; hence the refusal of Britain's Mohammedan subjects to be seduced by the attractions of a holy war. As Mr. Asquith recently remarked, England is "now gathering in, in the hour of trial, the fruits of a wise and far-sighted imperial policy."[1]

Best of all is the case of Ireland. After a century of agitation a British Government has conceded Home Rule, with what magnificent response from a grateful Ireland Germany knows to her own confusion. "I say to the government that they may to-morrow withdraw every one of their troops from Ireland. I say that the coast of Ireland will be defended from foreign invasion by her armed sons, and for this purpose armed Nationalist Catholics in the south will be only too glad to join arms with the armed Protestant Ulstermen in the north."[2] In these words, uttered in the House of Commons on 3 August, 1914, John Redmond produced his best argument for the cause he had so long advocated.

On paper the British Empire is not an empire at all. There is no single authority for the vast dominions which acknowledge the Union Jack. The interests of the component parts are by no means identical; in many cases there are actually conflicting interests which, on the eve of the Great War, threatened to strain the loose-jointed imperial fabric to the uttermost. In the self-governing dominions the forces of nationalism seemed to point away from a contracted imperialism. There was no imperial army, the navy was in large measure the creation of the United Kingdom. All attempts to create an imperial executive or an imperial legislature were defeated by the opposition of mother country and colonies alike. A few years ago it was difficult to discover any common bond which held the entire empire together, and many compe-

[1] Guild Hall, London, 19 May, 1915.   [2] 5 *Hansard*, lxv, c. 1829.

tent and experienced observers gave expression to the fear that it would not stand the test of a great European war.

With the world in the crucible, nothing is more astonishing than the unity of the British Empire and the enthusiasm of the outlying parts for the successful prosecution of a war waged far from their immediate touch. When one considers the haphazard imperial organization of the past and remembers the reluctance of the self-governing dominions to place their armed forces at the disposal of the British Government, it is evident that beneath the surface there has lain dormant a subtle and elusive spirit which defies calculation and responds only to the call of an all-pervading ideal. The British Empire is assuredly fighting for its interests, but it believes that it is also struggling for something greater and more ennobling, human liberty and humanity itself. As a French writer has said: "La conquête a pu fonder l'Empire. C'est la liberté qui le maintient." [1]

[1]Paul Leroy-Beaulieu, *Revue des Deux Mondes*, 1 January, 1912, p. 85.

CHAPTER III

THE GERMAN EMPIRE

"THE new German Empire is the most perplexing quantity in the modern world, and as unavoidable as it is perplexing." [1] So wrote an English observer two years before the war. That Germany was unavoidable the war itself is proof. And it may be fairly asked whether the war has made her any the less perplexing. Americans at least have not ceased to wonder why a nation which had kept the peace for forty-three years, and had reached a dizzy height of wealth and prosperity within that period, should risk this solid achievement by an appeal to the sword, and that, too, in an issue not of immediate concern to itself. Never was it more true that "the roots of the present lie deep in the past."

Nearly seventy years ago, or, to be precise, in 1848, Germany bore little resemblance to the mighty empire of to-day. The land still merited the name of "the Germanies," as the French, with their aptness for accurate expression, had long called it. Divided into thirty-eight states, and possessed of only a shadowy union in the confederation established by the Congress of Vienna, it was a prey to particularism and local jealousies, which were kept alive, on the one hand by autocratic Austria, and on the other by lesser princes who feared the growing prestige of Prussia and her traditions of aggression. The idea of German nationality was not popular in high political circles; it was cherished by a handful of professors and

[1] G. H. Perris, *Germany and the German Emperor*, preface, p. v.

35

historians, who painted the glories of the mediæval empire or glorified the un-German development of Prussia in
the last two centuries. Suddenly, as by a miracle, liberal
sentiment, which, though repressed by the system of Metternich, had not evaporated, produced a revolution that
forced the proudest monarchs, Frederick William IV of
Prussia and Ferdinand I of Austria, to grant constitutions
to their dissatisfied subjects, and sought, by means of a
national assembly, to transform the broken confederation
into a united Germany governed by its democracy. Almost
overnight Germany became a nation, in the sense that it
was animated by a definite ideal of union and liberty.

That movement failed, for reasons that need not here be
adumbrated, but amid the welter of those years, 1848 and
1849, two incidents stand out boldly. First, King Frederick William, on the outbreak of the troubles, proclaimed
that Prussia was henceforth merged in Germany. Second, relying on the royal promise, the democracy of Germany, assembled in the Frankfort Parliament, offered to
him the imperial crown which should be the symbol of a
new and free fatherland. The vacillating monarch declined the offer, if for sound *Prussian* reasons; but for
Germany a unique opportunity was lost. The particular-
ist spirit of the lesser princes had been broken, their governments had collapsed, and a great king would have found
in the Frankfort assembly the force required to deal with
the ambitions of Austria, who essayed to preserve indefinitely a disordered Germany subservient to her own interests.

It was not to be. Democracy had played its hand and
lost. For the future, blood and iron, not parliamentary
majorities, the genius of Otto von Bismarck, and not the
theories of 1848, must prevail. By the might of Prussian
arms, wielded in three successful wars against Denmark,

Austria, and France, the King of Prussia became German Emperor, and Prussia herself not only the bulwark of German union but the model according to which the other states of Germany were invited to fashion their own life in all its details. It is worth while to inquire (1) what this has meant for Germany and (2) how far Prussia has succeeded in her self-imposed task; for the modern German Empire is not the creation of the German people, who long disliked and distrusted Bismarck and his coadjutors and were reconciled to their work only after the glittering triumphs of the three wars.

It is notorious that the old Germany was highly idealistic, cultured, cosmopolitan. It was largely responsible for the Protestant Reformation, it produced some of the world's greatest philosophers, musicians, and men of letters: Leibnitz, Kant, Beethoven, Goethe, to name but a few of the illustrious galaxy of men who made German culture the heritage of the human race. But this liberal spirit, which was never concentrated in one capital, such as Paris or London, and thereby struck deep roots in the German character, was unconcerned with political affairs. The spectacle of a Goethe who was not humiliated by the Napoleonic conquest of Germany suggests, indeed, an abnormal view of life. Not until the nineteenth century did German thought attempt seriously to cope with the problems of internal disunion or foreign intrigue. Its remedy was parliamentary government, but the revolutions of 1848 showed the futility of such ideas; so that it was left for Bismarck, by seizing a tradition of order, discipline, thoroughness, and frankly material aims, to lead the German nation out of the shadows of the Holy Roman Empire and the Confederation of 1815 to the reality of a Prussian-governed autocracy.

Since 1871 Germany has been in the iron grip of Prussia.

For under the imperial constitution the governing force
is the Bundesrath, which is an assembly of delegates from
the confederated governments, and the votes are so arranged that Prussia's will is, for all practical purposes, law.
The chancellor and his ministers take their orders from
the Emperor, to whom alone they are responsible. The
Reichstag, though elected by universal suffrage, which was
Bismarck's one concession to the spirit of the age, in theory
holds the purse-strings, but, since no taxes can be changed
without the consent of the Prussian Government, it is
really little more than a debating society and sits powerless
in the palace guarded by the statue of Bismarck. Five
times since the foundation of the Empire has the Reichstag
been dissolved for resistance to the imperial will, and in
each election the opponents of the official policy have been
pilloried as traitors and invited to leave a country they
could not appreciate. It is scarcely too much to say that
there is no way for the people of Germany to limit the action of their government except by open rebellion, against
which the memories of 1848, a standing army of nearly
1,000,000 men, and an omnipresent and omnipotent bureaucracy have hitherto operated as effective restraints.

This ascendency of the executive over the legislature
has not passed unchallenged, for the Radical and Socialist
parties protest against it. The latter, in particular, realizing clearly that political reform must precede any social
revolution, has for years demanded a responsible ministry,
freedom of speech and of the press, control of war and
peace by the Reichstag, and the other concomitants of a
democratic state; all of which are anathema to the governing classes. Bismarck endeavored to repress the agitation
by harsh legislation, Emperor William has violently de-
nounced its supporters as grumblers and traitors, but with
each general election the movement has gathered force.

But for their refusal to co-operate with the other opposition parties, whom they despise as representing the black-coated and white-collared classes, the socialists would long since, on paper, have become a menace to the self-perpetuating government they profess to abhor.

ADVANCE OF SOCIALISM

Year	Total vote	Socialists	Percentage	Seats in Reichstag
1890.............	7,228,500	1,127,300	10.11	35
1893.............	7,674,000	1,786,700	19.74	44
1898.............	7,757,700	2,107,076	23.30	56
1903.............	9,495,586	3,010,771	31.71	81
1907.............	11,262,800	3,259,000	28.94	43
1912.............	12,206,806	4,250,329	34.82	110

Many competent students looked forward to the day when the socialist avalanche should overturn the autocratic system, and it is not impossible that the fear of this eventuality was among the factors which induced the imperial government to precipitate a war that promised to end speedily in a resounding triumph. But such estimates of the situation overlooked three important facts.

First, to make the chancellor responsible to the Reichstag would endanger Prussia's supremacy in Germany, for, under the existing arrangements, he is always the Prussian prime minister. The commons of England had to cut off the head of one king and drive his son from the throne to secure even partial control of the executive; France, since 1815, has indulged in three revolutions for the same end. Let the Reichstag choose the chancellor, and that mouthpiece of the Emperor may well be the bitter opponent of the Prussian King. Before granting such a concession, the Emperor is more likely to follow the advice of a well-known Conservative and send a lioutenant with ten men to "close up the Reichstag." [1]

Second, by no means one-third of the German people are Socialists. Most of those who voted the Socialist ticket in the Reichstag elections did so to protest against the government's policy and not against the government, which was chiefly criticised for its vacillating conduct of foreign affairs. Not more than a million genuine Socialists paid dues to the party organization; the other three millions were well aware that the Socialist programme was not a matter of practical politics, and if its realization had seemed probable they would promptly have rejoined one of the national parties.

Third, the Socialist members of the Reichstag have never really joined issue with the government. They have talked vaguely about disarmament and have rendered lip homage to the principle of arbitration, but they have always voted for the vast appropriations demanded for increasing the army and navy, which the government, cleverly enough, raised at the expense of the middle and upper classes. Thus the Socialists were able at once to save their principles and to further the national policy which could be represented as purely defensive. It is well to remember that after the Morocco crisis of 1911 Herr Bebel, the Socialist leader, declared that if Germany were attacked he would shoulder his musket and go to the front like all other good Germans. The Socialists accepted as fully as the other parties the necessity of national expansion, and to expect, as some writers have done since the war began, that they would raise their voices against a war upon which the future of German expansion depended, was to associate with them a philosophy of conduct which they never promulgated and never accepted. For this very reason

---

[1] Herr von Oldenburg, quoted by F. W. Wile, *Men Around the Kaiser*, p. 94

they never accorded their sympathy to the propaganda of Jaurès and the French syndicalists, who aimed at creating an international solidarity among the working classes that would render mobilization a farce.

But not only has popular control been excluded from the German constitutional system: south and non-Prussian Germany have been deprived of any real voice in the conduct of affairs, and these regions, traditionally rather liberal and easy-mannered, have in no small degree been infected by the Prussian spirit. According to Prince Bülow, whose *Imperial Germany* is an admirable statement of the Prussian official doctrine, German idealism has been in this fashion tempered by Prussian realism. Both are necessary for Germany, so that the government rules in Prussia with the help of the Conservative party, in the Empire with the support of liberalism. From the fusion of these two elements a national spirit is being evolved which will preserve the united fatherland from both the black peril of clericalism and the red peril of socialism. But he is thoroughly convinced that Prussia must bear the brunt of the burden.

That proud kingdom, he says very fitly and succinctly, "always has been, and still is, a nation of soldiers and officials," [1] and it could not well be otherwise. Prussia is not a geographical necessity, as is France or Italy, but an artificial patchwork of lands without natural limits on either eastern or western frontiers. Nor is it the heir of a great historical tradition, which provides Austria-Hungary with an excuse for existence. Three hundred years ago the Hohenzollerns ruled but the Mark of Brandenburg, a small district lying mainly between the Elbe and the Oder, and two small provinces in south Germany. Thus the Prussian state of our time is the creation of half a

[1] *Imperial Germany*, p. 227.

dozen warrior kings and a few more statesmen of tran scendent ability.

In the middle of the seventeenth century the Great Elector found himself possessed of disjointed dominions stretching from Königsberg to the Rhine. He therefore got rid of the mediæval estates which restricted his absolute authority, and established a standing army out of all proportion to the number of his subjects but abundantly useful for the acquisitive policy he elected to pursue. From the great principles thus laid down his successors have never departed. Reduced to a science and successfully applied by Frederick William I (1713–40) and Frederick the Great (1740–86), they did not save the kingdom from the Napoleonic onslaught and the humiliation of Jena (1806).

A new era seemed to open in Prussian history when, on 22 May, 1815, Frederick William III promised his people a constitution. But, under the influence of Metternich, the promise was speedily forgotten till vividly recalled by the revolution of 1848. At the end of that episode Frederick William IV granted a constitution which is still the public law of Prussia. This instrument was framed in the atmosphere of absolutism, and the King, in opening the first Diet, declared that he would never let a scrap of paper stand between him and his divine mission to govern the people of Prussia. The real power was left in the hands of the King, who appointed the ministry and retained complete control of the army. The legislature, though elected nominally by universal suffrage, was rendered harmless by the three-class system. The largest taxpayers, who together pay one-third of the taxes, form one class; the next largest class, paying another third, form a second class; and the rest of the voters a third. Each class in a constituency chooses the same number of electors, who in turn choose the deputy; the rich and the well-to-do inevitably control the Diet. At the election of 1908 the system worked as follows:

Party	Votes	Seats earned	Seats obtained
Social Democrats...........	598,522	112	7
Catholic Centre.............	499,343	94	104
Nationalists...............	404,343	76	19
Conservatives..............	354,786	67	152
National Liberals..........	318,589	60	65
Radicals...................	120,593	22	36
Free Conservatives.........	63,612	11	60
Total....................	2,360,247	443	443

As the Conservatives support the government unreservedly, there is no outlet or hope for democracy. Despite the liveliest discontent, the system has withstood all attacks, and the laws of the Medes and Persians were not more sacred than this antiquated franchise in the eyes of the privileged voters. And even if the Conservatives should go into opposition, a thing unthinkable, the government could, as Bismarck did from 1863 to 1866, rule without the Diet by means of the army.

Thus, in spite of the autonomy left to the other confederated states by the constitution of 1871, the control of Prussia over Germany is complete, which, to be sure, is merely the logic of history. Furthermore, that control is vested, not in the Prussian people, but in an autocratic government operating through the most efficient and highly organized bureaucracy in the world. Recruited, at least in its higher ranks, from those classes which have profited most from the enlightened absolutism of the past—the landowners, the capitalists, and the military—this bureaucracy resents the slightest concession to democracy. Numbering more than two million officials, it regulates the life of the land to the last detail; so that the cities are uncannily clean, the schools hall-marked for efficiency, and more things forbidden by ubiquitous notices than are dreamed of in our American philosophy. That the German people like this all-pervading governance, and, in fact, need its direction, has often been asserted, is probably true, and, true or not, is of no immediate concern to the outside world. But we are bound to observe that the deadening traditions of acquiescence in official action play into the hands of the government and permit it to march serenely along the course it has staked off, especially in foreign affairs.

Similarly, the German press is sharply differentiated from that of Great Britain or the United States, which subjects every act of government to meticulous criticism and creates that public opinion upon which free government is ultimately dependent. It would be a great mistake to suppose that all German newspapers are inspired by government departments or subsidized from secret funds; on the contrary, many of them are exceedingly outspoken, and convictions for *lèse-majesté* are quite common But, generally speaking, the function of German newspapers is to set forth a view of men and events that will aid and abet the plans matured in official circles; so that public opinion is rather a lever in the hands of the government than a check upon its activities—is, as it were, made to order and regulated according to the necessities of the moment. Especially has this been true in times of international crisis, when the tone of the press invariably reflects the attitude of the foreign office. The leading publicists are professors in the state-controlled universities, retired officials and military men, or aristocratic and titled landowners, all of whom are by tradition committed to the existing system. Against such forces a free-lance like Maximilian Harden, or the Socialist journals, tilt in vain. In the great reviews there is rarely an interpretation of international problems from any point of view not exclusively German; whereas reputable English periodicals have never hesitated to publish articles by foreigners bitterly denouncing British policy and all its works. Internal politics are, indeed, discussed with more freedom, but, when all is said, the imperial government seldom allows itself to be deflected from its policy by press utterances.

It may therefore be said, in answer to the first of our two questions, that Prussian ascendency has pretty thoroughly obscured any recollections of liberalism which may have survived the Bismarckian triumphs of half a century ago; whatever Germans may think, Americans cannot regard the loss of political liberty as desirable, even though efficiency and thoroughness are acquired in its place. As regards the second question, it was indubitable, before the war, that Prussian policy had not stimulated the real unity of Germany, despite the gilded trappings of the imperial edifice. "Bismarck," says the English publicist quoted at the beginning of this chapter, "found his country politically anarchic but morally united; he left it with a semblance of political union and a plague of moral anarchy that has become increasingly evident since the veil of his personality has been removed from the facts."[1] With every allowance for the Englishman's prejudice, the charge rings true across the fifty years that have elapsed since the great chancellor entered the Prussian ministry. Then men were willing to sacrifice everything for German unity; on the eve of the present war sectionalism and class feeling were rampant. The Germans themselves admit it. Are we not told, in private letters and public despatches, that the war has generated a feeling of unity hitherto unknown?

Germany, like ancient Gaul, is divided into three parts. East of the Elbe lie the Mark of Brandenburg and the old

[1] Perris, *Germany and the German Emperor*, p. 276.

duchies of East and West Prussia. Won by the sword in the Middle Ages, and retained by the energies of German colonists, these lands are the heart of the Prussian monarchy. They are thinly populated, given over to agriculture, and dominated by the landed nobility, who exercise quasi-feudal privileges. These gentlemen are described by Bismarck himself, who was one of them and knew the breed, as "the most reactionary class in Europe." Devoted to king, army, and church, whether Lutheran or Catholic, they are the pillars of the autocracy and look with bitter contempt upon the ravages of modern industrialism. Along the Rhine are the provinces secured by Prussia during the Napoleonic wars. Here are located the great industries which are the glory of modern Germany, here social democracy, the eternal enemy of junker privilege, has been most formidable and assertive. Then there is non-Prussian Germany. In south Germany, which joined the empire reluctantly in 1871 (the Prussian spirit was distasteful to its more liberal and democratic ideas), Prussianization has made considerable progress, for it has been found conducive to material prosperity and Catholic interests. But in the provinces acquired by Prussia in the last century—Posen, populated chiefly by Poles; Schleswig-Holstein, containing a number of irreconcilable Danes; and Alsace-Lorraine, with its cherished remembrances of the more liberal French rule—a Prussianizing policy has egregiously failed, as every such policy must fail which sins against the undying facts of national life and character. Finally, across the whole empire there looms the shadow of the Catholic Church, roused to life by the Bismarckian *Kulturkampf* and indifferent to ordinary political animosities, but ever ready for any bargain that will advance her interests; with the curious result that for thirty years the Protestant government of a Protestant empire has maintained a majority in the Reichstag only with the help of

the Centre or Catholic party! This, too, in spite of Prince
Bülow's argument that Prussia's mission is to preserve
Germany from socialism and clericalism.[1]

This lack of real unity is at the bottom of the autocratic
régime imposed upon Germany. "We are not a political
people," constantly asseverates Prince Bülow of his countrymen, and it is intelligible that German statesmen, recalling the long centuries of disunion and weakness, should
be unwilling to test the new-born unity by experiments in
self-government. Not unnaturally, perhaps, have they
argued that the age-old centrifugal forces could be obliter-
ated only by the power, dominion, and majesty of the Prussian state, and that the transformation could not be speedily
accomplished. They have yet to learn that self-government
and national unity go hand in hand, and that sectionalism
has been perpetuated precisely because the non-Prussian
regions distrust the Prussianizing policy of the imperial
government. Thus events move in a vicious circle, the
slightest manifestation of a provincial spirit being coun-
tered by the application of more rigorous Prussian methods.

The treatment of the conquered provinces fearfully illustrates the bankruptcy of Bismarckian and Guilelmian state-
craft. Until the Iron Chancellor conceived the idea of
Germanizing the province of Posen by expropriating the
lands of the Polish inhabitants and forbidding the use of
the Polish language, the Poles were loyal subjects of Prussia
who appreciated the blessings of ordered government in
comparison with the harsh treatment of their brethren in
Russian Poland. At a cost of $120,000,000 the Prussian
Government has established 110,000 Germans in the province, but their presence has been useless to the cause of
Teutonism, and the Poles have become not only martyrs
to the idea of nationality but actually dominant in economic as well as political affairs. Prince Bülow himself,

[1] *Imperial Germany*, part 2, chap. 2, "National Views and the Parties."

while ardently supporting the official policy, admits that
it has failed—and can suggest no alternative but more of
the same diet![1]

In Alsace-Lorraine inconsistency has been added to stupidity. In the opinion of the writer, Bismarck was justified in demanding the provinces from France in 1871, for,
if Napoleon III had been victorious in the war, he would
have extended the French frontier toward the Rhine at
the expense of Germany. But the official ground for the
annexation was that the people of Alsace and Lorraine
were German in descent and feeling, and must therefore
belong to a united Germany. If so, were they not entitled
to be treated like other non-Prussian Germans? Like
the Bavarians, for instance, who, although enemies of
Prussia in the war of 1866 and unwilling partners in the
enterprise of 1870, were allowed to retain autonomy and
the emblems of their historical sovereignty? But no. The
Alsatians and Lorrainers, transferred against their will,
were treated like Frenchmen and subjected to the full force
of Prussian bureaucratic methods. To their persistent demand for self-government, which would have reconciled
them to their new allegiance, no adequate answer was ever
given, for the constitution of 1911 preserved the reality of
power in the hands of the *Statthalter*, who was appointed
by the Emperor. If German statesmen had not been so
unwilling to learn from English experience, a reluctance
born of their horror of parliamentary government, they
would have at least conceded to the provinces privileges
similar to those granted to Quebec in 1774, which have
kept a population of bigoted French Catholics splendidly
loyal to the British crown. It is impossible to say whether
the people of Alsace-Lorraine desired reunion with France,
but no one will assert that they were satisfied with the
Prussian régime that culminated in the affair of Zabern.

[1] *Ibid.*, chap. 4, "The Eastern Marches."

In the autumn of 1913 an ardent lieutenant of the garrison reviled the inhabitants of Zabern for their attachment to France, and when the compliment was returned by the populace, he took to shopping under an escort of soldiers with fixed bayonets. One day he struck with his sabre a lame shoemaker who brushed him in the street. An uproar followed, martial law was proclaimed, and the colonel of the regiment threatened to "shoot up" the town. A man was arrested for laughing, and also several government officials who protested against the supersession of the civil authority. The climax was reached when a court martial exonerated the officers involved, and formally sustained the pretensions of the military; while the gallant colonel received the Order of the Red Eagle. Moltke, who in 1871 demanded Metz for military reasons, said that the provinces might be reconciled in fifty years; after Zabern all signs of friendliness disappeared, and the return of the Tricolor seems to have been enthusiastically hailed in Alsace.

The supreme test of statesmanship is the ability to govern well and to their own satisfaction a helpless and conquered people, and judged by this standard the German imperial system has ignominiously failed. To Americans, with an ancient heritage of self-government and political freedom, it is almost unintelligible why autonomy, which breeds loyalty and contentment, should have been denied to Prussian Poland and Alsace-Lorraine. But German political philosophy demands formal connection with and control by the central government of all phases of the national life, and behind this conviction, it must be admitted, there lies the peculiar history of Germany, which is in marked contrast to the slow and orderly, almost paradoxical, evolution of England.

The Norman conquest saved the island state from the worst evils of feudalism, and precisely because the English

king during the Middle Ages was able to maintain order
and to rest his military and financial system on sound
principles, he could concede to his subjects privileges and
liberties which the more absolute monarchs of the Continent
were bound to regard with abhorrence. In the fulness of
time a Parliament grew up and waxed strong, which was
the king's most valiant support as long as he respected
its rights, as was apparent when the brilliant Tudor monarchs of the sixteenth century erected a despotism practically with the consent of Parliament. Then, with this
despotic machinery to hand, the Stuarts endeavored to
dispense with Parliament altogether, but they found, to
their sorrow, that the liberties of Englishmen were far
stronger than any power the crown might secure, and their
fate we know. Since then the inalienable rights of Parliament and people have remained secure against all attacks.

On the other hand, even in the palmy days of the Holy
Roman Empire, the Emperor never exercised absolute
power. Feudalism ran its logical course in Germany, as in
no other country, for it managed to destroy the effective
power of the central government, which alone could protect the land against oppression and misgovernment by a
host of princes now responsible to no higher authority. In
such a system, or the lack of it, there was no place for
popular rights, so that in 1848 the Frankfort assembly
had to waste six precious months in elaborating the fundamental rights of the German nation. Not until very recent times was there in Germany any strong authority
which could satisfy the needs of the German people.
When order was finally evolved out of chaos by the will of
a single state, and Germans were thereby enabled to achieve
internal peace and material prosperity, it is small wonder
that they hastened to idealize and deify the state as something above themselves, upon whose strength and power
their own happiness depended. The very failure of the

movement of 1848, based as it was on the attempt to introduce English practises into Germany, and the resounding triumphs of 1864, 1866, and 1871 compelled a belief
in power and force and war. And an English scholar admits that "only a powerful state could disregard the grum-
blings of that provincial patriotism which was still so deeply
rooted in the German character, or could face with equanimity the international situation created by Bismarck's
policy of blood and iron." [1]

The most vivid expression of the doctrine of power is
to be found in the writings of Heinrich von Treitschke,
who from 1874 to 1895 was professor of history in the University of Berlin. Owing to the profound respect and approval with which professorial utterances are received in
Germany, the occupant of this chair has a unique opportunity to obtain a hearing; his position is decidedly more
inportant than in America is the presidency of Harvard
or Columbia University. Treitschke was also the editor
of the *Preussische Jahrbücher*, which is the German equivalent of the *North American Review*. His teachings were not
less calculated to please because he was by birth a Saxon,
and in his earlier years, before the wars of unification,
had been an advocate of liberal institutions. He had, as
it were, accepted the logic of events, and adjusted his political theories to the new situation. He was, however, no
toady. Deeply versed in ancient and modern history, he
tried to formulate his conclusions on the basis of human,
or rather national, experience. Nor is it always easy to
refute his argument, as when he says that "the state is
the public power of offense and defense," [2] that is, it exists to administer justice and to make war. At the time

[1] H. W. Carless Davis, *The Political Thought of Heinrich von Treitschke*, p. 134.
Though written after the outbreak of the Great War, the book is a fine piece of
scholarship and treats Treitschke with considerable sympathy.

[2] Mr. Davis's translations have been generally used; occasionally I have borrowed from A. L. Gowan, *Selections from Treitschke's Lectures on Politics*, 1914.

Treitschke wrote, such were the chief and almost the only functions of the state. It must also be remembered that he did not propose to elaborate a system of politics suitable to all peoples under all conditions; he wrote for Germans, and he sought to interpret their problems from the German point of view. If he was often prejudiced, especially against English practises and institutions, he must be given credit for entire sincerity and frankness. The extent of his influence in contemporary Germany is a matter of dispute. In his lifetime he was certainly the most noted apologist of the Bismarckian system, his theories found much favor with Pan-German writers after his death, and his interpretation of history was boldly appropriated by General Friedrich von Bernhardi for his *Germany and the Next War;* his ascendency among German political thinkers was also assumed by the late Professor Cramb in his *Germany and England.* But Mr. Sidney Whitman, whose experience of Germany goes back fifty years, states that Treitschke's influence has been on the wane for some time.[1] The point is perhaps immaterial, for his work had been done. He preached to the generation which now dominates Germany, and the doctrines he popularized have been highly regarded since the foundation of the empire.

The gist of his teaching, as exemplified in the *Politik* and as already suggested, is that the state is power. "Of all political sins that of weakness is the most reprehensible and the most contemptible; it is in politics the sin against the Holy Ghost." All other purposes are subordinate to the acquisition of power, which, in plain language, means the ability to make war. For without war, which "is the only remedy for ailing nations," as well as the instinct of mighty peoples, the state cannot indulge "the craving to impress the seal of its nature upon barbaric lands"; nor without war will Germany be able to acquire the colonies

[1] "Germany's Obsession," *Fortnightly Review,* October, 1914.

upon which her future depends. Consequently, the mechanism of the state must be ordered with the view of conducting a successful war. That is to say, individual rights, except the privilege of independent thought, cannot be tolerated, for they may conflict with the highest interests of the state, which the individual cannot appreciate. "On principle the state does not ask how the people is disposed; it demands obedience: its laws must be kept, whether willingly or unwillingly. It is a step in advance when the silent obedience of the citizens becomes an inward, rational consent, but this consent is not absolutely necessary."

"With reference to the best form of state, all that the historian can assert without presumption is that, since the state is primarily power, the form of state which will take the government into its own hands and make itself independent best fulfils the idea." Parliamentary government, which he admitted was admirably suited to eighteenth-century England, he disliked because the parties indulged in a struggle for office; it worked in England only because there was no difference of principles between the parties, both of which were aristocratic to the core. But in Germany, where "the kingship is almost the only force of political tradition which unites our present with our past" and where parties profess different principles that are irreconcilable, parliamentary government is ridiculous. The existence of the German state demands that any discrepancy between king and ministers be promptly reconciled, "however inconvenient this may be for the ministers concerned." In fine, the idea of popular government is in contradiction with the whole imperial system. "We have reason to congratulate ourselves that we do possess a vigorous monarchical civil service, which, in virtue of its own services, of its social position, and also of the authority of the crown, has a real and absolute importance. We have no ground whatever for wishing that it should be otherwise." Monarchy, in short, is the best form of government, for Germany at any rate, because "the will of the state is represented by one single individual," whose authority "is not transmitted, but rests on its own right." The monarch will be supported by the aristocracy, who, Treitschke says, must be maintained by the masses. "The masses will always remain the masses. There can be no culture without the masses." They may find "a certain superficial consolation from universal suffrage," but the nobility must do the governing, for they, and they alone, possess that will to rule which is the first principle of power.

Such, in brief and very inadequate form, is the philosophic justification of the German autocratic government, which has ever been indifferent to justification. The German people, as a whole, have no complaint about its working, and the very limited success of parliamentary government in countries outside of England does not suggest that it would be more suitable to Germany where every tradition is against it. There is, then, no ground for ridiculing or abusing Germans for not trying a system foreign to their history, and probably abhorrent to their character, which has always required leadership, direction, command for adequate development or assertion. But when the cult of power breeds an excessive devotion to distasteful ideals, it is necessary to repudiate the premises from which such conclusions follow and to express the belief that the extension of this system of life and political organization beyond the confines of Germany cannot only rouse no enthusiasm, but demands our hearty disapproval.

The second Prussian tradition, militarism and the religion of war, which is the concrete expression of the doctrine of power, finds no little justification from a historical point of view. The annals of the Hohenzollerns, from their purchase of the Electorate of Brandenburg in 1415 to the proclamation of the new empire at Versailles in 1871, are synonymous with military prowess: the two black episodes of Prussian history should convince even the antimilitarist that military weakness is the prelude to national disgrace and humiliation. In 1806 Napoleon shattered the inefficient Prussian army at Jena and proceeded to partition the kingdom. In 1850, when Austria had crushed the revolutionary movements in her own territories, she demanded that Prussia forego her plans for a German state under her direction and consent to the re-establishment of the old Confederation of 1815; and because of her military unpreparedness, Prussia was constrained to yield. The modern history of Germany may be said to date from this incident, for when the vacillating Frederick William IV (1840–1861) was succeeded by William I the first task of the new monarch was to reform the Prussian army in all its details. How Bismarck provided the genius to carry through the reform against the wishes of the Diet and then used the new army to achieve the unification of Germany, is a story that need not be told here. But we must not ignore the moral. Germany was created by the sword, and only the sword, firmly wielded, it was believed, could preserve her from the greed and jealousy of the older nations that resented her sudden and dramatic entry into the European family. *Ohne Armee kein Deutschland*, to borrow a saying of Bismarck.

No reasonable person has ever denied the necessity for Germany to maintain a strong army. Unless she was to undergo again the horrors of the seventeenth and eighteenth centuries, when her fair provinces were overrun by armies from every country in Europe, and her people suffered untold miseries, she must be a match for any probable combination of enemies. Also it was well recognized that, faced as she was on her western frontier by her hereditary enemy (even the Kaiser spoke of France as the *Erbfeind*),

and on the east by a Power possessing inexhaustible resources of men, that might and did ally itself with France,
Germany was entitled to be strong, to be prepared for
any eventuality, to be even "touchy" on the matter of
other nations' armaments. In addition, universal military service has been an important factor of internal
policy. Two years of barrack and camp life, after the
strenuous thoroughness of the schooling period, mean much
for the physical health and strength of the German people; there is also generated a sense of discipline and a
regard for authority which is quite necessary for both
government and governed if the existing political institutions are to be maintained or the German character to
remain what it is. Like many other aspects of German life
which are foreign to American ways of thinking, the German army finds no little justification in the light of German
history and German problems.

But Prussian ascendency in Germany has been responsible for foisting upon the country two unnecessary developments of the doctrine of conscription: the reckless and in-
human increase of armaments, which Germany's neighbors
have been compelled to emulate; and the deliberate exalta-
tion of the military spirit, which has not unnaturally made
other nations of Europe suspicious of her intentions.

It may be admitted that the first steps in the heaping up
of colossal armaments were taken by France. The German
imperial constitution provides that the army on its peace
footing shall represent one per cent of the population, and
as long as Bismarck remained at the helm of state this proportion was not exceeded. Starting at 401,000 in 1871,
the army was raised to 427,000 in 1881, and to 468,000 in
1887. France, however, had gone beyond this, especially
in the Boulanger law of 1886, which gave her an army of
above 500,000, although her population was less than 38,-
000,000. In fairness to Germany let it not be overlooked

that she has never kept as large a proportion of her people with the colors as has France, and Germans have not unnaturally argued that France must be preparing for a war to recover the lost provinces. As the French military attaché wrote in March, 1913: "Moderate persons, military and civil, glibly voice the opinion that France, with her 40,-000,000 inhabitants, has no right to compete with Germany in this way."[1] To which it may surely be retorted that Germany ought not to consider herself in the running with Russia!

The expansion of the German army is chiefly the work of William II. The half-million mark was passed in 1893, and further increases in 1899, 1905, and 1911 merely preserved the constitutional ratio of one per cent between army and population. But the law of 1893 reduced the term of service from three to two years, thereby increasing the number of trained men nearly fifty per cent. Twelve years later France followed the example of Germany, and by abolishing all exemptions and privileges was able to create a peace army of 567,000, including 28,000 colonial troops stationed in France. Even this left her behind Germany by more than 50,000. Indeed, it was this disparity in troops, threatening each year to become more marked by reason of her stationary population, that led the Republic to conclude the alliance with Russia, which has been its overwhelming offense against Germany. But France could scarcely do otherwise. She believed that the war of 1870 had been forced upon her by the malevolent intrigues of Bismarck; she was convinced that in 1875, and again in 1887, she would have been the victim of an unprovoked attack had not the Tsar interfered to restrain the military party in Berlin. On the other hand, the conclusion of the alliance gave Germany an excuse for increasing her own forces indefinitely.

[1] *Yellow Book*, no. 1, enclosure 1.

This was delayed for some years, for huge sums were lavished on the fleet, but after her diplomacy had failed in 1911 to solve the Moroccan imbroglio satisfactorily to herself Germany frankly abandoned the old ratio of one per cent. To the statement of the Prussian minister for war, in 1911, that "there was no government which either desired or was seeking to bring about a war with Germany," was opposed the chancellor's remark that "Germany was firmly resolved not to be pushed aside." The population stood at approximately 66,000,000; the army was, by the law of 1912, raised to 723,000. In addition, the machinery of mobilization was improved by raising ten corps on the frontier almost to their war footing and by creating an additional number of reserve officers; likewise various technical improvements, which by the law of 1911 were to be spread over a period of five years, were to be completed at once. The military budget, which in 1905 stood at 698,000,000 marks, was raised to 945,000,000, an increase of 129,000,000 over that of 1911.

But these measures were nothing compared with the herculean effort of 1913, when, according to the chancellor, "the events taking place in the Balkans had changed the balance of power in Europe." By this, the last army law before the Great War, the peace strength of the German army was fixed at 870,000 men. The cost of this colossal addition was met by increased taxation for the recurring expenditure (over £9,000,000 a year), and for the non-recurring expenditure by an extraordinary property levy, estimated at £26,100,000. Unquestionably the collapse of the Turkish power before the onward rush of the young Balkan states had deprived Germany of a potential ally in a general European war, and the aggrandizement of Serbia increased considerably the difficulties in the way of an Austrian forward movement in the Balkans, so that, if the Triple Alliance were at war with Russia, the bulk of the fighting would indubitably fall upon Germany. From this point of view and on the assumption that Germany, contrary to the advice of Bismarck, would make Austria's Balkan policy her own, a general strengthening of the army was imperiously necessary. But when the *Cologne Gazette*, without the slightest provocation, declared on 10 March, 1913, that "never has the relationship to our western neighbor been so strained as to-day, never has the idea of revenge been exhibited there so nakedly, and . . . that it is perfectly certain Germany will have to cross swords with France," the rest of Europe doubted whether the latest army measures were really directed against Russia, and could assert in good conscience that Germany, and Germany alone, was responsible for the burden of armaments.

It was inevitable that the other European countries should follow her example. France returned to the rule of three years' service, at a cost of £20,000,000, the bill being passed on 16 July, seventeen days after the German measure. Belgium introduced universal military service, which promised to give her an army of above 300,000 men in the course of several years. In Russia the term of service was lengthened to three and a quarter years, and some £15,000,000 provided for emergency expenditure in 1914. Great Britain alone of the *Entente* Powers, who were supposedly hostile to Germany, made no change in her military establishment. The proof, then, is absolute that in the last phase of the armament curse, "the white man's burden," the pace was set by Germany, and "it is difficult to believe that some startling *coup* was not even then being planned by the military party." [1]

This suggestion is thoroughly justified by the popularity in modern German thought of the religion of war. The bible of this doctrine is, of course, General Friedrich von

[1] *Why We Are at War*, by members of the Oxford School of Modern History, p. 46.

Bernhardi's *Germany and the Next War*, and, although the book has been widely read, a brief analysis seems called for. Germany, the general argues, can acquire that "place in the sun" which is her due only by a war of aggression, because the Powers of the Triple Entente—Russia, France, and England—, each and all endowed with vast possessions which they cannot adequately use, surround her with a ring of iron; yet to avoid the appearance of aggression she must "initiate an active policy which, without attacking France, will so prejudice her interests or those of England that both these states will feel compelled to attack" her. There is also a labored analysis of war as a "biological necessity"; "the maintenance of peace never has been, and never can be, the goal of a policy." Equally striking, perhaps, is the remark about the "dangerous agitation" of social democracy: "A war may be forced upon a statesman by the condition of home affairs." When the war comes, and we are told that an Anglo-German war is "inevitable," it is to be waged ruthlessly, "frightfully," with the object of destroying the balance in Europe and without regard to treaties or vested rights the neutrality of Belgium is only "a paper bulwark"; "in this war we *must* conquer, or, at any rate, not allow ourselves to be defeated, for it will decide whether we can attain a position as a world Power by the side of, and in spite of, England." From first to last the argument is directed against England. Thus, *"we must square our account with France* if we wish for a free hand in our international policy." It is a small matter that such a consummation could not be reached without the crushing of Russia as well, for the general, like all Germans, has a poor opinion of Russia's capacity for war, and he does not believe that "Russia would now be inclined to make an armed demonstration in favor of France." England, he admits, will make a hard fight, but her colonies will revolt, the Turks will attack Egypt, and her relations with America will increase the difficulties of her situation. Germany, therefore, needs but to increase her navy until it can cope with the armada of England and victory will be sure. "English attempts at a *rapprochement* must not blind us as to the real situation. We may at most use them to delay the necessary and inevitable war until we may fairly imagine that we have some prospect of success."

Such is the monstrous theory which seems primarily responsible for the present war. It is necessary to point out that the cult of militarism is an old story in Germany, or at least in Prussia. In 1836 Clausewitz, a Prussian general who fought against Napoleon and whose book on *War* is the basis of scientific study of the subject, laid down the doctrine that war is "the continuation of policy by other means," a doctrine the successful application of which in the unification of Germany not unnaturally commended it to the governing classes of the next generation. Even the great Bismarck was aware that militarist influence might escape the bounds which his personality and character imposed upon it. Discussing the question whether diplomacy can ever be justified in deliberately causing war, he says, in his *Reflections and Reminiscences:*

"I have always opposed the theory which says 'yes'; not only at the Luxemburg period, but likewise subsequently for twenty years, in the conviction that even victorious wars cannot be justified unless they are forced upon one, and that one cannot see the cards of Providence far enough ahead to anticipate historical development according to one's own calculation. It is natural that in the staff of the army not only the younger active officers, but likewise experienced strategists, should feel the need of turning to account the efficiency of the troops led by them and their own capacity to lead, and of making them prominent in history. It would be a matter of regret if this spirit of the spirit did not exist in the army; *the task of keeping its result within such limits as the nation's need of peace can justly claim is the duty of the political, not the military, heads of the state.* That at the time of the Luxemburg question, during the crisis of 1875, invented by Gortchakoff and France, and even down to the most recent times, the staff and its leaders have allowed themselves to be led astray and to endanger peace, lies in the very spirit of the institution, which I would not forego. *It only becomes dangerous under a monarch whose policy lacks sense of proportion and power to resist one-sided and constitutionally unjustifiable influences."* [1]

The reference to the present Emperor is obvious (the *Reflections and Reminiscences* were written after Bismarck's dismissal in 1890), but William II has from the beginning of his reign flattered, caressed, and exalted the military spirit. His first act, after his accession, was to issue a proclamation to his army, not to his people as his father Frederick III had done, and he has seized every occasion since then to preach from the same text. True, his speeches abound in phrases proclaiming his love of peace, but there is always the implication that peace rests upon the strength of the German army, which is ready for instant use if the interests of the fatherland are in question.

In no other country but Germany could seven thousand books dealing with war have been published in the ten years preceding the great conflict: General von Bernhardi is simply the ablest, the most scholarly, and the most sincere exponent of the militarist thesis. We in America remain convinced, despite the denials of German apologists, that he reflected the sentiments of his countrymen; as the late Price Collier put it: "It is a commentary upon the three countries that in Germany the soldier receives a reduced rate when travelling, in England the golfer pays a reduced rate, and in America, until lately, the politicians were given free passes." [2] The fact that the operations of the German army and the German navy in the war have followed so closely the strategy outlined by General von Bernhardi raises the suspicion that official inspiration had something to do with its writing.

[1] Vol. II, pp. 101–2.   [2] *Germany and the Germans*, p. 441.

Germany and the Next War appeared in the spring of 1912, or some six months after the last Moroccan crisis, in which Germany was badly worsted. That defeat was universally attributed, and properly, to the intervention of Great Britain. General von Bernhardi takes up the challenge in true Prussian fashion, at the very time when Norman Angell, in *The Great Illusion,* was insisting on the uselessness and improbability of war. It is surely symptomatic that the general's book could be written, and, if it did not commend itself to the "general reader" until a few months ago, it was thoroughly digested and reviewed in the leading journals of France and Great Britain, where it was accepted as a semiofficial statement of German policy. It was promptly translated into English at least. Even so, it was difficult for Englishmen to take its outpourings seriously.

"If General Bernhardi would come to this country," wrote Lord Esher to the *Times,* "and move among the best elements of our people, among our university students, among our workers in great cities, and among our peaceful agricultural population, it would amaze him not to find a single soul, unless it be here and there a lover of paradox, that could be got to understand his point of view. . . . For those of us who hope always to see Germans and French stand shoulder to shoulder with our own people in the van of enlightened thought, it is piteous to see a German writer, so distinguished in the technical field of military strategy and tactics, plunging so forlornly into a quagmire of international politics and ethics, created, let us hope, by himself." [1]

One is indeed reluctant to believe that any considerable or influential section of a nation, especially if that nation be distinguished for its industrial and commercial enterprise, and fond of asserting that its civilization is not only the glory of this age but the promise of generations to come, can have gone so completely war-mad. Nevertheless, am-

[1] Weekly edition, 5 April, 1912.

ple corroboration of such a melancholy temper may be found in a report on German public opinion prepared by French diplomatic agents in Germany and printed in the French *Yellow Book*. The document is not above suspicion, for, dated 30 July, 1913, it contains a reference to Herr von Kiderlen-Waechter, the German foreign secretary who died in the last days of 1912. But the materials on which the report is based may have been collected before the latter date; there is certainly no analysis of German sentiment with respect to the Balkan Wars of 1912-13, which were universally regarded as a decisive set-back for German policy. That the testimony of the French report was not a figment of the imagination may be seen from the interview with "An Ambassador" published by the Berlin *Lokal Anzeiger* in the spring of 1914. According to this anonymous personage, supposedly Sir W. E. Goschen, then British ambassador in Berlin:

"Jingoism has made indisputable progress in the German population. I am convinced that there exists among the German people a latent jingoism which is much more dangerous than that of England, Russia, or France. German jingoism recruits its partisans from the highest classes of the nation—nobility, clergy, army and navy, university and gymnasium professors and students, and the entire scholastic world. . . . Everywhere among the cultivated classes it is made a dogma that the German Empire does not take its proper part in world politics. Everywhere the great organs of public opinion spread the dangerous and irritating doctrine that German prestige is going down. And so patriots clamor for action." [1]

It therefore seems fair to cite the French report in this connection.

"German public opinion," it says, "is divided into two currents on the question of the possibility and proximity of war. There are in the country forces making for peace, but they are unorganized

---

[1] *Nation* (New York), 9 July, 1914, "Foreign Correspondence."

and have no popular leaders. They consider that war would be a social misfortune for Germany, and that caste pride, Prussian domination, and the manufacturers of guns and armor-plate would get the greatest benefit, but above all that war would profit England. The forces consist of the following elements: the bulk of the workmen, artisans, and peasants . . . those members of the nobility detached from military interests and engaged in business . . . numerous manufacturers, merchants, and financiers in a moderate way of business . . . Poles, inhabitants of Alsace-Lorraine and Schleswig-Holstein . . . finally, the governments and all the governing classes in all the large southern states—Saxony, Bavaria, Würtemberg, and the grand duchy of Baden. . . . These supporters of peace believe in war in the mass because they do not see any other solution for the present situation.

"People sometimes speak of a military party in Germany. The expression is inaccurate, even if it is intended to convey the idea that Germany is the country where military power is supreme, as it is said of France that it is the country where the civil power is supreme. There exists a state of mind which is more worthy of attention than this historical fact, because it constitutes a danger more evident and more recent. There is a war party, with leaders and followers, a press either convinced or subsidized for the purpose of creating public opinion; it has means both varied and formidable for the intimidation of the government. It goes to work in the country with clear ideas, burning aspirations, and a determination that is at once thrilling and fixed.

"Those in favor of war are divided into several categories. . . . Some want war because in the present circumstances they think it is *inevitable*. . . . Others regard war as necessary for economic reasons based on overpopulation, overproduction, the need for markets and outlets; or for social reasons, *i. e.*, to provide the outside interests that alone can prevent or retard the rise to power of the democratic and socialist masses. Others, uneasy for the safety of the Empire, and believing that time is on the side of France, think that events should be brought to an immediate head. . . . Others are bellicose from 'Bismarckism,' as it may be termed. . . .

"War alone can prolong the prestige of the aristocracy and support its family interest. The higher bourgeoisie, represented by the National Liberal party, the party of the contented spirits, have not the same reasons as the squires for wanting war. With few exceptions, however, they are bellicose. . . . Amongst the 'Bismarckians' must be reckoned officials of all kinds. . . . They find

disciples and political sympathisers in tho various groups of young
men whose minds have been trained and formed in the public
schools and the universities," which, "if we except a few distinguished spirits, develop a warlike philosophy. . . . Historians,
philosophers, political pamphleteers, and other apologists of German *Kultur* wish to impose upon the world a way of thinking and
feeling specifically German. . . . We come finally to those whose
support of the war policy is inspired by rancor and resentment.
These are the most dangerous. They are recruited chiefly among
diplomatists."[1]

The most conclusive proof of this bellicose temper was
vouchsafed in the fateful days of July, 1914. Early in the
month the German press vigorously demanded the severe
punishment of Serbia for the murders at Sarajevo. When
the Austrian ultimatum was presented, satisfaction was
universally expressed, and after war had been declared upon
Serbia by the Dual Monarchy there was general rejoicing
throughout Germany that at last the hated little nation
which blocked the designs of both Germany and Austria
was to be brought to book. Finally, the Kaiser's ultimatum to Russia, followed promptly by the declaration of
war, was the most popular act of his reign, if one may
judge from the excitement of the Berlin street crowds and
the truculent tone of the press. The hysteria of both Berlin and Vienna stands out boldly against the calm of Paris
and London; in St. Petersburg there was dignified enthusiasm, splendid determination, but no delirious outburst,
no thanksgiving that "the day" had come. We do not
hear that either press or populace in Germany regarded
the failure of the negotiations as an unspeakable calamity.
Not less than the French in 1870 did the nation enter upon
war "with a light heart," for, until Great Britain plunged
into the conflict, few doubted that the carefully prepared
plan of the general staff would make the war a short one
and that the profits would make the game worth the
expense.

[1] *Yellow Book*, no. 5.

No account of modern Germany would be complete without some reference, even at the risk of being hackneyed, to the Emperor William II. That redoubtable monarch is the most enigmatic individual of our time. Restless in his physical make-up, endowed by nature with an active mind and a picturesque imagination, possessed of a tenacious memory, and imbued with boundless self-confidence, he combines an ardent belief in mediæval political doctrines with an enthusiastic devotion to every phase of modern life. There would seem to be no branch of human knowledge or activity in which he has not participated or indulged an inordinate love of speechifying. Thus, in addition to the ordinary vocations of an emperor and king, he has shown an intense interest in the development of German commerce, preached stirring sermons on land and sea, criticised severely the national educational system, and attempted to dictate styles of architecture. He has designed yachts for the Kiel regatta, which he himself inspired, directed productions in the royal opera-house, conducted an orchestra, composed music, painted pictures, and discussed archæology with learned professors. Till the outbreak of the war the world was alternately alarmed and amused by the vagaries of the royal arbiter. Outside of Germany he was often regarded as a dilettante, but thousands of his subjects looked upon him as a genius who united in his own person the myriad talents of the German nation. This many-sided activity was partly explained by a feverish desire to lead the German people to great things and to impress them, if that were necessary, with the sense of their greatness; with it was coupled a deep-seated sense of responsibility and a personal charm that was universally admitted.

On the other hand, William II is the greatest living champion of reaction and militarism. Of the extent to which his people have been infected by the latter disease enough has already been said: the Emperor is more responsible for this than any other single person or circumstance, having for twenty-six years, by both speech and deed, labored to make the army the most important institution of the national life. His political philosophy is summed up in an unswerving allegiance to the divine right of kings, flaunted in innumerable speeches and practised at every turn. Thus, in 1890 he declared that "it is a tradition in our house to consider ourselves as designed by God to govern the people over whom it is given us to reign." In August, 1910, after a long period of comparative silence, he used these words at Königsberg: "Here my grandfather, by his own right hand, placed on his head the royal crown of Prussia, once more declaring with emphasis that it was bestowed upon him by God's grace alone, and not by parliaments, national assemblies, or the popular voice; so that he regarded himself as the chosen instrument of Heaven, and as such he performed his duties as ruler. . . . Looking upon myself as the instrument of the Lord, regardless of the views and opinions of the hour, I shall go my way." The imperial views were admirably summarized by the reactionary professor who enumerated *Pöbel, Presse, und Parlamentismus* as the three evils which must be exterminated from the life of Germany by the vehement assertion of the monarchical power.

On a par with these antiquated beliefs, which reveal some of the Hohenzollerns in a sorry light, and which even Thomas Hobbes, the great apologist of monarchy, did not care to defend, has been William's intolerance of opposition. His most famous utterance, perhaps, is: "There is but one master in this country—it is I, and I will bear no other." He has proclaimed that "an opposition of the Prussian nobility to their king is a monstrosity," and transformed the old Latin adage into *Voluntas regis suprema lex*. He has been his own prime minister, reducing his chancellors to the position of clerks and getting rid of each, from Bismarck to Bülow, at the least sign of insubordination, and he has persecuted to the limit of the law all who dared to criticise him or offer unwelcome advice. Much might also be made of his unusual ability, as a Protestant monarch, to rule his empire with the help of the Catholic (Centre) party and to cultivate an advantageous friendship with the Caliph of Islam; or his vacillations might be examined, for his policy has been now threatening, now pacific, in both tone and action. But William II must remain an enigma for yet a long time to come; indeed, it may well be doubted whether he has always known his own mind or thought out the problems he set himself to solve. It is highly characteristic that his exact measure of responsibility for the war is not yet determined. Had he planned with the Archduke Francis Ferdinand to resume a vigorous German-Austrian policy in the Balkans, or was he, when he returned from Norway late in July, overborne by the military party which thought its chance had come?

In any case William II is the embodiment of his people in their inconsistencies, their idealism, their will to power, and their utter inability to see any point of view not entirely their own, or to grasp the psychology of a situation. What is the world to think when it is told in the German *White Book* that Russia is responsible for the war, and that "shoulder to shoulder with England we labored incessantly" in the cause of peace; while the chancellor before the Reichstag accuses Great Britain of having precipitated the great struggle in order to preserve the balance of power? This lack of consistency, this confusion of thought is apparent in every phase of German life, from court and official circles to the socialists who are not socialists, and this chapter may well conclude with the sentence quoted at its beginning: "The new German Empire is the most perplexing quantity in the modern world, and as unavoidable as it is perplexing."

CHAPTER IV

GERMAN EXPANSION

UNDOUBTEDLY that feature of modern Germany which has commanded popular attention is her rise to the second position among the industrial and commercial nations of the world, and the promise that she would one day overcome the traditional supremacy of Great Britain. Yet there is nothing remarkable about this. Taking the country as a whole, the Germans were probably the most successful business people of the Middle Ages. Their practical genius found an outlet in the Hanseatic League of north Germany, which controlled the commerce of the Baltic and North Seas and exercised enormous political power in northern Europe. Along the Rhine and in south Germany cities like Cologne, Augsburg, and Nuremberg, located as they were on the trade routes between Italy and the north, throve splendidly. Not even the collapse of the mediæval empire and the subsequent growth of disorder could destroy the foundations of German prosperity, and at the opening of the sixteenth century, in the height of the Renaissance, the cities of Germany were famous for their comfort, wealth, and culture. Unfortunately, the failure of German rulers to create a strong national state, coupled with that schism in religion which ultimately led to the devastating Thirty Years' War, left the land a prey to foreign ambitions and local jealousies; so that in the seventeenth and eighteenth centuries it was the shuttlecock of diplomacy and the battle-ground of foreign armies, while frontier provinces which it could not defend were left open to foreign aggression. No wonder that its population fell below that of France, that its economic effort was pitiful compared with the marvellous outburst of English energy associated with the industrial revolution, or that no colonies were secured at a time when the maritime nations were appropriating desirable lands all over the globe.

Yet the heart of the nation remained sound. At the end of the eighteenth century the reforming zeal of Frederick the Great and some of the lesser princes promised well, the romantic movement indicated that a new spirit was awake, and, curiously enough, the cataclysmic wars of the French Revolution and the Napoleonic Empire actually advanced the clock of civilization. Not only were the three-hundred-odd states of Germany reduced to a tenth of their number; after the catastrophe of Jena in 1806, which placed Prussia and Germany at the feet of Napoleon, the Prussian Government set an inspiring example to the smaller states by abolishing serfdom and sweeping away the vestiges of mediæval restrictions and privileges. Nor were the lesser governments loath to act upon its advice, and by 1850 both agriculture and industry were free throughout Germany. The *Zollverein*, or customs union, founded by Prussia in 1828, and gradually extended until it included all the German states except Austria, laid the foundations of a new economic life which possessed boundless possibilities under a national government able to concern itself with the problems of the country as a whole. When unity was accomplished in 1871, Germany responded to the call of the shop and the factory with the enthusiasm that characterized her undertakings in the centuries when she was the dominant Power in Europe. It would, indeed, have been ridiculous if a nation which had fought its way to the political hegemony of the Continent and whose educational system was the envy of other lands had not proved its ability in the economic sphere as well.

Furthermore, Germany had to catch up with countries like England and France, which had achieved their national unity centuries before, were thoroughly industrialized, and had long dominated the markets of the world. Germany could meet their competition only by hard work and scientific endeavor. So, while rendering all honor and praise to the thoroughness of her business methods and the sustained enthusiasm of all classes for the national cause, let us remember that, in the light of her history and in the face of existing conditions, Germany was bound to make a tremendous effort, and her astonishing success has not unnaturally persuaded many neutral observers, not to mention the Germans themselves, that the Allies now ranged against her are actuated chiefly by motives of commercial jealousy.

The prodigious character of Germany's economic enterprise may be grasped from the following brief table— 1871 marks the first year of the new Empire, 1888 the accession of the present Emperor, 1900 the year in which the tension with England first attracted general notice, and 1913 the last for which complete figures are available.

	1871	1888	1900	1913
Population	41,060,792	48,693,836	56,367,178	66,505,825
Savings deposits..	....	....	M. 8,800,000,000	*17,800,000,000
Railways...	6,549 miles	24,036	31,173	*38,426
Revenue...	M. †596,726,300	1,225,926,000	2,025,770,000	3,696,033,200
Imports....	M. 3,464,600,000	3,429,400,000	6,043,000,000	10,695,000,000
Exports....	M. 2,465,200,000	3,356,400,000	4,752,600,000	9,912,600,000
Shipping...	982,355 tons	1,240,182	1,737,798	3,153,724

* Figures for 1911. † Figures for 1872.

The measure of this advance may be gauged from the fact that in less than half a century Germany has risen to second place in the struggle for economic supremacy. In 1913 the national wealth was estimated at 300,000,000,000 marks, the income at 40,000,000,000 marks, figures which are exceeded only by those of the United Kingdom.

Thus the early years of the twentieth century saw Germany well advanced along that road to economic supremacy which she believed to be her goal, and probably most Germans anticipated such a realization within the next ten or fifteen years. But about one condition of that triumph, the most essential condition, in fact, they were entitled to be anxious. They were well aware that the population of the fatherland had increased faster than its capacity for food production, an actual demonstration of the Malthusian principle, if the ability to purchase food abroad is not considered. In the last decade of the nineteenth century the average increase of population exceeded half a million yearly, more recently was above 800,000. Yet even this was not sufficient: for some years before the Great War it was necessary to bring in some 750,000 casual laborers annually from Russia, Poland, and Italy to harvest the magnificent crops of the eastern provinces. Emigration, which in 1880 amounted to 200,000 a year, dwindled to 20,000 after 1900, and of that number comparatively few were dissatisfied with the conditions of life they left behind. A competent authority estimated that, given normal conditions, there would be, in 1925, 80,000,000 people living within the boundaries of the German Empire. On the other hand, and this is the governing fact, 50,000,000 represented the maximum for which food could be grown within the same area.[1] But it was open to doubt if the land would receive such intensive cultivation, for the proportion of the people engaged in agriculture had both relatively and absolutely declined since 1871, as is evident from the following table:

[1] Paul Rohrbach, *Deutschland unter den Weltvölkern*, 1912, p. 17.

	Population	Agricultural	Percentage
1882.................	45,222,113	19,225,500	42
1895.................	51,770,284	18,501,300	35.6
1907.................	61,591,367	17,681,200	28.5

Indeed, without the stimulus of a protective tariff on agriculture, which the war would seem to have justified from a national as opposed to the consumer's interest, Germany would have been almost in the position of Great Britain, which practically depends on the produce of other nations. As it was, Germany ceased to be self-subsistent after 1883; in 1900 food imports amounted to 29 per cent of the total imports, and in 1912 to 30 per cent.

To pay for these foreign food supplies, two courses were open to Germany. She might pay cash or she might export in exchange native raw materials and manufactured articles. The first could take the form of investments abroad or the interest thereon, or be discharged by the services of German shipping. In both of these respects Germany had just cause to be proud of her achievements. The amount of capital invested abroad has been estimated at some 20,000,000,000 marks, the interest on which amounts to 1,000,000,000 marks.[1] The profits of the merchant marine amounted to more than 250,000,000 marks in 1899.[2] But, when all was said, exports had to constitute the bulk of the payments, and this would be increasingly true in years to come.

Now, next to cheap labor, the necessary condition of successful manufacturing is an adequate supply of cheap raw materials, and, unfortunately for Germany, she is less

[1] Dr. Karl Helfferich, *Germany's Economic Progress and National Wealth*, 1888–1913, p. 113, an English edition, issued by the Germanistic Society of America, of *Deutschlands Volkswohlstand*, 1888–1913.
[2] Henri Lichtenberger, *Germany and Its Evolution in Modern Times*, p. 46.

well endowed with natural resources than any of the Great Powers. She lacks in precious metals, the supply of coal and iron is limited, there is no native production of cotton or silk. In other words, Germany has to import practically all the materials consumed by the throbbing factories of Saxony and the Rhineland, copper, woods of various sorts, rubber, oils, and a large part of the minerals. Without a steady and sure supply of these and other stuffs her industries cannot live. Furthermore, it is essential that the finished articles shall find ready markets in foreign lands. Germany, in short, has become a replica of the United Kingdom, a nation living by its foreign commerce; let this cease, and she "would be the victim of a crisis compared with which the crisis in English industry when the American Civil War deprived its spindles of cotton would seem a child's play."[1]

Observing that Great Britain's commerce was most highly developed with her colonies, and that the proportion of this colonial commerce with respect to the total volume of British trade was steadily increasing, Germans not unnaturally argued that their commercial future depended upon the possession of large and flourishing colonies. The late German ambassador to the United States, Baron Speck von Sternberg, might declare that "Germany needs no colonies: what she wants is merely free co-operation on all seas, the open door, and the right to co-operate freely on an equal footing with all other commercial and industrial nations, in opening up and developing yet unopened districts and markets."[2] But the voluminous literature of the expansionist idea, the trend of official policy, and the increase of the navy warrant the belief that such statements were intended to dispel American suspicions

[1] Paul Rohrbach, "L'Evolution de l'Allemagne comme puissance mondiale," *Revue Politique Internationale*, July, 1914, p. 26.
[2] "The Truth about German Expansion," *North American Review*, March, 1908, p. 322.

and did not in any way represent the attitude of the German Government. The imperial chancellor's famous bid for British neutrality on the eve of the war—the promise to take only the French colonies in case of a German victory—revealed unblushingly the true purpose of German policy; as an English writer quite sympathetic with German ambitions remarked a few years ago: "Behind the colonial movement, as it has been reawakened and reinspired during the past few years, lies a virtually united nation,"[1] without distinction of party, from Conservative to Social Democrat. To such a people, who considered the lack of colonies the one defect in an otherwise perfect civilization, the teaching of Norman Angell, as set forth in *The Great Illusion*, that the political ownership of colonies does not in any way affect the wealth of the possessing country, was a voice crying in the wilderness.

As a matter of fact, the colonial question is not so simple and unprofitable as Mr. Angell would have us believe. All governments do not follow the English—and the German—practise of treating all nations equally in the matter of colonial trade. The French allow differential tariffs to their nationals throughout their extensive colonial dominions; the Japanese have been accused of similar sharpness in Manchuria, despite their treaty obligations to maintain the open door; and the Russians have always managed to keep their Asiatic possessions more or less as their own preserve. In the self-governing colonies of the British Empire preferential rates are imposed upon imports from the mother country, and since 1896 there has been much talk of an imperial customs union which would make England's astonishing aggregation of lands and peoples a self-sufficing economic entity. The fact that the trade of Germany with British, French, and Russian colonies is of modest volume has not deterred Germans from asking: What is

[1] W. H. Dawson, *The Evolution of Modern Germany*, p. 398.

to prevent any of these countries, in a moment of jealousy or blindness, from taking measures which would exclude German commerce altogether? And Germany does import a considerable share of her raw materials from British and French colonies. It is also true that the commerce of Germany with her own colonies is ridiculously small, considering the large sums that she has sunk in their development; indeed, the total amount, both imports and exports, represents less than one-half of the trade of those colonies, which in 1910 was valued at £17,387,000. In the same year Great Britain did business with her colonies to the extent of £329,853,099, and France, whose foreign commerce is far behind Germany's, carried on a colonial trade of £21,043,000. Is it any wonder that Germany believed overseas possessions to be both valuable and necessary, and declined to admit that, because she had made no great success of the colonies she did possess, she was doomed to similar failure if she were given a wider opportunity under more favorable conditions?

Patriotic Germans were willing to admit that, as matters stood in the business world, they were doing very well, but they doubted whether, a hundred years hence, when the vast dominions of Great Britain, France, and Russia, not to speak of the United States, had been adequately developed, the position of the fatherland would be secure: even if in old Europe she should completely outdistance her present rivals, they, by virtue of their far-flung empires, would wield political power far superior to her own. Also, without adequate colonies, Germany would be unable to spread her culture throughout the world and found daughter nations who should rise up and call her blessed, after the way of the English, whose imperial record it was desired to emulate and surpass. Thus the maintenance of peace, however much it might add to Germany's prosperity in the immediate future, must in the end tell against her, unless, which was not likely, her rivals were disposed to surrender to her some of the lands won by long years of persistent effort and enterprise.

Germany had, indeed, fared rather shabbily in the scramble for colonies which absorbed so much European energy in the nineteenth century, especially in the last quarter. Her first acquisitions were Togoland and Angra Pequena, in 1884. By 1900 she had added the Cameroons, Southwest Africa, East Africa, German New Guinea, with numerous islands in the Pacific, and the concession of Kiao-Chou in the Shantung peninsula of China: a total area of 1,130,-000 square miles and a population of more than 13,000,000, of whom, however, white persons represented, in 1910, only 25,758, and of that number officials of one kind or another accounted for 8,856. On the other hand, since 1871 France had acquired most of her enormous colonial dependencies (4,776,126 square miles; 41,653,650 inhabitants); Russia had pushed on into Central Asia till her frontier marched with that of British India; England had added Burmah, Egypt, South Africa, half a dozen other African colonies, and sundry Pacific islands; even little Belgium had, under the will of King Leopold, received in the Congo a domain more valuable than all of Germany's colonies together; and sleepy Portugal had consolidated the remnants of her former power into extensive holdings, which were abused by inefficient government and stagnated under the blight of slavery. Germany, whose colonies were the least valuable of all the African lands and were not suited for exploitation and settlement, must have her "place in the sun." "To talk of saturation, as in the time of Bismarck," said one of her sanest and most moderate publicists, "or of the possibility of Germany being satisfied with her present frontiers is, under all circumstances, rank foolishness." [1]

[1] Rohrbach, *Deutschland unter den Weltvölkern*, p. 23.

It is worth while to ask why Germany has been placed at such a disadvantage among the Great Powers of the world: and the historian is bound to answer that the great statesman to whom modern Germany owes its existence, Prince Bismarck, is primarily responsible. The colonial movement, in its present form of capitalistic exploitation, began in the 'seventies of the last century, when the exploration of Africa by Livingstone, Stanley, and others opened men's minds to the possibilities of that continent as an outlet for the surplus energy and capital of Europe. In those days Germany had every opportunity to stake out for herself a splendid colonial domain, inasmuch as the whole continent, except for Algeria, Cape Colony and Natal, and the Transvaal and Orange Free State, where French, English, and Dutch had already established themselves, was open to the first comer. But Germany neglected her opportunity. The people were interested in commercial and industrial development, the government was busy fighting the Catholic Church and the socialists, and a steady stream of emigration still directed itself to America and Australia, whose temperate climate was preferred to the fevers and jungles of tropical Africa. But even more decisive was the attitude of Bismarck. Not only did he oppose the acquisition of colonies by Germany—from his conversations with Dr. Busch, as recorded in *Some Secret Pages of Bismarck's History*, and from the diplomatic correspondence, we know that he encouraged France and England to colonial adventures with the expectation of fishing in troubled waters. The French occupation of Tunis, in defiance of Italian aspirations in that direction, effected a breach between the Latin nations which threw Italy into the arms of Germany and Austria; similarly, the rivalry of England and France in Egypt and elsewhere in Africa paralyzed the Continental policy of both countries for nearly twenty-five years. Nor, until 1883, would

the Iron Chancellor give any support to various German
explorers who, in English fashion, were seeking treaties
with native rulers in the hope that the pressure of opinion
at home would force the government to action. By such
expedients Bismarck managed to preserve his mastery of
Europe, but in the interval the future enemies of Germany
picked up the most desirable lands of Africa, Asia, and the
Pacific, and when the mighty empire finally claimed its
share of the feast it had to be content with the scraps.
Even then Bismarck had no heart for this policy, for he
was pushed into it by the Reichstag and the pressure of
public opinion, both of which he detested.

In the early 'nineties, when German trade began to
make enormous strides forward, public opinion awoke to
the unsatisfactory results of Bismarck's colonial policy,
and demanded more vigorous action by the government,
which, inspired as it was by the cult of power, confronted
by the challenge of Social Democracy in domestic politics,
and encouraged by the Emperor himself, was the more
disposed to welcome such manifestations of a truly national
sentiment The most positive expression of this idea was
observed in the Pan-German League (Alldeutscher Bund).
Founded in 1886, it had at first attracted little notice, but
after its reorganization in 1893, under the presidency of
Ernest Hasse, a Leipzig professor, it began a propaganda
on behalf of German expansion that no student of international affairs could either take very seriously or yet
ignore altogether. An organization counting but 50,000
members was scarcely representative of German opinion,
according to English and American standards, but German
political opinion was so machine-made, and the agitation
of the Pan-Germans was so vociferous that an accurate
measuring of its influence was impossible. Its close relations with the powerful and vigorous Navy League does
not suggest a state of innocuous desuetude, and it is worth

noting that its more provocative outbursts were usually followed by militant proceedings at the German foreign office and a period of great tension among the European Powers. On the other hand, the great newspapers were hostile, especially those of the capital which dared to cut loose from official *communiqués* and the inspiration of the Wilhelmstrasse. Very likely the average German was not a little confused between the ultimate goal for which the league stood and the programme it put forward for immediate execution.

The theoretical basis of Pan-Germanism is logical enough. Of more than 80,000,000 Germans in Europe fewer than 70,000,000 enjoy the blessings of the new Empire. Ten millions reside in Austria, a few more in Bohemia, where they are intermingled with the Czechs, and still others are found in Switzerland and the Baltic provinces of Russia. On the assumption that German nationality is synonymous with the German race, which, in reality, is far from the case, German unity is not complete. In addition, the Dutch are of Teutonic race, and their fertile country not only once belonged to Germany (up to 1648 in law, in practise to 1555), but actually controls the mouth of the German Rhine; Holland would also profit economically by being incorporated in the German Empire. This doctrine of racial kinship would make the Dutch of South Africa subjects of the Kaiser, and in southern Brazil there is a large German population. Finally, there was Belgium, whose historical connection with the Holy Roman Empire lasted till the French Revolution, and whose Flemish provinces could be claimed with as much justification as their Dutch neighbors to the north. If we remember how Louis XIV claimed the left bank of the Rhine for France on the ground that ancient Gaul had extended to that river, we can at least comprehend the historical reasoning which would justify the incorporation in the modern German

state of all lands which had ever belonged to the Holy
Roman Empire; and considering the favor with which
the doctrine of nationality has been received in the last
half-century, we should have to admit the moral right of
any German communities to join the German Empire if
they so wished.

As a piece of practical politics, the extension of Hohen-
zollern sovereignty over any such territories or peoples was
unimaginable, and the Pan-Germans themselves never set
a date for the apotheosis of their grandiloquent schemes,
which postulated the handling of provinces and nations
like pawns on a chess-board, after the fashion of the eighteenth century. Indeed, their argument, in spite of its
plausibility, was really fallacious. Was Bohemia, for example, to be included in Pan-Germany, and the Czechs
added to the already formidable list of irreconcilables, or,
if only Austria proper were taken over from the Dual
Monarchy, which the Germans of that province would
vehemently oppose, were the Germans of Bohemia to be
left to the tender mercies of Russia, toward whom Bohemia
would inevitably gravitate? The Dutch, though recognizing their kinship with Germany, were nothing if not
tenacious of their independence; so was Belgium, whose
culture, moreover, was rather French than German. In
the Baltic provinces only the nobility and townsmen were
German, the peasantry was Lithuanian or Finnish; geo-
graphically, also, any connection with Germany would be
ridiculous.

There is very little evidence to show that the people of
Germany were seriously enamoured of the Pan-German
ideal, although they might give it a theoretical approval,
and would probably have welcomed the incorporation of
Holland and Belgium in the present Empire. General von
Bernhardi, albeit a despiser of small states and the champion of aggression, does not mention Pan-Germanism by

name; on the contrary, he opines that any lands which
once belonged to Germany, but are now under other control, are "permanently lost," and does not in any form
demand territorial aggrandizement in Europe.[1] However
much he may wish to see the balance of power overturned to the profit of Germany, he would have that
revolution effected by superiority of armament and the
arbitrament of battle; Germany can then achieve her destiny in the colonies she has taken from the vanquished.
But so many distinguished professors have associated themselves with the Pan-German movement, its typical representatives have been so swashbuckling and jingoistic, and
the German masses have such a reputation for docility, that
foreign observers not unnaturally ascribed to Pan-Germanism an importance which it did not possess; as a definition
of the European ambitions of German policy, it can be
placed on a par with the American aspiration which demands the annexation of Canada as the consequence of our
"manifest destiny."

There was, however, another aspect of the Pan-German
movement which aroused much enthusiasm, namely, its
colonial programme, and it is therefore desirable to ascertain, with as much precision as possible, what Germany
hoped, or might reasonably expect, to obtain beyond the
confines of the old Continent. Here we are met by the
difficulty that the German Government never admitted
any definite ambitions, that is, of course, in the last twenty
years since the problem entered into the calculations of
its diplomacy. But by process of elimination we can arrive at certain plausible conclusions. At the opening of
the century, when the break-up of China seemed imminent,
Germany was fully determined to claim her share of the
booty; nor did she endeavor to prevent the Russo-Japanese War, which, had Russia been victorious, must have

[1] *Germany and the Next War*, p. 195.

hastened the collapse of the Celestial Empire. The triumph of Japan, however, meant the end of European expansion in the Far East, and since then Germany has been the champion of both Chinese integrity and the open door. The rich Dutch colonies in the Malay Archipelago were forbidden fruit unless Holland itself were absorbed.   Persia was practically divided between Great Britain and Russia.[1] India and Australasia were jewels of the British crown, and their conquest would be exceedingly difficult even if Great Britain were crushed and her sea power destroyed.   South America, where sundry German settlements might possibly become political outposts of the fatherland, was guarded by the Monroe Doctrine and the pride of the South American nations themselves.[2]   There were left Africa and the Ottoman Empire, the former in large measure under the dominion of other Powers, the latter still in the throes of that mortal illness diagnosed by the Tsar Nicholas I in 1853, when he described the Sultan as "the sick man of Europe."

In these two regions Germany seemingly desired and planned to satisfy her colonial ambitions. Her designs on the Belgian Congo were long suspected, and were admitted in the Franco-German treaty of 4 November, 1911. Not only did Germany receive from France two strips of the French Congo that brought the frontier of the Cameroons to the Congo River, which is the northwestern boundary of the Belgian Congo, but she induced France to forego her right of pre-emption over the Congo, any change in the status of which should henceforth be determined by all the African Powers.   The sudden Italian occupation of Tripoli is believed to have been stimulated by the sus-

[1] It will be seen in a later chapter that Germany cherished certain ambitions with respect to Persia, but her policy in that country was never very aggressive.

[2] Many persons, of course, believe that Germany has very real designs on South America; but obviously she could not prosecute them until she had disposed of her rivals in Europe, and particularly of England.

picion that Germany was herself preparing to seize it. An Anglo-German agreement of 1898 envisaged the partition of the Portuguese colonies in case Portugal were ready to part with them. Finally, German interest in Morocco, which kept Europe on tenter-hooks for six years, probably arose out of a desire to acquire some part of that country for colonizing purposes. As regards Turkey, German policy was equally determined, centring around the Baghdad railway scheme, but not overlooking the other possibilities of Asia Minor and Mesopotamia.

Morocco and Asia Minor, indeed, occupied a special place in German colonial plans. Quite apart from the desire for more colonies of the plantation or exploitation type, it had long offended the national pride that Germany, next to Russia the most prolific nation in Europe, possessed no settlement colonies comparable to those of England, France, or Russia. It was intolerable that a German emigrant was not able to settle in a land ruled by his Kaiser's government which was at the same time endowed with an equable climate, but must proceed to the United States, South America, or one of the British self-governing dominions, where he rapidly lost touch with his native land and was usually assimilated to his new surroundings. Of recent years, this aspect of the German colonial problem has been greatly modified by the decline of emigration, but in the 'nineties, when the new colonial movement took form, a considerable number of Germans were still leaving home each year, and a renewed impetus might at any time be given by economic depression or any of the other forces which have from time immemorial led men to try their fortunes abroad. This is clearly the thought of General von Bernhardi when he says: "The importance of Germany will depend upon two points: first, how many millions of men in the world will speak German? secondly, how many of them are politically members of the German

Empire?" Or again: "The dominion of German thought
can only be extended under the ægis of political power,
and unless we act in conformity with this idea we shall
be untrue to our duties toward the human race." [1]

Now, in the latter years of the nineteenth and the first
part of the twentieth century Morocco and Asia Minor
(up to 1899 the Boer republics as well) were precisely the
regions of the world that might be suitable for German
colonization; in fact, they were the only lands not already
appropriated by other Powers. They were, it is true, inhabited by a considerable indigenous population, but their
civilization, at once oriental and the prey of effete administration, seemed to clamor for German treatment; natural
resources were abundant, and in some parts the climate
was suitable for white settlement. Here Germans could
settle and spread their *Kultur*, which must sooner or later
take its place beside English imperialism as one of the
world's great dynamic forces; here German capital could
find an adequate opening for its energies, and German
business lay the foundations of a permanent prosperity.

There was nothing unreasonable in this ambition to make
Morocco and Asia Minor parts of the German Empire;
indeed, the programme was modest enough compared with
the actual conquests of England and France in various
parts of Africa or the advance of Russia in Central Asia.
Unfortunately, however, both Morocco and Asia Minor
were already ear-marked by the very Powers whose colonial
preponderance Germany wished to diminish; the former
was regarded by the French, established, as they were, in
Tunis and Algeria, as the natural limit of their North
African empire; the latter had long been dominated, politically and economically, by Great Britain and Russia,
while France had an outpost in Syria. Germans none
the less turned with longing eyes to these regions, and pub-

[1] *Germany and the Next War*, pp. 83, 77.

lic opinion quickly responded to any move of the foreign office which promised to advance the national ambition. The popularity of Heinrich Class's little pamphlet, *West-Marokko deutsch !*, not to mention other literature of the same description, and the expression, *Unser Baghdad*, which is said to have been widely used, indicated a genuine desire to see German policy triumphant in these Mediterranean lands, and it is safe to say that the people of Germany were not only convinced as to the justice of their cause but fully determined to support the government when the hour of decision should come.

Twenty years of striving, however, brought but a moderate success with the Baghdad railway, which was the epitome of German policy in Asia Minor, and, instead of a share of Morocco, only a small stretch of the French Congo, which was surrendered as the price of a French protectorate over Morocco. The disappointment in Germany was universal, being reflected in the language of the press, which the government made no effort to restrain. And Germans of all classes, instead of criticising the diplomacy of the imperial government, except to assert that it had not acted with sufficient vigor, convinced themselves that their legitimate ambitions had been blocked at every turn by the jealousy of Great Britain, as well in Morocco as for the Baghdad railway. The truth of this charge will be presently examined, but probably no amount of exposition and argument would have convinced Germany that she was not the victim of a grand conspiracy to deprive her of her coveted "place in the sun."

This conviction, which has been dinned into the masses by ardent publicists and a zealous press, throws an interesting light on German armaments. Prince Bülow notes the "curious fact that in the most military and warlike of the European nations"—a striking admission, in the face of German *post-bellum* propaganda—"the parties have re-

signed themselves so unwillingly to the new demands for
the defense of the empire that it has taken more than three
and a half decades to achieve unanimity, at least among
the middle-class parties." [1]   The Reichstag of 1907 was
the first to give the government a majority for its world
policy that was not dependent on the Centre, which is
opposed to colonial expansion; up to that time the Radicals
refused to vote for the numerous army and navy laws
which have been so prominent a feature of the reign of
William II.   The elections of 1907 were fought on the issue
of German imperialism, and the government got a majority
of Conservatives and Liberals, who were sympathetic with
its expansionist schemes.   In 1912 all the middle-class
parties supported the army and navy bills, and even the
Socialists indirectly, since they voted the supplies for the
increased establishments.   At last there was a national
majority for the national policy.   The government always
demanded additional troops or more ships in the interest
of German world-diplomacy; as one class after another was
converted to the imperialistic programme the opponents
of military expansion lost ground, until there stood behind
the Emperor and his government a united nation, which,
however torn by party faction and class feeling on matters
of domestic concern, was determined that Germany should
take her lawful place among the great colonial and maritime nations.   Throughout the summer of 1911, when the
Morocco controversy was in process of solution, public
opinion was, on the whole, more aggressive than the government, and after the settlement with France had been
disclosed there was a wild outburst of rage in the Reichstag from all parties, because the national interests had
been sacrificed to the Emperor's love of peace.   From that
time there was no difficulty in passing measures for the
increase of armaments, in spite of the fact that Germany's

[1] *Imperial Germany*, p. 193.

relations with England underwent considerable improvement and that the world was disposed to render a due meed of praise to the Emperor for not appealing to the sword in the Morocco business. Without asserting positively that the German people were itching for war, one is justified in saying that they wanted all the fruits of war, and from such a state of mind the transition to war itself is neither difficult to make nor long to be avoided.

The national attitude toward questions of foreign policy and armaments was prodigiously affected by a profound change in the German character, a change much remarked upon by innumerable travellers, students, and publicists for many years back. The generation which witnessed the wars of unification was still in the grip of that romantic and cosmopolitan feeling which had distinguished the early nineteenth century. Life was simple, for money was scarce; high thinking was the order of the day; the ideal of a free and united Germany still was widely cherished, except in official society. Treitschke himself, writing in 1861, could say:

"How lifeless, how sterile are the supporters of absolutism in their opposition to the demands of the nations for liberty! . . . Everything new which the nineteenth century has created is the work of liberalism. The enemies of liberty can only persist in negation, or waken to the semblance of new life the ideas of days which have long since been submerged." [1]

To-day the spirit of Germany is frankly material and expresses itself in commercial values. Nor is this surprising. The enormous increase of the population since 1870, the expansion of industry and commerce, the changed conditions of every-day life brought about by great wealth on the one hand and a restless proletariat on the other,

[1] From *Die Freiheit*, quoted by Davis, *The Political Thought of Heinrich von Treitschke*, p. 9.

and the cult of thoroughness and efficiency—all these and
other factors have intensified the struggle for bread and
pushed the humanities into the background. A German
writer has well described the transformation, not without
some lament for the old, easy days:

"One is often pained and overcome," writes Herr Fuchs, "with
longing as one thinks of the German of a hundred years ago. He
was poor, he was impotent, he was despised, ridiculed, and de-
frauded. He was the uncomplaining slave of others; his fields
were their battle-ground, and the goods which he had inherited
from his fathers were trodden under foot and dispersed. He shed
his blood heroically without asking why. He never troubled when
the riches of the outside world were divided without regard for
him. He sat in his little bare room high under the roof, in simple
coat and clumsy shoes; but his heart was full of sweet dreams,
and uplifted by the chords of Beethoven to a rapture which threatened to rend his breast. He wept with Werther and Jean Paul in
joyous pain, he smiled with the childish innocence of his naïve
poets, the happiness of his longing consumed him, and as he listened
to Schubert's song his soul became one with the soul of the universe.
Let us think no more of it—it is useless. We have become men,
and the virtues of our youth are ours no more. We can but face
the inevitable and overcome it." [1]

A professor at Jena asks:

"Have we Germans kept a harmonious balance between the
economic and the moral side of our development, as was once the
case with the Greeks? No; with the enormous increase of wealth
dark shadows have fallen on our national life. In the nation as
in the individual we see with the increase of wealth the decrease
of moral feeling and moral power."

Professor Paulsen complains:

"For new institutes of natural science and medicine new millions
are always ready, but is any liberality shown toward the modest
needs of philology or philosophy?"

[1] This and the two following quotations are taken from Dawson, *Evolution of
Modern Germany*, pp. 5, 8. For an excellent description of conditions in Germany
before 1870, cf. Sidney Whitman, *German Memories*, chap. 2.

It does not become an American to throw stones at the ideals of wealth or bigness, which are our besetting sins in the eyes of Germans themselves. But, with all our optimism and boastfulness, we remain an introspective and critical people. Germans, however, came to believe, with the Emperor, that they were "the salt of the earth," [1] and they looked with good-natured contempt upon their neighbors. The inability of the French to multiply and replenish the earth, the difficulties of the British in the Boer War, and the colossal failure of the Russians in Manchuria impressed unfavorably a people who performed their military service as a cheerful duty and smiled at the suggestion that the nations should turn their swords into ploughshares. The heads of all but the most conservative were indeed affected by the praises which a wondering world showered upon the upstart empire and its spectacular Kaiser. Wherever Germans turned they observed that their star, lately risen in the heavens, shone brilliantly amidst the dimmed rays of the older planets; its glory would be even more effulgent if some of the other stars were deflected from their ancient courses. Germany's place in the sun was not commensurate with her achievements in the other fields of human endeavor; her genius was correspondingly cramped and her "historical mission" unfulfilled.

Every self-respecting nation places a high value on its peculiar culture. Some years ago a famous British statesman, who is still living, dedicated a book to "those who believe that the British Empire is, under Providence, the greatest instrument for good that the world has ever seen." [2] A French professor has recently described the civilization of his country as the *forme exquise de justice et de vérité universelles*.[3] And there is the famous Russian prophecy that

---

[1] Speech at Bremen, 22 March, 1905.
[2] Hon. G. N. (now Lord) Curzon, *Problems of the Far East*, 1894.
[3] M. Alfred Croiset, in *Bulletin de la Société autour du Monde*, January, 1915.

"the Slavs stand on the threshold of the morning," while the other European peoples have already reached their apogee. But no nation has carried the obsession of its superiority to such a pitch as the present-day Germans. With all our marvellings at their progress in industry and commerce, our efforts to copy their system of municipal government, our fondness for their music, and our enormous debt to their science and philosophy, it comes as a distinct shock to read the following in the pages of General von Bernhardi:

> "No nation on the face of the globe is so able to grasp and appropriate all the elements of culture, to add to them from the stores of its own spiritual endowment, and to give back to mankind richer gifts than it received. . . . To no nation, except the German, has it been given to enjoy in its inner self, 'that which is given to mankind as a whole.' We often see in other nations a greater intensity of specialized ability, but never the same capacity for generalization and absorption. It is this quality which specially fits us for the leadership of the intellectual world, and imposes upon us the obligation to maintain that position." [1]

This is national egotism raised to the nth power, and the first impulse is to dismiss it as the ravings of a military fanatic. But the utterances of the gallant general can be duplicated at every turn. If the reader will consult a remarkable work entitled *The Foundations of the Nineteenth Century*, by Houston Stewart Chamberlain, an Englishman who married the daughter of Richard Wagner and has become thoroughly German, he will find developed there such astonishing theories as that Christ was not a Jew, or that all the races of Europe—Celt, Slav, Latin, and German—sprang from the same original stock and may therefore be called German. In the eyes of Chamberlain all that is best in European civilization is essentially German, and the Germans are the chosen people. His bulky book has

[1] *Germany and the Next War*, pp. 73-74.

sold by tens of thousands, and "is, by the majority of Germans, considered to be a higher revelation of truth unfathomable." [1] Other writers argue, on the basis of philology and archæology, that the great artists of the Italian Renaissance, and even Jesus himself, were Germans. Or there is the statement of Herr Alfred Kerr, a well-known critic, as reported by M. Georges Bourdon, in his valuable analysis of German opinion, *The German Enigma:*

"It is a law of history that the elder societies shall cede their place to the younger, and this is the condition of the perpetual regeneration of humanity. . . . Nothing has any power against the destiny of history. The German with his red corpuscles has arrived, and I believe his hour has come. The law of life ordains that the least strong shall be eliminated, and the real conquerors are the famished. That is to say, we Germans. The money that we have earned has given us the taste, and conquered prosperity has increased our appetite. When the German contemplates the rest of the world, he finds that he has not been spoiled, and that all that has been left him are the stale remains of a good dinner. But this share is merely a provisory one in his mind, and I believe that some day a new redistribution will take place." [2]

Only since the war began has it been fully understood to what extent the virus of national conceit has permeated the German consciousness. From no other country has there poured forth such a deluge of articles, books, and pamphlets asserting the superiority of German culture in all its aspects, and in many instances proclaiming that it must be forced on a reluctant world. The most astonishing outburst, that of Professor Adolf Lasson of Berlin, deserves to be quoted. In two letters to a friend in Holland, written at the end of September, 1914, he says:

"One cannot rest neutral in relationship to Germany and the German people. Either one must consider Germany as the most

[1] Emil Reich, *Germany's Swelled Head*, 1907, p. 13.
[2] Interview with Herr Alfred Kerr, p. 171.

perfect political creation that history has known, or must approve
her destruction, her extermination. A man who is not German
knows nothing of Germany.

"We are morally and intellectually superior to all: without peers.
It is the same with our organizations and our institutions.

"William II, *deliciæ generis humani*, has always protected peace,
right, and honor, although it would have been possible for him by
his power to annihilate everything. The greater his success, the
more modest he has become. His chancellor, Herr von Bethmann-
Hollweg, the most eminent among men who are now alive, does not
know any higher cares than those of truth, loyalty, and right.
Our army is, as it were, the image in miniature of the intelligence
and morality of the German people."

"We are breathing, with full chest, the full breath of history,
and we know nothing about this wretched bourgeois existence [of
Holland].

"We have no friends. All fear us and look upon us as dangerous,
because we are intelligent, active, and morally superior. We are
the freest people in the world. For we know how to obey. Our
law is our reason. Our force is the force of the mind; our victory
the victory of that. That is why we are able to triumph against
numerous enemies, as did Frederick II in other days.

"The European conspiracy has woven around us a web of lies
and slander. As for us, we are truthful, our characteristics are
humanity, gentleness, conscience, the virtues of Christ. In a
world of wickedness, we represent love, and God is with us!"

Such examples of perverted scholarship and distorted
history are amusing, but they are also significant. There
must be fire to produce so much smoke. And the fire has
evidently been burning for some time. The German literature of international politics, so voluminous in recent
years, abounds in references to decadent France, inefficient
Britain, mediæval Russia; the whole case for German expansion rests on the assumption that the world badly
needs German *Kultur* to reach the highest plane of development, and the conviction has become firmly rooted, as
any one who travelled in Germany or talked with Germans

was bound to discover, that the fatherland was fully capable of imposing its will upon the other Powers of Europe.

The world has not condemned Germany blindly; rather it has been convinced, against its will and from a study of the available evidence, that her ambitions are too subversive of others' rights and her people too militaristic for these peace-loving times. If her position among the imperial and colonial nations was less favored than seemed her due, the fault was her own, either of her tragic past or of her recent diplomacy. She made no brilliant record in the colonies she did possess; they were costly to maintain, unproductive from both commercial and human standards. With all of England's faults and despite the questionable methods often resorted to in the expansion of her empire, she has done much for the advancement and prosperity of her subject peoples. Germany can adduce no such claim. On the contrary, her mechanical and bureaucratic policy has more than once produced rebellions that were suppressed with great cruelty. Hence German colonial ambitions, legitimate as they often were, arouse no sympathy outside of Germany, and if the argument must be reduced to General von Bernhardi's formula, "world power or downfall," the unmistakable answer is that the world can and will get along without Prussian militarism, a Prussian reorganization, or even a Prussian world peace.

CHAPTER V

COMMERCIAL RIVALRY

It is a fixed idea with Germany and her sympathizers that Great Britain was drawn into the war from jealousy of Germany's advance toward the commercial conquest of the world. They point to the law of 1887, by which the British Parliament required all goods of that origin to be stamped "Made in Germany," lest Englishmen should unwittingly patronize foreign industries, and they laughingly remark that the law in no small degree failed of its purpose, because the superiority of German-made commodities soon commended them to English buyers. From the German point of view, British commercial supremacy has been in jeopardy for at least two decades from the extraordinary expansion of German trade; sooner or later it must succumb to the intensified attack of its rival. Therefore, when Germany found herself at war with France and Russia, the temptation to the nation of shopkeepers was irresistible. The armies of other nations would fight her battles on land, her own navy would bottle up German merchantmen, and British manufacturers and traders would recover the markets filched from them by the superior genius of Germans.

Such is the indictment, which rests on two assumptions: first, that Great Britain and Germany are rivals, one of whom must destroy the other; and second, that the United Kingdom cannot hold its own against the upstart Power across the North Sea. Before examining the argument in detail, let us frankly admit that Great Britain has not viewed the competition of Germany with pleasure or unconcern. From a host of writings bearing on the matter, the following quotations may be given because they are free from prejudice or envy:

Lady Phillips, in *A Friendly Germany: Why Not?*, writes:

" The rapid development of German trade within the last two decades undoubtedly bears part of the responsibility for the ill feeling harbored against Germany in some quarters."[1]

H. G. Wells, in *Social Forces in England and America*, writes:

"We in Great Britain are intensely jealous of Germany. We are intensely jealous of Germany not only because the Germans outnumber us, and have a much larger and more diversified country than ours, and lie in the very heart and body of Europe; but because in the last hundred years, while we have fed on platitudes and vanity, they have had the energy and humility to develop a splendid system of national education, to toil at science and art and literature, to develop social organization, to master and better our methods of business and industry, and to clamber above us in the scale of civilization. This has humiliated and irritated rather than chastened us, and our humiliation has been greatly exacerbated by the swaggering bad manners, the talk of 'Blood and Iron' and Mailed Fists, the Weltpolitik rubbish, that inaugurated the new German phase."[2]

An impartial American could say:

"In the great total of Germany's trade, and in the rapidity with which it has risen to its present volume and value lies the reason for the anti-German agitation in England. On the surface this antagonism is political, and relates to armaments, but its roots lie in the trade of the world, and it is fed upon commercial rivalry."[3]

The historical fact that the Anglo-Dutch wars of the seventeenth century arose out of English jealousy of Holland's control of the carrying trade, may perhaps be adduced to support the theory that Great Britain has declared "war on German trade." Or we may believe that the American Revolution came about because the greedy

[1] P. 78.   [2] P. 42.   [3] James Davenport Whelpley, *The Trade of the World*, p. 42.

merchants of Great Britain demanded the enforcement of the Navigation Acts in restraint of colonial trade. More recently, as far back as 1885, a royal commission on the depression of trade and industry suggested that British business men were making an ineffective opposition to German competition.[1] If it be added that the tariff reform movement, associated with the late Mr. Chamberlain, justified itself on the ground that only a protective tariff could preserve British industry from the vigor of the German attack, and that the consumers of the United Kingdom were invited by spasmodic appeals to insist upon British goods, it may sound absurd to assert that commercial considerations were not very much to the fore when the neutrality of Belgium was ostensibly the cause of Britain's declaration of war. Here, again, one is confronted with the difficulty of analyzing accurately the temper of a nation, but the available evidence points to the conclusion that English opinion had pretty thoroughly absorbed the teaching of Norman Angell, that war and business were contradictory terms. Sir Edward Grey, in his speech to the House of Commons on 3 August, 1914, certainly brushed aside commercial considerations. "Foreign trade," he said, "is going to stop, not because the trade routes are closed, but because there is no trade at the other end."[2] On this very ground the Radical wing of the Liberal party opposed his policy, and the Socialists conducted demonstrations against war, even after the violation of Belgian neutrality. The great banking houses of the city are also believed to have been against the war.

A few years ago Great Britain and Germany did appear to be locked in a death-struggle for the commercial domination of the world, for the statistics of the last generation

[1] Parliamentary Papers, cd. 4715. Second report of the royal commission on the depression of trade and industry, 3 March, 1886, pp. 21, 43–44, 48–50, 54, 57, 64, 67–68, 119–122, 124–125, 128, 130, 140, 193, 221, 265, 283.
[2] 5 Hansard, lxv, c. 1823.

showed German trade to have grown far more rapidly than that of England.[1]

| | In Millions of £ Sterling | | | (20 Marks= £1) | |
| | United Kingdom | | | Germany | |
	Imports	Re-exports*	Exports†	Imports	Exports
1870.........	303	44	200	173‡	125‡
1880.........	411	63	223	142	145
1890.........	420	64	263	214	166
1900.........	523	63	291	302	239
1910.........	678	104	430	465	382

*Of foreign and colonial produce.   †Of British produce.
‡Figures for 1872, the first year for which they are available.

In forty years British imports increased 130 per cent, as opposed to an advance of 170 per cent for Germany; for the export trade the figures stand at 115 per cent and 194 per cent, respectively (119 per cent for England, if re-exports are included).

It is quite evident, therefore, that in a general way the establishment of the new German Empire was followed by a prodigious expansion of foreign trade, beside which the slower progress of England was in marked contrast. Even in the first decade of the twentieth century, after Germany had made up for the time lost in a century of disunion, her effort was more pronounced than that of her long-established competitor. From all parts of the globe complaints began to pour in that Germany was displacing Great Britain in the markets which had belonged to the latter since the early days of modern industry. Whether one reads the reports of consuls and commercial attachés, or is content with articles in newspapers and reviews, there

[1] Except where otherwise indicated, the statistics cited in this chapter are culled from the *Statesman's Year Book*, the *Statistisches Handbuch des Deutschen Reiches* (1907), and the *Statistisches Jahrbuch für das Deutsche Reich* (annual).

is the same story. German business methods—cheap goods, efficient advertising, competent salesmen, catering to individual and national tastes, governmental assistance —were challenging the supremacy of the British trader. South America, Africa, the Ottoman Empire, China, and even British colonies figured in the imagination of scare-mongers, who could see no limit to German cupidity or German ingenuity, as lands where the British position would soon be seriously threatened.

In fact, the British nation was told by Joseph Chamber-lain that "during the last thirty years . . . our general ex-port trade has remained practically stagnant" (Newcastle, 20 October, 1903). "Cotton will go"; "wool is threat-ened"; "your iron trade is going." Such phrases of the Conservative statesman indicated a pessimism which de-manded either retaliatory measures or a complete over-hauling of the national industrial machine. Even the great staple industries seemed to be losing their hold, as the following statistics of production show:

Date	COAL PRODUCTION		IRON ORE PRODUCTION	
	United Kingdom	Germany	United Kingdom	Germany
	Tons	*Metric Tons*	*Tons*	*Metric Tons*
1880.........	146,969,000	46,974,000	18,026,000	7,239,000
1890.........	181,614,000	70,238,000	13,781,000	11,406,000
1900.........	225,181,000	109,290,000	14,028,000	18,964,000
1910.........	264,433,000	152,828,000	15,226,000	28,710,000

Date	PIG IRON PRODUCTION		CRUDE STEEL PRODUCTION	
	United Kingdom	Germany	United Kingdom	Germany
	Tons	*Metric Tons*	*Tons*	*Metric Tons*
1880.........	7,749,000	2,713,000	....	....
1890.........	7,904,000	4,651,000	3,579,000	2,232,000
1900.........	8,959,000	8,507,000	4,901,000	6,362,000
1910.........	10,012,000	14,794,000	6,515,000	12,281,000

1 metric ton = 2,204 pounds.

Even in the cotton trade Germany had become quite independent of England, as evidenced by the number of bales imported at Liverpool and Bremen.[1]

	Liverpool	Bremen
1885–1886......................	2,558,798	530,451
1911–1912......................	3,690,800	2,792,000

Finally, in a province wherein the English were wont to reign supreme Germany made marvellous progress, the shipping industry. The Hamburg-America Company and the Norddeutscher Lloyd are the two largest shipping concerns in the world. A generation ago they usually bought their ships in the British Isles, but no one will now dispute the ability of the German yards to build as good ships as any in the world. In most aspects of agriculture German production has, thanks to the high protection obtai ed by the Conservative party, forged considerably ahead of England.

To these undoubted facts of German competition may be added the pitiful misery of the lower orders of English society, which moved the late Sir Henry Campbell-Bannerman to declare that twelve millions of the people lived on the verge of hunger and "in the grip of perpetual poverty";[2] the collapse of many enterprises under the pressure of German competition and the inevitable growth of unemployment; the persistence of the tariff reform agitation for ten years; and the endless discussion as to what British manufacturers should do to prevent the capture by the Germans of the markets which were left. It is not surprising, therefore, if the casual observer assumed that Great Britain belonged to the nations with a past, and was correspondingly jealous of the new German state which promised ere long to become the wealthiest nation in Europe.

[1] These and the immediately preceding figures are taken from Hurd and Castle, *German Sea Power*, pp. 230–231, 297.

[2] At Perth, 5 June, 1903.

Yet the figures in the case do not reveal England as decadent and listless.   Unluckily for the tariff reformers, they
argued too closely from the condition of England on the
morrow of the Boer War.   The additional taxation which
that enterprise entailed was naturally reflected in the business world and, furthermore, the competition of Germany
was still so recent that the possibility of meeting it had
not been thoroughly grasped.   The statistics of British
and German foreign trade for the fifteen years 1899–1913,
during which the former is usually represented as at the
mercy of the latter, are very instructive.

	In Millions of Pounds Sterling				
	United Kingdom			Germany	
	Imports	Re-exports	Exports	Imports	Exports
1899.........	485	65	264	289	218
1900.........	524	63	291	302	239
1901.........	522	68	280	286	225
1902.........	528	65	283	290	241
1903.........	543	69	291	316	255
1904.........	551	70	301	343	265
1905.........	565	78	330	372	292
1906.........	607	85	376	422	324
1907.........	645	92	426	450	355
1908.........	593	80	377	404	324
1909.........	625	91	378	443	343
1910.........	678	104	430	465	382
1911.........	680	102	454	477	405
1912.........	745	112	487	550	454
1913.........	769	109	525	534	495

During the Boer War and a few years afterward British
trade remained practically stationary; that of Germany
expanded rapidly.   From 1905 to 1907 both countries felt
the stimulus of a world-wide boom, and both were badly
hit the following year by the collapse of credit which followed the American panic.   After 1909 there was a general

recovery, in which—and this is the point—Great Britain fared quite as well as Germany.

INCREASE 1909–1913
(In Millions of Pounds Sterling)

	Imports	Exports
Great Britain..............	146	148 (with re-exports 177)
Germany.................	91	152

But these figures do not consider the growth of population, which was greater in Germany than in the United Kingdom.

	1900	1910	Per cent increase
Great Britain.................	41,605,323	45,365,599	11.4
Germany.....................	56,367,178	64,903,423	15.1

Examined on this basis, the export trade of the United Kingdom is seen to have been increasing its margin of superiority.

EXPORTS PER HEAD OF POPULATION[1]

	UNITED KINGDOM			GERMANY		
	£	s.	d.	£	s.	d.
Average 1900–1904..............	6	14	9	4	1	3
Average 1907–1910..............	9	2	0	5	6	0
1912........................	10	3	7	6	10	0
Increase....................	3	18	10	2	18	9

To contend, as many have done, that Great Britain was falling behind as an industrial and commercial nation is obviously absurd.

The growth of the import trade was another sign of British prosperity. In America we are accustomed to think

[1] *Liberal Year Book*, 1913, p. 172.

that a balance of international trade "in our favor" is
essential to our happiness, and it is true that our greatest
prosperity has been attained under such conditions. "Our
English cousins look at these things from a different point
of view, for it is equally true that England's fattest years
have been those in which, as we say, her balance of trade
has been 'against' her. It is when her imports exceed
her exports by the most millions that business is good and
profitable."[1] The surplus of imports represented, not an
unfavorable balance of trade, but the tribute of the world
for the services of British shipping and the interest on
British investments abroad. The larger the excess of imports, the greater the activity of Britain's merchant marine, the more productive her capital in foreign countries,
and, of course, the greater the supply of commodities for
home consumption.

Despite the growth of Germany's merchant marine, despite the capacity of her shipyards, the United Kingdom
still enjoyed an overwhelming supremacy among maritime
nations. She owned approximately 50 per cent of the tonnage of the world, and she built more ships annually than
the rest of the world together. Her position was, indeed,
in little danger of being challenged for an indefinite period.

NET REGISTER OF TONNAGE

	UNITED KINGDOM		GERMANY	
	Total	Steam	Total	Steam
1870............	5,690,789	1,112,934	982,355	81,994
1880............	6,574,513	2,723,468	1,181,525	215,758
1890............	7,978,538	5,042,517	1,433,413	723,652
1900............	9,304,108	7,207,610	1,941,645	1,347,845
1910............	11,555,663	10,442,719	2,903,570	2,396,733
1912............	11,894,791	10,992,073	3,023,725	2,513,666

[1] J. D. Whelpley, *The Trade of the World*, p. 47.

If, on the one hand, Germany achieved a larger *percentage* of increase than the mistress of the seas, the latter strengthened her general lead by 4,162,632 tons and her ascendency in steam shipping by 7,447,467 tons. British supremacy was as fully apparent in the construction of new ships.

NEW TONNAGE

	United Kingdom	Germany
1881–1885.....................	3,313,431 tons	248,504 tons
1906–1910.....................	4,126,093 "	612,112 "

Britain's lead in the first quinquennium............3,064,927 tons
Britain's lead in the second quinquennium ....3,513,981 "

In 1912, the last year for which figures are complete, new tonnage to the amount of 1,738,514 gross tons was constructed in the shipyards of the United Kingdom, as opposed to 1,163,255 for the rest of the world, and 480,038 for Germany. In perhaps no other phase of world business was the ascendency of Great Britain so overwhelming, and there was no sign of a change for the worse.[1]

The capital invested abroad by Englishmen and Germans is difficult to estimate. Sir George Paish, the editor of the *Statist*, credited Britain with £1,681,000,000 in her overseas dominions and £1,837,000,000 in foreign countries, a total of £3,518,000,000, on 31 December, 1912. This was capital publicly subscribed, and the private investments probably brought the total up to £4,000,000,000, from which the nation derived an income of about £200,-000,000, or one-tenth of the national income.[2] The amount of German capital sent abroad has probably been exaggerated. For the year 1900 20,000,000,000 marks (£1,000,-

[1] Hurd and Castle, *German Sea Power*, pp. 305 ff.
[2] *Liberal Year Book*, 1913, p. 181.

ooo,ooo) was quoted by several authorities,[1] but Dr. Karl
Helfferich, director of the Deutsche Bank, writing in
1913, stated that "the estimate of 20,000,000,000 marks
for all Germany's investments of capital abroad seems
rather too high than too low," adding that "new investments abroad have, within the last few years, been considerably restricted owing to the enormous home demand
for capital for industrial and public purposes."[2]   The
ratio between Great Britain and Germany stood at four
to one, and was certainly not diminishing.

The export trade of Great Britain and Germany must be
further compared, as regards the geographical distribution.[3]

	In Millions of Pounds Sterling					
	United Kingdom			Germany		
	1899–1903	1904–8	1912	1899–1903	1904–8	1912
Average................						
Europe.............	108	132	175	173	224	337
Extra-European, ex-						
cept British Empire	75	111	128	43	65	91
British Empire.......	94	118	188	9	11	19

Two conclusions seem warranted from these figures.   First,
the bulk of Germany's foreign commerce was with countries of the European continent, and in these regions she
had pushed considerably ahead of England.   The latter,
on the other hand, did an increasing business with her
vast Empire, where Germany's hold was quite slender;
even though the mother country had refused to adopt a
protective tariff for the benefit of her colonies, her exports
went to them in increasing quantity and increasing per-

[1] E. g., Wolf von Schierbrand, Germany, p. 101.
[2] Germany's Economic Progress and National Wealth, 1888–1913, p. 113, an English edition, issued by the Germanistic Society of America, of Deutschlands Volkswohlstand, 1888–1913.
[3] Geoffrey Durham, "The Foreign Trade of Great Britain and Germany," in
Contemporary Review, October, 1910.

centage. It was, of course, only natural that Germany should have the stronger position on the Continent, for she was advantageously placed for developing close commercial relations. Similarly, political considerations, and in the case of the self-governing colonies preferential tariff treatment, secured Great Britain the commercial ascendency in her own Empire. Thus the main field for competition between Great Britain and Germany lay in the non-British territories outside of Europe. The results of that competition over a period of ten years are indicated as follows:

EXPORTS

(In £1,000; 20 marks = £1)

	UNITED KINGDOM		GERMANY	
	1902	1912	1902	1912
China......................	7,142	14,311	1,845	4,275
Japan......................	5,142	12,229	2,490	5,600
Dutch Indies................	2,155	6,233	1,175	3,765
Siam......................	251	1,086	110	320
Korea......................	50	319	110	20
Congo......................	102	367	30	100
French Colonies.............	2,319	3,867	290	1,100
Portuguese Colonies..........	1,596	2,357	295	620
German Colonies.............	117	583	357	2,865
Persia......................	369	878	55	180
Liberia.....................	52	93	35	70
United States...............	23,760	31,355	22,460	35,300
Argentina..................	5,871	20,505	2,360	11,970
Brazil......................	5,389	12,658	2,190	9,640
Chile......................	2,839	6,159	1,700	5,600
Rest of South America........	3,612	8,156	1,770	5,135
West Indies.................	2,379	2,956	710	1,805
Central America.............	718	1,352	325	630
Mexico.....................	2,170	2,508	1,705	2,263

In not a single region of the world was the British trade being expelled, or even seriously hampered, and the import figures would demonstrate the same fact with perhaps even more conviction.   Finally, not to dishearten the reader with endless figures, it may be remarked that Germany was the best customer of the United Kingdom, and exported to it more goods than any country except the United States. In 1913 the reciprocal trade of the two countries exceeded £121,000,000, not counting re-exports from England to the amount of £19,878,000.   Even if German imports to England increased more rapidly than the reverse trade, the fact remained that British commerce with Germany represented one-tenth of the trade of the country: a most excellent reason why war would be a calamity to both parties.[1]

Still, it may fairly be asked whether Englishmen accepted this point of view.   The most convincing evidence is that in three general elections (January, 1906, January, 1910, December, 1910) they declined to adopt the new gospel of tariff reform.   The baldly avowed purpose of a protective tariff was to save British industry from German competition, but ten years' discussion merely served to convince the majority of the voters that free trade was the only possible system for a country which imported the greater part of its food and the raw materials for its industries.

On the eve of the war tariff reform was quite distinctly in the background.   Similarly, as regards the imperial aspects of that controversy, Englishmen seemed instinc-

[1] The German view of Anglo-German trade rivalry is well expounded by Professor von Schulze-Gaevernitz in *Deutschland und England* (1908). He recognizes that Germany has profited enormously by the free-trade system of England, but believes that German competition will force the adoption of a protective tariff sooner or later; also that war is not impossible for this very reason. "Let us not forget" the fate of Holland; and "what the Spain of Philip II and the France of Louis XIV and Napoleon were, Germany is to-day: the enemy" (p. 33). But he concludes with the observation: "If once Germany and England realize that neither can be annihilated and that third parties will be the only gainers from a war between them, all danger thereof will disappear, despite all the jingoes on either side." See also his article in the *American Review of Reviews*, November, 1909. The book is reviewed by C. S. Goldman in the *Nineteenth Century*, February, 1909.

tively to realize that the best guarantee for the preservation of their Empire lay in maintaining a fair field for all, with favors for none; so that throughout the vast British dominions, except in the self-governing colonies, British manufacturers and traders enjoyed no privileges which were not equally available for Germans.[1] Nor is it without bearing on the question that the British Government, after years of hesitation, withdrew its opposition to the Baghdad railway, which was calculated to stimulate German commerce in the valley of the Tigris and Euphrates, a field of endeavor long sacred to British enterprise. So far as public sentiment was reflected in the great reviews, the bugbear of German competition disappeared when the trade figures showed that British exporters were getting their share of the increased volume of business so characteristic of the last decade. For two years before the war England experienced such a boom as she had not known for many a day, and if in the spring of 1914 there were signs of relaxation, the favorable conditions of English industry were indicated by the comparative lack of unemployment.

The impartial observer will probably recognize, in the pressure of German competition, a stimulus much needed by the easy-going Briton of the late Victorian era. The United Kingdom had so long dominated the markets of the world that the advent of a serious rival was difficult to imagine or understand. With true British insularity, her manufacturers had insisted on selling to foreign cus-

[1] Since these lines were written German propagandists in the United States have sought to create the impression that German trade is discriminated against in the colonies of the British Empire and that this policy is intended for further development. Nothing could be farther removed from the facts; except, of course, as regards the self-governing dominions. But in those countries the British Government has absolutely no control of fiscal policies. Canada, New Zealand, Australia, and South Africa have granted preferential treatment for British goods primarily for economic, and not for political, reasons, and it will be seen in Chapter VII that the German Government has accepted the principle that in tariff matters the British self-governing colonies enjoy complete autonomy.

tomers the same commodities that were acceptable to Englishmen. They expected peoples who spoke every language but English to peruse catalogues written in English. They ignored shipping directions, and they were indifferent about the appearance of their product. British goods were supposed to rest on their reputation for quality; if they were not acceptable as they stood, it was not the fault of their makers. And so *ad infinitum*. The carelessness and lack of initiative on the part of manufacturers, the inferior quality of their agents abroad, and the utter absence of governmental assistance, the conservatism of investors and the positive ignorance of foreign lands, all contributed to reduce British industry almost to stagnation.

This lassitude was not confined to business circles. The recklessness with which the country plunged into the Boer War, in the expectation of an easy victory, was an index of that feeling of smugness which Englishmen were wont to exhibit in their dealings with other people, and which had recently found expression in the Diamond Jubilee of 1897. The conduct of the war, however, suggested that national complacency had been carried to a dangerous pitch, and the Prince of Wales (now King George V) was moved to exclaim, in a famous speech, "England, wake up!" It was indeed high time that she did. Her educational system, according to the then prime minister, Mr. Balfour, was "chaotic, ineffectual, utterly behind the age." The Irish problem still remained unsolved; there were vast questions of social reform which must be faced unless the conscience of Englishmen was utterly dead, and a new period in international affairs was clearly opening. The pursuit of pleasure and the love of sport, the luxury of the rich and the indifference of the middle classes were slowly sapping the creative power of an ancient and famous people, who seemed to have forgotten their glorious past and were now content to rest complacently upon the laurels of a bygone age. In his book *England and the English* the late Price Collier has a brilliant chapter on "The Land of Compromise." Modern England, he suggests, has refused to face the problems of the modern world, and has sought refuge in her traditional policy of compromise; she is a national ostrich that hides its face in the sands, a twentieth-century Belshazzar who will not read the handwriting on the wall. "The world has changed, but the Englishman has changed least of all," and a casual reader of Mr. Collier's indictment must have despaired of a really United Kingdom or an Empire which was more than a name.

There can be little question, however, that in the last ten years a new England has been in the making. One does not need to defend all the policies and actions of the Liberal government which took office in December, 1905, to recognize that it honestly endeavored to cope with the multitude of problems accumulated in the late Victorian period. Social reform, economic readjustment, Ireland, even the constitution itself—nothing escaped the attention of this zealous and able cabinet. We cannot judge as yet of the value or soundness of their measures, but we are very much aware of a deep awakening in the national life of the most conservative people in Europe. Contemporary England is, indeed, a kind of Rip Van Winkle, roused from slumber by the loud and persistent energy across the North Sea, and neither the world at large nor England herself has fully realized the significance of this awakening.

What other country could have weathered so easily and so calmly the storms produced by the great strikes of a few years ago? Seamen, railway servants, transport workers, dockers, miners, etc., seemed suddenly to have been infested by the virus of syndicalism, and their intransigeance for a while threatened to destroy the entire edifice of national prosperity. They unquestionably possessed many just grievances, for of the increasing wealth of the country they were receiving little advantage, but were, on the contrary, adversely affected by the general rise of prices.   Nor is it clear how far these elements of English society were satisfied with the concessions which their employers made with tolerable good will.   Yet in spite of the very considerable dislocation of the national life caused by these recurring strikes, British commerce continued to expand rapidly (*cf.* table on p. 102) and the chancellor of the exchequer was able to count on a progress- ive increase of revenue from customs.   Between 1909 and 1914, a period during which the revenue increased from £151,442,837 to £188,853,233, there was no increase of taxation—a striking contrast with Germany, where the imperial government was able to make both ends meet only by heavy borrowing (£59,353,970).

"There is no sign of decadence in England. By contrast with the rapid development of Germany and of the United States she seems, however, to be progressing but slowly. It needs but a glance at the vast figures of her foreign trade, encompassing as they do the world wide field of human endeavor and industry, to gain some understanding of what has yet to be accomplished to retire her to second place. To British ports come vessels of every nation and to every seaport in the world are sent British-owned vessels on trading missions. Millions of tons of staples are bought by England in the country of their origin, loaded on British ships, and delivered to her customers elsewhere without touching British ports. In the warehouses along the Thames and elsewhere are concentrated the supplies of the world, in many notable articles of commerce. The ivory of India and Africa are first brought here. The furs of the world are sold at auction in the London fur-market. Mahogany logs lie on the London docks awaiting transshipment to countries much nearer to their native growth than England. In brief, this little island is the commercial heart of the world, and the slowing or quickening of its pulses is reflected on the bourses of the nations of the earth. With all the internationalizing of finance which has come about in recent years, England still keeps tight hold upon the purse-strings. The London bank rate is a governing factor from

New York to Peking. England has been for generations and still is the great creditor nation. More than £200,000,000 is scattered abroad annually. It is her money which builds the pioneer railroads, opens mines, dams the waters, and finances the lesser nations. From all these enterprises her people take their toll and seek new outlets for this increment. That too much money and too many men have been sent abroad attracted by promise of greater returns is probably true. She has bled herself too freely, and the heart now shows some signs of weakness. The rivalry of younger and more daring and strenuous peoples for the trade of the world is a severe test of her seasoned strength."[1]

Personal impressions are doubtless of little value, but in 1913, when the writer revisited England after an absence of five years, he was not conscious, either in conversation with Englishmen or in reading the daily press, of that national depression and pessimism which was so noticeable in the first decade of this century. Domestic politics, not foreign affairs, were the subject of controversy. Of anti-German sentiment there was little or no evidence. The country had got used to the German navy, and except for a few extremists welcomed Mr. Churchill's efforts to strike a bargain with Admiral von Tirpitz. Trade was flourishing, unemployment rare, prosperity general. The possibility of war had almost faded from the popular mind, the more so as Anglo-German relations had "sensibly improved" during the Balkan Wars.

It would be foolish to assert that when the war did come there was not in the back of the English mind the idea that if the royal navy could control the seas a severe blow would be inflicted on German foreign commerce, but such a result was regarded as the means to an end, not the end itself. There is no evidence at all to show that the destruction of Germany as an economic Power was considered by Parliament in deciding to support the policy of Sir Edward Grey. And since war was declared the sober and

[1] J. D. Whelpley, *The Trade of the World*, pp. 63–65.

responsible journals have insisted that the annihilation of Germany, of the German people, was neither possible nor desirable for Great Britain to accomplish. No looser statement can be made than that British participation in the great conflict was dictated by cupidity or jealousy, for if sheer profit were the only consideration England would never have risked her very existence in a struggle which must cost infinitely more than the sum total of Germany's foreign trade for many, many years.

As a matter of fact, in the summer of 1914 there appeared to be no reason for a war to destroy German commerce, even if one had been planned by Great Britain, for the economic condition of Germany was far from roseate. The first nine months of 1912, a period of great commercial expansion, were followed by a disorganization of the railway service which occasioned great losses. Then came the Balkan Wars and the consequent collapse of a profitable market, so that during the year 1913 the shortage of capital, first noticed at the time of the Agadir crisis, became quite serious. An issue of Prussian four-per-cent treasury bonds, offered at 99 and redeemable in 1917, was only half taken up in March; a second loan in June fared little better, and even imperial-government consols could be sold only to 80 per cent of the issue. New industrial enterprises decreased from £134,000,000 in 1911 and £146,000,-000 in 1912 to £87,000,000 in 1913; the throbbing factories of Westphalia had to curtail considerably; and the building trade, which had been depressed since 1911, was saved only by large orders from the military authorities. In Bavaria the toy, hat, pencil, brush, and india-rubber trades suffered considerably, and in the case of baskets, cane furniture, granite, and paint, which had been sent chiefly to England, the market was lost by the competition of British manufacturers! Unemployment assumed a dangerous dimension, and was the more serious because of the constant rise in the cost of living. It is also believed that the yield of the great war tax of 1913 was far less than had been expected. Economically, therefore, Germany on the eve of the war was getting into difficulties for the first time since the period of expansion began, nor was the outlook for better times favorable. This may well have weighed with the military authorities in deciding that the time for war had come; with equal emphasis it would suggest to Great Britain that she had only to wait for a financial crisis in Germany to recover whatever ground had been lost in the heyday of German prosperity.[1]

[1] This paragraph is a summary of the British consular reports, published in the appendix to Ford Madox Hueffer, *When Blood is Their Argument.*

CHAPTER VI

ANGLO–GERMAN RELATIONS TO 1890

THE relations of England and Germany, as regards modern international politics, begin with the year 1740. Not that before this date the two countries were disinterested the one in the other. The captivity of Richard the Lion-Hearted in the twelfth century; the election of Richard of Cornwall as King of the Romans in the thirteenth; the appointment of Edward III as Vicar of the Empire on the eve of the Hundred Years' War; the importance of the Steelyard in London as an outpost of Hansa commerce, an experiment which insular jealousy forced Queen Elizabeth to terminate; the inspiration which English reformers drew from the teachings of Luther and Zwingli; and the vacillating interference of James I in the Thirty Years' War: these episodes testify to a connection between the two lands usually political, sometimes economic, and latterly religious, but none the less constant if viewed in the perspective of centuries. In the interval between the close of the religious wars and the expansion of European politics to America and India, that is to say, during the growth of French ascendency in the age of Louis XIV, England and Brandenburg—the forerunner of Prussia, which was in turn the creator of Germany—discovered a mutual interest in the preservation of Holland from French acquisitiveness and in the protection of Protestantism against the onslaughts of the Most Christian King.

Throughout the eighteenth century Germans played an important part in English history. On the extinction of the house of Stuart in 1714, it was a German, the Elector of Hanover, who mounted the English throne as George I. Though his positive services to his adopted country were not conspicuous, he brought Handel to England, and, from his ignorance of the English language and English politics, made parliamentary government both possible and necessary. German soldiers were repeatedly the agents of British expansion. Thus, Gibraltar was captured, with the assistance of the British navy, by a force under Prince George of Hesse-Darmstadt. English battles on the Continent were fought by Hanoverians or other German troops in English pay, and in the War of the American Revolution Hessians were used in a manner quite familiar to us. Before that war there had begun an emigration of Germans to British colonies which continued unabated until a generation ago; many Germans went to England itself, and rose rapidly in the business world. "England and its dominions have wisely honored and welcomed these men, and no lists of notables in any part of the British Empire could be made without including some of German birth or German extraction." [1]

But not till the reign of Frederick the Great of Prussia did the mistress of the seas appreciate the importance of a fixed policy with respect to German affairs. That policy came to rest on two considerations, the possession of Hanover by English kings and a determination to resist French predominance in Europe. Of "Germany" or of its future there was no conception. As long as the house of Hapsburg remained the enemy of France, British statesmen found an Austrian alliance the natural basis of the balance of power. But the refusal of Maria Theresa to defend Hanover on the eve of the Seven Years' War and her overtures for an alliance with Louis XV threw England into the arms of the King of Prussia. From the Convention of Westmin-

[1] Lady Phillips, *A Friendly Germany, Why Not?*, p. 48.

ster (January, 1756) and later treaties under which William Pitt subsidized Frederick to the extent of £670,000 a year immense consequences flowed. Frederick raised Prussia to an equality with Austria, and began the creation of that Germany which in recent years has been the preoccupation, if not the terror, of Great Britain; while by conquering America and India on the plains of Germany the island kingdom laid the foundations of that colossal Empire which is to-day the envy of united Germany. In the light of this strange development, it is not surprising that German historians regard the abandonment of Frederick by Lord Bute and George III an act of treachery which might be repeated by a modern English cabinet to escape from an unprofitable alliance with the Germany of to-day. Frederick, it may be noted, recouped himself by leaving England to "stew in her own juice" when confronted by the Franco-American alliance of 1778.

During the Napoleonic wars British policy was at one with German interests, to achieve the overthrow of imperial France. That Great Britain thought mainly of her insular security and the preservation of her Empire did not deprive her action of results advantageous to Germany. Without her subsidies to the allied armies, the pressure exerted by Wellington's troops in Spain, and her resistance to the Continental system which impelled Napoleon to undertake the fatal Russian campaign—above all, without the example of her steadfast refusal to make terms with the Corsican adventurer, Germany to this day might have been, if not a province of France, at least an outpost of French culture, a travesty of race and national honor. German historians, although they contend that Waterloo was won by Blücher and his Prussians, and complain of England's refusal at the Congress of Vienna to allow the annexation of Alsace-Lorraine by Prussia, recognize the debt of the Continent to English wealth and English stubbornness from 1793 to 1815. Englishmen in turn have always thrilled at the thought of Prussia in 1813. Crushed, partitioned, and humiliated after the catastrophe of Jena, her people, under the guidance of Stein, Scharnhorst, Gneisenau, and Hardenberg, had risen as a nation in arms and given to the world an inspiring picture of what may be accomplished by a great idea and a lofty purpose. If the relations of England and Germany in the following century had continued the traditions of Napoleonic days, the two nations would have avoided the death-struggle in which they are now locked and have stood shoulder to shoulder as the apostles of peace and progress. *Dis aliter visum*.

During the great peace, from 1815 to 1848, Great Britain settled down to the work of political regeneration, economic development, and humanitarian legislation. She quickly recovered from the strains of the war, and became the workshop of the world. Her colonial Empire expanded on all continents, her fleets policed and dominated the seas, and her institutions became the model for Continental nations. Still struggling to be free, and rent by internal dissensions, the latter enjoyed, if they did not merit, the mingled contempt and dislike of the island Power, to whose interest it was that they remain in a condition of innocuous desuetude. The pages of Thackeray reflect the attitude of aristocratic society toward the European peoples among whom they sought their pleasures, and the middle or lower classes were too prejudiced or too ignorant to regard "foreigners" dispassionately. English insularity was probably at its worst in the years before nationality began to be the controlling factor in European affairs.

Germany, unfortunately, entered upon an inglorious period in her history. In 1815 Frederick William III of Prussia was hailed as the leader of Germany, for he was to achieve its unity and endow it with those liberal institutions which were considered the secret of English greatness. But his acceptance of the German Confederation, by which the Congress of Vienna restored Germany to the tutelage of absolutist and obscurantist Austria, destroyed the hopes of his people, and for the rest of his reign Germany groaned under the oppression of Metternich. The King himself adopted the Austrian system, which reduced Prussia to the rank of a second-rate Power, and thereby earned the obloquy of English liberals who conceived their own philosophy to be a panacea for all evils existent and potential.

For this state of affairs Great Britain was in part responsible.[1] She had it in her power to dictate the settlements of the Congress of Vienna. Had she seen fit to demand the creation of a strong and united Germany, which should satisfy the aspirations of the German people, she might well have accomplished it. The Tsar Alexander ardently supported the claims of Prussia to the whole of Saxony, and Prussian statesmen demanded Alsace-Lorraine as well. But Alexander, who was then posing as a liberal, was distasteful to Castlereagh, the British plenipotentiary, and his designs on the Ottoman Empire were suspected; Austria was the traditional ally of Great Britain, except in the Seven Years' War, and was the opponent of Russian designs in the Balkans. Castlereagh, therefore, joined with Metternich and Talleyrand, the French representative, to upset the Prusso-Russian schemes, and to force the Confederation upon Germany. Perhaps German unity was yet only an ideal, but if British statesmen could have looked ahead fifty years and perceived how British policy in the Italian wars of unification would cement an abiding

---

[1] For the German attitude toward English policy up to 1871, see Erich Marcks, *England and Germany*, 1500–1900 (1900), Richard Graf von Moulin-Eckart, *Englands Politik und die Mächte* (1901), and Heinrich Oberwinder, *Die Aufgaben des Deutschen Reiches* (1905). Lord Palmerston is severely criticised by Sir Spencer Walpole in his two works, *History of England from* 1815 and *History of Twenty-Five Years*.

friendship between England and Italy, they might well have done something for the great nation of central Europe. Intelligible as was Castlereagh's attitude in the light of narrow "British interests," it is to be regretted that he had no vision of a Europe reconstituted on the basis of liberty and nationality.

In the reaction which followed the Congress of Vienna, German liberals looked across the North Sea for light, for with the passing of Castlereagh, in 1822, English policy became distinctly liberalizing, in both foreign and domestic affairs. The Carlsbad Resolutions of 1819 gave the German governments absolute control over the intellectual life and political activities of their peoples; in comparison, England, even before the Reform Act of 1832, was free and enlightened. Not even the unconstitutional régime in Hanover, which was still bound to England by a personal union, and until its severance refused to join the *Zollverein*, could dampen the enthusiasm of German professors for the institutions and liberties of England. In official circles, on the other hand, English policy was not popular, more especially after Palmerston, speaking in the House of Commons, advised the German princes to restrain their reactionary tendencies.

The name of Palmerston hangs like a dead weight over Anglo-German relations till the days of Bismarck. Controlling the foreign relations of Great Britain for the greater part of a generation, he certainly achieved some remarkable successes. The independence and neutrality of Belgium, the establishment of British influence in China, and the checking of French and Russian designs in the Near East are not less conspicuous than his benevolent neutrality in Italian politics, without which Italy might never have been made. But with respect to Germany, his attitude was deplorable. He described the country as "a land of damned professors," and quoted with favor the aphorism of Voltaire, that its people should be content to rule the clouds, while France ruled the land and Britain the seas. While the Frankfort Assembly of 1848 purchased a fleet to protect Schleswig-Holstein from Danish acquisitiveness, he airily remarked that the "German" flag was unknown to international law, and that British cruisers might treat the ships of the Confederation as "pirates"! His policy was regarded as meddlesome, high-handed, and treacherous. The famous doggerel,

"Hat der Teufel einen Sohn,
Ist er sicher Palmerston,"

reflects accurately German antipathy to the great Englishman. His dismissal from office in 1851, for a too prompt recognition of Louis Napoleon's *coup d'état*, was hailed with delight at the German courts, and his diplomacy was felt to be an important factor in the maintenance of British economic supremacy, which aimed to keep Germany divided in the interests of its own monopoly. But his worst offense was to exclude Prussia from the Congress of Paris, which met after the Crimean War, until the terms of peace had been settled, although as a neutral nation Prussia had no legal claim to participate.

As Lord Palmerston enjoyed boundless popularity among all classes of Englishmen they accepted his view of a country about which they knew little and cared less. The typical German, as portrayed in literature and on the stage, was "a genial, wool-gathering professor in a formidable pair of spectacles, untidy of habit, and far from athletic in form, the dedicated slave rather than the possessor of several large note-books and a collecting-box." [1] Not even the old universities were free from the prevailing prejudice, perhaps because they were strongholds of Anglicism and suspected the "undisciplined freethinkers" (Palmer-

[1] *The Round Table*, September, 1914, p. 617.

ston) of Germany.[1]   Prince Albert was long disliked as a foreigner scarcely worthy to be the consort of an English queen, in spite of the deep regard of Frederick William IV for Queen Victoria[2] and the partiality of Bunsen, his minister at the court of St. James, for English institutions.[3] Finally, the international exhibition of 1851, held to demonstrate the complete superiority of English civilization and the ineffable blessings of peace, was considered a kind of rebuke to Germany for the revolution of 1848 and the backward "Kultur" which produced them.

On the other hand, says Sir Harry Johnston, "the marriage of Queen Victoria gave a fresh impetus to the Germanization of Britain.   Notable Germans were more or less directly brought to this country by those far-seeing helpers of England, Leopold and Albert of Saxe-Coburg. They explored unknown lands for the British Empire, founded colleges of music and chemistry, schools and museums of art, studios in philology, ancient and modern, improved both theatre and drama, extended horticulture,

---

[1] See W. Tuckwell, *Reminiscences of Oxford*, p. 147.

[2] In 1848 he addressed to Queen Victoria the following remarkable letter: "Most Gracious Queen and Sister . . . God has permitted events [the Paris revolution of February, 1848] which decisively threaten the peace of Europe. . . . If the revolutionary party carries out its programme, 'the sovereignty of the people,' my minor crown will be broken no less certainly than the mighty crowns of your Majesty, and a fearful scourge laid upon the nations: a century of rebellion, lawlessness, and godlessness. . . . God has placed in your Majesty's hands and the hands of the two Emperors, and in those of the German Confederacy and in mine, a power which, if it acts now in union and harmony, with reliance on Heaven, is able, humanly speaking, to enforce with certainty the maintenance of the peace of the world. . . . The power I mean is 'the power of united speech.' In the year 1830 the use of this immeasurable power was criminally neglected. . . . On both knees I adjure you, use, for the welfare of Europe, '*Engellands England*.' With these words I fall at your Majesty's feet." (*Letters of Queen Victoria*, vol. II, p. 151.)

[3] The comment of a Pan-German is worth reading. Bunsen was "the worst choice that could have been made. Instead of being a man of the old Prussian type, he was a weak and fanciful representative, whose Anglomania was accentuated by his English wife." He desired an Anglo-German alliance, "forgetful of what such an alliance had cost Prussia" in the time of Frederick the Great. And "the almost sickening prejudice of Frederick William IV was increased by Bunsen's effusive reports." (Moulin-Eckart, *Englands Politik und die Mächte*, p. 60.) This is practically a paraphrase of Treitschke, *Deutsche Geschichte*, vol. V, pp. 125–6.

and assisted to make Kew Gardens and the Herbarium what they are and have been to an Empire in which economic botany is a matter of necessity, not a pretty luxury as some of our home-bred statesmen have imagined. Glance through the eminent names which have become famous during the nineteenth century in British colonial and imperial history, in British exploration, biology, metallurgy, painting, music, journalism, banking, law making and expounding, soldiering and seamanship, and note how many are of recent or immediate extraction." [1]   There follows a truly astonishing list of notabilities who gave England their best efforts, and were well rewarded by a grateful country.   Between none of the countries now at war did there exist such close and intimate personal relations of long standing as between England and Germany.

When the movement for German unification began to take definite shape, Queen Victoria lent her sympathy and her influence to the Prussian cause,[2] but Bismarck's defiance of the Prussian Diet aroused much indignation.   The foreign office had no definite policy, although it did not stand alone in this respect, for Bismarck's designs were nowhere understood, not even in Germany itself.   Palmerston had once written (22 November, 1850):

"We should have no objection to see Prussia take the first place; on the contrary, a German union, embracing all the smaller states, with Prussia at its head, and in alliance with Austria as a separate Power, would have been a very good European arrangement." [3]

With such remarkable prescience did Palmerston envisage the future organization of central Europe, but when the crucial moment came he abandoned this view for a policy of bluster.

---

[1] *Views and Reviews*, p. 104.
[2] *Cf.* Sir Sidney Lee, *Life of Queen Victoria, passim.*
[3] Ashley, *Life of Lord Palmerston,* vol. II, p. 171.

The unification of Germany began when Bismarck interested himself in the problem of Schleswig-Holstein. That question was one of the most complicated which ever confronted European diplomacy. As Palmerston explained, only three persons had ever understood it: the Danish prime minister, who had lost his mind; the late Prince Albert; and himself, who had forgotten it.[1] It did not occur to him that the Prussian statesman had thoroughly grasped the possibilities of the situation, and as the status of the duchies rested on an international agreement of 1852 Palmerston supposed in 1863, when the attempt of Denmark to annex them brought both the German Confederation and Prussia on the scene, that the Concert of Europe would settle the matter. Hence his statement that, if any violent attempt were made to overthrow the rights or interfere with the independence of Denmark, those who made the attempt would find that they would not have to contend with Denmark alone. A more unfortunate declaration could not have been made, because England was not prepared to use force on behalf of Denmark, even if the Prince of Wales had just married a Danish princess, and diplomacy was quite unable to prevent Bismarck from taking both Schleswig and Holstein for Prussia.[2] "The war of 1864 was one of the great cross-

[1] The problem itself and the insufficiency of British diplomacy is admirably presented in the *Memoirs and Letters of Sir Robert Morier, 1826–1876*. Sir Robert was one of the few Englishmen who possessed an adequate knowledge of German affairs. He was attached to the Berlin embassy, and had his advice been followed the question would probably have been peacefully settled; which doubtless explains Bismarck's bitter dislike of him and his rejection for the Berlin embassy after the unification of the empire.

[2] "When in the year 1864 the sudden death of the King of Denmark opened up the Schleswig-Holstein question, the British Government proposed to France that they should oppose the advance of Prussia and Austria-Hungary, that is, they should interfere in the internal affairs of Germany, with a view to hindering the advancement of German unity." (So Heinrich Oberwinder, *Die Weltkrise und die Aufgaben des Deutschen Reiches*, p. 37.) This is, of course, a ridiculous overstatement, because the Schleswig-Holstein question had been internationalized by the Treaty of 1852, and no one, not even the Germans themselves, who were far from approving of Bismarck's policy, anticipated his real intentions. Until after the war with Austria

roads of British history," observes a competent student of
naval affairs, and he opines that England "took the wrong
turning. The great German chancellor candidly admitted
that the possession of Kiel and a strategic canal through
Holstein were two of the principal objects which Prussia
had when she drew the sword. . . . A war which should
have left Schleswig-Holstein in the hands of Denmark
would have been . . . exceedingly advantageous, eco-
nomical, and opportune for Great Britain."[1]   But royal
interference restrained Palmerston and Russell, and Bismarck had achieved the first of his great triumphs.

Not until the defeat of Austria in the war of 1866 and
the establishment of the North German Confederation did
England comprehend the progress of events in central
Europe. But as the policy of Napoleon III grew more
reckless, English sentiment began to see in the new Germany an important bulwark for the balance of power.
The annexation of Savoy and Nice by the French Emperor after he had withdrawn from the Italian War of
Liberation, had been deeply resented in England, and his
negotiations with Bismarck for "compensation" on the
morrow of Sadowa branded him as a veritable highway-
man. His raising of the Luxemburg question in 1867
ended by involving England in a difficult pledge to protect its neutrality. And as it became evident that the
Second Empire was tottering he was expected to stake all
on a last desperate throw.

For these reasons English opinion, in the early stages
of the Franco-German War, was decidedly favorable to
Germany. She had been attacked after conceding the
essential point in the preliminary diplomacy. On 25 July,
1870, the *Times* published a draft treaty, in the hand-

Bismarck was generally regarded as a traitor to the German cause. Herr Oberwinder's remark admirably illustrates the fashion in which history has been distorted to serve modern political ambition.
[1] Hurd and Castle, *German Sea Power*, p. 87.

writing of the French ambassador in Berlin, which provided for the annexation of Belgium to France, and to the
same newspaper Thomas Carlyle, then at the height of
his influence, sent a long letter in praise of Germany.[1] The
Queen's sympathy was known to be with the German
legions. In short, politicians and publicists were agreed that
a strong Germany was essential to Europe and to England;
to quote the *Times*, *à propos* of the adhesion of the South
German states to the North German Confederation, "in
this the policy of past generations of English statesmen
will be fulfilled."[2] The first French defeats aroused no
sympathy—they were considered a proper punishment for
a reckless and uncalled-for declaration of war.

But the disinterested spectator could not remain indifferent to the fate of France. Bismarck's protest against
the sale of coals and ammunition to France by Newcastle
and Birmingham, and the refusal of the German military
authorities to let an English gunboat ascend the Seine to
remove British subjects from France were not kindly received, and when, after Sedan and the collapse of the
Empire, it was realized that the Germans would make
peace only for a heavy price, English opinion began to
rally to France. To the feeling that France should not be
unduly punished for the mistakes of a government she
had repudiated, the desire was added that the city and
people of Paris should be spared the horrors of war. Lord
Granville therefore endeavored to bring about an armistice
before the capital should be bombarded. Bismarck spoke
of this proposal as so much "rubbish," pretending to believe that slow starvation and the horrors of a siege were
worse than a bombardment; in his *Reflections and Reminiscences* he declared that the Commune was directly caused
by conditions arising out of the siege. In the same place,
and even more in Moritz Busch's *Bismarck : Some Secret*

[1] 11 November, 1870.   [2] 10 December, 1870.

Pages of His History, his irritation against England finds constant expression: now a complaint that the Crown Princess, who was the daughter of Queen Victoria, was influencing the King or her husband; now a lament that the two men were more anxious to be praised in the English press than to further the interests of Germany. Nor was Bismarck pleased when Lord Granville protested vigorously against Russia's repudiation of that clause of the Treaty of Paris which restricted her from building warships in the Black Sea, for he himself had urged this action upon Prince Gortchakoff, the Russian chancellor; and in the London conference which met to consider the Russian demand, the Prussian representative voted steadily with his Russian colleague. In such an atmosphere the suggestion of Queen Victoria that King William should be "magnanimous" in the final terms of peace was ignored; while Gladstone's protest against the annexation of Alsace-Lorraine inspired Bismarck with a permanent dislike for the great Englishman and a contempt often manifested in the title "Professor" Gladstone.[1]

British policy, throughout this period of Bismarckian triumphs, was frankly opportunist, and perhaps it was a mistake not to take sides more resolutely. "A great English statesman would either have prevented the uni-

[1] Sybel in his *Begründung des Deutsches Reiches*, of course, follows the cue of Bismarck. Oberwinder and Moulin-Eckart, in the works cited, are very bitter because Great Britain did not prevent the war with France, as if Bismarck had not boasted, in the *Reflections and Reminiscences*, that he had contrived to make the war inevitable! Professor Marcks writes: "The unity of Germany was accomplished without the aid, and somewhat against the wishes, of England. The historian understands how the interests of Great Britain caused her indifference and unfriendliness, but he also understands how her course of action affected Germany. The German mind does not understand, and has not yet forgotten, how the land it had hitherto so greatly admired, and which was so closely akin to it, so bitterly disappointed it." (*England and Germany*, 1500–1900, p. 50.) As a matter of fact, Lord Granville did endeavor to mediate between France and Germany in the two weeks before the war, and his policy as regards the neutrality of Belgium was scrupulously impartial. *Cf.* Morley, *Life of Gladstone;* Fitzmaurice, *Life of Lord Granville;* Lord Augustus Loftus, *Diplomatic Reminiscences*, second series; Wemyss, *Memoirs and Letters of Sir Robert Morier.*

fication of Germany or have loyally welcomed it as a guarantee of the peace of Europe." [1] But British interests were not directly involved; "watchful waiting" and a strict neutrality were seemingly called for in the circumstances of the moment. Thanks to its ignorance of German affairs, English opinion had not grasped the necessity of German unity—it could not see that "Germany" deserved its sympathy quite as much as "Italy." English assistance was invaluable to Garibaldi and Cavour ; why should it be denied to Bismarck and Moltke?

The answer, of course, is that Cavour fought for an intelligible purpose; from the first the unification of Italy was his acknowledged aim, and his policy enjoyed the enthusiastic support of the Sardinian Parliament and the people of Italy. When Italy was made, parliamentary government became the basis of her national life, union and liberty went hand in hand. Such a cause appealed strongly to all classes of Englishmen. But they were utterly unable to understand the devious ways of Otto von Bismarck. His defiance of the Prussian Diet in the interests of the army; his unblushing destruction of the liberties of Schleswig-Holstein to protect which had been the ostensible purpose of his policy; and the annexation of Hanover and other small states after the war of 1866, were disgusting and repugnant to the English mind. Had a liberal Prussia, such as was struggling to be born when Bismarck thrust his sinister personality into the balance, struck for the unity of Germany, had the liberal ideas of some of the lesser princes been more favorably received by the Prussian Government, England would doubtless have rallied to the German national cause with the same enthusiasm which enabled Palmerston and Russell to support the Italian patriots against a reactionary Austria. But

[1] Sidney Whitman, "England and Germany," in *Harper's Magazine*, April, 1898, p. 783.

Bismarck cared little for German nationality he thought only of Prussian supremacy, and Englishmen could not respond to the autocratic and military ideals of Prusso-Germany. Even so, the events of 1862–71 received sympathetic treatment at the hands of Mr. C. A. Fyffe, whose *History of Modern Europe* long was, and perhaps still is, the standard account of nineteenth-century history.

We shall not be far from the truth if we say that Englishmen were taken aback by the meteoric rise of Prussia to the headship of a great nation, the more so because her methods were contrary to English traditions, but there was no disposition to ignore the new Power. To contend, as some superpatriotic Germans have done, that Great Britain tried to prevent the unification of the fatherland or to "embitter the proudest moments of our victory by phrases about civilization and humanity," [1] is absurd, *pace* Bismarck and Busch. Whatever the unpleasant features of the new Power, they were expected to disappear when the Crown Prince should inaugurate a more liberal system upon his accession to the throne. For twenty years after the creation of the German Empire— that is, until the dismissal of Bismarck—the attitude of Great Britain was decidedly friendly, in spite of many disagreeable incidents, and the possibility of a fatal quarrel between the two countries was beyond imagination.

The unification of Italy and Germany fixed the map of Europe, outside of the Balkans, for forty-three years—from 1871 to the beginning of the Great War. The new Germany was immeasurably stronger than the old Prussia, whose part in international politics since 1815 had been negligible. South of the Alps an entirely new Power had arisen. The war of 1866 with Prussia and the compromise with Hungary in the following year had transformed

[1] Moulin-Eckart, *Englands Politik und die Mächte*, p. 76.

Austria into a dual monarchy. The future of France, shorn of two fair provinces and equipped with a genuine constitutional system for the first time in her history, was problematical. Only England and Russia had experienced no organic changes.

It was natural, therefore, that for some years international politics should be in a state of flux. For Bismarck the great problem was: Will defeated France accept the new situation? She could undertake a war of revenge, he saw clearly, only if she were allied with Austria or Russia. So, to keep the new Republic isolated, the chancellor in 1872 devised the Three Emperors' League, an elastic agreement between the Tsar, the Austrian ruler, and the German Emperor, whose nominal purpose was the preservation of monarchical principles in Europe. As room in this combination was left for Italy, and Great Britain was eschewing an active part in Continental politics, Bismarck's ascendency was complete. France was helpless, and was quite aware of the fact.

Then occurred one of those incidents which have done so much to prejudice Germany in the eyes of other nations. In 1874–5 the military party in Berlin professed much alarm at the rapid recovery of France from the effects of the war, and in particular at the reorganization of her army. The *Kulturkampf* was then at its height, and Bismarck was disposed to relieve the internal pressure by a vigorous foreign policy. The international atmosphere suddenly became thick with rumors of a second Franco-German war, nor were they dissipated when the French Government communicated to the *Times* a report from its ambassador in Berlin on German war preparations. Bismarck always denied that war was in sight at this time; on the contrary, he asserted that he had restrained the military enthusiasts. But the evidence is against his contention. Queen Victoria wrote to Bismarck and Emperor William, and at the

critical moment Gortchakoff descended on Berlin, from
which, after an interview with the Emperor and Bismarck,
he issued a circular beginning: "Peace is now assured."
The peace was not broken, but Europe was stunned to
observe that in four years Germany had "learned and exaggerated the besetting vice of the people she had conquered,"
with the distinction that while French chauvinism was
"spasmodical and undisciplined," hers was "methodical,
calculating, cold-blooded, and self-contained." [1]

The repercussions of this war scare were soon felt. Bismarck was furious with Gortchakoff, whose conduct could
be regarded as either an insinuation or an affront; the
Three Emperors' League was doomed. As the Turkish
crisis of 1875–8 developed and revealed Russia and Austria
as rivals in the Balkans, Bismarck drew closer to the latter
Power, and at the Congress of Berlin consistently supported
the Anglo-Austrian pretensions against Russia. It was
also clear that Russia would not permit France to be crushed
at the convenience of German militarism, and that Great
Britain, under the leadership of Lord Beaconsfield, was
conscious of her duty as a European Power. Russian opinion deeply resented this ingratitude for Russian neutrality
during the wars of unification; it suddenly gave vent to
much abuse of Germany, and early in 1879 Russo-German
relations became very strained.

Under these circumstances Bismarck negotiated an agreement with Austria which was expanded into the Triple
Alliance by the adhesion of Italy in 1882. So far as is
known the purpose of the combination was purely defensive. Austria was not pledged to act against France, nor
Italy against Russia. In this form the Triple Alliance endured for thirty-three years as one of the "hard facts"

[1] Wemyss, *Memoirs and Letters of Sir Robert Morier*, II, p. 346. The evidence
is discussed in J. Holland Rose, *The Development of the Modern European Nations*,
1905, chap. 12: "The Triple and Dual Alliances." See also Lord Newton, *Life of
Lord Lyons* vol. II, pp. 67–84.

(Prince Bülow) of Continental politics. Thus the three Powers which had been born or reorganized in the third quarter of the century were united to preserve the new settlements; furthermore, they formed a compact block in the centre of Europe, recalling after a fashion the old Holy Roman Empire, and their united military strength was irresistible.

Here was a fact of which British statesmen were not slow to take advantage. Since 1815 British policy had endeavored to restrain the aggressive tendencies of France, and to check the advance of Russia toward the Mediterranean or the frontiers of India. Thanks to German arms, France had ceased to be dangerous; but the revision of the Treaty of Paris in 1871 and Lord Beaconsfield's diplomacy in the crisis which culminated in the Congress of Berlin had aggravated Anglo-Russian bickerings almost to the point of war. On the other hand, German assistance had been invaluable in securing the "peace with honor" (Treaty of Berlin), and Bismarck had formally stated that there was no conflict of interests between England and Germany. Lord Salisbury, who held the foreign office from 1878 to 1880, welcomed the news of the Austro-German alliance as "good tidings of great joy." [1] According to one account, Bismarck proposed an Anglo-German alliance to Lord Beaconsfield on the morrow of the Berlin Congress, and the idea was cordially received, but the election of 1880 drove the Conservative statesmen from office before the negotiations were complete. It is likewise stated that in 1887 Bismarck wrote a personal letter to Lord Salisbury, to urge that England join the Triple Alliance, but that the latter was then too obsessed by his policy of "splendid isolation." [2]

Generally speaking, the British Government co-operated

[1] Speech at Manchester, 17 October, 1879.
[2] *Daily Telegraph*, 12 May, 1912. Special correspondence from Vienna.

with the Powers of the Triple Alliance as long as Bismarck
was chancellor of the German Empire. England and Austria equally desired the exclusion of Russia from the Balkans; Lord Granville accordingly sought and secured the
help of Bismarck in carrying out the treaty of Berlin.
England and Italy were at one in opposing the pretensions
of France in the Mediterranean, especially after the latter's
occupation of Tunis; in 1888 some kind of bargain was
made between the first two Powers, and a British squadron
appeared in Italian waters when Franco-Italian relations
became difficult. "In Egypt," Bismarck declared, "I
am English." If the decade from 1880 to 1890 be viewed
as a whole, Anglo-German intimacy must be credited with
evicting Russia from the control of Bulgaria and prevent-
ing General Boulanger from precipitating a war of revenge.

Disputes there were between London and Berlin. Bismarck refused to tolerate the marriage of Prince Alexander
of Battenberg, the deposed ruler of Bulgaria, with the
daughter of the Crown Princess, an arrangement upon
which Queen Victoria had set her heart. His treatment
of the Crown Princess, amounting almost to persecution,
and his conduct toward the Emperor Frederick during his
brief reign of three months (March–June, 1888) aroused
much resentment in England. He boasted to Busch, his
Boswell, that he encouraged the colonial ambitions of
France to make bad blood between Paris and London;
he frequently complained that Great Britain was endeavoring to use Germany as a catspaw in her quarrels with Russia; he often discanted upon that hypocrisy which most
Germans believe is the dominant trait of the English character. He raised no objection when Russia provoked the
Pendjeh incident on the Afghan frontier shortly after the
death of Gordon at Khartoum; and he was not opposed to
a Russian occupation of Constantinople provided Austria
was given a free rein in the western Balkans.

In the difficult question of colonial expansion, which was now coming to the fore, there was considerable wrangling between England and Germany; at times the tension was acute, as the *Life* of Lord Granville clearly reveals. But the statement of Professor Hans Delbrück, that, "immediately on taking her first steps to share in the exploitation of the earth, Germany encountered the negative of England and, in consequence of the English attitude, acquired during a quarter of a century only very few and very unimportant colonies," [1] is an exaggeration. In two instances Great Britain did impose her veto. In 1884 the British flag was hoisted at Santa Lucia Bay, on the east coast of Africa, shortly before a German man-of-war arrived for a similar purpose; and the following year Bechuanaland was occupied, to prevent a junction between the Transvaal and German Southwest Africa. The refusal to surrender Walfisch Bay to the last-named colony may also be considered a legitimate grievance, although the Union Jack was hoisted there before Germany manifested any interest in the region; for that matter, the London authorities would probably have surrendered the possession except for the emphatic protests of Cape Colony.

For the rest, Downing Street made a point of admitting the claims of Germany where they did not conflict with a well-recognized and clearly established British interest. In some cases anterior British rights were renounced in order to humor Germany. Lord Granville withdrew the British claims to Angra Pequena (Luderitz Bay), which became the nucleus of German Southwest Africa. He welcomed the protectorate over Togoland, on the ground that Germany was a more desirable neighbor than France, which would then have surrounded the Gold Coast on three sides; and he made it possible for a German agent to ac-

[1] "The Price of a German-English Entente," *Contemporary Review*, February, 1911, p. 13.

quire the Cameroons for the fatherland He yielded to German remonstrances against an Anglo-Portuguese convention of 1884 which would have secured the control of the lower Congo region by the signatories. Finally, he restricted the British claims in New Guinea, in order that Germany might have a share of the island, in spite of vigorous objections from Australia.

The only serious rivalry between England and Germany concerned Zanzibar, where each had strong claims. In the end Lord Salisbury arrived at a complete understanding with Count Caprivi, which was recorded in the convention of 1890. Germany's claims to what is now—or was, before the war—German East Africa were admitted, except that the island of Zanzibar remained a British protectorate; Great Britain in return secured a free hand in Uganda. But, in the light of later developments, the most important provision was the cession of Heligoland, for which Bismarck had been clamoring since 1884. This must always remain the conclusive proof that Great Britain was not jealous of a legitimate German expansion, for that would have been impossible so long as Heligoland gave the British navy a base of operations on the very coast of Germany. If Germany was not satisfied with her acquisitions in Africa and the Pacific, the blame must rest, not upon Great Britain, but with the policy of Bismarck, who deliberately encouraged France to a programme of colonial adventure in order to divert her thoughts from Alsace-Lorraine and a war of revenge.

The truth is, Bismarck never allowed any difference with England to become serious. Mr. Sidney Whitman, who knew the prince better than any Englishman, has said that "he was free from that petty dislike of England so often imputed to him." [1] In his *German Memories*, the same writer has stated:

[1] *Conversations with Prince Bismarck*, p. 173.

"I know for a fact that Bismarck's final verbal instructions to German officials, such as consuls and diplomatic agents to India and Egypt, invariably culminated in the words: 'Do all you can to obtain the good will of the English.   You need never use a cipher in telegraphing, for we have nothing to conceal from them.   It would be madness for us to quarrel with England, or she with us.' "[1]

Various statements of Bismarck to the Reichstag might be quoted to show his appreciation of England's position with respect to Germany: it will suffice to recall that upon the conclusion of the convention of 1890, which was not popular in Germany because Zanzibar was conceded to England, although Heligoland was given in exchange, he declared that the good will of England was more important to Germany than the whole of Africa, and he might have added that Germany had secured the colonies she then possessed in Africa through the good will of the British Government.[2] Whatever the mistakes or evil deeds of the Iron Chancellor may have been—and he can be charged with a good many of both; however much he might differ with Great Britain in even important matters, till at times his relations with London were severely strained—he was under no illusions as to the danger which the permanent hostility of the British Empire would be to the splendid edifice of German power he had been at such pains to construct.   In no phase of his policy did he show more strikingly his ability to distinguish between the possible and the impossible.   This is not to say that Bismarck would not have broken with England if he had remained in office till his death, but one thing is certain—he would not have risked such a quarrel until he had squared Germany's account with France and have arranged with Russia for a diversion against British interests in Asia.

In England there was no disposition to regard Germany as an enemy.   Sir Charles Dilke, easily the most acute

[1] P. 125.   [2] This appears clearly in Fitzmaurice, *Life of Lord Granville*.

observer of international politics in his day, presented a sympathetic view of Germany in his *Present Position of European Politics* (1887), and was able to say: "Little harm has been done to English interests by Germany since she became the foremost of Continental Powers, and few occasions of serious difficulty between the countries are likely to arise." [1]   He thought that the German general staff, underrating the military capacity of England, would attack France through Belgium in case of another war between the two nations, but he credited Germany with a desire to keep the peace, and believed that if Belgium strengthened her army, so that it might offer effective resistance, war in western Europe might be indefinitely postponed.

To-day two kindred nations, who have more in common than any other European nations as regards natural characteristics, and who have through the centuries usually stood shoulder to shoulder in the great movements of European history, whose best interests, separate and reciprocal, would have been best served by the permanent enjoyment of peace, are locked in a struggle to the death. Even if a drawn battle is the ultimate result the loss to each country will be enormous, almost irreparable; more likely one will be badly defeated by the other and will sink from the high position it has hitherto enjoyed in the world.   Is it possible to determine with any approach to accuracy or fairness where the responsibility for this lamentable rupture should rest?   An overwhelming majority of Americans have close ties with either England or Germany; they would rejoice to see a lasting peace established between the two most progressive countries of the Old World.   In the succeeding chapters an effort will be made to discuss these problems as dispassionately as possible, and, if possible, to establish the responsibility for the rupture of 1914.

[1] P. 55.

CHAPTER VII

THE QUARREL

THE last decade of the nineteenth century is a very confused period for the student of international politics. It opened with an Anglo-German convention which seemed to dispose of all serious disputes between the two governments; at its close the world had become aware of an Anglo-German rivalry that boded ill for the peace of Europe. In 1890 the Triple Alliance was well-nigh omnipotent in Europe; in 1900 it was confronted by a hostile alliance of France and Russia, with which Powers, however, the German Empire had managed to preserve tolerably cordial relations. The position of Great Britain had changed most of all. Lord Salisbury and Prince Bismarck were in substantial agreement in 1890; in 1900 Anglo-German relations were so delicate, thanks to the inflamed state of public opinion on both sides of the North Sea, that the most careful handling of the difficulties arising out of the Boer War was required of the German Government to prevent an open rupture. Four years later, on April 8, 1904, France and England signed a series of agreements, which not only adjusted numerous disputes of long standing, but rescued England from the "splendid isolation" to which the policy of Lord Salisbury condemned her, and effected a diplomatic revolution comparable only to the reversal of alliances on the eve of the Seven Years' War. The essential point lay in the fact that Great Britain passed over to the side of Germany's hereditary enemy, France, and by her action restored a semblance of equilibrium to a Europe long dominated by Germany.

The most striking characteristic of these fifteen years is the absence of any guiding hand in the international game, for William II was a poor substitute for the great Bismarck. The Iron Chancellor had insured the predominance of Germany by "keeping the wire open to St. Petersburg." William II, in 1890, refused to renew the secret "reinsurance" treaty, out of loyalty to Francis Joseph, his formal ally, and Bismarck resigned shortly afterward. His passing removed the last obstacle to that Franco-Russian alliance which he had always feared, and which had been foreshadowed by Russian loans in Paris, not to speak of Russian warnings to Berlin in 1875 and 1887 that the Tsar would not allow France to be crushed. The alliance was concluded sometime between 1891, when a French fleet visited Cronstadt, and 1896, when the Tsar came to Paris, probably in 1895. The treaty has never been published; its purely defensive character and its limitation to European affairs, however, have always been assumed. For some years the French unquestionably cherished the hope of recovering Alsace-Lorraine with the help of Russia, and Germans were able to stigmatize the alliance as unnatural, on the ground that a democratic and republican country could have nothing in common with an autocratic empire. But their own policy was primarily to blame for this development, and they must be held in large measure responsible for the enormous armies of recent years. After all, France was merely reviving the policy of her Valois and Bourbon kings, who always maintained an alliance with some state of Eastern Europe against the predominant power in Germany. Whatever the motives of the Republic may have been, Germany was henceforth compelled to reckon with the possibility of a simultaneous attack on both frontiers. William II, therefore, tried to handle the situation by diverting the new alliance to his own purposes.

There is some reason for believing that it was directed,

in the first instance, against Great Britain. Here was Germany's opportunity. She was resolved to become a world, as distinct from a European, Power; she believed that England was the chief obstacle to her success in such a policy, and English opinion, it may be admitted, had not taken kindly to her first ventures in this field. Furthermore, in the lack of an adequate German fleet, the assistance of France and Russia was essential for any humiliation of the island Power.

It happened that the French foreign minister from 1894 to 1898, M. Gabriel Hanotaux, was by no means averse to a policy of "pin-pricks" which would cause embarrassment to Great Britain in various parts of the world. Since the dismissal of Bismarck William II had in various ways tried to cultivate friendly relations with France. So it was easy for Paris and Berlin to strike up a temporary accord. In 1894 they protested successfully against an Anglo-Congolese treaty which would have given Great Britain a connecting strip of territory between Rhodesia and the Uganda Protectorate. The following year Germany supported the Dual Alliance in "advising" Japan to give back Port Arthur, which China had surrendered by the Treaty of Shimonoseki, and winked at its subsequent seizure by Russia, who had made no opposition to the German occupation of Kiao-Chou. Next, Germany was certainly aware of, and may possibly have abetted, the expedition of Major Marchand, which the French Government sent into the Sudan in the hope of blocking the recovery of that region by the Anglo-Egyptian forces under Sir Herbert (now Lord) Kitchener; when the expedition was abruptly stopped at Fashoda by Lord Kitchener's victory near Khartoum, Germany offered, so Englishmen believe, to make a demonstration in South Africa if France would hold firm. In the same year Prince Münster, the German ambassador in Paris, proposed an alliance

with France in order to nullify the British guarantee of
the Portuguese colonies, which was understood to be the
price of a free passage for British troops through Delagoa
Bay into the Transvaal. As all these overtures required
a tacit recognition by France of the Treaty of Frankfort,
they led to nothing definite, but generally speaking Germany
supported the aggressive policy of both France and Russia,
who were still the rivals of Great Britain. If she gained
little for herself, the Austro-Russian agreement of 1897 for
preserving the *status quo* in the Balkans removed a serious
obstacle to her own programme of commercial and railway
development in Asia Minor.

William II had very early appreciated the importance
of the Ottoman Empire in that scheme of expansion which
was the great idea of his reign. To win the friendship of
the Sultan, the German ruler opposed the British plan for
reforming the Ottoman administration, which the Armenian massacres had completely discredited, and he dis-
creetly refused to join in settling the Cretan problem
against the wishes of Abdul Hamid. Finally, in 1898, he
visited the Sultan at Constantinople, from which place he
proceeded to Jerusalem as the latter's guest. In a famous
speech he there declared that Germany was the only true
friend of Islam, for she was the only European Power
which neither possessed Moslem subjects nor coveted
Moslem territory. The rise of German influence at Constantinople was detrimental to British interests throughout the Ottoman Empire, and this rivalry between the two
Powers, begun at a time when England's attention was
being directed more and more to South Africa, was destined
to acquire very great importance when England's hands
were free again.

The year 1898 witnessed the Spanish-American War.
There is every reason to believe that a coalition of the
European Powers to help Spain against the United States

was proposed by Germany, but was quashed by Lord Salisbury's intimation that Great Britain would support the United States. Similarly, in the harbor of Manila, when Admiral Dewey had trouble with the commander of the German fleet, the British admiral probably had orders to give our admiral all necessary assistance.

All such incidents, however, might be regarded merely as moves on the diplomatic chess-board, although they intimated that the intimacy of Bismarckian days was gone. What first brought home to Englishmen the reality of German hostility was the Kaiser's telegram to President Krüger on the morrow of the Jameson raid:

"I express to you my sincere congratulations," William II telegraphed on 3 January, 1896, "that without appealing to the help of friendly Powers, you and your people have succeeded in repelling with your own forces the armed bands which had broken into your country and in maintaining the independence of your country against foreign aggression."

This message, as we now know, emanated from the Berlin foreign office rather than from the Emperor himself.[1] There was nothing objectionable in the protest against such an international misdemeanor, and the sentiment of the civilized world approved the imperial action. But it intimated, and the foreign secretary, Baron von Marschall, formally stated in the Reichstag, that the independence of the Boer republic fell in the scope of German interests. From that moment till the outbreak of war eighteen years later, Great Britain and Germany were seldom sincerely in accord, though their relations were

[1] According to the Paris correspondent of the *Times*, 29 October, 1908, as soon as the news of the raid reached Berlin, Baron Marschall visited M. Herbette, the French ambassador, to inquire whether France would join Germany with a view to securing the integrity and independence of the Boer states. M. Herbette demanded as a *quid pro quo* German assistance in the Egyptian question, and the matter got no farther. Prince Bülow admitted in the Reichstag on 12 December, 1901, that the telegram was a *ballon d'essai* and that he was disappointed by its reception in France.

now and again friendly and usually "correct"; also, there
was created between the two peoples a barrier of suspicion,
if not of jealousy, which seriously militated against the
belated efforts of their governments to arrange an understanding.   The situation, however, was not yet beyond
control, as was shown by the events of 1899–1900.[1]

The first step toward an Anglo-German *détente* was an
agreement with respect to the Portuguese colonies, which,
though never published, was understood to provide for
their disposition in case Portugal wished to sell.   As Germany was well treated in the division, her interest in the
Fashoda affair rapidly declined, and Lord Salisbury dictated his own terms to France in March, 1899.   Cecil
Rhodes journeyed to Berlin, where he was cordially received by the Emperor and, in default of the Cape to Cairo
railway, arranged for a telegraph line which should pass
through German territory.   A most important convention,
to which the United States was a party as well as Great
Britain, settled the ten-year-old quarrel over Samoa on
terms distinctly to Germany's advantage (Prince Bülow).[2]
In announcing the agreement Lord Salisbury declared that
the relations between England and Germany were all that
could be desired, and that for years there had been friendship and sympathy with Germany as with no other country.
Indeed, late in the year 1899 Count Bülow (as he then was)
called on Joseph Chamberlain, the colonial secretary, in

[1] "The Jameson raid and the Emperor's telegram did something to inflame the
mutual distrust and jealousy already growing between England and Germany.
The sentiment was carefully watched by both governments, and was not permitted
to produce any adverse effect on their political or diplomatic action.   But, though
the two foreign offices kept their tempers admirably, a bitter warfare of tongues and
pens was raging between England and Germany during the final years of the century, and was at its height when Queen Victoria's reign came to a close."   (Low
and Sanders, *Political History of England*, XII, "The Reign of Queen Victoria,
1837–1901," p. 437.)

[2] *Imperial Germany*, p. 116.   This admission is quite important, for it disposes
of the contention often met with in German writings that England in this matter
was playing her favorite game of blocking the expansion of Germany.

London, and three days later (30 November) the latter in a speech at Leicester proclaimed the necessity of an Anglo-German alliance.

Unfortunately, the Boer War had already begun. That struggle, which put an end to German aspirations for the incorporation of South Africa in a Greater Germany, was the great landmark in Anglo-German relations. All over the Continent British policy was bitterly criticised, but the German press exceeded all others. It did not stop at vilification, at distortions and falsifications—it demanded action from the government. The caricatures of the aged Queen Victoria were often vulgar, and anything, however unreasonable, was printed and believed. Especially objectionable in German eyes were the concentration camps for Boer non-combatants. Ultimately Mr. Chamberlain reminded the Germans of the conduct of their own troops in the war of 1870; Count Bülow replied that to criticise Germany was like biting granite, and the evangelical clergy of the Rhenish provinces protested against the "wanton audacity" of comparing their fathers and brothers with "the craven bands of mercenaries who placed Boer women and old men in front of their ranks in battle in order to protect themselves against the bullets of the Boers."[1] At this time professorial lucubrations, which ransacked the past for proofs of English hostility to Germany, began to make their appearance. To all this hue and cry the British press replied with spirit, and the recollections of those unfortunate days were never eradicated from the minds of either Germans or English.

The German attitude was explained by Englishmen as an aftermath of bungling diplomacy.[2] Moderate Ger-

[1] For details about this exchange of compliments, see the *Annual Register* for 1900, 1901, and 1902.

[2] "The most intelligible explanation of this state of affairs was not creditable to Great Britain, which was her attitude in the affair of Angra Pequena in 1882, and more recently in 1895 in the Armenian question. In the latter matter Italy, the

mans like Theodor Mommsen, who had formerly admired
the free institutions of England and desired their development in Germany, were revolted by "the repetition of
Jameson's raid by the English Government dictated by
banking and mining speculators." [1]

"When the burghers of the two little Teutonic republics were
fighting to resist annexation to the British Empire we had the
same feelings as every Englishman would have if the German
Government—*absit omen*—should take the fancy to add to the
German Empire the German-speaking Swiss republics." [2]

But neither a few moves of British diplomacy nor sympathy with a kindred race would scarcely have aroused the
German people to a passionate display of hatred for England. Germans spoke freely, if frankly, because they
perceived clearly that the mistress of the seas must be
humiliated before their own plans of Empire could be realized.

In marked contrast to this, the attitude of the German
Government would seem, throughout the war, to have
been not only studiously "correct" but actually friendly
to England. In June, 1899, President Kruger had been
warned to come to terms with England.[3] When the war
broke out Prince Muravieff, the Russian foreign secretary,
three times endeavored to organize a demonstration against

ally of Germany, had been invited to join with Great Britain to force Turkey to
more humane treatment of her Armenian subjects. With the consent of Germany,
and with the assurance of her support, Signor Crispi had thrown himself heartily
into the British policy, only to find himself saddled with the Abyssinian War and
the hostility of Russia and France. Lord Salisbury thereupon disinterested himself altogether in the trouble of which he had been the principal cause. This deser-
tion of Italy, behind whom Germany was standing, and ready to support her, impressed German statesmen and writers with such a sense of selfishness of British
policy that they came to the conclusion that no understanding with England was
possible." (*Annual Register*, 1900, pp. 7–8.) The accuracy of this interpretation
may be questioned, for Germany consistently opposed all efforts to reform the administration of Turkey.

[1] *North American Review*, February, 1900.
[2] *Independent Review*, November, 1903.
[3] *Annual Register*, 1900, p. 313.

England, in which the Kaiser, according to his own statement, refused to participate.[1] He seems also to have sent some military advice to the British Government,[2] and he declined to receive President Krüger for a personal interview. Doubtless William II was not playing the part of a disinterested knight,[3] and he expected due consideration from the British Government for German interests in Africa,[4] but, whatever the motive, his policy allowed Great Britain a free hand in South Africa. Only when some German steamers were seized by British cruisers on the ground that they were carrying contraband to the Boers, was there any friction between the two governments, and this was speedily adjusted by the release of the steamers and the payment of damages.

That the Boer War had little bearing upon the official relations of Great Britain and Germany is clearly seen from the convention of October, 1900, by which the two governments agreed to uphold the integrity of China and to observe the principle of the open door in their commercial dealings with that country. In fact, the identical character of British and German interests in the Far East came near culminating in that Teutonic alliance of which Joseph

---

[1] Interview in *Daily Telegraph*, 28 October, 1908.

[2] In the *Daily Telegraph* interview, the Emperor said that he had sent a plan of campaign to the war office, "which can be found in the archives of Windsor Castle." Actually, it would seem to have consisted of "some general aphorisms on military tactics" contained in a letter to the Queen, and the British Government denied that it had ever received such a document as the Emperor described. (Perris, *Germany and the German Emperor*, p. 411.)

[3] According to the Paris correspondent of *The Times*, 29 October, 1908, the proposed coalition fell through because France and Russia refused to guarantee the *status quo* in Europe, *i. e.*, the treaty of Frankfort, apart from the fact that M. Delcassé, the French foreign minister, ardently desired to effect a general settlement with England. On this last matter, see Bérard, *La France et Guillaume II*, p. 23. On 18 October, 1899, one week after war was declared between England and the Boer republics, the German Emperor spoke of "the bitter need of a strong German navy," with which "we should be able to further our flourishing commerce and our interests overseas."

[4] Lady Phillips, *A Friendly Germany, Why Not?* pp. 63–64, quoting special correspondence of the *Daily Telegraph*, sometime in 1912.

Chamberlain had dreamed and spoken.   When the Marquis
Ito opened those conversations with the British Government which produced the Anglo-Japanese alliance of 30
January, 1902, "there was a German suggestion of a triple
alliance between Germany, Great Britain, and Japan, and
for some time Germany was kept *au courant* with the negotiations by Lord Lansdowne." [1]   She "was finally ignored,"
according to a competent authority, because she demanded
"terms which might have involved Great Britain in heavy
responsibilities in Europe, Africa, and America, without
involving Germany in any corresponding responsibilities
in Asia."   The German idea was that the Japanese alliance would protect British interests in Asia, and "leave us
[England and Germany] both free to co-operate in other
quarters where our interests might be found to approxi-
mate much more closely."   But even supposing an Anglo-
German agreement, "it is more than doubtful whether, in
view of Germany's relations with Russia, Berlin would ever
seriously have entertained the idea of Germany's open
adherence to the Anglo-Japanese alliance, even if it had
commended itself to Japan "[2]

About an Anglo-German alliance Prince Bülow has
written:

"Germany might perhaps not have been disinclined to conclude
a treaty with England on a basis of absolute equality, and with
mutual obligations.   German interests would have gained nothing
by stipulations which England might disregard in the event of a
change of ministry, or the occurrence of any other circumstances
over which we had no control, while we continued bound by them.
Nor would it have sufficed us that some minister or other was in
favor of an Anglo-German treaty.   To make a lasting agreement

[1] Hayashi revelations, *Times* (weekly edition), 12 September, 1913.
[2] Sir Valentine Chirol, *Times* (weekly edition), 19 September, 1913.   He has
since stated that at the time of the German intervention, after the war with China
in 1895, Marquis Ito said emphatically to him that "Japan would never forgive
Germany"—and she never did.   ("The Origins of the Present War," *Quarterly
Review*, October, 1914.)

the whole cabinet, and above all the prime minister, would have had to support it. Bismarck pointed out how difficult it was to establish firm relations with England; because treaties of long duration were not in accordance with English traditions, and the expression of opinion of English politicians, even those in a prominent position, and the transitory moods of the English peers were by no means equivalent to immutable pledges. For many reasons English public opinion is more favorable to France than to us, for England no longer looks upon her as a rival, and certainly not as a serious competitor, at sea; consequently France occupies a different position from ours with regard to England. In consideration of the wide-spread jealousy roused in England by Germany's industrial progress, and especially by the increase of the German navy, it was only on condition of absolute binding pledges on the part of England that we could have set foot on the bridge of an Anglo-German alliance. We could only thus unite ourselves with England on the assumption that the bridge which was to help us over the real and supposed differences between England and Germany was strong enough to bear our weight.

"At the time this question of an alliance was being ventilated the European position differed in many respects from the present one [1913]. Russia had not then been weakened by the Japanese war, but intended to secure and expand her newly won position in the Far East, in particular on the Gulf of Pechili. Owing to the Asiatic questions pending between the two empires, relations between England and Russia were then rather strained. The danger was imminent that if Germany allied herself with England she would have to undertake the rôle against Russia which Japan assumed later single-handed. But we should have had to play this part under very different conditions from the very favorable ones which Japan found at her disposal in her conflict with Russia. The Japanese war was unpopular in Russia, and it had to be waged at an immense distance, like a colonial war. If we had allowed ourselves to be thrust forward against Russia, we should have found ourselves in a far more difficult position. A war with Germany would not, in these circumstances, have been unpopular in Russia, and would on the part of the Russians have been carried on with that national enthusiasm which is peculiar to them when defending their native soil. France would have preferred the excuse of the *casus fœderis*, and would have been able to wage her war of revenge under favorable circumstances. In the event of a general conflict, we Germans would have had to wage strenuous war on land in two directions, while to England would have fallen the easier task of expanding her colonial Empire without much trouble and the profiting by the general weakening of the Continental Powers. Last, but certainly not least, while military operations were going forward on the Continent and for a long time after, we should have found neither strength nor means nor leisure to proceed with the building of our navy, as we have been able to do. Thus the only course left to us was not to intrench upon English interests, and to avoid both a hostile encounter and a docile dependence." [1]

The failure of this project, which, had it been successful, would have ranged the greatest naval and the greatest military powers of the world against the Dual Alliance, and profoundly changed the course of European history, may be regarded as the last effort of both Germany and England to find a basis for a common policy. For Great Britain the rise of the German navy and the outburst of Anglophobia during the Boer War were at once disturbing and surprising; Germany in turn was exceedingly disgusted to see the Boer republics incorporated in the British Empire, for ever since the Jameson raid the opinion had been ventilated in countless newspapers and pamphlets that only in South Africa could Germany acquire a settlement colony in a temperate climate. Official circles in both countries might argue that conditions had not changed, that an alliance was both possible and desirable, or the close relationship of the two royal families might be considered a barrier to an irreconcilable quarrel; but after 1900 the two peoples were so mutually suspicious that cordial co-operation between their governments would have been exceedingly difficult. In such circumstances it was doubly unfortunate that a clash of national interests should be suddenly revealed by the bad faith of one or the other party.

By article 3 of the Anglo-German convention of October, 1900, it was stipulated that, "in case another Power should

---

[1] *Imperial Germany*, pp. 39–42.

take advantage of complications in China to obtain territorial advantages in any form whatsoever, the two contracting parties bind themselves to conclude a preliminary
agreement with respect to measures eventually to be taken
for the protection of their respective interests in China."
The very case seemed to have arisen when the Russian contingent of the allied army which rescued the legations in
Peking from the Boxer warriors, instead of retiring beyond
the Amur River, remained in occupation of Manchuria;
which permitted the cabinet of St. Petersburg to negotiate
with China an arrangement that practically made Manchuria a Russian province. Lord Lansdowne desired the
Wilhelmstrasse to join in a formal protest to Russia against
these proceedings, but Count Bülow stated in the Reichstag (15 March, 1901) that "the agreement had no reference
to Manchuria" and that Germany had "no important
national interest" there. Between his contention that
"during the negotiations we left no doubt that Manchuria
was in no way involved" and Lord Lansdowne's reply
that "the agreement referred not only to China proper,
the Eighteen Provinces, but to Manchuria as well," it is
impossible to pass judgment until more information is
vouchsafed by one party or the other.[1] But the result of
the controversy was quite definite. In British eyes, Germany was deliberately encouraging Russia in a line of action detrimental to British commercial interests, in order
that German diplomacy might have a freer hand in the
Near East, where British interests were already suffering
from German competition; and Germany was once more
able to argue that British diplomacy was playing its favorite game of using a Continental Power to exert pressure
on Russia.

From this *malaise* there gradually developed an atmosphere of hostility. When in 1902 Great Britain and Ger-

[1] Lémonon, *L'Europe et la Politique brittanique*, 1882–1909, p. 225.

many, in co-operation with Italy, interfered in the affairs of Venezuela, "profound and almost universal annoyance" was manifested by Englishmen that "His Majesty's Government had gone into the business in alliance with a country which had shown itself during the South African war thoroughly disaffected toward [themselves]"; [1] and the following year, when Great Britain had to decide whether she would participate in the Baghdad railway, public opinion forced the Balfour government to withdraw the support which had practically been promised to Germany. It was further held against Germany that she had abetted Russian designs in the Far East, and that she was the mainstay of the Red Sultan, Abdul-Hamid, whose intolerable misgovernment of Macedonia had produced a general outbreak in that unhappy country.

One delicate matter between Great Britain and Germany had, indeed, been adjusted, but not without much irritation on both sides. In 1897 the Canadian Government granted a preferential tariff to British imports. Under the treaty of 1865 between Great Britain and the Zollverein, German products were granted in the British colonies a footing of equality with those of the mother country, and to escape the German demand that the Canadian tariff should be overruled, Her Majesty's Government terminated the treaty. Lord Salisbury would negotiate no new treaty which did not recognize the fiscal autonomy of British colonies, and Germany threatened to withdraw the most-favored-nation treatment from British trade unless the Canadian preferences were disavowed. In June, 1898, the Bundesrath excepted Canada from the benefit of the most-favored-nation clause, in spite of the British protest that colonies of other Powers which differentiated in favor of their metropolitan countries were not so treated. The controversy dragged on for five years. In

---

[1] *Annual Register*, 1902, p. 240.

April, 1903, the Canadian government imposed a surtax
of one-third the general tariff upon German imports, and
Lord Lansdowne gave warning that "should the German
Government persist in the attitude which they have taken
up in this matter, . . . a very wide and serious issue must
inevitably be raised involving the fiscal relations of this
country and the German Empire." The German Government precipitately retreated, and nothing more was heard
of interference with imperial reciprocity, probably because
German trade with Canada was of no great volume. But
had the Conservative policy of a British imperial customs
union reached maturity, a serious issue might have been
raised between Great Britain and Germany.[1]

Such were the relations between Great Britain and Germany when on 8 April, 1904, Lord Lansdowne and M. Paul
Cambon, the French ambassador in London, signed a
series of conventions which not only guaranteed the neutrality of England and France in the Russo-Japanese War,
which had begun in February, but also swept the slate
clean of a multitude of differences which had in the past
often produced great tension between London and Paris.
This *entente cordiale* ushers in a new period in diplomatic
history which was to end disastrously in the Great War
of 1914. That the British Government should reconcile
itself with its enemy of centuries, was explained partly by
a genuine desire to adjust its differences with all the world,
and no wiser step in the direction of a sound diplomacy
had been taken in many years. But England also felt
herself face to face with a greater problem—the challenge
of a new Power, whose commercial advance, colonial aspirations, and naval ambitions seemed to take the whole world
for its field of operations, and at certain points to threaten
the safety of the British Empire.

[1] The correspondence between the British and German Governments may be
conveniently read in Barker, *Modern Germany*, pp. 148–174 (edition of 1912).

Unfortunately for the world, the Anglo-German quarrel was not restricted to the wranglings of Downing Street and Wilhelmstrasse—it was quickly taken up by the two peoples and by them transformed into a struggle for ascendency between two antagonistic civilizations. And precisely because Englishmen and Germans were closely related, because they had, in fact, long regarded each other as cousins, their animosity was distinguished by that virulence, unreasonableness, and resentment which usually accompanies a family quarrel.[1] Given the necessary good will, diplomatists can usually patch up the most threatening dispute, but if the peoples whose interests they represent seem to be spoiling for a fight, their task is well-nigh hopeless. Such was the condition of Anglo-German relations for many years, and the possibility of an understanding was not grasped until too late.

For this melancholy state of affairs the press of both countries is very largely to blame. For nearly twenty years publicists and journalists engaged in the pleasing business of dissecting Anglo-German relations from every conceivable point of view, and the more irresponsible of them delighted to exaggerate differences and minimize points of common interest. On both sides facts were garbled, motives imputed, official statements belittled, and a most outrageous lack of perspective revealed. There was not enough effort to discover the other nation's point of view, and when once it is assumed that a contradiction of interests exists, an infinite deal of labor is required to prove the contrary. In England it was frequently charged that the campaign in Germany derived inspiration from official sources, for the Bismarckian methods of using the press were well known, and the semiofficial character of many newspapers was notorious. This, however, could scarcely

---

[1] "The existence of race kinship has only added bitterness to the feud." (Sidney Whitman, "England and Germany," *Harper's Magazine*, April, 1898.)

explain the voluminous output of pamphlet literature, in which German writers excel, and which passed for the work of scholars and responsible thinkers, many of them professors in the great universities or men high in the business and official world. The English opposition to Germany was voiced primarily in the Conservative journals of London and by a small group of military and naval enthusiasts. Few Englishmen of standing indulged in abuse of things German, except indeed German policy; rather the tendency was to praise the extraordinary achievements of Germany since 1870, and to argue that the hostility manifested in certain quarters of both countries did not reflect the sentiments of either people.

German writers never tired of quoting a famous article in the *Saturday Review*, which created an extraordinary impression at the time, and which was probably the most provocative diatribe in the annals of newspaper effrontery. After pointing out how the superior British navy could bottle up the German harbors and sweep German merchantmen from the seas, the organ of Tory chauvinism argued that "were Germany destroyed to-morrow there is not an Englishman in the world who would not be the richer," and proceeded to the conclusion expressed in the paraphrase *Germania est delenda*.[1] However intelligible such an outburst may have been in the light of what the German press had been saying, it must ever be a regret to those who sympathize with Great Britain in the present war that a great journal with an established reputation could descend to such depths of ignorance and folly. For Germans would not and did not understand that this weekly journal represented but a small section of English opinion, that is, the military and upper-class world of London.

Certain London newspapers, notably the *Daily Mail*,

[1] 11 September, 1897.

and to a lesser degree the *Times* and the *Morning Post*, were frankly pessimistic about Anglo-German relations, and often treated their readers to inflammatory articles. But the industrial centres, which are the heart of England and the source of her power, were conscious only of commercial rivalry, which they endeavored to meet in good spirit by adopting German science and German methods.[1] The men of Lancashire and Yorkshire were under no illusions as to the ruinous cost of even a victorious war. The Liberal press, with the *Manchester Guardian* (one of the most influential newspapers in England) at its head, and the organs of financial circles, especially the *Economist*, never ceased to plead for moderation and fairness. No one will deny that there was a strong current of opposition to all things German in twentieth-century England, and that the needs and ambitions of Germany were often misunderstood and misrepresented; but there also existed a powerful party which honestly strove to create a better atmosphere, and which unquestionably gained prestige with the passage of time.

The same temper cannot be predicated of modern Germany. The perusal of a considerable quantity of the German literature of international politics has convinced the present writer that the animus of Germany toward Great Britain was far more bitter and deep-rooted than the reciprocal feeling among English people, and that the seed of the press polemics was sown in Germany.

It is, of course, difficult to estimate accurately to what extent the dislike for one nation penetrated the national life and consciousness of the other. But it may be very safely said that from 1896 to the outbreak of the Balkan wars the tone of public discussion in Germany, as regards relations with England, was consistently bitter; the occasional protests of clear-headed patriots against the folly

[1] Charles Trevelyan, in *England and Germany* (1912), p. 98.

of chauvinism were like voices crying in the wilderness.[1] Men there were who perceived that a permanently hostile England would be the most serious obstacle to Germany's imperial ambitions—the late August Bebel, Karl Lieb-knecht, and Eduard Bernstein.[2] But such critics were not heard, probably because they belonged to the Social Demo-cratic party; the nation preferred the teaching of Hans Delbrück and the *Preussische Jahrbücher*, Karl Lamprecht of the University of Leipzig, and Paul Rohrbach, whose travels made him the best equipped of German publicists. These men were not exactly anti-English; indeed, they were anxious for an understanding with England;[3] but the terms of the agreement they conceived were to be dictated by Germany, and they consistently preached the idea that England refused to recognize Germany as an equal.[4] In the hands of lesser men, especially the writers of the Pan-German League, just criticism of English policy degener-ated into malignant abuse and gross misrepresentation. As long ago as 1898, Mr. Sidney Whitman, an Englishman with ardent German sympathies, remarked upon "the intense political distrust and dislike for England in Ger-many," which he ascribed to the Anglophobe historical works of German professors; and as for English jealousy of Germany, it "was resented and paid back in kind . . .

[1] "The world power of England does not obstruct the interests of Germany in any particular. I do not know on what grounds Germany could desire the British Empire to go to pieces. . . . Nothing would be more profitable than a permanent alliance between the greatest sea power and the greatest military state. It would be the best guarantee for the free and peaceful development of the world, and far more effective than all the speeches, writings, and congresses of the pacifists." (Rudolf Martin, *Deutschland und England*, 1908, pp. 89, 91.)

[2] *Cf.* Bernstein, *Die englische Gefahr und das deutsche Volk*, 1911.

[3] *Cf.* Delbrück, in *Preussische Jahrbücher*, March, 1912.

[4] Dr. Rohrbach's books afford the best insight into Germany's needs and as-pirations: scholarly, moderate, and written from a historical point of view, they are in striking contrast to the dangerous polemics of most German writers. *Die Bagdadbahn*, 1902; *Deutschland unter den Weltvölkern*, 1908, 1912; *Der deutsche Gedanke in der Welt*, 1912 (English translation, *German World Policies*, 1915); *Der Krieg und die deutsche Politik*, 1914.

with a large amount of malignant envy added to the score." [1]

Mr. Whitman further points out that the fall of Bismarck was welcomed in England because he was reputed anti-English, and William II was expected to be pliable, even obedient, to the wishes of his grandmother, Queen Victoria. German opinion in the 'nineties was, indeed, thoroughly suspicious of British policy. Lord Salisbury was represented as desiring an Anglo-German alliance in order that Great Britain might have the assistance of a Continental army in her inevitable war with Russia, and Germans were fain to ask how such a campaign would profit themselves. But even if all the counts against England are returned in the court of civilization, the historian is entitled to say that Germany is responsible for the bitterness of feeling and the violence of language which long characterized the discussion of Anglo-German relations. The testimony of Germany's sanest publicist may be invoked against her.

In his *Deutschland unter den Weltvölkern* Dr. Paul Rohrbach has written:

"It cannot be denied that if the utterances of the German press at the time of the Krüger telegram are considered, they were excellently calculated to convince an Englishman that England was regarded by us with a far more powerful and general aversion than was to be explained by the mere sympathy with that happy stroke by which the Boers resisted the plot against their independence. It must, furthermore, be admitted, from the highly explosive outbursts of Anglophobia in the whole German press, without regard to party and feeling, that public opinion with us was hostile *per se* to England, and that it not only did not begrudge the Boers anything good, but also wished the English the worst of everything. To make this clear is quite important, for in judging the political relations of England and ourselves, much depends upon what people on the other side believed they had in general to expect from us. There can be no doubt in the mind of an impartial political observer

---

[1] "England and Germany," *Harper's Magazine*, April, 1898, p. 779.

that the idea was not first mooted in England that Germany presents a danger to England, and must be struck down before it is too late, but that, on the contrary, Germany was thinking of attacking England at a favorable opportunity, and enriching herself at her expense. Accordingly, it is not particularly surprising that in English eyes the German Emperor, the German nation, and the German press were thrown together and taken for one, and even less does it appear wonderful that Germany's economic expansion which was gradually becoming noticeable, and the very disagreeable and surprising experiences with German competition which the English business world was beginning to encounter in all corners and regions overseas, must very soon serve the purpose of providing a basis for the plans ascribed to Germany." [1]

Doctor Rohrbach explains the attitude of his countrymen as "an emotional reaction against the high-and-mighty condescending air with which Englishmen were formerly accustomed to treat us, socially, commercially, and politically as poor relations." But he is bitter against the irresponsibility and bad manners of the German press, which, he says, "have wrought the greatest damage to Anglo-German relations," and when he advises the hack-writers of an unrestrained press not to advocate policies which they could not carry out if intrusted with political power, he puts his finger on the most insidious of the many offenses for which modern journalism is responsible.

At this point it is fitting to speak again of Treitschke, whose *Deutsche Geschichte im Neunzehnten Jahrhundert* is a "great fact" (Richard Meyer) and who "devoted all the resources of a mordant rhetoric, a pitiless invective, and a vitriolic ridicule to making Britain odious and contemptible in the eyes of the generation which heard him with enthusiasm in the class-room, and read his book as a gospel." [2] The late Professor Cramb wrote of him:

[1] Pp. 53–55. A similar admission is made by Dr. Theodor Lorenz, *Die Englische Presse*, in *England in deutscher Beleuchtung*, 1907, Heft 9, pp. 76, 136.
[2] Vigilans sed Æquus (W. T. Arnold), *German Ambitions as They Affect Britain and the United States*, 1903, p. xv.

"More than any other single character in German political life he is responsible for the anti-English sentiment which blazed out during the Boer War, which still reigns in German society and the German press, which in the Reichstag reveals itself in the frigid or ironic applause with which any references to 'our amicable relations with England' are greeted. The foundations of that sentiment, of course, lie deeper than the creative power of an individual intellect or will. They are . . . beyond the control of any passing generation, rooting themselves in the dark forces which determine the destinies of peoples and of the universe itself. But Treitschke, beyond any other German, stands forth as the interpreter of these forces." [1]

It is significant that his famous dictum, "With Austria, with France, with Russia, we have already squared accounts; the last settlement—with England—seems likely to be the longest and the hardest," [2] was quoted with equal approval by Pan-German agitators and British jingoes. It is not entirely true that he was unknown in England until his name was found in the writings of Professor Cramb or General von Bernhardi. English publicists who read German discussions of international politics certainly found repeated quotations in castigation of their own country, and some of these were translated for English readers. His *Deutsche Geschichte* was one of the books recommended by the Oxford faculty of modern history for a study of the nineteenth century. But there was no wide-spread knowledge of his teaching, no appreciation of the place he occupied in German life; which is the more remarkable because rabidly anti-German organs like the *Daily Mail* and the *National Review* were always searching for fresh proofs of German designs upon English liberties, and surely no one ever pursued England with such relentless and bitter hatred as this apostle of Neo-Germanism and *Realpolitik*. Treitschke did not write directly upon English history,

---

[1] *Germany and England*, p. 70. (English edition.)
[2] *Deutsche Kämpfe, Neue Folge*, p. 349.

but he frequently diverted from the topic in hand to discuss certain problems of the island state. Thus in the *Deutsche Geschichte* the main events of English history up to 1848 are discussed at length, and British foreign policy is the subject of several essays, printed in *Deutsche Kämpfe*. He can be credited with entire sincerity, for he sought to abide by the canons of historical writing; much of what he says is true; he expressed himself with no little eloquence, and, according to all reports, he aroused in his hearers or readers the same passionate desires which he himself felt so deeply. His great purpose was to construct an indictment of Great Britain which should make Germans regard her as the inevitable enemy that must be crushed before Prussia could accomplish her divine mission of leading the world into the way of truth and righteousness of life. In his glowing pages, stored with facts and replete with bitter invective, three sins of England are constantly held up to the withering scorn of honest and idealistic Germany.[1]

First, "England is at the present day the unblushing representative of barbarism in international law. It is England who is to blame if naval warfare, to the shame of humanity, still bears the character of privileged robbery."[2] Again and again he returns to this congenial theme, that the right of a belligerent to capture enemy ships on the high seas is "an organized form of piracy"; that "it is the common task of all nations to establish on the sea that balance of power which had long existed on land, that healthy equilibrium which should make it impossible for any state to do just as it pleased and to secure for all alike the protection of a humane system of international law." It was therefore Germany's mission to

[1] The translations used in the following quotations are borrowed from H. W. C. Davis, *The Political Thought of Heinrich von Treitschke*, 1914, which is the most sympathetic, yet critical, study of Treitschke in English.
[2] *Deutsche Kämpfe*, II, p. 362. Quoted hereafter as *D. K.*

"mitigate that oppressive alien despotism" which the British fleet exercised in all the waters of the world.[1]

Second, Treitschke is very scornful of English commercialism, which he regards as the ordinary motive of British policy. Cobden's "doctrine of a universal free exchange of commodities was based on the tacit assumption that England was to control the wholesale industries of the whole world, and that only the primary industries, and a few others, which would be difficult to transplant, should be left to the other nations. Just as Canning and Palmerston had relied on the phrase 'constitutional,' so Cobden relied on the phrase 'free trade' as a profitable article of export, which should make the tour of the globe, and enlist all the nations in the interest of British trade supremacy."[2] "Such a gospel of mammon-worship threatened to mutilate the human race"; but it has been the constant inspiration of the British foreign office. Thus Canning, "in the midst of peace, ordered the marauding expedition against Copenhagen because the interests of English trade demanded this act of violence."[3] For the same reason did he break with the Holy Alliance at the Congress of Verona, when it was proposed to intervene in Spain against the revolutionists and help the King to recover his revolted American colonies: "If England were the first to express formally that recognition of the independence of South America which was, in fact, already partly ratified, the British flag would win the lead in the newly opened market, and might possibly secure in the West another greater Portugal and the commercial and political exploitation of a vast territory." In 1877, when the Russians were nearing Constantinople, Treitschke remarked that "Great Britain desires at any price to preserve the existence of the Ottoman Empire, because the

---

[1] *Deutsche Geschichte*, V, p. 63.   Quoted hereafter as *D. G.*
[2] *D. G.*, V, p. 477.   [3] *D. G.*, III, p. 263.

ridiculous commercial policy of the Turks has opened a
vast hunting-ground to the English trader";[1] "the economic helplessness of the slumbering Balkan peoples," he
said in another place, "offered such a convenient market
to the British merchant."[2] With regard to the repeal of
the Corn Laws he wrote:

"A commercial spirit pervaded the whole life of the nation.
That last indispensable bulwark against the brutalization of society
—the duel—went out of fashion; the riding-whip supplanted the
sword and the pistol; and this triumph of vulgarity was celebrated
as a triumph of enlightenment. . . . The gulf between German and
British manners widened more and more. Such traces as remained
of the Puritans of Shakespeare's merry England were completely
submerged in the prose of commercial life. Therefore the attitude adopted by the island kingdom toward the other states of the
world was more than ever determined by the calculations of a
commercial policy."[3]

Third, Treitschke never tired of parading, in order to
criticise it, the habit of interfering in Continental politics
—what he called "Palmerston's old policy of secretly disturbing the peace of the world."[4] This interference was
now in the name of liberalism, now to the tune of nationality; but its real object was to perpetuate "that condition of veiled dissension which England needed for her
plans." "Like Canning, Palmerston wished to preserve
the peace of the world, in order not to injure British trade;
but, like his master, he desired with equal intensity that
the Continent should always be threatened with a simmer-
ing danger of war, in order that England might have a
free hand for extending her colonial Empire, and for securing the markets of the whole world." Another notion
also animated the "paltry statesmanship" of "a policy
which, like that of Metternich, merely strives to preserve

[1] D. K., II, p. 396.
[3] D. G., V, p. 480.
[2] D. G., III, p. 265.
[4] D. G., V, p. 63.

existing conditions because they exist, lives from hand to
mouth. . . . In their blissful seclusion, the inhabitants
of this rich island have preserved an antiquated notion of
a European balance of power, and they torment their
brains with horrid visions which, since the revolutions in
Italy and Germany, have lost any justification."[1] But
it is all cant, sheer hypocrisy. England will not recognize
the right of other nations to become as rich, as strong, as
famous, as herself, and therefore she does not scruple to
restrain their development by every means and at every
turn. "Overrich and oversatiated, vulnerable at a hundred points of their widely scattered dominions, the British feel that they have nothing more in the world to wish
for, and that to the young and developing forces of the
century they need still only oppose the mighty weapon
of a vanquished age."[2]

Thus, in the name of impartial history, Treitschke drew
a picture of England as a great robber state which clamored
vainly for peace, although it had waged more wars than
any nation in Europe. "England! the successful burglar,
who, an immense fortune amassed, has retired from business, and, having broken every law, human and divine,
violated every instinct of honor and fidelity on every sea
and every continent, desires now the protection of the
police!"[3] Such unctiousness would have been less distasteful to Treitschke had he not cherished the conviction
that modern England was a colossus with feet of clay, a
nation decadent in every fibre and utterly unable to accomplish the mission she proclaimed with intolerable
egotism. Professor Cramb, in his *Germany and England*,
has explained Treitschke's feelings in these words:

"Britain's world-predominance outrages him as a man almost
as much as it outrages him as a German. It outrages him as a

---

[1] *D. K.*, II, p. 464.   [2] *D. K.*, II, p. 362.
[3] Cramb, *Germany and England*, p. 44.

man because of its immorality, its arrogance, and its pretentious security. It outrages him as a German because he attributes England's success in the war for the world to Germany's preoccupation with higher and more spiritual ends. But for her absorption in those ends and the civil strife in which that absorption resulted, Germany might, in the seventeenth and eighteenth centuries, have made the Danube a German river and established a German predominance from the Bosphorus to the Indus. . . .

"His strongest motive is the conviction, which becomes more intense as the years advance, that Britain's world-predominance is out of all proportion to Britain's real strength and to her worth or value, whether that worth be considered in the political, the social, the intellectual, or the moral sphere. It is the detestation of a sham. 'In this universe of ours the thing that is wholly a sham—wholly rotten—may endure for a time, but cannot endure forever.' This is the protest of the stern apostle of reality. He frequently rings the changes on the nation of shopkeepers, pointing with aptness and justness to the general meanness and gradually increasing sordidness of English political life. That which Treitschke hates in England is what Napoleon hated in England —a pretentiousness, an overweening, middle-class self-satisfaction, which is not really patriotism, nor the high and serious passion of Germany in 1813 and 1870, but an insular, narrow conceit, in fact, the emotion enshrined in that most vulgar of all national hymns, 'Rule Britannia!' . . .

"For Treitschke it is not genuine, it is not valor, it is not even great policy, as in the case of Venice, which has built up the British Empire; but the hazard of her geographical situation, the supineness of other nations, the measureless duplicity of her ministers, and the natural and innate hypocrisy of the nation as a whole. These have let this monstrous Empire grow—a colossus with feet of clay. Along with this he has the conviction that such a power can be overthrown. And with what a stern joy and self-congratulation would not the nations acclaim the destruction of the island state! 'Old England!'—old, indeed, and corrupt, rotten through and through!" [1]

If the reader doubts that the conception of England as a colossus with feet of clay was widely cherished in Germany, let him read Alexander Tille's *Aus Englands Flegel-*

[1] Pp. 92–94.

jahren ("England's Hobbledehoyhood"), published in 1901 by a sometime teacher in Glasgow University who was compelled to give up his post during the Boer War. Every aspect of English life or English policy is held up to scathing criticism, and the United Kingdom is pictured as almost on the verge of dissolution. Or there is Mariano Herggelet's *England's Weak Points and Germany's Position in Europe*, published in both countries in 1912. The author states that "in the whole of England there are about 150,000 really capable men, according to German ideas," [1] and summarizes the British philosophy of life in these words:

"Dream, live in a pleasant mist of unreality, take refuge in delightful meditation about money and games, sleep late, live well, do a little work, spend a quarter of an hour daily in abuse of the scandalous behavior of the other side in politics, pay your taxes, be content, believe firmly in the natural superiority of the British race, and, for the sake of appearances, always look pleasant and be pleasant to every one." [2]

The complaint that Britain refused to recognize Germany as her equal found constant expression. Englishmen knew nothing of Germans, whom they looked upon as "an inferior race, living on all kinds of impossible things, and satisfied with an economic and political existence which is semislavery." [3] Thus, the *Saturday Review* printed four columns about "dirty, dusty, nasty, smelling, unromantic Germany." [4] And Mr. Sidney Whitman lamented that "somehow or other the German race has never succeeded in getting itself accepted by the English as on a parity." [5] To a people who conceived their civilizing mission in large and vigorous terms, who looked upon

[1] P. 17.   [2] P. 15.
[3] Fritz Schneider, *We Germans and Our British Cousins* (1909), p. 19.
[4] 14 August, 1897.
[5] "England and Germany," *Harper's Magazine*, April, 1898, p. 779.

themselves as "the salt of the earth," this contemptuous attitude of the island race was exasperating in the extreme, not less so because in the field of social legislation and scientific achievement the latter openly copied the methods of Germany! "We want nothing better than to love the English, but they will not let us," Bismarck had once remarked. Similarly, in the twentieth century many Germans frankly ventilated the opinion that war with England was bound to come, because in no other way could Germany secure adequate recognition as the equal of the older European states, who were being organized by England in a coalition to keep Germany in swaddling-clothes.[1]

The German view of England has been admirably stated by Mr. Bernard Shaw in *The Man of Destiny*. When that play was published, in 1898, France was the principal opponent of British policy, and the dramatist used Napoleon for the expression of his caricature. In point of fact, the words put into the Corsican's mouth reflected with substantial truth the opinions of the historical Emperor, who, it may be noted, has become almost a hero to Pan-German writers, because he endeavored to destroy the world Empire of Great Britain. In this speech we have the best possible exposé of English hypocrisy, about which Germans have written so much.

"No Englishman is too low to have scruples; no Englishman is high enough to be free from their tyranny. But every Englishman is born with a certain miraculous power that makes him master of the world. When he wants a thing he never tells himself that he wants it. He waits patiently until there comes into his mind, no one knows how, a burning conviction that it is his moral and religious duty to conquer those who have got the thing he wants.

[1] "We owe the North German Confederation to the dualism between Austria and Prussia. We owe the German Empire to the jealousy of France. We shall have to thank the dualism between Great Britain and the German Empire for the new Greater Germany." (Rudolf Martin, *Kaiser Wilhelm und König Eduard*, 1907, p. 58.)

Then he becomes irresistible. Like the aristocrat, he does what
pleases him and grabs what he covets; like the shopkeeper, he pur-
sues his purpose with the industry and steadfastness that come
from strong religious conviction and deep sense of moral responsibility. He is never at a loss for an effective moral attitude. As
the champion of freedom and national independence, he conquers
and annexes half the world, and calls it Colonization. When he
wants a new market for his adulterated Manchester goods he sends
a missionary to teach the natives the Gospel of Peace. The natives
kill the missionary: he flies to arms in defense of Christianity;
fights for it; conquers for it; and takes the market as a reward
from heaven. In defense of his island shores he puts a chaplain
on board his ship; nails a flag with a cross on it to his topgallant
mast; and sails to the end of the earth, sinking, burning and destroying all who dispute the empire of the seas with him. He
boasts that a slave is free from the moment his foot touches British
soil: and he sells the children of his poor at six years of age to work
under the lash in his factories for sixteen hours a day. He makes
two revolutions, and then declares war on our one in the name of
law and order. There is nothing so bad or so good that you will
not find Englishmen doing it; but you will never find an Englishman in the wrong. He does everything on principle. He fights
you on patriotic principles; he robs you on business principles;
he enslaves you on imperial principles; he bullies you on manly
principles; he supports his king on loyal principles and cuts off
his king's head on republican principles. His watchword is Duty;
and he never forgets that the nation which lets its duty get on the
opposite side to its interest is lost." [1]

And, as the *Round Table* admitted, "there is much truth
in the general charge that the national characteristic of
the Briton is not only to ignore the other man's point of
view but to believe that indefeasible right lies behind his
own." [2]

Englishmen, if they gave any heed to the problem of
Anglo-German relations, formed their opinions in three
main directions. Those few who possessed any knowledge
of German history ascribed to the government of William

[1] *Plays Pleasant and Unpleasant*, II, pp. 200–201.
[2] "Britain, France, and Germany," December, 1911, p. 41.

II the same brutal, unscrupulous, and aggressive aims that characterized the policy of Bismarck from 1862 to 1871; wherefore they concluded that imperial Germany was trying to shuffle the cards of diplomacy in such fashion that Great Britain would be left isolated, upon which consummation the Kaiser would promptly declare war. Others drew the same inference from the rapid construction of a German navy; when it was large enough, or when the British fleet had been lured away from British waters, it would sally forth to challenge the mistress of the seas. Still others harked back to the outbursts of Anglophobia in Germany during the Boer War and afterward; not being aware that England had given offense to Germany, they argued that Germany must be envious of England's wealth and England's colonies. The Emperor, his government, his people were thus credited with the plan of attacking England and destroying her Empire, and that, too, without warning or provocation. To quote Professor Cramb:

"There beyond the North Sea is the stern watcher, unsleeping, unresting, bound to her own fate, pursuing her own distant goal undeviatingly, unfalteringly, weighing every action of England, waiting for every sign of England's weakness." [1]

Conscious of their own desire for peace, many Britons believed that Germany desired war, and interpreted the policy of her government since the accession of William II as a Machiavellian plot to usher in the struggle when the circumstances seemed favorable to German success. Four times between the opening of the twentieth century and July, 1914, Europe was faced with the possibility of war. Each crisis was precipitated by Germany or her ally, Austria-Hungary: by Germany in 1905 and 1911 in Morocco; in 1908 and 1912 by the Dual Monarchy in the Near East. In each case peace was preserved by British

[1] *Germany and England*, p. 130.

diplomacy, so at least Englishmen believed; except after
the Balkan settlement of 1913 Germany vented her indignation in press campaigns against England and by adding to her navy. Englishmen may have been wrong, they
may have misjudged the intentions and ambitions of Germany; but they were at least sincere.[1] They looked upon
Germany not as a rival but as a probable enemy, and they
allowed their government to take all precautions against
the arbitrament of war, even though such precautions involved a reversal of many sacred traditions of British policy;
even though the new policy, by irritating Germany, actually brought nearer the danger it was intended to forestall.
And the undoubted fact that Germany resented the policy
of England only persuaded Englishmen the more that Germany's own policy was directed primarily against themselves. The British attitude was admirably stated by the
Round Table in the following question:

"If a nation constantly proclaims that it is the strongest and
greatest people on earth, that its destiny is to dominate the world,
that it will do so by the use of the mightiest armaments the world
has ever seen, and that it will use them instantly and mercilessly
against those who thwart its will, what wonder that its neighbors
take it at its word, and insure one another's prosperity and safety
by *ententes* and understandings?"[2]

The interests of Britain and Germany were not irreconcilable. But the essential preliminary to an understanding was proof positive that the aims of Germany did not

[1] Among anti-German publications in England may be noted: Emil Reich,
Germany's Swelled Head, 1907; Rowland Thirlmere, *The Clash of Empires*, 1907;
W. N. Willis, *What Germany Wants*, 1912; Charles Sarolea, *The Anglo-German
Problem*, 1912. *The Spectator* for years maintained the thesis that the danger to
England lay in the incalculable ambitions of the bureaucracy which completely
controlled the policy of Germany; it freely admitted the right of Germany to
build as large a fleet as it could pay for, also the justice of the German desire for
more elbow-room in the world. Only, it insisted, Great Britain must be prepared
for all eventualities.
[2] "Britain, France, and Germany," December, 1911, p. 51.

threaten the interests of the British Empire, or that it was not her policy to squeeze and cajole weaker nations at the risk of plunging the world into war. Not until the Balkan crisis of 1912–13, however, did the imperial government or the German press make a serious effort to disabuse Englishmen of their suspicions, to translate into action their oft-professed desire for an accommodation with Great Britain. If during the ten or fifteen years preceding the *rapprochement* of 1913 German policy was sincerely pacific, then its directors committed an irreparable error in not taking note of English susceptibilities; on the other hand, if its intentions were equivocal, as English opinion was not unjustified in believing, the reserve of Sir Edward Grey and the watchfulness of the London press[1] were measures of elementary prudence.

A fitting conclusion to this chapter may be found in two quotations. From the *Round Table :*

"Ignorance spells suspicion, and the British and the Germans, being extraordinarily ill-informed about one another's affairs and being fed largely on reports of the extravagances of extremists, came to believe that their rivals were incredibly efficient and far-sighted, were malignantly hostile, and by some miracle were so free from internal difficulties that they were able to pursue their baneful designs with relentless labor night and day." [2]

In large measure each nation did make identical accusations against the other.[3] Not until too late did either recognize any justice in the position of the other, or perceive

[1] Certain English newspapers and writers made a practise of collecting from German newspapers, pamphlets, and books innumerable expressions of hostility to England and the Empire. Such outbursts can scarcely be explained away as the extravagances of extremists, for they represented all shades of opinion; if they were not spontaneous, then the German Government must be held responsible for deliberately encouraging or restraining, as the political situation demanded, a dangerous and execrable habit. Examples of these pronunciamentos may be found in J. Ellis Barker, *Modern Germany*, and A. D. Maclaren, *An Australian in Germany* (1912).

[2] "Britain, France and Germany," December, 1911, p. 40.

[3] *Cf.* Sigma, "The Tu Quoque Quarrel," *Contemporary Review*, June, 1907.

that concessions on both sides might open the wide world to the energies of both peoples. Asking "what were the roots of the jealousy that gave such fruits?" Mr. G. H. Perris says, in *Germany and the German Emperor*:

"Fear, of course. Fear, on the part of England, of an unprecedented competition, both in commerce and armaments. On the part of Germany, fear of a kindred race, an old friend turned enemy, one not content with possessing a quarter of the land surface of the globe, but claiming also to be 'mistress of the seas' and holding the power at any moment to sweep away every German ship and to seize every German colony. The fear of an old state, its nerves shaken by the strain of a petty expedition grown into a first-class war; the fear of a young state, instably constituted, politically ill-equipped, trying its new strength in an unwonted field. A pitiful spectacle history will call it." [1]

[1] P. 423

CHAPTER VIII

THE ADMIRALTY OF THE ATLANTIC

IN the preceding chapter we have seen how, within a period of fifteen years, the British Government exchanged its traditional friendliness with the Powers of the Triple Alliance for an unexpected intimacy with the French Republic, which was a member of the Dual Alliance. The growth of bitter feelings between the peoples of Germany and England was also described at some length. But the primary and most lasting cause of Anglo-German rivalry was not referred to at all: the rise of a German navy, which, in the eyes of Englishmen, was intended to filch from them the supremacy of the seas and thereby endanger the safety of the United Kingdom and the British Empire. In the treatment of that question it will be convenient to set forth chronologically the bald facts concerning the navies of Germany and Great Britain up to the outbreak of war; after which the merits of the controversy can be more easily discussed, and the responsibility for the burden of naval expenditure properly attributed.

The German navy has been created in the reign of William II. In 1888, when he ascended the throne, it consisted of "floating forts placed at the estuaries of the rivers on which stood the rising commercial centres," [1] together with an excellent torpedo-fleet; it was administered by military men who considered it of secondary importance to the army, a view inculcated and sustained by the full force of Bismarck's personality. But by this time

[1] Hislam, *Admiralty of the Atlantic*, p. 13.

"the national mercantile marine had risen to the third place among the trading Powers, and the Emperor clearly saw the futility of endeavoring to defend it by coast-defense gunboats and torpedo-craft." [1]   He therefore created an imperial navy office (*Reichsmarineamt*) in charge of Admiral Hollman, who induced the Reichstag to provide for five battleships and three small cruisers.

The next stage was a campaign to educate public opinion in naval affairs. Not much success was achieved until the formation of the Navy League (*Deutscher Flottenverein*) in April, 1898, an organization of which the Krupps have been the chief financial supporters. But the decisive step was the appointment, in 1897, of Admiral Tirpitz as secretary of state for the navy. An efficient officer, risen from the ranks, who believed with the Emperor that "Neptune with the trident is a symbol that we have new tasks to perform . . . and that trident must be in our hands," [2] he has been the chief craftsman of the German fleet and "the most dangerous international mischief-maker of our time." [3] Chancellors and ministers have come and gone, but Grand Admiral von Tirpitz, as he now is, has survived them all, for the fleet has been the Emperor's hobby and Tirpitz an extraordinarily efficient minister.

The German navy in 1898 consisted of 9 battleships (excluding coast-defense vessels), 3 large cruisers, 28 small cruisers, and 113 torpedo-boats; there were building 3 battleships, 7 cruisers; the personnel comprised about 25,-000 men. [4] Concentrated in the Baltic, this fleet was of little concern to the mighty British navy of 54 battleships, 14 coast-defense ships, 104 cruisers, and several hundred torpedo-vessels. Immediately upon taking office Admiral Tirpitz decided to inaugurate a policy which has

---

[1] *Ibid.*, p. 15.   [2] Cologne speech, 4 April, 1897.
[3] Collier, *Germany and the Germans*, p. 529.
[4] Parliamentary papers, 1912, cd. 6513. *Admiralty Memorandum*, sec. 2.

been consistently pursued ever since. Its four elements
were:

(1) The creation of a high-seas fleet (*Hochseeflotte*).

(2) The establishment by law of a fleet of fixed size and
character.

(3) The replacement of old ships after a definite interval.

(4) Argument with and persuasion of the Reichstag, in
place of Admiral Hollman's policy of coercion, and the
moulding of public opinion through an elaborate campaign
waged in the press and by the Navy League.

The first-fruits of the new course were gathered in the
Navy Law of 1898, which revealed ambitions far exceeding
the modest demands that Admiral Hollman had failed to
carry through the Reichstag. The law provided for 19
battleships, 8 coast-defense vessels, 12 large cruisers, and
30 small cruisers. Battleships were to be replaced in
twenty-five years, large cruisers in twenty, and small
cruisers in fifteen. Although the entire programme was
to be completed within six years, it "bore no reasonable
relation," says an English writer, "to Germany's growing
trade and overseas interests." [1] But greater things were
at hand.

The Boer War began on 11 October, 1899. A week later
the Emperor, in an impassioned speech, declared:

"We are in bitter need of a strong German navy. If the increases
demanded during the first years of my reign had not been continu-
ously refused in spite of my warnings and continued entreaties,
how differently should we now be able to further our flourishing
commerce and our interests oversea!"

Though the Emperor declined to take any measures against
England during the course of the war, the German people
understood his meaning: it was impossible to interfere as
long as the British navy controlled the seas. Public opin-

[1] Hurd and Castle, *German Sea Power*, p. 118.

ion was further stimulated by the seizure of several German steamers in South African waters. The Navy League increased its membership to 200,000, and Admiral von der Goltz issued a statement to the effect that "we are almost defenseless against England at sea." The press fell in line, with what deplorable results upon the future of Anglo-German relations has been noticed in the last chapter.

So in 1900, in spite of Admiral Tirpitz's declaration the year before that there was no intention of altering the programme of 1898, a new law was passed, by which in 1920 the German fleet was to consist of 38 battleships, 14 large cruisers, and 38 light cruisers, with the necessary torpedo and auxiliary craft. Two battle squadrons and a flag-ship, 17 battleships in all, were to be kept permanently in commission, and the age of replacement for battleships was fixed at twenty-five years.

What gave exceptional interest to this programme, which definitely announced Germany's intention to become a mighty naval Power, was the memorandum annexed to the law.[1] The important passage reads as follows:

"To protect Germany's sea trade and colonies, in the existing circumstances, there is only one means: Germany must have a battle fleet so strong that even for the adversary with the greatest sea power a war against it would involve such dangers as to imperil his own position in the world.

"For this purpose it is not absolutely necessary that the German battle fleet should be as strong as that of the greatest naval Power, because a great naval Power will not, as a rule, be in a position to concentrate all its striking forces against us. But even if it should succeed in meeting us with considerable superiority of strength, the defeat of a strong German fleet would so substantially weaken the enemy that, in spite of a victory he might have obtained, his own position in the world would no longer be secured by an adequate fleet."

[1] The text of all the German navy laws, in English, is given in Appendix I of Hurd and Castle, *German Sea Power*.

And in an exposition of naval strategy published at the same time by Admiral von der Goltz, a former chief of the admiralty staff, occur these words:

"Let us consider the case of a war against England. In spite of what many people think, there is nothing improbable in such a war, owing to the animosity which exists in our country toward England and, on the other side, to the sentiments of the British nation toward all Continental Powers, and in particular against Germany. . . . Our chances of success in a war against England grow more favorable day by day.

"The maritime supremacy of Great Britain, now [1900] overwhelming, will certainly remain considerable in the future; but she is compelled to scatter her forces all over the world. In the event of war in home waters, the greater part of her foreign squadrons would, no doubt, be recalled; but that would be a matter of time, and then all stations overseas could not be abandoned. On the other hand, the German fleet, though much smaller, could remain concentrated in European waters.

"With the increases about to be made, it will be in a position to measure its strength with the ordinary British naval forces in home waters; but it should not be forgotten that the question of numbers is far less important at sea than on land. Numerical inferiority can be compensated for by efficiency, by excellence of material, by the capacity and discipline of the men. Careful preparation permitting rapid mobilization can insure a momentary superiority." [1]

In this language there is nothing threatening, but much that is illuminating. Whatever Germany might intend to do, she was clearly of the opinion that her fleet would at least be a good match for the British, which appeared to be incapable of defending British interests. It is therefore necessary to examine the condition of the British navy at the opening of the twentieth century.

The British fleet in its modern form dates from the Naval Defense Act of 1889, which provided for the construction of 70 men-of-war, including 10 battleships, within seven

[1] Quoted in Hurd and Castle, *German Sea Power*, pp. 121–123.

years, at a cost of £21,500,000. The avowed object of
the measure was to create an "establishment on such a
scale that it should be at least equal to the naval strength
of any two other nations."[1]   Under this two-Power
standard 30 more ships of the line were laid down before
the end of the century, thanks to which the Boer War had
been conducted without interference by any Continental
Power.   By 1904 10 others were built or building, making
a total of 50 battleships not more than fifteen years old.
It might seem that only jingoism or jealousy could, under
such circumstances, regard the new German navy as a
danger to the overwhelming British fleet.

As a matter of fact, the royal navy was in a very parlous
condition.   Except for the desultory operations of the
Crimean War and the bombardment of Alexandria in
1882, it had lived on its reputation since the Napoleonic
struggle that ended in 1815.   How lax discipline had become, how inefficient the gunners were, how far a general
slackness had permeated the whole naval administration,
was known only to the inner circles of the admiralty and
a few officers afloat.   Moreover, innumerable ships were
kept in commission which had long outlived their useful-
ness, while more modern vessels were rendered useless
from the shortage of crews; eighteen types of ships actually figured in the navy list, and many of them were divided
into classes, so that homogeneity, an essential attribute of
an efficient battle fleet, was notoriously lacking.   But this
was not all.   The two-Power standard had been devised
against the Powers of the Dual Alliance, France and Russia,
and the strategic distribution of the British squadrons was
determined by the possibility of war with those countries.
The most powerful ships were stationed in the Mediterranean; the Atlantic fleet was as important as that sta-

---

[1] Lord George Hamilton, first lord of the admiralty, House of Commons, 7 March,
1889.   (3 *Hansard* cccxxxiii, c. 1171.)

tioned in the Channel. Strong squadrons were maintained in the Far East to watch the designs of Russia, and others in American waters for no particular reason except habit. In the North Sea there were only antiquated or obsolescent ships, which were used chiefly for training purposes. Also it was deemed necessary for political motives to show the White Ensign[1] in all parts of the world, so that cruisers and gunboats had to be kept in service wherever British interests had assumed any importance. In other words, circumstances, tradition, and necessity had combined to leave home waters, in particular the North Sea, practically defenseless.

Yet it was from across the North Sea that a direct challenge seemed to have been flung at the heart of the British Empire. To rouse public sentiment in favor of a large fleet, the German press and the Navy League had openly spoken of England as the eventual enemy; the language of the two memoranda quoted above seemed to convey a clear warning; the diplomatic situation did not indicate any slackening of the tension between the two countries. But this was not all. The Russo-Japanese War relieved Germany from any danger on her eastern frontier, and thus upset the balance of power in Europe; while the success of Japan, England's ally since 1902, insured the safety of British interests in Asia. Events in the Balkans demanded the attention of British statesmen. There was also only too much reason to believe that neither the French army nor the French navy, as they had been administered by General André and M. Pelletan, were prepared to risk a combat with Germany if the policy of the latter should become aggressive.

These circumstances explain the momentous measures taken by the British Government in the year 1904. First

---

[1] The name usually applied to the British naval flag. The red cross of St. George is shown on a white field, with the Union Jack in the upper corner.

of all, the agreement with France, the famous *entente cordiale*, and the situation in the Far East permitted a wholesale redistribution of the British squadrons. Those in the North Pacific and South Atlantic were abolished, and the Mediterranean and China fleets were almost denuded of battleships. The Channel fleet was correspondingly strengthened. An Atlantic fleet resting on Gibraltar, and *a home fleet stationed in the North Sea*, for which public opinion had been clamoring,[1] were also envisaged, and made their appearance in 1906. Thus was begun that concentration of British naval strength against Germany, the silent pressure of which has been one of the marvels of the Great War.

Of equal, perhaps greater, importance was the appointment of Sir John Fisher as first sea lord at the admiralty, whose one ambition was to put the British fleet in a state of "instant preparedness for war." His first step aroused considerable opposition among sentimentalists, for he "scrapped" 180 obsolete ships of no fighting value. Not only was the heavy charge for up-keep abolished and the money freed for purposes of new construction; the crews and officers thus released were sent to fighting units hitherto kept in reserve and the first step taken toward simplicity of organization and efficiency in practise.

Much more sensational was the introduction of the *Dreadnought* type of battleship. In the early years of the century the admiralty had materially reduced its programme of construction, while the German fleet was advancing toward its statutory limits. Under such circumstances the 4 battleships which the Balfour government proposed to lay down annually would not suffice to maintain the two-Power standard. Moreover, the Russo-Japanese

---

[1] In February, 1903, a meeting was held in London to discuss the "desirability of creating a North Sea squadron and of establishing a naval base on the east coast." It was voted that the "proposed measures are urgently required in view of the continuous increase of the German navy." (*Annual Register*, 1903, p. 35.)

War was held to have demonstrated the comparative inefficiency of medium armaments, and ships which should carry only guns of heavy caliber had already been foreshadowed by American and Italian designers. British tendencies were in the same direction. The ships built before 1900 were regularly provided with four 12-inch and twelve 6-inch rifles; the 8 *King Edwards* (1901–1903) were equipped with four 12-inch, four 9.2-inch, and ten 6-inch; the 2 *Lord Nelsons* (1904) had four 12-inch and ten 9.2-inch guns. The transition to the *Dreadnought*, therefore, was not so revolutionary as is usually supposed. This famous ship, laid down in October, 1905, and commissioned before the end of 1906, carried ten 12-inch guns on a displacement of 17,900 tons, which made possible a speed of twenty-one knots, or at least two knots more than had been attained by any battleship heretofore. Three other ships, known as battle-cruisers, with eight 12-inch guns and a speed of twenty-eight knots, were also laid down and completed within two years, which now became the recognized period for construction. Since then practically all capital ships in all navies have been *Dreadnoughts*.

Beyond a doubt the admiralty had achieved a triumph not only of engineering skill but, for the moment, of diplomacy: from the summer of 1905 to July, 1907, no battleship was laid down in Germany. The first 4 German *Dreadnoughts* were not completed until May and September, 1910, by which date the British navy possessed 10 of these monsters. Furthermore, the cost of construction per ton was smaller than for the old type of ship, and the maintenance per year less by £50,000. But it is equally clear that, by inaugurating the *Dreadnought*, the admiralty condemned the magnificent collection of older ships to an earlier uselessness than would otherwise have been the case. With respect to the new type, Germany was able to start the race on fairly equal terms, and at the beginning

of the Great War possessed 17 modern ships of the line
to England's 29.   In addition, the enthusiasm created in
England by the *Dreadnought* and the battle-cruisers gave
a new fillip to the propaganda of Admiral von Tirpitz and
the Navy League, who for a campaign cry asked nothing
better than an undoubted increase of British superiority.

In 1906 a third navy law was passed by the Reichstag.
Six large cruisers, which the Reichstag of 1900 had refused
to grant, were added to the 14 provided for in the earlier
law.   Anglo-German naval rivalry now began in earnest.
The preceding year had been one of great tension, for Great
Britain intervened in the Morocco dispute between France
and Germany, and the German Government took advantage of the new outburst of Anglophobia to carry through
the naval increment.   Most unfortunately, it also declined to respond to British overtures for a reduction of
armaments.

When the crisis of 1905 had been adjusted by the Algeciras Conference, the Liberal and Radical press in England, taking up Prince Bülow's statement that Germany
thought as little of challenging British maritime supremacy
as of building a railway to the moon,[1] began a strenuous
campaign for a limitation of armaments.   The movement
reached its height when Sir Henry Campbell-Bannerman,
the prime minister, published an article in the first issue of
the *Nation* (London),[2] a new Radical weekly, in which he invited Germany to discuss the whole problem;   only to encounter an obstinate refusal from Prince Bülow.[3]

Sir Henry's sincerity, which Germans were not inclined
to admit, cannot be doubted.   His government had taken
office pledged to a vast policy of social reform, which promised to be very costly.   So the Cawdor programme had

---

[1] August, 1906, to a correspondent of the *Daily Mail;*   quoted in Bardoux, *L'An-
gleterre radicale*, 1906–1912, p. 340.
[2] 2 March, 1907.   [3] Reichstag, 30 April, 1906.

been abandoned, only 3 ships being laid down in 1906, and again in 1907; this *after* the German increase of March, 1906. The British Government also earnestly strove to have the limitation of armaments discussed at the second Hague Conference, in 1907. But the German Emperor, who in August, 1906, expressed to Sir Charles Hardinge, then permanent undersecretary for foreign affairs, the opinion that the coming conference was "great nonsense," refused to be represented at it if the question of disarmament were to be brought forward.[1] Nevertheless, at the conference the British delegate read a declaration that Great Britain was ready to exchange naval estimates in advance with any other Power in the hope that the exchange might lead to a mutual reduction.

In the autumn of 1907 the Emperor William visited England and, in a speech at the Guild Hall, professed emphatic sentiments of amity toward the country of his grandmother; but during the time of his stay he probably received the impression that the British reductions were dictated by weakness. Otherwise he would hardly have dared write to Lord Tweedmouth, then first lord of the admiralty, a letter reassuring him as to German naval plans and protesting against "this perpetual quoting of the German danger" as "utterly unworthy of the great British nation, with its world-wide Empire and mighty navy."[2] His Majesty's belief in British decadence must have been confirmed by Lord Tweedmouth's reply, which communicated the naval estimates for the coming year, 1908-9. Providing for only 2 battleships and reaching the lowest figure for new construction since 1898, they

---

[1] Sir Edward Cook, *How Britain Strove for Peace* (1914), p. 11. This is a "record of Anglo-German negotiations, 1898–1914, told from authoritative sources," evidently the British foreign office. The narrative presented has not been denied, except in one detail, by the German Government or its apologists. The pamphlet is the most valuable contribution to the subject of Anglo-German relations that has appeared since the war began.

[2] First published in the *Morning Post*, 30 October, 1914.

could have only one meaning for tho German admiralty. Might not a supreme effort practically destroy the British superiority in modern ships?

So in March, 1908, a fourth navy law was passed, by which the period of replacement was reduced for battle-ships from twenty-five to twenty years, that is, *Dreadnoughts* would take the place of old ships five years earlier than originally planned.   To give effect to the new plan, the programme of 2 battleships a year, which had been increased to 3 in 1907, was now increased to 4; so that between 1906 and 1908 9 German *Dreadnoughts* were actually authorized to England's 8.

In the summer of 1908 the British Government once more endeavored to make an arrangement with Germany. King Edward VII, with Sir Charles Hardinge, visited the German Emperor at Cronberg and explained to the latter that "the naval rivalry set on foot by Germany was sure to provoke suspicions as to its ultimate intentions, and thus to embitter relations, then perfectly friendly and natural, between the two countries."[1]   William II flatly refused to discuss his naval armaments with a foreign government, and, it is understood, "avowed his intention to go to war rather than submit to such a thing."   The German foreign office repelled the British overtures with equal emphasis.   Proceeding to Ischl, where he met the Emperor Francis Joseph, the King urged the Austrian monarch to exert his influence with the German Emperor, but to no purpose, doubtless because German assistance might be needed in the coming annexation of Bosnia and Herzegovina.[2]   King Edward is believed to have returned to the charge on the occasion of his visit to Berlin in February, 1909.

An awakening was now at hand.   The continued re-

[1] Sir Edward Cook, *How Britain Strove for Peace*, pp. 13–14.
[2] Maximilian Harden, *Monarchs and Men*, p. 33.

fusal of the German Government to discuss a limitation of armaments; the interview with the Kaiser published in the *Daily Telegraph*, in which he stated that the majority of his people were hostile to England; the contention of Lord Cromer that the money intended for old-age pensions should be devoted to battleships; some fiery letters in the *Daily Mail* by Robert Blatchford, a socialist; the agitation carried on by Lord Roberts for national military service and the sensation produced by the play "An Englishman's Home"; and the crisis in the Balkans from October, 1908, to March, 1909—all prepared the way for the "panic" of March, 1909. In submitting the naval estimates for 1909–10 Mr. McKenna pointed out that the British navy then possessed 5 *Dreadnoughts*, which would be increased to 12 in 1911. In the same year Germany would have 9, according to the announced programme; but in 1908, when only 2 British ships were laid down, the German Government had accelerated the construction of 4 ships, so that there would be 13 German *Dreadnoughts* in 1911, as opposed to the 12 British. By the autumn of 1912 there would be 17, and, if acceleration were again resorted to, by April, 1912. To meet this emergency the admiralty proposed to build 4 capital ships at once, which would raise the British strength to 16 by November, 1911; if the German ships of 1911 were accelerated, 4 more British ships would be laid down, which when completed in March, 1912, would give Great Britain 20 *Dreadnoughts* as opposed to the German 17.[1]

It was subsequently proved that these figures were based on a mistaken estimate of German capacity. The imperial government declared that it would not possess 11 *Dreadnoughts* till April, 1912, and that there would be no further

[1] House of Commons, 13 March, 1909. (5 *Hansard* ii, cc. 930 *ff.*) Mr. Balfour declared that Germany would have at least 21 *Dreadnoughts* in April, 1912, and perhaps 25, and that therefore not even a one-Power standard was being maintained by the mistress of the seas!

acceleration, that is, there would be only 13 ships ready in the autumn of 1912.[1] But public opinion in England paid no attention to these assurances. Ignoring, wisely, as events have shown, the enormous preponderance of England in older ships, the Conservative newspapers took up the cry, "We want eight and we won't wait"; the opposition in Parliament demanded a clear-cut two-Power standard without exceptions, so as to avoid offense,[2] and the by-elections began to indicate popular uneasiness. On 26 July the government conceded the 4 contingent ships, in spite of the protests of its followers, thus taking the first step toward securing that preponderance in ships of the line which has been of such incalculable importance in the war. Advantage was taken of the delay, it should be noted, to equip 6 of the 8 ships with 13.5-inch rifles, so that they go by the name of *super-Dreadnoughts*.

This episode was not really a "panic." The 4 contingent ships merely filled up the shortage in the Cawdor programme, from which the Liberal government had departed for three successive years (8 ships instead of 12, 1906 8). When the Germans did not respond to the British overtures for disarmament, it was inevitable that the old programme should be restored and its deficiencies remedied. There was, to be sure, much unnecessary fire-eating on the part of irresponsible journalists in England, but no corresponding outburst across the North Sea occurred. On the contrary, the fatherland was greatly impressed by the resolute determination of a Liberal government to maintain that "unassailable supremacy" (Mr. Asquith) at sea which it had previously seemed to let pass.

---

[1] Admiral von Tirpitz, in the Reichstag, 17 March. Even these forecasts were not realized, for in March, 1911, there were only 5 *Dreadnoughts* in commission; in March, 1912, only 9.

[2] On 12 November, 1908, Mr. Asquith said that the government accepted the two-Power standard as defined by Lord Cawdor, that is, a ten-per-cent margin above the two next strongest Powers. (4 *Hansard* cxcvi, c. 560.)

In the budget of 1909 Mr. Lloyd George easily raised the huge sums required for the naval estimates; Prince Bülow was defeated in the Reichstag when he demanded new taxes to pay for the vast armaments authorized during his chancellorship.   Perhaps for this reason the Kaiser did not demand a new naval law from the Reichstag in reply to the British programme.   Whether Germans realized the fact or not, they had been too clever in 1906–8, for the situation was now less favorable to them than it had been previous to their efforts to catch up with England.[1]   In addition, the British Channel fleet was now absorbed in the home fleet, which comprised 16 battleships on a war footing and 16 more in reserve.

For the next three years the rivalry went silently on, in spite of British efforts to stop it.   In the summer of 1909, after the resignation of Prince Bülow, overtures were made by the new chancellor, Dr. von Bethmann-Hollweg, to secure British neutrality in the event of a Continental war, in return for which Germany was willing to "retard her rate" of construction without abandoning her programme mapped out up to 1918.[2]   The offer was naturally refused as inadequate, but new negotiations were opened the following year.   After informal views had been exchanged for some months, the chancellor declared that "a frank and sincere interchange of views followed by an understanding as to the economic and political interests of the two Powers offered the surest means of allaying all distrust."[3]   He would seem to have been willing not to increase the German programme in return for a general understanding with England, and "the British Govern-

---

[1] The German Government denied that definite proposals had ever been made by Great Britain (Reichstag, 29 March, 1909); this in reply to Mr. Asquith's statement (House of Commons, 16 March) that "informal" communications had taken place with regard to a reduction of armaments.

[2] Sir Edward Cook, *How Britain Strove for Peace*, p. 20.

[3] Reichstag, 10 December, 1910.

ment were considering their reply when the German Emperor informed the British ambassador that he would on no account ever consent to any agreement binding Germany not to enlarge her naval programme." [1] The chancellor himself crushed all hopes of an agreement by his speech in the Reichstag on 30 March, 1911.

"I consider," he said, "any control of armaments as absolutely impracticable, and every attempt in that direction would lead to nothing but continual mutual distrust and perpetual friction. Who would be content to weaken his means of defense without the absolute certainty that his neighbor was not secretly exceeding the proportion allowed to him in the disarmament agreement? No, gentlemen, any one who seriously considers the question of universal disarmament must inevitably come to the conclusion that it is insoluble so long as men are men and states are states."

Germany meanwhile adhered to her programme of 4 ships each year until 1912, when she was expected to lay down only 2. But it soon became clear that she intended to build 58 *Dreadnoughts*, instead of the 38 capital ships authorized by the law of 1900, for the large cruisers would gradually be replaced by battle-cruisers.[2] The British Government was therefore compelled to increase the Cawdor programme, and laid down 5 ships in both 1910 and 1911. Even so, at the beginning of 1912 England possessed but 30 *Dreadnoughts*, built and building, as opposed to Germany's 19. Nevertheless, in preparing the estimates of 1912, the admiralty assumed that Germany would lay down only 2 ships, according to previous announcements and reduced its own programme to 4.

Unfortunately, the Agadir crisis of 1911 had aroused intense indignation in Germany. Within two weeks of the announcement of the British plans the German Government presented a new fleet law for the consideration of

[1] Sir Edward Cook, *How Britain Strove for Peace*, p. 25.
[2] So Colonel Gaedke, in *Berliner Tageblatt*, 23 February, 1910.

the Reichstag.   As passed without amendment, it added
3 battleships to the familiar 38, but its main feature was
an increase in the striking force of ships of all classes which
would be available—immediately available—at all seasons
of the year.   A third squadron of 8 battleships was created
and maintained in full commission as part of the high-seas
fleet, which was henceforth to consist of 25 battleships,
8 battle or large armored cruisers, 18 small cruisers, and 99
destroyers; in short, four-fifths of the entire German navy
was to be kept constantly and instantly ready for war.
Fifteen thousand men were added to the personnel, which
in 1920 was to number 107,000 apart from the reserves.[1]
When completed, this fleet would be the most powerful
aggregation of war-ships the world had ever seen.   No
wonder an English writer exclaimed: "For the first time
in history a Great Power definitely asserted its intention
of being supremely powerful both by sea and land." [2]

Once more Great Britain endeavored to arrange some
agreement to stop the insensate naval rivalry.   The German chancellor had declared that the settlement of the
Morocco difficulties had "cleaned the slate" as regards
Anglo-German relations, and at the invitation of the Emperor Lord Haldane went to Berlin to discuss the naval
problem, although only two days before his arrival the new
navy law had been announced.   But the German Government would not offer more than a temporary retardation
of their existing programme, even in return for a political
understanding with Great Britain which the latter was
quite willing to conclude.   Nothing, therefore, came of
the negotiations.   A month before Sir Edward Grey had
indicated the British acceptance of a proposal that the
two governments should exchange information on naval

---

[1] Mr. Churchill's summary, House of Commons, 24 July, 1912. (5 *Hansard*,
xli, cc. 838–840.)

[2] A. S. Hurd, *The Command of the Sea* (1912), p. xvi.

matters; this was left unanswered, and also came to
naught.[1] From this time to the outbreak of the Great
War no further overtures were formally made to Germany
by the British Government, so far as is known, for a limitation of armaments. But it was barely possible that
public opinion would succeed where official negotiations
had failed.

Under the various navy laws 35 German *Dreadnoughts*
should be in commission in 1920. A two-Power standard
for England, without a ten-per-cent margin, would require
70 British ships of the same type. In March, 1912, 16
of these monsters were completed, 12 were building, and 2
provided for, a total of 30. In the next eight years to
build 40 capital ships would be a herculean task, and Mr.
Churchill, first lord of the admiralty since October, 1911,
recognized the fact. Speaking in the House of Commons
on 18 March, 1912, he discussed the situation with entire
frankness, on the ground that plain speaking would be
welcomed in both Germany and England. The principle
of the two-Power standard was no longer applicable to
Europe. In recent years the admiralty had maintained
a superiority of sixty per cent in *Dreadnoughts* over the German fleet, and would continue that standard for the next
four or five years. But England stood on the defensive,
so that any reduction in the German programme would
be immediately imitated. If the Germans built no ships
in a given year, neither would England, and on this basis
a limitation of armaments could be effected without formal
agreement or any restrictions of national sovereignty.
The futility of this appeal was apparent when the German
navy law of 1912 was passed through the Reichstag by an
overwhelming national majority.

Mr. Churchill's programme, as outlined in July, 1912,
provided for 25 *Dreadnoughts*, spread over the next six years.

[1] Sir Edward Cook, *How Britain Strove for Peace*, p. 25.

This would have given 55 to the German 35, which did not represent a superiority of sixty per cent; they would, however, provide a margin of a little more than sixty per cent above the 33 German ships, which could be foreseen in commission in 1920.   But to achieve this result in the North Sea, all the *Dreadnoughts* must be withdrawn from the Mediterranean, where by 1916 Austria and Italy were due to have 4 and 6 *Dreadnoughts* respectively.[1]   The problem of manning the British fleets was also beginning to attract attention.   It was estimated that, instead of the 134,000 enrolled in 1912, 170,000 would ultimately be required, and while the additional quotas could doubtless be raised they would be very expensive, whereas German ratings were conscripted and therefore cheap.[2]

In these circumstances Mr. Churchill's efforts to lessen the naval rivalry were quite intelligible, nor was he discouraged by the chilling reception of his first overtures. When Admiral von Tirpitz in February, 1913, stated that the ratio of sixteen to ten for the construction of battleships was "acceptable" to Germany, he was formally invited by Mr. Churchill to proclaim a "naval holiday."[3]   It was at once objected in Germany that the net result would be to increase the superiority of England, for the Canadian Government was then proposing to present 3 capital ships to the mother country; and that Germany could not afford to let her plants and workmen stand idle; moreover, the

[1] There was talk of creating a Mediterranean squadron which should be truly imperial in character and intrusted with the defense of the highway of the British Empire: the *Australia*, presented to the imperial government by the Commonwealth in March, 1909, but stationed in Australian waters; the *New Zealand*, presented at the same time, and lent for use in the North Sea temporarily; the *Malaya*, presented by the Federated Malay States; and 3 ships which the Canadian Government was then proposing to build.   As the Canadian ships were not finally authorized, the proposal came to nothing.

[2] Most German discussion of British naval problems assumed that England could not raise the necessary quotas, but there was no real foundation for this theory, which merely served to stimulate German ambitions.

[3] House of Commons, 26 March, 1913.   (5 *Hansard* l, c. 1759.)

navy laws stood in the way. But the British statesman was indomitable. On 18 October, 1913, speaking at Manchester, he renewed his offer, with a detailed proposal. If Germany would put off for twelve months the beginning of her 2 ships of the 1914 programme, Great Britain, "in absolute good faith," would postpone for the same period the laying down of her 4 ships, provided that other Powers fell in line with the idea. This proposal commended itself to neither British nor German public opinion and was quietly dropped. But in one matter Mr. Churchill had succeeded. The British and German Governments agreed to exchange information about naval matters, so that "scares" would be difficult to organize in the future. On the eve of the war recrimination had practically ceased, and many believed that an Anglo-German *rapprochement* was not impossible.

In spite, however, of the more cordial relations reflected in the last paragraph, the concentration of the British fleet in home waters proceeded. In 1912 Mr. Churchill announced that the navy would be organized in three fleets: the first, of four squadrons of 8 battleships each, in full commission, with a fleet flag-ship; the second, of two squadrons with nucleus crews;[1] the third, of two squadrons, one with nucleus crews, the other of the oldest ships of the line. To complete the active battle fleet of 33 capital ships, it was necessary to recall the Atlantic fleet to the Channel, and the Mediterranean fleet, hitherto resting on Malta, to Gibraltar, besides reducing the strength of the latter from 6 battleships to 4 battle-cruisers. Thus the Mediterranean was practically abandoned,[2] in spite of the

[1] Enough men were retained to keep all the machinery of the ships in order—about two-thirds of the full complement.

[2] "England has suffered her first defeat, her first moral defeat. She has had to withdraw her fleet from the Mediterranean. That sea was once ours—an English lake. It is no longer ours. Our power is concentrated, watching our dearest friends, those Germans who have no intention whatever of coming near England!" (Cramb, *Germany and England*, p. 37, note 1.)

fact that through it came about fifty per cent of the grain consumed in England. But, inasmuch as in March, 1913, there would be 13 German *Dreadnoughts* in the North Sea, British interests in the Middle Sea had to be left in charge of France, against whom the British fleet had been concentrated ten years before in the same waters, but whose own fleet was concentrated there in the autumn of 1912. But the sea is all one, and the principal business of a British fleet in case of war would be to destroy that of the enemy. Sound strategy, therefore, demanded the strongest possible armament in the North Sea.

The situation in 1914 was as follows: England possessed 29 modern battleships,[1] Germany 17; they were building 15 and 11 respectively. In older battleships the proportion was exactly two to one—40 British, 20 German. There were 125 British cruisers built and building, as opposed to 55 German. In torpedo-craft the figures stood at 237 for Britain, 154 for Germany; in submarines, 99 British, 45 German. The Berlin correspondent of the *Times* predicted an increase of the foreign-service cruiser squadron, but he went on to say:

"Every effort is being made, and will be made, to sterilize the rivalry with Great Britain and to shift the scene of action, or rather the arguments for eventual expansion, from the North Sea to the Baltic. To all appearances we are going to hear a great deal more about the naval strength of Russia, and to a minor extent of France, than about the naval strength of Great Britain."

The ratio of sixteen to ten in the construction of battleships was "still acceptable" to Admiral von Tirpitz, who said:

" If it were really desired to come to an armaments agreement, it was only natural that England, as by far the most powerful sea

[1] Including the *New Zealand;* the *Malaya* is included among the ships building. Both ships were gifts to the imperial government. Two others, taken over from Turkey, raised the total to 46.

Power In the world, would have to make the positive proposals. He had no doubt that such proposals would be examined by Germany most minutely."

He added that "if a general reduction of displacement were to set in he would welcome it";[1] which was not unlikely, for England and France had agreed that their ships should not exceed 26,000 tons for the future.[2]

One cannot say that Anglo-German naval rivalry had subsided when the murder of the Archduke Francis Ferdinand disturbed the diplomatic situation; but the calm temper in which the first lord of the British admiralty and the German naval secretary now discussed their problems was in marked contrast to the feverish excitement previously attendant upon a striking move by either government. English opinion had somehow got used to the German fleet. Germany, on her side, had taken to heart Lord Haldane's statement: "Whatever efforts Germany may make, she must reckon upon our making efforts which will be still greater, because sea power is our life, and in sea power we intend to remain superior."[3] Furthermore, the predictions of economists like Professor von Schulze Gaevernitz,[4] that English resources would be unequal to the strain of German competition, had been disproved by the enormous expenditure in the five years preceding the war, which, it should be noted, had been met entirely from the increased yields of taxation, whereas the German fleet had been built very largely from the proceeds of loans. Similarly, the idea so prevalent in the early years of the twentieth century, that the British navy was rotten to the core and living on its traditions,[5] had been dissipated by the reforms

[1] *Times*, 6 and 10 February, 1914.   [2] *New York Times*, 15 February, 1914.
[3] House of Lords, 23 July, 1912. (5 *Hansard* xii, c. 668.)
[4] "England and Germany—Peace or War?," *American Review of Reviews*, October, 1909.
[5] See Ernst Meyer, *Los von England*, translated in *Contemporary Review*, July, 1902.

carried out since 1904.   Germans had abundant proof that
Great Britain was not a colossus with feet of clay.   Probably they had also come to see that their challenge of
British naval supremacy was stimulating, as nothing else
could do, the organization, perhaps the federation, of the
British Empire.   But, above all, the policies of the British
and the German Governments had been found less antagonistic than was previously supposed; at least, this was the
lesson drawn from their co-operation during the Balkan
wars of 1912–13.   If a political understanding could be
reached between London and Berlin, the naval question
would ultimately settle itself, as it was already in a fair
way of doing.   And the tragedy of the Great War lies in
the fact that early in the summer of 1914 a substantial
agreement had been reached between Great Britain and
Germany on those matters about which they had previously
disagreed.

From this narrative of events we may now turn to discuss the merits of the Anglo-German naval controversy.
The British Government certainly exhausted the resources
of diplomacy and persuasion to secure from Germany an
agreement to limit the expenditures upon naval armaments.
Failing in that policy, it faced with courage and resolution
the task of maintaining that supremacy of the sea which
has belonged to Great Britain since the Napoleonic wars.
Was such an attitude justified, or has she been guilty of a
"navalism" comparable to that militarism of Germany
which has been counted the chief cause of the Great War?
The case for a German navy was admirably summarized,
in its broad outlines, by the great expositor and champion
of sea power.

"The only shore-line of the German Empire," wrote the late
Admiral Mahan, in his *Interest of America in International Condi-*

tions, "Is that of the North Sea and the Baltic Sea. All the river ways of Germany, so extensively developed and utilized, interconnected by canals already existing or planned, constituting a huge internal system of water communications, find their outlet in one or other of these two seas through which all sea-borne trade enters or departs. The whole external commerce of Germany, going or coming, focusses there. The North Sea, if it be covered by hostile cruisers, is little over sixty miles long from the Ems to the Elbe. The Baltic seaboard is much more extensive; but all access to it from the Atlantic is through the Skager-Rack, the external approach to which is less than a hundred miles wide. . . . Directly across all lines of communication to the Atlantic, and so to every ocean, lie the British Islands. Most of us carry in our mind's eye the width of the English Channel and the Straits of Dover, along the full length of which, moreover, is English land containing two principal naval stations; but the other way round, by the north of Scotland, the North Sea itself is nowhere four hundred miles wide, and in places only three hundred. In case of war between the two countries, no German ship, as international law now stands, can use this stretch of water without liability to capture; while a successful blockade of the German harbors on the two seas puts a stop to all commerce as well by neutrals as by Germans." Even supposing that through the use of the Kiel Canal the ports of the Baltic or the North Sea can be kept open, "the neutral tonnage would be quite inadequate to the necessary transportation to German ports. . . . Americans who recall what Cuba once meant to our international policy may appreciate what the British Islands by situation mean to German commerce. . . . The supremacy of Great Britain in European seas means a perpetual latent control of German commerce." [1]

The above quotation represents quite fairly the official view that Germany's growing commerce must be adequately protected. Closely connected with this was the complaint that through her occupation of Gibraltar, Egypt, Aden, South Africa, and innumerable coaling-stations in all oceans, Great Britain effectively controlled the trade routes of the world; Germany not only possessed no such stations, except some islands in the Pacific, but could not

[1] Pp. 53–61, *passim.*

secure any, because of British opposition.[1]   The idea was also ventilated that the supremacy of the seas on the part of a single Power was an anachronism in an age when the commercial interests of all the Great Powers demanded that the seas be kept open.[2]   In the same strain, Germans argued that England refused to treat them as equals in the affairs and politics of the world.   Germany would be "most willing," said Prince Bülow, "on the basis of mutual consideration and absolute parity, to live with England in peace, friendship, and harmony."[3]   "The English . . . are not willing to admit us to a political and national equality in the world," declared Dr. Paul Rohrbach.[4] As a German admiral put it:

"The source of misunderstanding resides in the fact that England refuses us equal maritime power, and only recognizes us on land, or in the realms of culture and the like."[5]

Finally, we may quote Herr Arthur von Gwinner, the manager of the Deutsche Bank:

"That sea supremacy is, for Great Britain, a life-and-death question is understood and appreciated in Germany as well as it is in England.   Can public opinion on the other side of the North Sea not be convinced likewise that the possession of a strong fleet is for Germany, if not to such a complete extent, still to an important degree, also a question of vital importance?"[6]

----

[1] This point is well developed by L. von Amran, *Englands Land-und-See Politik und die Mächte*, 1902.   The author proposed the neutralization of all straits then under British control, as well as their adjacent territories; if the Ottoman Empire, which he foresaw shorn of its European provinces, were similarly treated, England could surrender her points of vantage with equanimity, and if she refused, the other European Powers were to unite for the purpose of executing the plan.

[2] Professor von Schulze-Gaevernitz, "England and Germany—Peace or War?" *American Review of Reviews*, October, 1909.

[3] Reichstag, 16 December, 1900.

[4] *Der deutsche Gedanke in der Welt* (1912), p. 196.

[5] *England and Germany* (1912), p. 156.

[6] *Ibid.*, p. 113.

Politically, the case was put by the Emperor when he said: "We need a fleet to protect ourselves from arrogance." [1]   Or when he remarked:

"Every German war-ship launched is one guarantee more for peace on earth, yet it also means that our adversaries will be so much less inclined to pick a quarrel with us, while it renders us by an equal amount more valuable as allies." [2]

Professor Hans Delbrück was less cautious, if more frank:

"The German navy is not, and never will be, sufficiently strong directly to menace England; yet it is strong enough to necessitate a cautious English policy and to compel England continually to consider her relations with Germany. . . . If Germany had been content to maintain her position of thirty years ago as a Continental Power, and had built no war-ships in addition to her few cruisers, England's power on the seas would be boundless." [3]

Germany must, he contends, restrict the movements of England to prevent them becoming hostile to herself.

Finally, Germans never tired of asserting that their fleet was intended only for defense, that it would never be used offensively against Great Britain; whereas the naval history of England, they contended, was largely one of aggression. When the Dutch in the seventeenth century managed to secure the carrying trade of Europe, had not the English used their navy to secure that trade for themselves? Had not the Earl of Chatham explained the Anglo-French wars of the eighteenth century as a struggle for the mastery of the sea?   In 1807 an English squadron had bombarded Copenhagen and brought the Danish fleet to England as a prize of war: this when Great Britain and Denmark were at peace!   Within the present generation Alexandria

[1] I have not been able to discover the time and place of this remark, although it is often ascribed to the Emperor.
[2] Bremen, 22 March, 1905.
[3] "Why Germany Builds War-ships," *Contemporary Review*, October, 1909.

had experienced the same fate at the orders of a Liberal British government; and during the Boer War German mail steamers had been taken into port by British cruisers. So no nation is safe from the tyranny of the British fleet, which alone is responsible for the continued liability of private property at sea to capture.   In short, *Nieder mit dem englischen Seeräubertum !* [1]

Such is the indictment which for the past fifteen years and more, especially since the Great War began, German officials and German publicists have drawn up against the mistress of the sea.   And if the British fleet has been a danger, actual or potential, to Germany, then she was well advised not to accept British overtures for a limitation of armaments, but, on the contrary, to strain every nerve in the hope of some day overcoming the British supremacy.   It is therefore necessary to examine the counts of Germany's indictment with an open mind.

First, as regards the protection of their commerce, Germans would seem to have been guilty of deliberate misrepresentation or much loose thinking, for they often talked as though the British navy was a continual menace to their overseas trade.   Of course, this was not true.   From the creation of the German Empire to August, 1914, the seven seas were just as free to the ships of Germany as to those of Great Britain and her colonies; and Germans made full use of that freedom to develop a merchant marine second in general importance to that of England.   Only during the Boer War were German steamers molested in the slightest degree by British cruisers, and then they were released as soon as complaint was made.   The British position was made clear some years ago by an English writer on military problems:

"It ought to be made clear to all the world," wrote Mr. Spenser Wilkinson, "that, whatever may be the language used in English

[1] Paul Rohrbach, *Der Krieg und die deutsche Politik* (1914), p. 100.

discussions, Great Britain makes no claim to suzerainty over the
sea, or over territories bordering on the sea not forming parts of
the British Empire; that, while she is determined to maintain a
navy that can, *in case of war*, secure the 'command' of the sea
against her enemies, she regards the sea, in peace, and in war except against her enemies, as the common property of all nations—
the open road forming the highway of mankind." [1]

Thus, only if Germany were involved in war with Great
Britain would her commerce be in the slightest danger
from the British fleet. Was such a contingency probable?
Not if England's wishes were to prevail. In the account
of Anglo-German relations up to 1904, it was pointed out
that Anglo-German relations were satisfactory enough
until William II began to give a distinctly anti-English
bent to German policy; and in the following chapters it
will be seen that in the decade before the Great War
British policy toward Germany was essentially defensive.
In other words, an Anglo-German war would result only
from German aggression, and Germans denied that they
were planning such a war. True, they accused Great
Britain of a desire to destroy the German navy; but if such
was the main purpose of British policy (which can by no
means be admitted), then to increase the German navy
so that it might become more distrusted than ever by the
British was surely a paradox of reasoning and the negation of statesmanship. The truth is, the British navy
could become a danger to Germany only if her own policy
was so devised as to endanger the legitimate interests of
Great Britain, in which event the main German argument
against the British navy falls to the ground.

Next, as to the contention that the control of the seas
by a single Power could not be tolerated in these days of
international commerce, and that Germany must be recognized as the equal of Great Britain. "For reasons abso-

[1] *Britain at Bay* (1909), p. 92.

lutely vital," said the late Admiral Mahan, "Great Britain cannot afford to surrender supremacy at sea."[1]   The frontiers of Germany are, in the main, land frontiers; in the matter of food she is largely self-supporting or fed overland.   The British Isles, on the other hand, must import most of the food they consume, and *such imports must come by sea*, for there is no contiguous country through which the necessaries or the luxuries of life may come.   The closing of the trade routes would be the prelude to famine, revolution, national collapse.   To quote Sir Edward Grey:

"There is no comparison between the importance of the German navy to Germany and the importance of our navy to us. Our navy is to us what their army is to them.   To have a strong navy would increase their prestige, their diplomatic influence, their power of protecting their commerce; but it is not the matter of life and death to them that it is to us."[2]

To Englishmen, devoid as they were (with some exceptions, to be noted presently) of aggressive intentions toward Germany, the German fleet was bound to appear a "luxury," as Mr. Winston Churchill once called it.[3]

Could Great Britain have solved her problem by consenting to make private property at sea immune from capture in time of war?   Theoretically, at least, there could then be no interruption of her food supplies.   The traditional British view, however, has been that the ability to destroy an enemy's sea-borne trade is at once the surest means of defeating him in war and of restraining him from making war.   It is also urged that as war interrupts all commerce on land between belligerents, a similar interruption must occur on the sea.   The analogy, indeed, between

[1] *Interest of America in International Conditions*, p. 61.
[2] House of Commons, 29 March, 1909. (5 *Hansard* iii, cc. 60–61.) As long ago as 1862 Francis Urquhart said: "England will be the sea's victim on the day she ceases to be its queen."
[3] Speech at Glasgow, 9 February, 1912

private property on land and at sea is not complete, for
the latter is almost entirely the means or the articles of
commerce, not the paraphernalia of every-day life, and
a belligerent always restrains the land commerce of his
enemy in every way possible. Finally, would the immunity of British trade be actually respected by a belligerent possessed of strong naval power?

For these reasons the British Government opposed any
change in the existing rule at the second Hague Conference.
But Sir Edward Grey "expressly intimated to the German
Government his readiness to make the concession, if it
were made the basis of an agreement for the restriction of
naval armaments," only to meet with an absolute refusal.[1]
Hence the statement of Mr. Edwin D. Mead, who has
long advocated the change:

"One of the ablest statesmen in England declared to me his belief, shared, he assured me, by many like himself, that, if England
had voted at The Hague for the inviolability of ocean commerce
in war, Germany would have been at war with her in less than two
years."[2]

Nevertheless, in May, 1914, Sir Edward Grey declared that
England would not offer "a blank opposition to this question on the next international occasion," if she could secure
the conditions which would make her ocean trade absolutely safe. He added this promise:

"If it is understood that we must have conditions, I should be
quite prepared to take up the attitude that we should not on the
next occasion refuse to negotiate, but should come forward ourselves with the actual conditions which we regard as essential and
fair in the matter with the possibility of a settlement."[3]

[1] J. M. Robertson, M.P., who says he had "special means of knowing the facts,"
New York Times, 3 August, 1915.
[2] "England and Germany," *Atlantic Monthly*, March, 1908.
[3] Sir Edward Grey, House of Commons, 6 May, 1914. (5 *Hansard* xlii, c. 410.)

It is plain, therefore, that the British Government was ready to concede the essential point if that were the price of a limitation of naval armaments; while the German Government, although it put forward the necessity of protecting German commerce as the *raison d'être* of its fleet, did not respond to any overtures to remove the grievance of which it complained.

Quite apart from the duty of keeping the trade routes to England open, another equally important task devolves upon the British navy—the defense of the British Empire. Not one of the numerous colonies or dominions of England would be able, alone, to defend itself against aggression, and the time is far off when the mother country can confide to her children the burden of self-defense. It is usually overlooked that until England felt her own situation imperilled by the rise of the German navy the British fleet was actually employed for the defense of British dominions *on the spot*. And since more and more ships have been withdrawn to home waters at least two self-governing colonies, Canada and Australia, have felt constrained to begin the construction of their own fleets at their own expense. In the existing organization of the world an enormous fleet is needed for the protection of an Empire which comprises a fifth of the land of the globe and contains a quarter of its inhabitants; whether that fleet is maintained by the Empire as a whole or by the metropolitan nation is entirely a matter of imperial, as opposed to world, politics. So, from whatever angle the question may be viewed, it is evident that Britain is bound to maintain a navy superior to that of any other Power.

And curiously enough, paradoxically even, Germans on paper conceded this point, which was the fundamental issue in the Anglo-German quarrel! While he was chancellor of the Empire Prince Bülow repeatedly declared that Germany did not aspire to wrest the control of the seas from Great Britain, and in his *Imperial Germany*, written after his retirement, he said: "English policy has remained true to itself up to the present time, because England is still, as she was formerly, the first sea Power." [1] Admiral von Tirpitz was equally positive that Germany had no intention of challenging the supremacy of Great Britain; he renewed the assurance whenever a new navy law added to the strength of the German fleet. Count Reventlow, the well-known naval critic; [2] Herr Ernst Bassermann, the leader of the National Liberal party; [3] and several admirals[4] could be quoted as proof that thinking Germans accepted the necessity for England to maintain a predominant navy. Even more interesting was the admission of the *Kreuzzeitung*, the well-known Conservative paper, the foreign columns of which are edited by Professor Schiemann, the personal friend of the German Emperor.

"England," it wrote on 28 January, 1911, "must protect her enormous imports of food against every disturbance, especially in time of war. Therefore the English Government is compelled to maintain a navy strong enough to open all trade routes, and if possible to blockade all hostile squadrons in their ports in order to protect the British Isles against the danger of starvation and a panic affecting the prices of foodstuffs." [5]

Yet, in spite of these admissions, both official and private, whenever the British Government proposed a limitation of armaments the German reply invariably was that any agreement would have the effect of making the British supremacy permanent! The conclusion can scarcely be avoided that Germany *did* aspire to the admiralty of the

---

[1] P. 33.
[2] "Die englische Seemacht," in *England in deutscher Beleuchtung*, Heft 5, pp. 1–2.
[3] *England and Germany* (1912), p. 149.
[4] E. g., Vice-Admiral Karl Gaster, in *England and Germany*, p. 143.
[5] Quoted by J. Ellis Barker, *Modern Germany* (1912 edition), p. 245.

Atlantic,[1] and that she expected to achieve it. "The maintenance of Great Britain's naval supremacy has become impossible in the future. . . . That is the great historic process which we are witnessing." [2]

With respect to British naval policy in the past, some of the German criticism is justified; but it is scarcely fair to judge the twentieth century by the canons of the seventeenth and eighteenth. Even so, at the time of the Anglo-Dutch wars "England was not yet a great Power; Holland and England fought as rivals and on equal terms, in a feud which subsequent alliances have healed, over a policy which England has long since renounced as mischievous and futile." [3]   The bombardment of Copenhagen in 1807 was a great wrong; in extenuation it may be noted that the British Government had learned of the plan of Napoleon and the Tsar to seize the Danish fleet for use against England.   The high-handed impressment of American seamen for the British navy was one cause of the War of 1812 between England and the United States; but that policy has not been reinvoked in the somewhat similar conditions of a hundred years later.

Since 1815 the British navy has been used with great restraint. Apart from the Crimean War, which was not primarily concerned with European politics, Great Britain kept out of the numerous struggles which occupy so large a page in the history of the nineteenth century. Her naval power has not been used to prevent the legitimate development of any European state, except where British interests have been directly threatened; and she has endeavored to keep that naval power within bounds. Of course, the wide sweep of British interests throughout the world

---

[1] In August, 1902, at Revel, the German Emperor is said to have signalled to the Tsar: "The admiral of the Atlantic greets the admiral of the Pacific."

[2] *Deutschland sei Wach !* (1912), quoted in *Fortnightly Review*, June, 1912.

[3] *Why We Are at War*, by members of the Oxford faculty of modern history (1914), p. 121.

has involved England In many disputes, somo of which were unnecessary or unjustified. But, when all is said, it can be admitted that from 1815 to 1914 the British navy was but twice used for aggressive purposes against a European Power: in 1853, when Great Britain declared war on Russia to prevent the destruction of Turkey, and again in 1878, when she threatened war against the same Power for the same purpose. All things considered, England's record for the nineteenth century is better than that of any Great Power except, perhaps, that of Italy.

When the Anglo-German naval rivalry became acute Germans professed to believe that England would one day pounce upon their fleet as she had upon the Danish in 1807. They could point to the famous article in the *Saturday Review*, to which reference was made in the last chapter. They were told how Mr. Arthur Lee, civil lord of the admiralty in the Balfour government (1902–5) had said at a dinner that England might strike the first blow before Germans had read in the newspapers that war had been declared.[1] The *Army and Navy Gazette* had remarked that "once before we had to snuff out a fleet which we believed might be employed against us," and the *Daily Chronicle*, a Liberal paper, had written that "if the German fleet were destroyed the peace of Europe would be assured for two generations." After the Morocco crisis of 1911, Captain Faber, M.P., asserted that on 18 September the British squadrons were ready to attack the German fleet preparatory to landing a British army in France, and the admiralty admitted that precautionary measures had been taken.[2] And unquestionably there was a feeling in cer-

[1] This and the next two quotations are borrowed from Paul Rohrbach, *Der deutsche Gedanke in der Welt ;* they are reproduced in Prince Bülow's *Imperial Germany*.
[2] 17 November, 1911, at Andover. In December the *Illustrirte Zeitung* (Leipzig) published a series of maps showing the distribution of the British fleet at different times in the summer of 1911. In none of them is the fleet represented as concentrated in the North Sea. Vice-Admiral Karl Gaster ridiculed the idea that a surprise attack was being planned. (*England and Germany*, p. 145.)

tain English circles that, "if England were ever going to check the rapidly growing German navy, the sooner she did it the better, before it got any larger; the smashing would be easier now than later."[1] Germans were, perhaps, the more inclined to ascribe such madness to England because it seemed to them a natural proceeding, thoroughly in keeping with those Bismarckian traditions which dominated the policy of their own foreign office.[2] But England wisely refused to listen to its jingoes, who were splendidly described as "false guides, bad strategists, and worse statesmen."[3] In August, 1905, Mr. (now Lord) Bryce, after a consultation with the leading men of both political parties, assured Germany that "no English politician of standing, no leader in any department of English thought, had the slightest idea of a war with Germany, or would contemplate its advocacy by reckless writers with anything but abhorrence and dismay."[4]

Such evidence, however, is no more conclusive than similar statements by representative Germans that Eng-

[1] Edwin D. Mead, "England and Germany," *Atlantic Monthly*, March, 1908. Thus Sir Edmund C. Cox ("England and Germany: How to Meet the Crisis," *Nineteenth Century*, April, 1910) demanded an ultimatum to Germany that she should stop the construction of her fleet. "Not a shot need be fired. . . . The whole of Europe, with the exception of Austria, would gladly support England in an ultimatum demanding the instant cessation of this universal danger." "An Englishman" (*The German Menace and How to Meet It*, 1911) proposed "a diplomatic notification to Germany that her naval programme will be interpreted as indicative of intended conflict with this nation and must be arrested. It would be notified to Germany that an agreement must be come to without delay, limiting the strength of her navy: that failing such an agreement the laying down of any batteships after a given date would be regarded by this country as a *casus belli*. If this notification were disregarded and further *Dreadnoughts* were laid down after the specified date, war would be declared, and Germany's naval power and mercantile marine, as they now exist, would, in six months, become things of the past " (p. 33). One would have thought that Englishmen were sufficiently aware of Napoleon's failure in restricting the Prussian army after Jena to forego another such experiment.

[2] Æneas O'Neill, "Six German Opinions on the Naval Situation," *Nineteenth Century*, May, 1909; R. C. Long, "Naval Armament Delusions," *Fortnightly Review*, January, 1910.

[3] Spenser Wilkinson, *Britain at Bay*, p. 102.

[4] *Nation* (New York), 17 August, 1905.

land had no reason to fear an attack from Germany.
Much more to the point is the policy pursued by the British Government. At least twice since the tension with
Germany controlled its international relations the United
Kingdom could have precipitated a war with Germany
had it been so minded: in 1908 over the Bosnian crisis,
and again in 1911 in the last stages of the Morocco dispute. Each year that passed decreased the superiority
of the British fleet over that of Germany, yet Great Britain
did not strike, and, as will be seen in a later chapter,
she was ready to pledge herself never to undertake a war
of aggression against Germany. And surely, if Great Britain had desired war with Germany, she would not have
striven so manfully for peace in the last days of July, 1914,
would not have withheld any promise of assistance to France
until the latter had received an ultimatum from Germany.

Equally important for the student of history, is the consistent refusal of successive British governments to create
a military establishment on Continental models. At any
time after 1896 war with Germany was a possibility. Now,
whenever England has been involved in European wars in
the past, the decision has invariably been secured by land
warfare. In many cases the pressure of the British fleet
has seriously reduced the fighting capacity of the enemy,
but it has never won Great Britain's victories. Napoleon
was overthrown by the campaign in Spain and the "crowning mercy" of Waterloo, and similarly England could not
defeat Germany by merely destroying her fleet. Nevertheless, the British army for service abroad was not increased above 160,000 men—a mere bagatelle compared
with the hosts of Germany. For home defense a territorial
army of about 300,000 volunteers, reorganized by Lord
Haldane in 1907, was deemed sufficient, and even that
force never reached its legal establishment.[1] Yet in spite

[1] Duke of Bedford, "The Territorial Force Fiasco," *Nineteenth Century*, June, 1913.

of the agitation ably conducted by the late Lord Roberts for some kind of universal military service, in spite of the fact that in the fleet manœuvres of 1912 the "enemy" succeeded in landing an armed force on the east coast, both the government and public opinion resisted the propaganda of the military party, on the grounds that even Great Britain could not maintain both a supreme navy and a conscript army,[1] and that such an army would everywhere be regarded as the proof of aggressive intentions and would indeed stimulate British diplomacy to an aggressive policy.   A nation bent on war would not have neglected its preparations to such an extent that when war did come the conduct of operations would have been seriously hampered by the utter lack of supplies and munitions of every kind, such as was actually revealed in the winter of 1914–15.

Lastly, we come to the question whether England should frankly have accepted the frequent German asseverations that their fleet was meant only for defense.   In other words, is there any reason for believing that the German navy was a positive danger to England?   Germans often complained that, although until very recently the American navy was stronger than their own, English opinion never used hard words about *it*, never looked upon *it* as a menace to their liberties and their happiness.[2]   To begin with, Englishmen were profoundly impressed by the achievements of Bismarckian diplomacy.   In their eyes, the great chancellor had isolated diplomatically, then attacked, and finally despoiled—for the profit of Prussia—Denmark, Austria, and France, in turn;   they were aware that a noisy section of the German people clamored for a repetition in the twentieth century of the exploits of 1864–71, and regarded war,

---

[1] *Edinburgh Review*, April, 1913; "An Islander," *The Naval and Military Policy of the British Isles* (1913); J. A. Spender, *The Foundations of British Policy* (1912); J. L. Garvin, in *England and Germany*, p. 82.

[2] This is a favorite idea of Dr. Paul Rohrbach, and finds expression in his various books.

In Mirabeau's phrase, as the "national industry." It was notorious that the Pan-German League represented England as the great obstacle to the realization of its ambitions, and that the Navy League, which was little more than a department of the German Government,[1] openly pointed to the British fleet as the main reason for increasing the German navy. There was the widely believed story that in the wardroom messes of the German navy the favorite toast was "To the Day!" that is, the day when the Kaiser's fleet should engage that of his Britannic Majesty for the mastery of the seas. Likewise, the Emperor's famous dictum, "Our future lies on the water," had for British ears an ominous ring. To some extent Englishmen's nerves were certainly affected, but the cumulative effect of innumerable expressions of Anglophobia in Germany, the circumstances in which the German fleet was constructed, and the generally hostile tone of German foreign policy from 1896 to 1912 were admirably calculated to inspire a strictly commercial people with a genuine dread, not to say positive terror, of the most military and efficient nation in the world.

In the second place, many Englishmen believed that Germany actually contemplated an invasion of England. It has been stated that "the British Government, by those means which are always open to the Power ready to pay for information, came into the possession of a matured scheme for the invasion of this country which had not only been submitted to the German Government, but had been adopted as a plan of campaign that could be put into

[1] Prominent government officials were responsible for its organization and have always held the chief offices; private patronage is a sure road to official favor; the Reichsmarineamt supplies it with information and the Emperor has more than once interfered in its affairs. Its membership fluctuates around a million, in striking contrast with the private Navy League of England, which numbers about 20,000. *Die Flotte*, its monthly journal, is said to have the largest circulation of any paper in Germany. *Cf.* Hurd and Castle, *German Sea Power*, pp. 207–213; J. Ellis Barker, *Modern Germany*, pp. 324–344.

operation at almost any moment with the minimum of ostentation and the maximum probability of success." [1] At a time when the British fleet was away from the North Sea a military force was to be embarked in the steamers always available in German harbors and convoyed to the Humber. At the same time the high-seas fleet would seize Dover. The landing force would then march across England to Liverpool and by paralyzing the industrial life of Lancashire dictate peace to the British Government.

Whether this plan was more than one of the campaigns which the German general staff had worked out for war against any country there is no way of knowing; and as the British military authorities had for some years before the war consulted with those of France and Belgium with reference to joint operations in case of a war with Germany, the mere existence of a German plan of campaign against England cannot be considered proof of hostile intentions. What did make the matter serious was the frequency with which the possibility of invading England was discussed by German military and political writers, and the confidence they expressed that such an undertaking was quite feasible. [2] For many years the question was vigorously debated in the English press, and the Balfour government thought the problem serious enough to have it discussed by the committee of imperial defense. Gradually the view that "a serious invasion of these islands is not a possibility which we need consider" was accepted, [3] although the danger of a "sudden raid" was officially admitted. [4] The relatively long time required by Italy to transport her Tripolitan expedition across the Mediterranean doubtless lulled popular

---

[1] Hislam, *Admiralty of the Atlantic*, p. 75.

[2] *Ibid.*, p. 144; Edelsheim, *Operationen über See*, translated in Barker, *Modern Germany*, pp. 345 ff.; Rudolf Martin, *Deutschland und England* (1908).

[3] Mr. Balfour, House of Commons, 11 May, 1905. (4 *Hansard* cxlvi, c. 77.)

[4] The secretary of the admiralty, House of Commons, 5 March, 1907. (4 *Hansard* clxx, c. 662.)

suspicions.[1] In 1912 the admiralty took the unusual step of publishing, over the initials of the first sea lord, a reasoned argument against the possibility of invasion, on the condition, of course, that British naval supremacy was maintained.[2] But if that supremacy were surrendered, then all was lost, for not even an invasion would be required to humble Britain in the dust; she could be starved into submission.

Lastly, when the purely defensive theory of the German navy was examined, it was noted that the German coast was already defended against the landing of an English army. The German fleet could not protect German commerce on the high seas, because that function appertained to fast cruisers, of which Germany had built few, and because the necessary coaling stations were conspicuously lacking. Germany had no point of contact with Japan or the United States; naval operations against Russia or France would be of little use, and their fleets were far from formidable. Yet a war armada like the German high-seas fleet was not built for nothing: by process of elimination, England must be its objective.[3] It would be too much to say that Englishmen really believed Germany to be meditating an unprovoked attack upon their country, although they undoubtedly feared that such might be the case. Their feeling simply was that they must be prepared for the worst, and their political instinct told them that "the moment the German navy became strong enough to confront that of Great Britain without risk of destruction British influence in Europe would be at an end, and the Continent would have to follow the direction given by

[1] *Cf.* Archibald Hurd, "Italy's Bolt from the Blue," *Fortnightly Review*, December, 1911.
[2] As an appendix to the second edition of Sir Ian Hamilton's *Compulsory Service.* The first sea lord was Sir Arthur Knyvet Wilson.
[3] *Naval Supremacy: Who?* (1908); *Edinburgh Review*, April, 1912; Captain Hartwig Schubert, *Die deutsche Schlachtflotte eine Gefahr für Deutschlands Machtstellung* (1911).

German policy." [1]   After that Germany could subdue England at her leisure and convenience.   To quote Admiral Mahan:

"The British navy is left the sole military force in the world superior to anything that Germany can as yet bring into the field. . . . This removed, neutral, or fallen in power, Germany, under present anticipations, which accord with reasonable probabilities, becomes the dominant naval state of the world, as well as the predominant country of Europe." [2]

Here, indeed, is the root of the whole controversy.   Britain never aimed at, never acquired, the hegemony of Europe: Germany did dominate the Continent; and whatever her precise ambitions might be, the world would lie at her feet if she secured the control of the seas as well.

The British view was well formulated by two eminent statesmen, one an ex-prime minister, the other a leading member of the present government.   In a letter written for the German magazine *Nord und Süd* in May, 1912, Mr. Balfour said:

"If recent years have produced a change in the way in which ordinary Englishmen judge of German policy, it is due to no national prejudice, to no underestimate of German worth, to no want of gratitude for German services in the cause of universal culture. . . . If Englishmen were sure that a German fleet were only going to be used for defensive purposes, *i. e.*, against aggression, they would not care how large it was. . . . But does Germany make it easy for Britain to take this view?   The external facts of the situation appear to be as follows: the greatest military Power and the second greatest naval Power in the world is adding to both her army and her navy. . . . It is conceivable that all this may be only in order to render herself impregnable against attack.   But unfortunately no mere analysis of the German preparations for war will show for what purposes they are designed.   A tremendous weapon has been forged; every year adds something to its efficiency and power; it is as formidable for purposes of aggression as for

[1] Spenser Wilkinson, *Britain at Bay*, p. 93.
[2] *Interest of America in International Conditions*, pp. 67, 68.

purposes of defense. But to what end it was originally designed, and in what causes it will ultimately be used, can only be determined, if determined at all, by extraneous considerations. . . .

"The danger lies in the coexistence of that marvellous instrument of warfare which is the German army and navy, with the assiduous, I had almost said the organized, advocacy of a policy which it seems impossible to reconcile with the peace of the world or the rights of nations. For those who accept this policy German development means German territorial expansion. All countries which hinder, though it be only in self-defense, the realization of this ideal, are regarded as hostile; and war, or the threat of war, is deemed the natural and fitting method by which the ideal itself is to be accomplished."

Disclaiming any intention to criticise the theories held and preached by German students, Mr. Balfour went on:

"Do not let them ask Englishmen to approve. We have had too bitter an experience of the ills which flow from the endeavor of any single state to dominate Europe; we are too surely convinced of the perils which such a policy, were it successful, would bring upon ourselves as well as upon others, to treat them as negligible." [1]

In a speech to the House of Commons on 27 November, 1911, Sir Edward Grey remarked.

"German strength is by itself a guarantee that no other country will desire or seek a quarrel with Germany. That is one side of the shield of which the Germans may well be proud. But I think it ought to be remembered by German public opinion that there is another side of the shield, and that if a nation has the biggest army in the world, if it has a very big navy and is going on to build a still bigger navy, then it must do all in its power to prevent what would otherwise be natural apprehensions in the minds of others who have no aggressive intentions against that Power, lest that Power with its army and navy should have aggressive intentions toward them."

Without positively ascribing such intentions to Germany, Sir Edward added:

[1] Reprinted in *England and Germany*, pp. 1-7.

"I think it must be realized that other nations would be apprehensive and sensitive, and, of course, will be on the lookout for any indication of aggressive intentions." [1]

No responsible Englishman denied the right of Germany to build as large a fleet as she could man and pay for; what was wanted was an assurance that such a fleet would not be used aggressively against England, for German policy seemed to point in such a direction.   That assurance Germany would never give, although the British Government was willing to undertake most solemnly never to be a party to aggression upon Germany.   It is in the light of this circumstance that we must now consider which of the two rivals—England or Germany—was responsible for the burden of modern naval armaments.

The German thesis from the first has been that her navy was being built to further the interests of Germany, without regard to the size of other navies—if Great Britain chose to build two battleships for every one laid down in Germany, the fault was hers; if she found the burden intolerable, the remedy was to abandon the two-Power standard.   Even English radicals and social reformers took much the same ground,[2] and Sir Edward Grey admitted that England built the first *Dreadnought*.[3]

But Germany's case would be infinitely stronger if she had been willing to negotiate upon the matter of disarmament.   As it was, she invariably took refuge behind her navy laws, which she alleged could not be changed without the consent of the Reichstag; as if the British programme was not subject to the approval of Parliament, and as if the Reichstag was not frequently called upon to

---

[1] 5 *Hansard* xxxii, cc. 59–60. As an illustration of Sir Edward Grey's criticism, Germany in 1911 fixed her army establishment for the next five years, and declared that her navy was satisfactory; the chancellor said that Germany was at peace with all the world, but quite ready for war if it were forced upon her. Yet in 1912 she increased her army and passed a new navy law.

[2] *E. g.*, F. W. Hirst, *The Six Panics* (1913).   [3] Manchester, 3 February, 1914.

change the existing laws *in an upward direction!* As for the two-Power standard, it first appears *eo nomine* in the Naval Defense Act of 1889; but its principle had been acted upon ever since the Napoleonic wars. Neither France nor Russia, which nations were usually hostile to Great Britain throughout the nineteenth century, had found the British supremacy of the seas injurious to them, primarily because, in spite of innumerable disputes with Great Britain, both perceived that the British navy was the bulwark of the European balance of power.

An analysis of the programmes of construction and of the moneys voted for that purpose shows clearly that British policy, viewed over a period of twenty years, was remarkably constant, in marked contrast with that of Germany:

BATTLESHIP CONSTRUCTION

Period	Great Britain	Average	Germany	Average
1889–1898............	30	3	9	$\frac{9}{10}$
1898–1905............	23	$2\frac{7}{8}$	15	$1\frac{7}{8}$
1905–1909............	12	3	11	$2\frac{3}{4}$

Or take the amounts voted for new construction, which is the real key to naval expenditure:

Year	Great Britain	Battleships	Germany	Battleships
1901–1902........	£10,341,780	3	£4,653,423	2
1902–1903........	9,282,217	2	4,662,769	2
1903–1904........	12,398,133	5	4,388,748	2
1904–1905........	13,184,419	2	4,275,489	2
1905–1906........	11,368,744	4	4,720,206	2
1906–1907........	10,480,397	3	5,167,319	2
1907–1908........	8,849,589	3	5,910,959	3
1908–1909........	8,521,930	2	7,795,499	4

Thus Great Britain, up to 1909, took little notice, in concrete fashion, of the development of the German navy;

she built, on the average, approximately the same number of ships annually, before and after 1898, and the expenditure for new construction showed a persistent tendency to diminish.

For the five years preceding the Great War it is more difficult to form an impartial judgment. The figures are as follows:

Year	GREAT BRITAIN			GERMANY		
	Construction	Ships	Person-nel	Construction	Ships	Person-nel
1909–1910..	£11,227,194	8	127,968	£10,177,068	4	53,946
1910–1911..	14,957,430	5	130,817	11,392,850	4	57,373
1911–1912..	17,566,877	5	132,792	11,710,859	4	60,805
1912–1913..	17,271,317	4	136,443	11,393,340	4	66,810
1913–1914..	17,361,850	5	142,500	10,719,787	3	73,176
1914–1915..	18,676,080	4	151,000*	19,902,859	2	79,386

The German estimates do not include votes for aeronautics; the British estimates have *exceeded* the actual payments for construction by amounts ranging from £200,000 to £2,000,000.

* Estimated number.

The verdict must depend largely upon the point of view. If the German contention be accepted,—that British sea power is simply piracy brought up to date,—then the addition of 31 *Dreadnoughts* and *super-Dreadnoughts* to the first dozen was a crime against humanity and an unnecessary burden upon a country as heavily taxed as modern England.   On the other hand, those who believe that the growing German fleet was a positive danger to the United Kingdom and the British Empire—and a large number of Englishmen did so believe—will acquit the British Government of reckless extravagance, and will argue in good conscience that an abdication of British naval superiority would have been a premium upon stupidity, a confession of cowardice, an act of treason; more especially as the British Government made repeated efforts to keep its naval expenditure within bounds, but invariably encountered the obstinate refusal of Germany to discuss even the principle of disarmament.

It is not out of place to remember, in conclusion, that nothing succeeds like success. Prince Bülow, in his *Imperial Germany*, argues that the entry of Germany into the world politics of the twentieth century was made possible by the building of her fleet, and that she had gained both profit and glory in the adventure.[1] What are the facts? Between 1884 and 1899, during which period the German fleet was a *quantité négligéable*, Germany secured all the colonies she possessed at the opening of the Great War, with the exception of what was surrendered by France in 1911 in return for a protectorate over Morocco. Between 1900 and 1914, while the German fleet was building, England disarmed the French opposition in Egypt; France secured Morocco; Italy seized Tripoli; Austria-Hungary regularized her position in Bosnia; Russia practically annexed northern Manchuria and established a protectorate over Mongolia. Even the little Balkan states despoiled the unspeakable Turk, who was the cherished friend of Germany. Spain received part of Morocco, and Belgium the Congo as the legatee of King Leopold. Germany alone got nothing, or next to nothing, for the Congo concessions of 1911 did not satisfy her appetite. Whether or not the Powers of the Triple Entente were responsible for this starvation of a hungry nation, it is evident that the German fleet produced no adequate return upon the colossal sums borrowed for its construction; nor has it been of appreciable value to Germany in the conduct of the war. Judged by the standard of results, the whole policy associated with naval expansion has been a lamentable failure, and a blunder for which Germany is paying by the participation of Great Britain in the Great War.

[1] P. 119.

CHAPTER IX

THE TRIPLE ENTENTE

THE ten years from 1904 to 1914 form one of the most stormy periods in the history of European diplomacy. Four times did the spectre of war stalk across the horizon— in the summer of 1905, in the winter of 1908–9, again in the summer of 1911, and lastly in the winter of 1912–13. In not all of these crises were the interests of Great Britain directly affected; yet because indirectly her position in the world and her honor as a Great Power were called in question, she was an active participant on each occasion, and the experience and knowledge she thereby gained of German policy was the secondary cause of her ultimatum to Germany in August, 1914. Three of the four disputes found England and Germany in opposite camps, and as crisis followed crisis, it became increasingly clear that the real issue was a test of strength between the two Powers, however much disguised by the circumstances of the moment.

Anglo-German relations became strained in the early years of the twentieth century, or in the last years of the nineteenth if the first symptoms of hostility be considered, because two great questions hitherto distinct were fused into a single issue. Those questions were the balance of power in Europe and the division of certain non-European lands which had thus far escaped effective penetration or absorption by white men. From 1870 Germany dominated the Continent of Europe, whereas she took but a limited interest in the problem of expansion; France and Russia, on the other hand, pursued an active colonial policy, which involved many disputes with Great Britam. Hence a policy of splendid isolation commended itself to British statesmen of both political parties. But when with the accession of William II to the throne Germany began to manifest an intense interest in the disposition of unappropriated lands, when the increase of her population, the accumulation of wealth, and the heaping up of great military and naval armaments threatened to overturn the balance of power in her favor, and when the direction of her policy became unmistakably anti-British, it was inevitable, first, that England should emerge from the isolation by drawing closer to one or more Continental Powers; and, second, that Germany should encounter the opposition of the island Power on every hand. For the moment the question may be passed whether the British attitude was offensive or defensive: it is sufficient to recognize that the ramifications of Anglo-German rivalry were endless and that the peace of the world was bound up with the issue of their antagonism.

The real cause of that hostility was, of course, the development of the German navy. To the pacifist and the advocate of disarmament, the danger to either Power from the navy of the other seemed to belong distinctly to the future, and for that reason he could not or would not admit the reality of the latent conflict. Yet the question has a very practical bearing upon the policy of each country, as Prince Bülow has rather naïvely confessed.

"The fleet was to be built," he writes in his *Imperial Germany*, "while we maintained our position on the Continent, without our coming into conflict with England, whom we could not as yet oppose at sea, but also while we preserved intact our national honor and dignity."

Or again:

"Patriotic feeling must not be roused to such an extent as to damage irreparably our relations with England, against whom our sea power would for years still be insufficient."

And *à propos* of the Boer War:

"Our navy was not strong enough for us forcibly to achieve a sufficient sea power in the teeth of English interests." [1]

Whatever may be thought of British sea power, Great Britain can scarcely be blamed for taking every precaution to meet the challenge of the German navy; for she believed the maintenance of her supremacy to be absolutely vital to her safety.

In the chapter on "German Expansion" it was pointed out that German colonial ambitions were to be satisfied, so far as may be guessed, in Morocco and Asia Minor. For reasons that will presently be set forth, a complete success of the German plans as regards those regions would prejudice England's interests severely, either by cutting into her trade, or by leaving her isolated diplomatically. Germany was fully entitled to carry through her schemes if she could, and the impression one gets from a study of her policy is that she aimed to present England with *faits accomplis*, which are the strongest arguments in the armory of diplomacy. Unfortunately for Germany, England refused to be taken by surprise, and endeavored to block the German designs in one way or another. Some will have it that British policy was dictated by jealousy. In any case, the interests of the two countries were for many years frankly contrary, and for that reason diplomatic tension was inevitable; which fact made difficult, if not impossible, a sincere co-operation in those fields where there was no conflict of interests.

Another factor in the situation was the attitude of public opinion in both countries, which had been lashed to fury by the Boer War and its attendant circumstances. Repeated efforts were made to restore confidence, and no little success had been achieved; so much, indeed, that

[1] *Imperial Germany*, pp. 23, 24, 38.

until the violation of Belgian neutrality English opinion
was far from convinced that English intervention in the
war was necessary.   But up to 1912 the difficulties of Downing Street and Wilhelmstrasse were certainly enhanced by
the conviction of many sections of both peoples that war
was inevitable.

The emergence of Great Britain from her cherished isolation was a gradual rather than a sudden development,
and was accomplished against her wishes and in spite of
repeated attempts to prevent it.   A more melancholy fact
can hardly be imagined than that the Anglo-French reconciliation of 1904, designed to secure a lasting peace between
England and France, should prove one of the main causes
of war between England and Germany!

The *entente* between England and France was the work
of three men: M. Delcassé, French minister for foreign
affairs from 1898 to 1905;   Mr. Thomas Barclay, sometime
president of the British chamber of commerce in Paris,
and the late King Edward VII.   Upon taking over the
Quai d'Orsay in November, 1898, when the Fashoda incident was still fresh in men's minds, M. Delcassé said to
M. Victor Bérard, the noted publicist: "I do not intend
to leave this office until I have re-established good relations
with England." [1]   Six years passed before the definitive
conventions were signed, but the thoroughly correct attitude of the French foreign office during the Boer War,
when there were rumors of an anti-English coalition, paved
the way.   Queen Victoria was decidedly pro-German in
her sympathies, and Lord Salisbury entertained a deep
distrust of all things French.   These obstacles were removed by the death of the Queen in 1901 and the retirement of Lord Salisbury from the ministry in July, 1902,
and in the late summer of 1902 M. Delcassé made over-

[1] Victor Bérard, *La France et Guillaume II* (1907), p. 23.

tures to London for a joint settlement of the Egyptian and Moroccan questions. Lord Lansdowne was sympathetic, but the South African situation and a dispute with Venezuela postponed active negotiations until the summer of 1903.[1]

Meanwhile unofficial influences were at work. In the summer of 1899 Mr. (now Sir Thomas) Barclay determined to bring about a reconciliation between England and France. At his suggestion, and with the cordial approval of the French Government, the chambers of commerce of the United Kingdom held their annual meeting in Paris during the exposition of 1900 as guests of the British chamber of commerce, and from that time Englishmen flocked to the exposition in great numbers. Mr. Barclay then began a campaign in favor of an arbitration treaty between England and France, in which he enlisted the enthusiastic support of the chambers of commerce and the trade unions of both countries. It was no small undertaking to break down the prejudices of centuries and the time-honored belief in both countries that their respective interests were conflicting; and not the least obstacle was the attitude of Sir Edmund Monson, the British ambassador in Paris, who did not consider a *rapprochement* possible and possessed a capacity for making tactless speeches. But in the end provincial opinion on both sides of the Channel was converted. Only the two capitals remained suspicious. Finally, in May, 1903, King Edward, who as Prince of Wales had been adored by the Parisian populace and who was an ardent admirer of France, visited Paris and was respectfully received. The return visit of President Loubet in July was an even greater success, so that it only remained for the two governments to translate their friendly sentiments into concrete agreements.[2]

[1] William Morton Fullerton, *Problems of Power* (1913), p. 57.
[2] For the history of the *entente cordiale*, see Sir Thomas Barclay, *Thirty Years' Reminiscences*, 1876–1906, especially pp. 175–326.

This was done by the arbitration treaty of 14 October, 1903, and the epoch-making political conventions of 8 April, 1904. The details of these treaties have been given in the chapter on "Modern England," and need not be here recited; nor will their historical importance lie in the fact that the two countries adjusted sundry colonial disputes in various parts of the world. A perspective of only ten years was needed to show that the *entente cordiale* marked a new period in recent history, the chief characteristic of which, internationally considered, was the freedom enjoyed by both France and England in their dealings with Germany. Such freedom was the more desirable because the outbreak of the Russo-Japanese War, in February, 1904, deprived France of any possible assistance from her ally, and for practical purposes left Germany in absolute control of the Continent.

The balance of Europe was restored by the *entente*, as Prince Bülow subsequently admitted, but this was apparently the result rather than the cause of the *entente*. There was nothing in the conventions themselves, which were being negotiated before the war in the Far East, to indicate any *arrière-pensée* toward Germany, and they were obviously designed simply to end the long strife between France and England. Lord Lansdowne "strongly repudiated the assumption that because there had been an approximation between Britain and two great and friendly Powers, there must necessarily be an estrangement between ourselves and any other Power or Powers." [1] To the German ambassador in Paris the Anglo-French arrangement seemed "perfectly natural," [2] and his government declared its acceptance of what was regarded as a new pledge and guarantee of the peace of the world. Prince Bülow's remarks in the Reichstag, on 12 April, 1904, are conclusive of Germany's opinion at the time.

---

[1] 6 November, 1905; quoted in *Annual Register*, 1905, p. 228.
[2] French Yellow Book, *Affaires du Maroc*, 1901–1905, p. 122.

"We have no cause," he said, "to apprehend that this agreement was levelled against any individual Power. It seems to be an attempt to eliminate the points of difference between France and Great Britain by means of an amicable understanding. From the point of view of German interests we have nothing to complain of, for we do not wish to see strained relations between Great Britain and France, if only because such a state of affairs would imperil the peace of the world, the maintenance of which we sincerely desire."

"There was another reason why Germany would rather welcome than find fault with the agreement. The general impression in Germany throughout 1904 was that the *rapprochement* between France and Great Britain tended to weaken the alliance between France and Russia. Any enduring friendship with both, owing to existing political conditions in both the Middle and Far East, seemed impossible. The public excitement in England caused by the Dogger Bank affair and the exploits of the Russian cruisers *Petersburg* and *Smolensk* accentuated, if anything, this impression."[1] As it turned out, the German assumption that England and Russia were of necessity hostile and irreconcilable, an assumption that governed the weekly reviews of foreign politics written by Professor Theodor Schiemann for the *Kreuzzeitung*, was to prove Germany's undoing, for when England and Russia made up their differences Germany had no policy prepared to meet the new situation, and the ultimate result of that deficiency was the war of 1914.

Thus the *entente cordiale* of 1904 augured well for the peace of the world. Yet it must be recognized that the agreement commended itself to the public opinion of both France and England, and to their respective foreign offices, because at the very least each country would enjoy a free hand against Germany, and might, in certain contingencies, count on the diplomatic support of the other.[2] Ger-

[1] Barclay, *Thirty Years' Reminiscences*, p. 261.
[2] This is admitted by Sydney Brooks, "England and Germany," *Atlantic Monthly*, May, 1910, p. 624.

mans subsequently convinced themselves that M. Delcassé's policy was inspired solely by the desire to secure British support in a war of revenge, and that King Edward VII was at the bottom of a matured scheme to effect the diplomatic isolation of Germany.[1] Here, then, was a situation full of dangerous possibilities. Would either France or England, or both of them, pursue an aggressive policy toward Germany? or would the latter endeavor to break up the new friendship before it had been consolidated as an effective force against a German hegemony of Europe? In either case the peace of Europe was bound to be seriously threatened; so that the agreement concluded between Great Britain and France for the purpose of avoiding war on account of numerous questions in which they were both interested actually opened up the vista of war between one or both of them and Germany!

As it happened the initiative in testing the new situation came from Germany. Although she had raised no objection to the Anglo-French convention at the time of its publication, even though it had not been formally communicated to her,[2] the prospect of a permanent reconciliation between the two old enemies was far from pleasing to her; for her colonial policy had hitherto profited from the jealousy of London and Paris, not to mention her ascendency in Europe. But when the Russian armies, in February, 1905, met defeat at Mukden, it was obvious that France could expect no assistance from her ally in case of trouble with Germany. The temptation was too strong for the latter. Count von Bülow, the chancellor, stated in the Reichstag that Germany was ignorant of any agree-

[1] *Inter alia*, Dr. Paul Rohrbach, *Deutschland unter den Weltvölkern*, pp. 243–247. Innumerable references could be cited.

[2] The British Government notified the Powers of its undertakings with respect to Egypt. France unofficially informed Germany of the Moroccan clauses of the agreement, and the latter made no protest at the time. Personal motives seem to have inspired M. Delcassé in neglecting the formal communication to Germany.

ments as to Morocco recently made between France and England, and to reinforce the position Emperor William II appeared at Tangier on 31 March, 1905, where he spoke to this effect:

"It is to the Sultan in his position of an independent sovereign that I am paying my visit to-day. I hope that under the sovereignty of the Sultan a free Morocco will remain, open to the peaceful rivalry of all nations, without monopoly or annexation, on the basis of absolute equality. The object of my visit to Tangier is to make it known that I am determined to do all that is in my power to safeguard efficaciously the interests of Germany in Morocco, for I look upon the Sultan as an absolutely independent sovereign."

This speech produced the most serious diplomatic crisis that Europe had known since thirty years before, when a Franco-German war was threatened by the attitude of the German military party. For Germany now challenged the principle of the Anglo-French convention, that "it appertains to France, more particularly as a Power whose dominions are coterminous for a great distance with those of Morocco, to preserve order in that country and to provide assistance for the purpose of all administrative, economic, financial, and military reforms which it may require." [1] In brief, Germany demanded that Morocco be placed under international control, while France seemed disposed to insist upon her ascendency in its affairs. As the French policy was peculiarly the work of M. Delcassé, a German ultimatum that France should consent to the meeting of an international conference was tantamount to a demand for the dismissal of the Republic's foreign minister, and was so regarded, both then and since. France, unable to face a war with her mighty neighbor, yielded, and Germany seemed to have scored a distinct triumph at the expense of the new *entente*, for, although the British Government was willing to assist France by landing

[1] Anglo-French Declaration (public), Art. II.

100,000 troops in Schleswig Holstein, the French cabinet declined to support M. Delcassé in a policy of resistance, and he resigned.[1]   After long negotiations, extending over the summer of 1905, it was arranged between France and Germany that the conference should meet at Algeciras, opposite Gibraltar on the Spanish mainland, in January, 1906.

Inasmuch as the agreement with France only bound the British Government to afford its "diplomatic support" to obtain the execution of the Morocco clauses, it is not surprising that Germany considered the offer of military assistance an evidence of England's unfriendliness, and that there was a renewed outburst of Anglophobia in the German press toward the end of 1905.   The Morocco question was, indeed, one of the few definite issues between the two countries, although Great Britain was not involved as a principal.   It is therefore necessary to explain what the problem was, and, if possible, to express some opinion as to the merits of the controversy.

Morocco, or the Shereefian Empire, was the last independent state of Africa Minor, as the southern littoral of the Mediterranean is sometimes called.   In the course of the nineteenth century all the surrounding regions had been appropriated by European Powers, and by 1900 the frontier of Morocco marched with that of the French possessions, except in the extreme south, where it touched a Spanish colony.   The government was no more successful than that of Mohammedan states elsewhere; the country was, in fact, a feudal state of the variety to be found in

---

[1] A special envoy, Prince Henckel von Donnersmarck, was sent to Paris by the German Government to warn the prime minister, M. Rouvier, that M. Delcassé was *persona non grata* to Germany, and that both the interests of France and the peace of Europe required his dismissal.   So the *Gaulois* (Paris) in June, 1905. M. Delcassé took his revenge by disclosing in the *Matin*, in October following, the details of the British offer of assistance.

Europe about the year 1000. Geographical divisions worked against national unity, even if there had not been many strong tribes much addicted to fighting and a tradition of corruption which prevented the working out of an efficient administrative system. Even the strongest sultans could maintain some semblance of order only by travelling about the Empire and quartering themselves upon powerful tribal chieftains. The last great ruler was Mulai Hassan, who died in 1894, and had prevented excessive European interference by protecting such Europeans as resided in the land for purposes of commerce; his policy, however, was continued by the grand vizier, Ben Hamed, down to 1901, when death removed the one man who understood the situation clearly.

The Sultan Abdel Assiz achieved considerable notoriety by his addiction to photography and other refinements of European life. But civilization led to bankruptcy, which could be liquidated only by European assistance; and tribal restlessness, culminating in the revolt of El Rogui in 1903, created a dangerous and difficult position for European residents. As the land had long been the arena of European intrigue without falling a prey to it, the unhappy Sultan was likely to be overwhelmed by applications from Powers anxious to give his country their respective types of colonial organization.

Historically Spain enjoyed the greatest interest in Morocco, on account of the long struggle between Christianity and Islam for the control of the Iberian peninsula. But at the opening of the twentieth century her holdings were confined to four *presidios* on the Mediterranean littoral and a small settlement on the Atlantic coast. Her friendship with Great Britain guaranteed that no other Power would be allowed to secure the Mediterranean coast lest it be used as a balance to Gibraltar.

Great Britain's interest was entirely commercial, except

that she could not tolerate an occupation by a hostile Power which might control either the Suez or the South African route to India. She had several times tried to secure reforms in the Shereefian Government, but, failing that, was content with some forty per cent of the trade of Morocco. Her diplomatic agents and her merchants enjoyed the confidence of the Sultan, who regarded the English friendship as the surest barrier to the introduction of European influences; so that in 1901 a protectorate was practically offered to the British Government.

The Power with a vital interest in the future of Morocco was France. Ever since Algeria became a French colony the anarchy which reigned on the Morocco-Algerian frontier had been a constant source of trouble; also of profit, for by perpetuating the disorder the French Government provided itself with a convenient excuse for intervening in Morocco should a favorable occasion ever arise. After the occupation of the last Sahara oases in the 'nineties, Morocco came to be regarded as the keystone of the French African Empire, and the colonial party in France openly avowed its desire for a French protectorate, or for an annexation, if possible. French commerce stood second to that of Great Britain, being reckoned at about twenty per cent. And some patriots, keenly aware of the ever increasing discrepancy of France and Germany in population, looked forward to the time when the Republic might use African troops to supply the deficiency of the regular army; for which purpose the fighting tribesmen of Morocco would be of great value. Furthermore, in the event of a European war, the position of France throughout northern Africa might be seriously compromised by the activities of Mohammedan secret societies operating from an independent Morocco. On the whole, therefore, France's moral claim to the reversion of the Shereefian Empire may be fairly admitted.

There remained Germany, who was not disposed to allow her western neighbor a free hand in dealing with the
decaying Moorish state, partly because of her own definite
interests therein, partly because, as the Emperor once remarked, "without Germany and the German Emperor, no
important step in international policy should be taken,
even beyond the seas."[1] Unfortunately, it is well-nigh impossible to determine whether the German Government
ever had a definite policy as regards Morocco itself, for its
conduct in the years 1905–11 was curiously inconsistent.
Prince Bülow repeatedly stated that the interests of Germany were purely economic, and that she would be content
if the open door and the sovereignty of the Sultan were
adequately maintained. At the end of the last century
German commerce with Morocco amounted to only nine
per cent of the total trade, but it was displaying the usual
German energy and was rapidly increasing. Well aware
that the French occupation of Tunis had led to sharp
differential treatment in favor of French goods and that
in Madagascar practically all non-French goods had been
excluded by a high protective tariff, Germany insisted
upon equal treatment for all nations in Morocco, and
might reasonably expect the support of other governments.
Her point was well taken because the Anglo-French agreement bound France to maintain the open door for thirty
years only and did not in any manner insure the rights of
other nations after that period.[2] So long, therefore, as
German policy envisaged the maintenance of the independence and integrity of Morocco, together with a recognition of the sovereignty of the Sultan, as a guarantee of
the open door, it occupied a strong position. In addition,
a convention signed at Madrid in 1880 by all the European
Powers and the United States made Morocco a kind of

[1] Kiel, 3 July, 1900.
[2] Anglo-French Declaration (public), Art. IV.

International hunting ground. True, that agreement had reference to the protection of European residents in the Shereefian Empire and was not concerned with trading rights; but Article XVII declared that "the right of most-favored-nation treatment is recognized by Morocco for all the Powers represented at the Conference of Madrid." The most-favored-nation treatment was also promised to Germany in the commercial treaty signed by Germany and Morocco in 1890.

On the other hand, it is difficult to believe that Germany did not cherish ambitions of another description. Throughout the period during which the Morocco controversy kept Europe on tenter-hooks the agitation for "a place in the sun" was at its height, and Morocco figured prominently in the programmes of the Pan-German League and the Colonial Society. In the propaganda of these associations the Shereefian Empire was described as a veritable Golconda; nor was this a distortion of the truth. With an area of 219,000 square miles and a population of only 5,000,000, the land was capable of receiving a large number of European settlers; the climate, more especially in the southwest, was salubrious; the agricultural possibilities were boundless, for the soil was both rich and sparsely cultivated; above all, from a German point of view, the earth was known to be extraordinarily rich in iron and other ores in which Germany was either lacking or increasingly dependent upon imports. A further recommendation could be found in the fact that Morocco was practically the last semicivilized region of the globe that was not mortgaged to some European Power or was not entangled in the meshes of Pan-American or Asiatic politics. The acquisition of Morocco would probably have gone far to satisfy German colonial ambitions, and, whether or not the imperial government aimed to secure the whole or a part of the spoils when the Sultan capitulated to European pressure, public opinion fully expected the fatherland to obtain its proper share of the prey.

For political reasons as well as economic considerations Germany would find Morocco useful. For some time she had felt keenly the need of a coaling station somewhere on the route from Europe to her African colonies—Togoland, Cameroons, and Southwest Africa. For that purpose the western coast of Morocco offered many possibilities. Furthermore, a German Morocco would neutralize French Algeria in case of a European war. But most important of all, Germany would become a Mediterranean Power, at least in its western area. Then, if her Baghdad railway could be put through and her hold on Asia Minor established; if also her ally, Austria-Hungary, were to carry through an ambitious naval programme, then the Germanic Powers might in time acquire a preponderant position in the Middle Sea, that is, across the most important trade route and the strategic centre of the British Empire. It must be frankly admitted that the above interpretation of Germany's Moroccan policy is inferential, for the imperial government never admitted that it cherished territorial aspirations in Morocco. But if Germany were merely championing the open door, it is difficult to understand why Great Britain opposed so resolutely every forward move of the Berlin foreign office, for her own trade was bound to profit by the success of the German policy. Either Germany *did* aspire to a part of Morocco—and in the negotiations preceding the Great War, she declined, be it remembered, to guarantee the integrity of the French colonies, of which Morocco was surely the most desirable; or she was using the Morocco question as a means of testing the Anglo-French *entente*. The one did not exclude the other, for that matter. If Germany avowed her designs upon Morocco, the *entente* would speedily become an alliance; on the other hand, if she could break up the *entente*, Mоrоссо would be hers for the asking, as France was in no position to undertake a war single-handed. But from whatever angle the matter is viewed, it is clear that Great Britain, deeply concerned as she was at the growth of the German navy, was bound to resent the establishment of German influence in Morocco, which would prejudice her position in the Mediterranean, or to draw nearer to France if the latter were subjected to any threats at the hands of Germany. If Germany's interests obviously demanded a forward policy in Morocco, British interests equally required that such a policy be blocked; and beyond that point it is neither useful nor possible to refine the dispute.[1]

After the foregoing statement of the attitude of the several Powers toward the Moroccan question we may narrate the course of events in the Shereefian Empire which led up to the Conference of Algeciras.

The first step toward securing a hold on Morocco was taken by France in 1901, when her relations with England were still problematical and when the latter was still engaged in the Boer War. In July of that year, after a French squadron had repaired to Tangier (a French subject had recently been murdered), a treaty was concluded which prepared the way for that *pénétration pacifique* so dear to modern diplomacy and pledged France to maintain the independence and integrity of the Sultan's dominions. This was followed in April, 1902, by another convention, which regulated the policing of the Morocco-Algerian frontier in a manner distinctly favorable to France. Shortly after this M. Delcassé opened negotiations with Germany

---

[1] Gustav Diercks, *Die Marokkofrage und die Konferenz von Algesiras* (1906); *Krieg mit Frankreich? Wohin muss die deutsche Marokkopolitik führen?* (1907); Heinrich Class, *West-Marokko deutsch!* (1911), 60,000 copies being sold; Dr. Albrecht Wirth, *Die Entscheidung über Marokko* (1911); Dr. Wilhelm Arning, *Marokko-Kongo* (1912). André Tardieu, *La Conférence d'Algésiras* (1906); Augustin Bernard, *Le Maroc* (1913). E. D. Morel, *Morocco in Diplomacy* (1912), bitterly critical of British policy, but containing all the essential documents.

to buy off her opposition, and proposed to Spain a partition of what did not yet belong to France. But nothing came of the former, and Great Britain got wind of the Franco-Spanish scheme and blocked it. This check was probably the decisive factor in deciding the Republic to give up its claims in Egypt in return for England's consent to its Morocco policy. The agreement with London was then concluded on 8 April, 1904.

The published articles of the Anglo-French convention bound the two governments not to "alter the political status" of either Egypt or Morocco, but in secret articles, which were not published until 1911, they considered "the event of either government finding itself constrained, by the force of circumstances, to modify the policy in respect to Egypt or Morocco," and they promised mutual assistance in securing "reforms" in either country. The published declaration recognized the interests of Spain on the Mediterranean littoral of Morocco, and France was bidden to come to terms with her. On 3 October, 1904, the French and Spanish Governments, in a public declaration, stated that they were "firmly attached to the integrity of the Moorish Empire under the sovereignty of the Sultan"; but secretly they arranged a treaty of partition which, according to agreement, was communicated to the British Government and which bound Spain never "to alienate or to cede in any form, even temporarily, the whole or any part of the territories" awarded to her—a precaution, perhaps, against a German purchase or lease.[1] Thus, while the world was led to believe that Morocco's position would be maintained intact by France, Spain, and Great Britain, those very Powers were privately agreed that the Sultan's dominions should be divided among two of their number, and the third was pledged to give its diplomatic support to the proceedings.

[1] Art. VII.

It was not a creditable business for the negotiators.
True, the possession of Morocco by France was the logical
corollary of the British occupation of Egypt, and a public announcement might easily have precipitated a war.
Probably not otherwise could the Western Powers have
scored at the expense of Germany, but their diplomacy
was placed in a false light; just as was Germany's by her
refusal to pursue a consistent policy fairly and squarely.
Whether or when Germany learned of the secret articles,
cannot be said; but it has been argued that the sudden
change of front made by Germany after the battle of
Mukden was dictated by the knowledge that a partition
of Morocco was being prepared,[1] and the explanation is
not unreasonable, as important secrets have more than
once leaked out of the Quai d'Orsay. In any case, the
Germans had reason to be alarmed, for in June, 1904, the
Maghzen, as the Shereefian Government is called, had
raised a loan of 62,500,000 francs in Paris, and the programme of reforms presented to the Sultan by the French
minister in February, 1905, would have made Morocco
practically a French protectorate.[2]

The Algeciras Conference had, therefore, to decide
whether it would establish an international control over
Morocco or recognize the peculiar interests of France and
Spain. Germany had a strong case, beyond a doubt, but
the strong-handed methods of her diplomacy militated
seriously against her. She had raised the question in a
brutal fashion, and her representatives at the conference
assumed a domineering and hectoring attitude that was
most distasteful to the polished agents of the other Powers.

---

[1] So Morel, *Morocco in Diplomacy*, p. 98, who bases his opinion on the text of a
Reuter despatch of October, 1904.

[2] According to the German minister to Morocco, his French colleague pressed the
reforms on the Sultan by the argument that he was acting in the name of the European concert. M. Saint-René Taillandier denied explicitly that he had used such
language.

Hence, in the really vital questions, she enjoyed the support only of Austria-Hungary, her ally. Her other ally, Italy, consistently voted against her, and even the neutral American delegates favored the French contentions. To a large extent, the question debated was not so much the future of Morocco as the strength of the several Powers. An unreserved German victory would have consolidated firmly the new position in Europe she had acquired since Russia's defeat in the Far East. The result of the conference, accordingly, was a theoretical acceptance of the German doctrine of internationalization, but a practical disavowal of it by the grant of a privileged position to France and Spain.

In securing this the assistance of the British Government was invaluable to France. Sir Edward Grey, who had just taken over the foreign office, said to the French ambassador:

"If war was forced upon France then on the question of Morocco —a question which had just been made the subject of agreement between this country [England] and France, an agreement extremely popular on both sides—if out of this agreement war was forced on France at this time, in his view public opinion in this country would have rallied to the material support of France." [1]

Sir Edward made no promises, but he conveyed his opinion to the German ambassador as well as to the French; he used no threats, but the German Government knew that it could not break up the *entente cordiale* by an aggressive policy toward France. Without committing the British Government, the foreign secretary also authorized the consultation of British and French military experts. Thus German policy had succeeded in cementing the *entente* into something more than a mere combination for diplo-

[1] House of Commons, 3 August, 1914. (5 *Hansard* lxv, *c.* 1811.)

matic manœuvroo, without, as later events showed, taking the lesson to heart.

The Act of Algeciras, in one hundred and twenty-three articles, accepted "the threefold principle of the sovereignty and independence of his Majesty the Sultan, the integrity of his dominions, and economic liberty without any inequality." Apart from regulations for the suppression of the traffic in arms and for the better collection of taxes, the essential provisions were those concerning the organization of a police force and a state bank. The former task was intrusted to French and Spanish officers. As regards the bank, its capital was divided into fourteen equal shares, of which one was allotted to each of the twelve signatory Powers, and the other two to the French banks interested in the loan of June, 1904; France and Spain, therefore, secured two-sevenths of the capital. Also, the bank was organized under the laws of France. In theory, France and Spain were to act as agents of the Powers, but in reality they were awarded a privileged position; and it soon became apparent that the authority given them as agents of the Powers was not sufficient to cope with the problems that arose.

Prince Bülow, in a speech to the Reichstag on 5 April, 1906, sought to justify his policy. The Morocco question, he said, had been "one affecting the prestige of the German Government and the dignity of the German Empire," and he argued that these had been vindicated and safeguarded by the conference and its decisions. He also insisted that Germany did not begrudge France her friendship with England or her reconciliation with Italy. But public opinion in Germany was not so easily satisfied. The press, the pamphleteers, and many parliamentarians felt that in reality little had been gained for so much effort; that the Act of Algeciras would not persuade France to abandon her policy toward Morocco, and that other nations were not sympathetic with German ambitions. As one writer remarked:

"We are now isolated, unloved, hated, because we have gradually established our right to take part in the settlement of international problems, because we have zealously come forward to support our interests." [1]

This was in large measure true, and it was much remarked upon at the time that in his Reichstag speech of 14 November, 1906, Prince Bülow, whose attitude had been rather haughty since the beginning of the Russo-Japanese War, was at some pains to demonstrate the friendliness of Germany with all the Powers of the world. But, he went on to say:

"A policy that aims to hem Germany in, to draw around us a circle of Powers for the purpose of isolating us, would be a very dangerous policy for the peace of Europe."

Nevertheless, the year 1907 witnessed a series of agreements which, avowedly growing out of the Morocco imbroglio, went far toward accomplishing the very result against which Prince Bülow had delivered his warning. On 16 May the French and Spanish Governments, in identical declarations, announced their intention to "maintain the *status quo* in the Mediterranean and that part of the Atlantic which washes the coast of Europe and Africa"; in case new circumstances necessitated any change in the *status quo* they would consult together with a view to common action. Similar declarations were made by Spain and Great Britain, for which the way had been prepared by the marriage of Princess Ena of Battenberg to King Alfonso the preceding year.[2] Thus Spain, which had long

[1] Diercks, *Die Marokkofrage und die Konferenz von Algesiras*, p. 170.
[2] About the same time Spain decided to reconstruct her fleet, which had been neglected since the war with the United States, and British capitalists arranged to provide the necessary loans.

been in close relations with the government of Berlin, was, by her interests in Morocco, brought within the orbit of the *entente cordiale*, to the intense annoyance of her former friend. It should also be noted that the Anglo-Portuguese treaty of alliance, which contained a guarantee of the integrity of the Portuguese colonies, had been renewed in 1903. From this time an active German policy in the Mediterranean was destined to meet with opposition from the four Western Powers.

With these Powers Italy was now, for practical purposes, closely associated. From the days of unification Italy had cultivated and enjoyed the close friendship of Great Britain, chiefly as a protection against the hostility of France, and she had persisted in this policy even after her ally, Germany, had fallen out with England, a fact recognized by visits of King Edward to Victor Emmanuel III in 1903 and 1907. More important was the *rapprochement* with France, which became possible after M. Delcassé, in 1901–2, had recognized the "rights" of Italy to Tripoli when a convenient season should come for asserting them. As the Anglo-French *entente* developed, Franco-Italian relations steadily improved, as evidenced by the Italian support of the French claims at the Algeciras Conference. No formal convention between the two countries was signed, except an Anglo-French-Italian agreement guaranteeing the independence and integrity of Abyssinia, but their interests were sufficiently identical to insure a harmonious co-operation. Italy, indeed, remained a member of the Triple Alliance, but she was a silent partner, whose ambitions in the Adriatic were directly opposed to those of her ally, Austria-Hungary. Prince Bülow insisted that the Triple Alliance was as efficient as ever, but he did not succeed in convincing his countrymen by his argument.

The last straw, from the German point of view, was the

Anglo-Russian convention of 31 August, 1907. This was perhaps the soundest move of British diplomacy for a hundred years, for it dispelled the long-imagined bogie of a Russian attack on India, whose safety is one of Britain's first considerations. But to Germany it was intolerable —first because Anglo-Russian rivalry had played an important part in the shaping of her policy; next because it was doubtful if the traditional friendship of the German and Russian Emperors could stand the strain of Anglo-German hostility; and lastly because, as the Russian foreign minister said,[1] the agreement made possible the re-entry of Russia into European politics, from which she had stood aloof since the days of Bismarck and her absorption in Far Eastern affairs. To be precise, Russia was henceforth to take an active interest in the Balkans, to support the policy of reform which Great Britain, to the disgust of both Germany and Austria, was urging for Macedonia, and in general to oppose the *Drang nach Osten* of the Germanic Powers.

Germans had not believed an Anglo-Russian reconciliation possible, and the renewal of the Anglo-Japanese alliance, which was originally directed against Russia, in August, 1905, seemed to confirm their view. But Russia had stood by England and France at Algeciras; on 10 June, 1907, France and Japan adjusted their relations by an agreement to respect the independence and integrity of China and the principle of the open door; on 30 July Russia and Japan drew closer together by a formal recognition of their possessions and treaty rights in China and Manchuria. These preliminaries removed the last obstacle to the accord between London and St. Petersburg, which was stimulated by the advance of German influence in Asia Minor and the Persian Gulf, to be noticed presently. Their bargain respecting Tibet and Afghanistan was of

[1] A. Viallate, *La Vie politique dans les deux mondes*, 1906–1907, p. 7.

no interest to Germany. But the practical partition of
Persia did not augur well for Germany's growing commerce
in that country, nor was she pleased to see Russia concede
British supremacy in the Persian Gulf. Henceforth Germany would not possess a free hand in the Near East, just
as her activities in the Mediterranean were restrained by
the agreements between the Mediterranean Powers.

It must be admitted that the situation was not pleasant
for Germany. As late as 1904 her influence in Europe
had been scarcely challenged, and the one check upon it,
the Dual Alliance, was seriously compromised by Russia's
reverses in the Far East. By 1907, in addition to the
Franco-Russian alliance, Germany was confronted by a
network of agreements involving Great Britain, Spain,
Italy, and Japan, of which Powers two were closely connected with the Dual Alliance. The Triple Alliance was
now opposed by a Triple *Entente*, which was in a position
to restrain the policy of Germany and Austria in the very
regions they regarded as the theatres of their political and
economic expansion. Indubitably the strength of the new
combination lay in the support which British sea power
could give to the military pressure exerted by France and
Russia. Germans had convinced themselves that Great
Britain must desire the destruction of Germany before the
latter forged ahead as a commercial and naval Power:
they therefore, not unnaturally, argued that the *entente*
had been engineered by Great Britain with the object of
isolating Germany diplomatically and with the ultimate
purpose of precipitating a war against her. Englishmen,
on the other hand, insisted that the agreements with France
and Russia were made merely as means of protection against
German aggression; they remembered the unscrupulous-
ness of Bismarck, they regarded the German navy as a
challenge to their traditional maritime ascendency, and
they pointed to the recurring diplomatic crises as convinc-

ing evidence of German forwardness. As long as Europe remained split into two hostile camps, only a miracle could avoid war between them.

The time is far off when we can know the truth about the so-called *Einkreisungspolitik* of England. It became "a matter of faith even among those who were her best friends,"[1] and Germans will probably never be convinced that King Edward VII and Sir Edward Grey were not playing a Machiavellian game. The King rather than the foreign secretary was held primarily responsible, but the latter passed for the arch-type of English hypocrisy, partly, it may be suggested, because he spoke but seldom in Parliament and took but little interest in the social life of London; his time must, therefore, be consumed in plots and intrigues against Germany. The basis of the charge against King Edward was his extraordinary fondness for travelling. From his coronation to his death not a year passed in which he did not pay a round of visits to his brother monarchs of Europe, and as he was a man of uncommon tact and urbanity it was easy to imagine that this activity was closely connected with British foreign policy. But those who ascribed to him the personal direction of that policy overlooked the fact that as a constitutional ruler he could not initiate a policy of his own; that on his many journeys he was accompanied by only officials of the foreign office, not by ministers responsible to Parliament, who alone could authorize actions binding the British Government. The King was certainly the agent of the foreign office, for he was excellently equipped to explain its intentions to Continental sovereigns who did enjoy control of their national policies; but as his official biographer has said:

[1] R. C. Long, "Germany and the Entente," *Fortnightly Review*, October, 1909, p. 738.

"Foreign statesmen and rulers knew that no subtler aim really underlay his movements than a wish for friendly social intercourse with them and the enjoyment of life under foreign skies quite unencumbered by the burden of diplomatic anxieties."

Some "unguarded remarks" in Paris, in the course of 1905, which reached the Emperor William had "an unfriendly sound," but "no deliberate hostility to the German people can truthfully be put to the King's credit." In short, British foreign policy "was unaffected by the royal progresses." [1]

These progresses, it should be noted, were impartially distributed. If he preferred to visit France and the Mediterranean lands, or sometimes journeyed to Russia and the Scandinavian countries, he did not neglect the Germanic sovereigns. He visited William II in 1904, 1906, 1907, 1908, and 1909, in the last year as an official guest in Berlin; Francis Joseph was similarly honored in 1903, 1905, 1907, and 1908. The real purpose of the King's visits was to induce the German Emperor to consider a limitation of naval armaments—that is, to prepare the ground for formal negotiations between the British and German foreign offices; and he sought to make use of the traditional friendship of England and Austria as a means of exerting pressure upon the ally of the latter. The verdict of Germany's most fearless publicist, Maximilian Harden, deserves to be quoted:

"Edward VII, son of a Coburger, grandson of a Saxon princess, was never an enemy of Germany. As a Briton he knew that England must not abandon the command of the sea and the predominant position in Islamic countries, if it did not wish to see the roots of its power destroyed. As the patron of Sir John Fisher he knew the opinion of English naval experts: 'Dreadnoughts alone, not the ships of yesterday, will decide any future war, and Germany may soon be devilishly near us in Dreadnought strength.' As a business

[1] Sir Sidney Lee, "King Edward VII," *Dictionary of National Biography*, second supplement, vol. I, pp. 592–596.

man he said to himself that the 63,000,000 of Germans would not quietly submit to the destruction of their fleet and the loss of their colonies, and that Great Britain, the market and clearing-house of the inhabited earth, could not sustain a century of constant menace of war, even after a great victory. He desired, therefore, an understanding as to extent of naval armaments instead of war." [1]

Harden's was a voice crying in the wilderness, except for the protests of Social Democrats, who were not heeded. The conviction as to British hostility and her policy of isolation subsisted in German minds. Thus Herr Bassermann, the National Liberal leader, at Essen, in September, 1905:

"England works for fresh coalitions against Germany in order to get great forces together for a final reckoning with Germany. . . . Peace with England will be assured when our fleet is so strong that England will not dare fall upon us."

Or again at Magdeburg, in April, 1907:

"England is everywhere, England's King is everywhere. . . . In every corner of the world England is pursuing a policy which is unfavorable to Germany." [2]

In June, 1908, the Emperor himself was full of the idea. In a speech at Döberitz he said:

"It seems likely that people wish to isolate and provoke us. We shall be able to put up with it. The Teuton has never fought better than when he has been brought to bay. So let them attack us; we shall be ready!" [3]

British statesmen endeavored to dispel the illusion that their policy was one of encirclement. Sir Edward Grey admirably defined his position in a speech made shortly before he took over the foreign office:

"Nothing we do in our relations with Germany," he said, "is in any way to impair our existing good relations with France. In

---

[1] *Monarchs and Men* (1912), p. 28.
[2] Quoted in *Annual Register*, 1905, p. 293; 1907, p. 306.
[3] A. Viallate, *La Vie politique dans les deux mondes*, 1907–1908, p. 162.

other words, it must be, in my opinion, a condition of any improve
ment in the public relations between Germany and ourselves that
the relations of Germany with France on all matters which come
under the French agreement should be fair and good also." [1]

This attitude he consistently maintained to the very outbreak of the Great War, and it may be stated that the relations of the British and German Governments, from 1904
to 1914, became strained only when the latter became truculent in its relations with France. As regards Russia, Sir
Edward was equally explicit. He warmly supported Sir
Charles Dilke in deprecating the idea that the Anglo-
Russian agreement aimed at the isolation of Germany,
and said that he had no objection to any alliances Germany might conclude.[2] For this reason, during the Bosnian crisis of 1908-9, which intimately affected the interests of Russia, "anything more than diplomatic support
. . . was never asked from us, more was never given,
more was never promised." [3] And after the Morocco crisis of 1911, Sir Edward Grey declared that "one of the essential conditions of our friendships with France and with
Russia in the last few years has been the certain knowledge
that neither they nor we wished to pursue a provocative
or aggressive policy." [4]

On the other hand, he made it quite clear that Great
Britain was willing, even anxious, to enjoy the friendship
of Germany, provided such a friendship was not at the
expense of Britain's existing friendships with France and
Russia; and it will presently be seen that he attempted
to give concrete expression to such a policy. The difficulty was explained by Sir Frank Lascelles, who was British ambassador in Berlin from 1895 to 1908, when he wrote:

[1] London, 20 October, 1905.
[2] House of Commons, 27 July, 1908. (4 *Hansard* cxciii, cc. 955, 970.)
[3] House of Commons, 3 August, 1914. (5 *Hansard* lxv, c. 1811.)
[4] House of Commons, 27 November, 1911. (5 *Hansard* xxxii, c. 59.)

"It became my duty to speak at dinners, and I noticed that whilst the expression of a sincere desire for good relations on the part of England was cordially applauded a coldness seemed to come over my audience when I pointed out that it must be clearly understood that friendship with one country did not imply hostility to any other, and although we desired to be friends with Germany we were not prepared to abandon the friendships into which we had entered with other Powers and which certainly did not imply any hostility toward Germany." [1]

That England adjusted her difficulties with France and Russia from fear of Germany, and by so doing created the Triple *Entente* is in large measure true, but no evidence has ever been produced to show that the immediate or ultimate aim of that policy was war with Germany, or that the *Entente* was ever regarded by England as other than a means of defense against the incalculable policy of Germany, which managed to challenge British interests first in one, then in another, quarter. If Germany has been the victim of a conspiracy hatched by Great Britain, she has published no evidence which can stand in the court of history. Indeed, such facts as are known point to Germany as the aggressive Power, for each of the four European crises preceding the Great War—1905, 1908–9, 1911, and 1912–13—were precipitated by the action of Germany or her ally Austria-Hungary; and on each occasion the crisis was due to the mailed-fist diplomacy of the Teutonic allies.

The relations of the British and German Governments from the Algeciras Conference to the Bosnian crisis of 1908–9 were chiefly concerned with the question of naval armaments, and the result has been noted in the chapter entitled "The Admiralty of the Atlantic." On the surface the only difficulties were met with in the delicate question of Macedonian reforms. But at the second

[1] "Thoughts on the Anglo-German Problem," *Contemporary Review*, January, 1912, p. 7.

Hague Conference (summer of 1907) British and German policies were poles apart. The atmosphere was somewhat cleared by the Emperor's visit to England in the autumn of 1907, despite a savage attack on Prince Bülow in the columns of the *Times*.[1] The Emperor was well received wherever he went, and he stayed on for some weeks in a private capacity. His speech at the Guild Hall made a profound impression. Referring to a visit to the same place in 1891, he said:

"I said then, on this spot, that my aim was, above all, the maintenance of peace. History, I venture to hope, will do me justice in that I have pursued this aim unswervingly ever since. The main prop and base for the peace of the world is the maintenance of good relations between our two countries, and I will further strengthen them so far as lies in my power. The German nation's wishes coincide with them."

In characteristic fashion the Emperor proceeded to undo the effects of these remarks: first, by his letter to Lord Tweedmouth;[2] second, by the navy law of 1908; and, above all, by the interview which he gave to an English diplomatist and which was published in the *Daily Telegraph* on 28 October, 1908:

"His Majesty," ran the principal passage of the statement, which was intended "as a message to the English people," "spoke with impulsive and unusual frankness, saying: 'You English are as mad, mad, mad as March hares. What has come over you that you are completely given over to suspicions that are quite unworthy of a great nation? What more can I do than I have done? I declared with all the emphasis at my command in my speech at the Guild Hall that my heart was set upon peace and that it was one of my dearest wishes to live on the best terms with England. Have I ever been false to my word? Falsehood and prevarication are alien to my nature. My actions ought to speak

[1] 10 October, 1907.
[2] See Chap. VIII, "The Admiralty of the Atlantic," p. 183.

for themselves, but you will not listen to them, but to those who misinterpret and distort them.

"'This is a personal insult which I resent; to be forever misjudged, to have my repeated offers of friendship weighed and scrutinized with jealous, mistrustful eyes taxes my patience severely. I have said time after time that I am a friend of England, and your press, or at least a considerable section of it, bids the people of England to refuse my proffered hand and insinuates that the other hand holds a dagger. How can I convince a nation against its will?'

"Complaining again of the difficulty imposed upon him by English distrust, his Majesty said: 'The prevailing sentiment of large sections of the middle and lower classes of my own people is not friendly to England. I am, therefore, so to speak, in the minority in my own land, but it is a minority of the best element, just as it is in England respecting Germany.'"

The rest of the interview presented the imperial view of recent diplomatic events, and need not be quoted here; it ended with the stereotyped justification of the German navy.

As a statement of facts, the interview was to some extent justified, for the ill feeling between Germany and England was very strong at the time, and was perhaps stronger in England than in Germany.[1] But it was singularly unsuccessful as a harbinger of better relations, for in both England and Germany there was intense indignation, which was in no wise diminished by the crisis in the Near East and the conflicting policies followed by Great Britain and Germany in that matter. Fortunately the statesmen of both countries kept their heads. Mr. Asquith, Sir Edward Grey, and Prince Bülow made conciliatory speeches, and the incident was gradually forgotten.

In February Edward VII visited Berlin, where he was

---

[1] "The ill feeling seems to me much commoner and more menacing in England than in Germany." (Edwin D. Mead, "England and Germany," *Atlantic Monthly*, March, 1908, p. 398.) But he records that the other English papers rebuked the *Times* for its savage attack on Prince Bülow.

most cordially received, and it was considered a happy
augury that during his stay a Franco-German convention was signed which promised to give a definitive solution to the Morocco question. But the royal visit "exercised no lasting effect in abating the popular apprehension
of German designs." [1] Indeed, shortly after the King's
return, the naval scare of 1909 was sprung, and Germans
said that they had been duped. The intervention, therefore, of the Wilhelmstrasse in the Balkan crisis to support
Austria against the demands of the Triple *Entente*, and the
complete rout of the latter were regarded as a fitting reply
to British duplicity, even though Europe was left in two
sharply drawn diplomatic groups in which Germany was
supported only by her ally.

No amount of official optimism or of private assurances
could conceal the harsh realities of the situation. Sincere
efforts were made in both countries. A British Anglo-
German Friendship Committee, organized in 1905, soon
had its counterpart in Germany. Visits of representative men were arranged on each side. Ministers, journalists, public officials, workingmen, and students from each
country visited the other, and professed themselves satisfied that the hostility reflected in the press was artificial
and did not represent a real conflict of interests. Many
writers in English reviews argued that each people accused
the other of the same hostile and diabolical designs, and
that only the armament firms profited by the insensate
naval rivalry. Englishmen hailed Germany as the land
of Goethe, Schiller, and the world's greatest musicians;
Germans gave fitting recognition to the genius of Shakespeare, and acknowledged their indebtedness to England
in all matters of commerce and industry. But nothing
could remove the *malaise* that oppressed the people of both
countries, and it was precisely this feeling that a conflict

[1] *Annual Register*, 1909, p. 8.

was inevitable which enabled both governments to construct the huge navies that actually did create an issue and materially increased the chances of a fatal outcome. Years of hard work by enlightened patriots in each country ultimately prepared the way for more cordial relations, more especially after the Morocco question was settled. But the reconciliation had not been effected when the crisis of 1914 arose; the old animosity reappeared, and Sir Edward Grey had behind him a practically unanimous nation when he called upon Germany to respect the neutrality of Belgium, while Germans were at once persuaded that the struggle with Great Britain was the real issue of the war. Public opinion must bear with diplomacy its share of the blame for the Great War, and the historian will be reluctant to say that in this respect one nation was entirely guilty and the other quite blameless.

Domestic politics in both countries reacted unfavorably upon their international relations. The Liberal government of Great Britain was pledged to a costly policy of social reform, and many of its supporters in the House of Commons were, for various reasons, admirers of Germany, with whom they insistently demanded an understanding. Under such circumstances the money required to keep up the two-Power naval standard was not forthcoming, and the foreign office could not, even if it so desired, make a formal defensive alliance with France and Russia. British policy was actually a compromise that was far sounder than most people suspected, but in many quarters it was not understood, and because devised by a Liberal ministry it was supposed to be weak and vacillating. This played directly into the hands of Germany, for the elections of January, 1907, had been fought on the question whether, to quote the *North German Gazette*, "Germany was at all capable of developing from a European Power into a world Power." The triumphant vindication of the government's policy and the defeat of the Social Democrats necessitated vigorous action, to which the foreign office was nothing loath, and whether by accident or design such action invariably involved British interests or British relations with the other Powers of the Triple *Entente*. Hence Anglo-German relations were at their worst during the five years' life of the Reichstag elected in 1907; whereas they improved materially after the elections of 1912 had gone against the government and revealed the popular disapproval of the Wilhelmstrasse's methods and policy alike. Also, in the course of time the German foreign office learned that Sir Edward Grey was not a man of wax, but was prepared to stand firm when British interests were affected. But again, the realization came too late, or the lesson was not taken to heart, and the Great War was the result.

From this analysis of the general situation we may proceed to examine the two great questions with regard to which Great Britain and Germany were ranged on opposite sides in the last years of peace: viz., Morocco and the aftermath of Algeciras, and the problem of the Near East, more particularly the question of the Baghdad railway. Chronologically the latter takes precedence and will be discussed first.

CHAPTER X

THE NEAR EAST

"The Near Eastern question may be defined as the problem of filling up the vacuum created by the gradual disappearance of the Turkish Empire from Europe."[1] Beginning with the treaty of Carlowitz in 1699, by which Hungary was restored to the Hapsburgs, the process was not finally completed by the treaty signed in London on 30 May, 1913, which left to the Sultan eastern Thrace and Constantinople itself. But down to the Crimean War and the treaty of Paris (1853-6), the Turkish possessions still extended to the Danube River and the Carpathians, and the animosities bred by their partition was one of the main causes of the Great War of 1914. The conviction that the Turk must depart from Europe gradually spread among all the European peoples, even the English, who fifty years ago believed that the safety of India depended upon the maintenance of the Ottoman Empire. But the problem of the Turk was not restricted to Europe. His possession of Asia Minor, Mesopotamia, and Arabia, and, until within a generation, of northern Africa as well, determined the policy of more than one Power with respect to the situation in the Balkans.

The problem is due to the Turks themselves. A nomadic tribe out of the heart of Asia, they conquered their vast dominions by the sword, and by the sword they held them. Of the arts of peace they knew nothing; in the six centuries of their domination they contributed little to the economic,

[1] William Miller, *The Ottoman Empire*, 1801-1913, p. 1.

political, religious, or literary life of their subjects. Worse
than that, they did not even govern, except so far as to
collect taxes and to raise armies for innumerable wars.
Furthermore, the Turks proper, who constituted the bulk
of the governing classes, represented only a minority of
the total population. In the European provinces the inhabitants were almost entirely of European stock, except
in certain small localities where there was some Turkish
immigration. In Asia also the bulk of the people was
anything but Turkish, being Arab, Armenian, Kurdish,
Jewish, or Greek. Only in Asia Minor was a Turkish peasantry to be found. From time to time clever individuals
of each of the subject races rose to high place in the Ottoman Government; but the main features of Ottoman political life—inefficiency, corruption, inertia, the playing off
of one race against another—were not counteracted, rather
they were intensified by the purely selfish ambitions of
these capable individuals.

Of recent years, as the doctrine of nationality has gathered force all over the world, the preservation of the Ottoman power has become increasingly difficult. Everywhere
the subject races have revolted against oppression and
tyranny, and one frontier province after another has escaped from the control of Constantinople. Indeed, the
final crash would have come long since but for the weaknesses and jealousies of the Sultan's subjects and the ambitions of the European nations, and the present war will
not have been fought in vain if it provides a lasting solution of the Near Eastern question. But it is necessary to
point out that only the Great Powers can furnish an adequate solution, for much more is involved than the fate of
the various peoples hitherto or still under Ottoman dominion.

The vast extent of her territory and the difficulty of
navigating the Baltic during half the year make Russia's

natural outlet the Bosporus and the Dardanelles, over which Constantinople stands guard; for the greater part of her grain crop, which is the chief item of her export trade, is raised on the black lands in the southern provinces of her European Empire. The fact that many ships loaded with Russian grain were cooped up in the Black Sea when Italy attacked the Dardanelles in 1912, amply justifies the national demand for a free passage to the Ægean and the Mediterranean. But long before economic considerations had assumed their present importance, historical and political forces were driving the Russians along the *chemin de Byzance*. They ever regarded themselves as the heirs of the old Greek Empire, from which they took their two-headed eagle. They aspired to plant the Cross once more on the church of Santa Sophia, and they cherished warm sympathies for those Southern Slavs who were cut off from the main Slav stock by a solid barrier of Germans, Magyars, and Rumanians, and groaned under the oppression of the Turk. To reach her goal, Russia resorted to endless intrigue, formed diplomatic combinations galore, waged nine wars—without, however, advancing her frontier perceptibly beyond the Rumanian barrier. But if the main Russian current made little progress, if Constantinople did not become Tsarigrad,—to the great satisfaction of other Powers,—Russia's wars were primarily responsible for the resurrection of five Christian states which might serve as outposts of Russian influence in the Balkans.

Greece received her independence after the war of 1828–9; but she was far away, and until recently too weak to be of particular service. Rumania secured autonomy as an aftermath of the Crimean War; but when her troops had saved the Russians before Plevna, in the war of 1877, she was "rewarded" by the seizure of Bessarabia, a trans-Danubian province inhabited by Rumanians. Consequently, for more than thirty years she cultivated the close friendship of Austria-Hungary, even though the Russian victory had secured her independence.

The war of 1877 also placed Bulgaria, Serbia, and Montenegro on the map. New states, with slender resources and thoroughly Slav in spirit, they seemed excellently suited to serve Russian designs—that is, as a result of their expansion and development, Russia might hope to secure that access to the sea which had been denied to herself. For twenty years after the Congress of Berlin Russia aimed to control the domestic politics of Bulgaria; later she transferred her attention to Serbia. In each case her policy was selfish, often brutal. Nevertheless the Balkan peoples did not forget that they owed their freedom to Russian arms, and if they resented some features of Russian conduct they showed no enthusiasm for the expansionist policy of Austria-Hungary, Russia's great rival. Only fair treatment was needed to make the Balkan states devoted adherents of Russia's great ideal.

Sharply opposed to this were the interests of Austria-Hungary. Bounded on the north by a nation whose commercial progress was the wonder of the world, the Dual Monarchy found the chief outlet for its trade down the Danube and toward the Ægean. Moreover, the traditional policy of the Hapsburgs, as revealed in the annals of four centuries, was one of territorial expansion, and after her expulsion from Italy and Germany fifty years ago, Austria regarded the western Balkans as her theatre of operations, with probably Salonika as the ultimate goal. Accordingly, she was permitted, in 1878, to "occupy and administer" Bosnia and Herzegovina, as they constituted the *hinterland* to her Dalmatian provinces. But she could not hope to advance farther along the Adriatic coast, because Italy, her ally since 1882, also had designs on Albania and would have resisted an Austrian occupation.[1]

---

[1] The Triple Alliance, as renewed in 1887, is said to have contained a clause imposing mutual forbearance upon the rival Powers as regards Albania, and in 1897

Incidentally Montenegro, whose guns on Mount Lövchen commanded the Austrian harbor of Cattaro, had long been a Russian protectorate.

Austria was therefore compelled to regard Serbia, which she surrounded on two sides, as the only region open to her expansion. A hundred years ago, when the Serbians, under Kara George, were seeking to emancipate themselves from Turkish rule, they repeatedly asked to be annexed to the Hapsburg crown. The request was refused, doubtless to the regret of later Austrian statesmen; but throughout the nineteenth century Austrian influence was dominant in Serbia, for the family of Obrenovitch, which usually possessed the throne, needed the assistance of Vienna against its rivals the Karageorgevitches. So it was easy for Austria to secure a favorable tariff for her goods, in return for which Serbia was encouraged to export her live stock to Austrian markets, and the Magyars of Hungary were able to lord it over the unhappy Croatians, who are closely akin to the Serbs, without fear of trouble from Belgrade. The true character of Austrian friendship was demonstrated to Serbia in 1885, when the union of Eastern Rumelia and Bulgaria was carried through, contrary to the Berlin treaty. At Austria's instigation the Serbians attacked Bulgaria, only to be badly defeated; the Dual Monarchy then intervened, and prevented the victorious advance of the Bulgarian army. After that the Belgrade politicians were as clay in Austrian hands, and from 1897, when Austria and Russia agreed to maintain the *status quo* in the Balkans, Serbia seemed to have become the permanent vassal of her great northern neighbor.

This situation was upset by the Serbians themselves. In 1903 King Alexander and his consort were murdered in their palace by Serbian officers who resented his sub-

a special agreement to maintain the integrity of Albania was concluded. See *Spectator*, 11 October, 1913; also Dr. Hans F. Helmolt, "La Triplice en Orient," *Revue Politique Internationale*, April, 1914.

servience to Vienna and the scandals of his court   As he
was the last of his line, Peter Karageorgevitch, who was
Russian in sympathy, was placed upon the throne; owing
to the circumstances of his accession he determined to
rule as a constitutional monarch, and, left to their own devices, his ministers soon broke with Austria.   Meanwhile
the Bulgarians had tired of the hectoring Russian protectorate and were cultivating the friendship of the Hapsburg monarchy.   From this time to the outbreak of the
present war the rivalry of Austria and Russia was acute,
because the *protégé* of one Power blocked the southward
expansion of the other.

This rivalry would become dangerous, however, only
on the collapse of the Ottoman Empire, and neither Austria nor Russia was prepared to face that eventuality:
Austria because of her internal racial problems; Russia
because of her approaching struggle with Japan.   So in
1903 they produced a scheme, known as the Mürzsteg
programme, for reforming the administration of Turkey
in Europe, lest the Balkan states should attempt forcibly
to relieve the lot of their brethren in Macedonia and
thereby forestall both Austrian and Russian ambitions.
Such was the Balkan situation when Great Britain and
Germany were discovered as rivals in another quarter of
the Sultan's Empire, viz., Mesopotamia and Arabia.

For a century Great Britain had been the traditional
upholder of Turkish independence and power.   She had
exhausted the resources of diplomacy in impressing upon
successive sultans the necessity of setting their house in
order.   In the Crimean War she was the active ally of
Turkey, and in 1878, when the Russian armies were at
the gates of Constantinople, she intervened to compel the
Tsar to revise that treaty of San Stefano which almost
expelled the Turk from Europe.   For the rest of the century British diplomacy, acting upon Lord Beaconsfield's

assertion that "Turkey was not a worn-out state," continued to urge reforms as the surest means of blocking the advance of Russia, and after 1903 the foreign office undertook to convert the Mürzsteg programme into a workable plan, under the direction of the Powers.

Nevertheless British policy gradually underwent a profound change. Its attitude had always been dictated by the necessity of guarding, for both political and commercial reasons, the Mediterranean route to India. Translated into practical politics, this meant that no strong Power should establish itself in the eastern Mediterranean, and that England should block the advance of Russia in the Balkans. But the treaty of Berlin recorded a distinct defeat of Russia's plans, and the difficulties experienced by the Tsar's Government in controlling the young Bulgarian state promised to postpone indefinitely a Russian conquest of Constantinople. Moreover, for her services to Turkey at the Congress of Berlin Great Britain had received Cyprus; in 1875 she had acquired control of the Suez Canal and in 1883 she had occupied Egypt; with Gibraltar and Malta in her hands her position in the Mediterranean seemed fairly secure. After 1894, when Russia began her aggressive policy in the Far East, British interest in Turkish affairs was limited to demanding, in diplomatic terms only, vengeance for the Armenian massacres and to providing a solution of the troublesome Cretan question. But about 1900 it became evident that another Power was assuming the Russian rôle of adviser-in-ordinary to the Sultan, and was securing for itself economic and political advantages which would either guarantee its hold on Turkey when the ultimate collapse came or make Turkey a vassal of itself. That Power was Germany, and the enterprises she was observed to be promoting were considered a direct and serious menace to British interests. Thus there was added to the general rivalry of the two countries a specific dispute which was typical of the Anglo-German problem as a whole—the challenge of a new Power to a nation long established in a strong position and determined to yield nothing of its just rights or legitimate interests.

During the crisis that led up to the Congress of Berlin Bismarck had made his famous remark that the whole Eastern question was "not worth the bones of a Pomeranian grenadier." But in 1883 General von der Goltz of the German army was, at the request of the Sultan, despatched to Constantinople to reorganize the Turkish army. In 1889, and again in 1898, the Emperor William II visited Constantinople, on the latter occasion proceeding to Damascus, where at the grave of Saladin he declared: "The 300,000,000 Mohammedans that are scattered through the world may rest assured that the German Emperor will eternally be their friend."[1]   At the moment this was no idle boast.   Christians had recently been massacred by thousands in Armenia, but with the assistance of Germany Abdul Hamid had successfully resisted the British demand for administrative reforms.   During the Greco-Turkish War of 1897 German officers had rendered signal assistance to the Ottoman forces.   That war had been caused by an insurrection in Crete; Germany declined to join in forcing the Sultan to grant autonomy to the island.

Most important of all, perhaps, was the appointment of Baron Marschall von Bieberstein as German ambassador to the Porte.   Easily the foremost of the Kaiser's diplomatists, a champion of colonial expansion, an expert in manipulating the press, and a bitter opponent of Great

[1] Dr. C. Snouck Hurgronje, one of the greatest authorities on Islam, has recently pointed out that this appeal made little impression on the Mohammedan world, because "in the Mohammedan East Saladin's name has long been forgotten, except by the few students of history and literature." Dr. Hurgronje remarks that German scholars were disturbed by the incident, which well illustrates the dilettanteism of the German Emperor and the unscientific basis of his foreign policy. (*The Holy War: "Made in Germany"* (1915), pp. 70–71.)

Britain, he readily obtained the ear of the Sultan, and was for fifteen years (1897–1912) the guiding spirit of Turkish foreign policy. He seems to have convinced Abdul Hamid, who had maintained his position only by setting the Powers at odds, that Germany was a sincere and the only friend of Turkey; for Germany alone of the Great Powers, it was urged, had no designs upon Turkish territory, and she was willing, even anxious, to promote the economic development of Asiatic Turkey, in contrast with other Powers, who were always clamoring for reforms. Baron von Marschall also encouraged Abdul Hamid in the hope of recovering Egypt, and pointed out that with the help of Germany he could ignore the inevitable Russian demand for the opening of the Straits to Russian men-of-war.

Finally, Germany aided and abetted the Pan-Islamic schemes so dear to Abdul Hamid. That wily monarch was fully aware that his Empire existed on the sufferance of the Great Powers: to their armies and wealth might he not oppose the unity of Islam, of which he was the titular head? The idea was the more attractive because his two greatest enemies (so Germany convinced him) were Russia and Great Britain, both Powers with more Mohammedan subjects than Abdul Hamid himself could boast of. If these millions could be weaned from their allegiance to the Tsar of all the Russias and the Raj of India, those sovereigns would be restrained from pushing on their designs of annihilating the Ottoman Empire and its Sultan might become the leading prince of the Mohammedan world.

According to the most competent authorities Pan-Islamism was very largely a figment of vivid imaginations.[1] There was, to be sure, an active Mohammedan propaganda in Africa when that continent began to pass under Euro-

[1] In addition to the work of Dr. Hurgronje, just cited, reference may be made to a lecture by Professor Edward G. Browne, the distinguished Cambridge scholar, "Pan-Islamism," in *Lectures on the History of the Nineteenth Century*, edited by F. A. Kirkpatrick (1902).

pean control, and it met with no little success; also, agents
of Abdul Hamid were at work throughout the Mohammedan world preaching disloyalty to the Christian governments.   But there was no real danger.   The basis of Abdul
Hamid's schemes was his possession of the title of Caliph,
which was supposed to be a kind of Mohammedan papacy.
But the claim of the Ottoman sultans to that dignity was
never recognized by the whole Mohammedan world.   It
had been wrested from the last Abbasid sultan of Egypt
when that ruler was defeated by Sultan Selim I in 1517,
and compelled to give up Egypt and Arabia, with the
holy cities of Medina and Mecca, to the Ottomans.   But
the sultans of Constantinople were not descendants of
the Prophet Mohammed, in whom alone the title of Caliph could vest, according to Mohammedan law, and four
centuries of de facto possession could not establish their
claim de jure—a fact which the non-Turkish Mohammedan
world did not forget, in spite of the practical usurpation
by the Turkish Sultan.   In the second place, the Caliphate
does not connote the spiritual headship of Islam.   In the
days when the title possessed any reality it implied the political overlordship of the Mohammedan world; and even
in the period of their greatest power, that is, the sixteenth century, the Turks never controlled all the lands
where Islam was the dominant religion, and in the latter
half of the nineteenth century their dominion was so severely shaken that its complete extinction was seen to be
only a matter of time.   For such a state to assert its suzerainty over the Mohammedan peoples was clearly absurd.
Finally, the unity of Islam is a myth.   Its political unity
really ceased within a few years after the death of Mohammed and has never been restored.   More important is
the century-old schism of the Sunnite and Shiite sects.
Their theological disputes do not concern us here.   But
Persia, which is the stronghold of the Shiites, lies wedged

between the Ottoman dominions and those Mohammedans of British India and Russian Central Asia whom Abdul Hamid aspired to use for political ends. The Arabs of the desert also, who resent the Ottoman assumption of the Caliphate, would never allow themselves to be reduced to political servitude in the name of Islam by a ruler whose very title they questioned.

Thus, however regarded, Pan-Islamism is seen to have been and to be a danger which was not very dangerous. To what extent the governments of Great Britain, Russia, and France (the last has millions of Mohammedan subjects in Africa) considered the matter serious it is impossible to say. They were doubtless well informed of any intrigues which Abdul Hamid and the Young Turks who succeeded him may have carried on; they may have believed that the "talk of an organization of Pan-Islamism . . . was without foundation," and that Turkey "was little qualified to lead an international movement";[1] publicly they took no steps to protect themselves. But the French and English press were persuaded that Pan-Islamism might easily become a grave danger, and soundly berated the Germans for encouraging it. The latter, on their side, were completely fooled. Their eagerness to involve Turkey in the present struggle, in order that a *jihâd*, or holy war, might be proclaimed, shows how confident they were that the Pan-Islamic propaganda had undermined the loyalty of the Allies' Mohammedan peoples. In their antebellum discussions of Near Eastern problems German writers frequently emphasized the identity of interest between Pan-Germanism and Pan-Islamism, and there can be no doubt that German diplomacy strove valiantly to forge an instrument which it believed would deal a hard, if not a vital, blow to the probable opponents of German ambitions. Whatever strength Pan-Islamism possessed it

[1] Hurgronje, *The Holy War*, pp. 25, 26.

derived from the support of the German Government, for the Sultan would never have undertaken a campaign against Great Britain, France, and Russia without the assurance of support from another Great Power, and that Power could be only Germany.

It is now time to inquire as to what were the motives of German policy in Turkey. For what purpose had she acquired practical control of the Ottoman Government and prevented it from carrying out those reforms which, in the opinion of disinterested observers, could alone save it from utter collapse? Viewed as part of the national *Weltanschauung*, the object was to provide Germany with a route to the Orient, with its teeming commerce, enormous wealth, and boundless possibilities of a political character. The commerce of the Far East has always been one of the great prizes for which the European nations have struggled, and in this blatantly commercial age Germany could not afford to be left behind. Great Britain bestrode two routes, the one around the Cape of Good Hope, the other through the Suez Canal; Russia was established in Central Asia at the gates of India; she was pegging out another route by the trans Siberian railway and her advance in Manchuria. A Germanized Turkey would give the fatherland an outlet on the Persian Gulf, from which steamship lines could carry German influence farther eastward; Persia might be brought under the spell; and even India itself might succumb to Teutonic attraction when the sceptre of England should fall from her nerveless hands and the sun set at last on her colossal Empire. It was a part of this audacious programme, of course, that Austria-Hungary should become the dominant Power in the Balkans; a consummation that, in the late 'nineties, when the German vision began to unfold itself, seemed not unlikely to be realized; for Serbia was still under Obrenovitch rule, Bulgaria was chafing under Russian dictation, Rumania was almost a member of the Triple Alliance, and Russia was busy in the Far East. To overpower the feeble resistance of Great Britain to an energetic *Drang nach Osten* might well seem like child's play to the vigorous, pushing, well-organized Germanic Powers, who dominated Continental Europe and who had established their ascendency in the councils of the decrepit Ottoman Government.

There was nothing objectionable *per se* in this German *Weltpolitik;* it was as reasonable as the ambitions of Russian or British imperialism, and its successful application would mean the introduction, in some measure at least, of European efficiency and order into a region which had been the cradle of civilization but which had for centuries suffered from the blight and inertia of oriental despotisms. England had reformed Egypt amidst the applause of the world: would not a German regeneration of Asia Minor and Mesopotamia be equally worth while? Before suggesting an answer it will be well to examine the German plans in detail.

It is most unlikely that Germany contemplated a conquest of the old-fashioned kind. A few years ago there was considerable talk of German colonization in Asiatic Turkey, but that was soon seen to be impracticable. Asia Minor was already inhabited by Turks—was, indeed, the *foyer* of the race—and the climate of Mesopotamia was unsuited for Europeans; nor would such immigrants as might be attracted from Germany consent to become Turkish subjects, which was the only condition on which the Ottoman Government would have encouraged such a settlement.[1] There is also no reason for believing that Germany intended to replace the Ottoman Government by a full-fledged Prussian bureaucracy. What she did desire was a practical protectorate over Turkey and a complete

[1] Dr. Paul Rohrbach, *Die Bagdadbahn* (1911), p. 10.

control of its economic resources. The fiction of sovereignty would be left, just as in Egypt, which remained in theory a province of Turkey; but the "advice" of German diplomatists and generals would be forced on the officials of the Sultan in the fashion adopted by the British in Egypt. There would, in short, be a German "occupation" of Turkey, but the *amour propre* of the Powers would be respected, and, it was asserted, their commercial interests would be not only considered but stimulated. By such means the integrity of the Ottoman Empire, which all the European Powers were pledged to respect, would be maintained; Germany's expansionist ambitions would be satisfied; and a fruitful source of international strife would be effectually closed.

This programme was to be realized by *pénétration pacifique*, or commercial exploitation; of which the chief instrument was the Baghdad railway.[1] As far back as 1888 a German company had received a concession for a railway, which had been duly built, from Ismidt, on the Asiatic mainland opposite Constantinople, to Angora, a distance of 301 miles (485 kilometres). By 1896 a branch had been constructed from Eski-Shehir, half-way between Ismidt and Angora, to Konia. After the second visit of the Emperor William to Constantinople (1898), the Anatolian Railway Company prepared for greater things—for nothing less than an extension of its line to the Persian Gulf, and in November, 1899, the concession was granted by the Sultan. The final step was not taken till 1903, when a *firman* was published constituting the Baghdad Railway Company as an Ottoman corporation and authorizing the building of a railway from Konia across the

---

[1] Dr. Paul Rohrbach, *Die Bagdadbahn*, first published in 1902; André Chéradame, *Le Chemin de Fer de Bagdad* (1903); Victor Bérard, *Le Sultan, l'Islam et les Puissances* (1907); René Pinon, *L'Europe et l'Empire Ottoman* (1908), chaps. 7, 8; David Fraser, *The Short Cut to India* (1909); T. A. O'Connor, "The Baghdad Railway," *Fortnightly Review*, February, 1914.

Taurus range and the Mesopotamian desert to Mossul, thence along the Tigris to Baghdad; from that point the line was to follow the right bank of the Euphrates to Bassorah, below the confluence of the two great rivers, and terminate at a point on the Persian Gulf. The original plan had been to prolong the Angora line through Armenia to the upper reaches of the Tigris, but Russia was unwilling to allow a railway—which could be used for the transport of troops—brought so near her Caucasus frontier, and it was necessary to follow the southern route, which would be more costly to construct and would pass through a much poorer section of country.

The estimated length of the line, with various branches, was 2,800 kilometres (about 1,740 miles). For purposes of construction it was divided into sections of 200 kilometres, each of which was to be constructed separately and the first within eight years. The capitalized value of each section was fixed at 54,000,000 francs, for which Turkish four-per-cent bonds were to be issued to the company before work was started. The company was to receive an annuity of 11,000 francs for each kilometre constructed and 4,500 francs additional toward the expenses of operation. At the end of ninety-nine years all rights and property of the operating company were to revert to the Ottoman Government. No date was fixed for the completion of the line. The first section, reaching to Eregli, near the foot of the Taurus, was promptly built, to the great profit of the promoters,[1] but after 1904 so great were the financial difficulties of Turkey that she could not meet any further kilometric guarantees, and, owing to British and French opposition to the railway itself, it was impossible to raise money in the London and Paris markets.

But before recurring to the main topic—Anglo-German

[1] Fraser, *The Short Cut to India*, calculates that the promoters were the richer by £1,243,000, or more than 21,000,000 francs.

rivalry—a word must be said about the general importance
of the Baghdad railway. The Germans liked to speak of
"our Baghdad" (*unser Bagdad*) or to talk of the "BBB"
—Berlin-Byzantium-Baghdad.   Now the railways of Turkey in Europe and the Balkan states were very largely
owned by German and Austrian banks.   When the Baghdad had been built, the Germanic Powers would control
the most direct line of communication from Europe to the
Far East, and by virtue of this control they might hope to
dominate the economic life of the vast region stretching from the North Sea to the Persian Gulf!   No wonder
that they were determined to carry through their plans
at all cost; no wonder that those plans should be closely
scrutinized by other nations whose political or commercial interests might be seriously prejudiced by a German
monopoly.   For, however much the Germans might explain their projects, it was clear that they aimed to solve
in their exclusive interest a question which had from its
very inception been regarded as an international matter,
and that their solution would upset, to the detriment of
other Powers, the balance of power in Europe, which for
a century has rested on the existence of an independent
Ottoman Empire.

If the history of the Baghdad railway be considered
from its inception in 1899 to the outbreak of the European
War in 1914, it is evident that the opposition of France,
Russia, and Great Britain was due not to the project itself but to certain features and details, the proof being
that in 1910 Russia came to terms, and that on the eve of
the war an agreement was initialed by London and Berlin
according to which the former withdrew its opposition
in return for certain concessions by Berlin.

The first British objection was concerned with the financ-
ing of the railway.   Not even its promoters contended
that the line would pay its way until many years after its

construction. Ultimately cotton might be grown along the Anatolian sections; northeast of Baghdad there are naphtha wells which can be developed; in the lower Tigris valley, below Baghdad, the irrigation schemes of Sir William Willcocks will restore millions of acres to cultivation. But the essential condition of success is a great increase in the population, at present very meagre, and, considering the climate, the only source of immigration is India or China! The concessionaires of the line, therefore, insisted on the kilometric guarantees and drove a hard bargain. By the terms of the agreement the charge upon Turkish revenues would amount annually to 43,400,000 francs—a sum utterly beyond the paying capacity of Turkey. Something could certainly be raised by increasing the customs; but in this matter Turkey does not enjoy a free hand, for the tariff is fixed by international agreement. Among the nations having commercial relations with Turkey, Great Britain had for a century enjoyed the supremacy, but here as elsewhere considerable German competition was developing.[1] Under such conditions it cannot be seriously argued that the British Government should consent to an increase in the Turkish customs, the object of which was to enable a German company to pocket handsome profits! Moreover, there was no little feeling that any increase in the revenues of Turkey should be devoted, not to the building of an unprofitable railway, but to the improvement of the internal administration of the Empire, especially in Macedonia, in which business Great Britain had come forward as the leader of the Powers and the promoter of a genuine scheme of reform.

[1] German imports to Turkey:

Year	German imports to Turkey	German exports from Turkey
1890	34,000,000 marks	9,600,000 marks
1895	39,000,000 "	22,100,000 "
1900	34,200,000 "	30,000,000 "
1905	70,800,000 "	51,500,000 "
1910	104,900,000 "	67,400,000 "

The other recourse for raising money was to the bourses of London and Paris. This solution was boldly put forward by Germany, for if the moneyed classes of England and France could be persuaded to invest in the Baghdad railway they would have an interest in its success, and would exert such pressure on their respective governments that the latter would not dare oppose the German plans upon which success depended. In 1903, accordingly, Germany proposed that she, France, and England should each raise thirty per cent of the required funds, the remaining ten per cent being left to Russia, or the smaller states if the latter would not participate. But at the same time the Sultan's *firman* enabled Germany to appoint six of the eleven directors of the Baghdad company; so that, although France and England were to contribute sixty per cent of the money, they would be effectually debarred from any voice in the management of the line. The bonds to be taken up were Turkish government securities, but the general financial situation of Turkey and the certainty that the railway would not be self-supporting made a depreciation almost inevitable; the *Deutsche Bank*, which was the financial backer of the grand project, would then buy in the bonds at a small figure, and Germany would acquire for a song the ownership of a railway which might do infinite damage to the very Powers whose money had been used for building it. Here again it is impossible to take seriously the German contention that France and Great Britain refused their help to a great economic enterprise out of jealousy and fear; quite apart from the fact that neither government exerted the slightest diplomatic pressure on Turkey to prevent the granting of the Baghdad concession,[1] they were both bound to safeguard the inter-

---

[1] In 1899 British influence would seem to have been exerted at Constantinople in favor of the concession, for this was the period when Joseph Chamberlain was advocating an Anglo-German alliance. Count Bülow's visit to London and the grant of the concession synchronized nicely.

ests of their investors and if possible to insure Turkey
against a financial collapse. Sound business and sound
politics alike demanded that London and Paris should
decline the German offer. Germany could not build the
Baghdad railway herself because she lacked capital; that
was her misfortune, but she could not expect other countries to build it for her and at the same time retain all the
advantages for herself.

In the second place, the British were not unnaturally
suspicious of the political aspects of the situation. They
understood thoroughly that the Baghdad line would place
Turkey under the tutelage of Germany; that they might
concede, under certain conditions, but surely they were
entitled to protect their own interests. Long before Germany had put the issue in the forefront of her policy her
diplomacy had opposed that of Great Britain in all quarters
of the globe; she had definitely challenged British naval
supremacy; and in 1905 she made a demonstration against
France, with the double object of breaking up the newly
formed *entente cordiale* and of establishing a hold on Morocco. She was not successful, but she might return
to the charge and another time she might gain her point:
that is, she would isolate England and she would establish
herself in Morocco. In view of this possibility, it was
unthinkable that Germany should be allowed a free hand
in the Baghdad railway, for she would then become the
mistress of the Mediterranean, and she could at her leisure
prepare to destroy the lonely British Empire by attacking
it in Egypt and the Persian Gulf.

It may not, at first sight, be clear how a line across
Asia Minor to the gulf could menace Egypt, protected as
it would be by the Arabian Desert and the Red Sea. To
begin with, a Turkey which was the vassal of Berlin would
offer no objections to the use of its Mediterranean ports
by German men-of-war. Still, a land attack would be

necessary for the recovery of Egypt. Now, in 1900 Abdul
Hamid had determined to construct a railway from Damascus southward to Medina and Mecca. The ostensible
object of the line was to facilitate pilgrimages to the holy
cities, and the Sultan cleverly appealed to the Mohammedan world for money and materials to build it; with
such success, indeed, that in 1908 the rails reached Medina.
Yet the real purpose of the line was political. The tribes
of the Hedjaz and the Yemen had for years resisted the
efforts of the Turkish Government to exercise real authority in western Arabia, and in this policy they had unquestionably been encouraged by the British Government,
which feared that the strengthening of Turkish influence in
Arabia would react unfavorably upon Egypt. The Hedjaz
railway could now be used for transporting troops to the
disturbed regions; connected with the Baghdad line, when
the latter should reach Aleppo, it would enable the Sultan
to concentrate large military forces along the eastern frontier of Egypt. And behind the whole enterprise England
saw the hand of Germany, even though the line had been
rather ostentatiously constructed by the Turks without
foreign assistance. The German attitude was frankly revealed by Dr. Paul Rohrbach in the second edition of his
book, *Die Bagdadbahn:*

"England can be attacked and mortally wounded by land from
Europe in one place only—Egypt. The loss of Egypt would mean
for England not only the end of her control of the Suez Canal and
her connections with India and eastern Asia, but probably the loss
of her possessions in Central and East Africa as well. The conquest
of Egypt by a Mohammedan Power like Turkey would react most
dangerously upon England's 60,000,000 Mohammedan subjects in
India and would prejudice her position in Afghanistan and Persia.
Turkey, however, cannot dream of recovering Egypt until she pos-
sesses a developed railway system in Asia Minor and Syria, and
until, through the progress of the Anatolian railway to Baghdad,
she can withstand a British attack on Mesopotamia; until her army

is increased and improved, and her economic and financial situation advanced."

For these reasons, Dr. Rohrbach says, Germany must give Turkey every assistance, and, though he insists that the German policy is defensive, he remarks:

"Egypt is a prize which for Turkey would well be worth the risk of taking sides with Germany in a war with England." [1]

The possibilities of the situation were foreseen in an incident of the year 1906. By that time the Hedjaz railway had been built considerably beyond Maan, a point just east of Akaba, which is at the head of the gulf of that name and lies within striking distance of Suez. In February a detachment of Turkish troops suddenly appeared at Akaba, and proceeded to occupy Tabah, on the other side of the gulf, with the object of pushing the Turkish frontier westward to the southern entrance of the canal. Needless to say, the British foreign office lost no time in asserting the rights of Egypt, which rested on the correspondence exchanged between Constantinople and Cairo, in 1892, upon the accession of the Khedive Abbas II. The Porte yielded, but not until a British squadron had been despatched to the eastern Mediterranean. "The diplomacy of the Emperor William II was officially disinterested in the Tabah incident, but the power of insinuation was stronger than the wishes of statesmen: German influence was so preponderant at Constantinople, the advice of the imperial ambassador was so heeded and so complete, so general was the dovetailing of Turkish and German interests, that public opinion in all countries was bound to regard the occupation of Tabah by Ottoman troops as the result of advice or encouragement from Berlin. . . . Great Britain and the whole of Europe were persuaded that behind the Turko-Egyptian dispute there must neces-

[1] Pp. 18-19.

---

sarily be lurking an episode of Anglo-German rivalry, a preliminary skirmish foreshadowing the harsh struggle for influence waged by the two great European empires over the ruins of Turkey." [1] Passing from surmises to facts, it is sufficient to recall, in justification of British apprehensions, that in the autumn of 1914 Turkey went to war with England at the behest of Germany, and actually used the Hedjaz railway in preparing for her attack on the Suez Canal.

The third and most important aspect of the Baghdad question was concerned with the Persian Gulf. The concession of 1903 authorized the building of the railway from Baghdad to Bassorah, and thence to some point on the gulf. Bassorah, the only commercial town south of Baghdad, was the logical terminus of the line, but owing to the bar at the mouth of the Shatt-el-Arab (as the fusion of the Tigris and Euphrates is called) it could be reached only by small ships. A gulf port was therefore desirable, and Koweit was the logical choice. But the Sheikh of Koweit denied that he was a vassal of the Sultan,[2] and when in 1900 the Germans endeavored to buy terminal facilities and lease a large concession he politely refused; for in January, 1899, he had secretly accepted the protection of the British Government in return for a promise not to cede any territory without the consent of Great Britain. For the next few years the Sheikh had to be protected by British cruisers against German intrigues and Turkish attempts to use force; but in 1901 an Anglo-Turkish agreement practically confirmed his independence and secured for him an increase of territory. The question came to

[1] Pinon, *L'Europe et l'Empire ottoman*, pp. 387, 389.
[2] In 1870, in return for his assistance to Midhat Pasha, he was given the title of kaimakam (the head of a sanjak) by the Sultan, but the duties were quite honorary, and no recognition of Turkish suzerainty was ever made by the sheikh, who throughout the nineteenth century was an independent potentate in fact quite as much as in theory.

a head with the announcement by Lord Lansdowne, then foreign secretary, in May, 1903, that Great Britain "would regard the establishment of a naval base or a fortified port in the Persian Gulf as a very grave menace to British interests, and would certainly resist it by all means at her disposal." [1] By what right did Great Britain thus proclaim a Monroe Doctrine for a body of water which washed the shores of independent countries (Turkey and Persia)? Did the Baghdad railway threaten the interests of England in the gulf so severely that she was justified in vetoing that section of the line from Baghdad to the gulf?

The British flag was first flown in the Persian Gulf in 1618, the year that saw the opening of the Thirty Years' War in Germany. In 1622 a treaty was concluded with Persia by which the British undertook "to keep two men-of-war constantly to defend the gulf"; [2] the number was subsequently increased to five, and ever since Great Britain has enjoyed paramountcy in those waters. It is not generally realized that the British were in the gulf some two hundred and fifty years before the Turks. The latter acquired nominal control of Mesopotamia and Arabia early in the sixteenth century, and their flag was hoisted at Bassorah in 1668; but until Midhat Pasha became governor of Baghdad, in 1869, no effort was made to assert Turkish authority on the western shores of the gulf. Even then Arabia was never reduced, and after Midhat's recall in 1873 Turkish interest again languished until stimulated by German ambitions.

During this long period the East India Company, and later the British Government, undertook the work that properly belonged to Turkey and Persia. At a consider-

---

[1] House of Lords, 5 May, 1903. (4 *Hansard* cxxi, c. 1348.)

[2] Quoted in *The Times History of the War*, 1914, vol. III, p. 84. The story of British policy in the Persian Gulf, the Gulf of Aden, and Arabia is well told by Dr. Rouire, *La Rivalité anglo-russe au XIXme siècle en Asie* (1908), part 1. Only the barest outline has been given in the text.

able expenditure of blood and treasure both piracy and the slave-trade were suppressed and gun-running reduced to a minimum. A hydrographic survey was begun as early as 1785. The lighthouse service was established by the British. Their sanitary measures helped exterminate the plague, which was for long endemic. Finally, the British resident at Bushire, on the Persian side, was the arbiter of local disputes and the guarantor of peace and security, especially during the date and pearling seasons, when local notables were apt to get out of hand. Great Britain may fairly claim to have discharged her duty as policeman with reasonableness and honesty.

Such a policy was, of course, dictated by enlightened self-interest, for disorder was prejudicial to British trade, and British trade has enjoyed almost a monopoly in the region, amounting to some £7,000,000 a year. The local products—wool, dates, barley, rice, and pearls—are exchanged for the cottons of Manchester and the coal of Wales, and English or Indian money is almost the medium of exchange. These goods are carried almost exclusively in British ships. Since 1834 the navigation of the Tigris as far as Baghdad has been controlled by Messrs. Lynch, whose steamers are better, faster, and infinitely more regular in their sailings than any which the Turkish Government has placed in service. Baghdad is also important as a distributing centre for the trade of Persia, and a British consul was appointed in 1798.

Germany began to invade this preserve of British commerce in the last decade of the nineteenth century. There is no need of repeating the familiar story of her success, which rested upon the cheapness of German goods, the foresight of her bankers, and the capacity of her local representatives. After the Hamburg-America Line established a monthly service to Bassorah, in September, 1906, German progress was steady and rapid, and, although her

trade remained far behind that of Great Britain, the outlook was distinctly favorable when the Great War began.
With the coming of the Baghdad railway greater things
were hoped for, because the railway was to make Mesopotamia once more a garden of prosperity, and would
provide a direct connection with Germany and western
Europe.

"It may be argued that Germany had an entire right to establish and extend her trade around the shores of this inland sea [the
Persian Gulf]. Of course she had. No one has ever dreamed of
questioning her right to trade or to build railways. What was
questioned were her motives and some of her acts. It was the combination of commercial effort with political action, so lucidly explained by the *Berliner Tageblatt*, which roused British hostility
to the doings of Germany in the Persian Gulf. On innumerable
German platforms the ultimate aims of Germany in the Middle
East were expounded with arrogance and without reserve. Countless German books dealt with the same theme. The intention was
to supplant and replace British influence in these regions, and not
to supplement it. To that great end all the German efforts were
in reality directed." [1]

No one ever denied that from the economic point of view
the Baghdad railway was a laudable enterprise, although
objections were raised to its financial methods. Its competition was recognized as desirable, for the freight rates
charged by British shipping companies engaged in the
gulf trade were outrageously high. It might carry the
Indian mails and much of the Indian passenger traffic,
especially if the trans-Persian line were built. In short,
British trade was bound to benefit by an improvement in
local economic conditions, and this fact was fully recog-

---

[1] *The Times History of the War*, 1914, vol. III, p. 101. The reference to the *Berliner Tageblatt* is to a statement made in 1907, that "commerce and politics can no
longer be divided," and that Germany could attain commercial success only by
"energetic political action."

nized in both England and India   British capitalists were quite ready to invest their money in the Baghdad line as soon as their government withdrew its opposition.

On account of the danger to India from a hostile naval force in the Persian Gulf, Great Britain has always insisted that no European Power should secure a foothold there. She made no political conquests for herself (except the Bahrein Islands); she enforced the same rule on others. The Germans, however, were fully determined to acquire a port on the gulf, and secured the right in Article XXIII of the convention of 1903.   From the Sheikh of Koweit they tried first to secure Koweit itself, and later the island of Bubian, which belonged to him.   They persuaded Abdul Hamid to grant a pearl monopoly on the island of Halul, which did not belong to him, but which might become an oriental Heligoland; but only a sharp word from London was required to quash the scheme.   The Germans, who worked through the commercial house of Wonckhaus, in Bahrein, next endeavored to secure the island of Abu Musa, where there were deposits of red oxide.   The Sheikh of Shargah, to whom the island belonged, objected to Wonckhaus acquiring the concession, and with the help of a British cruiser removed the invaders; whereupon the German Government formally protested and publicly challenged the position of Great Britain in the gulf. Finally, great pressure was put upon the Sheikh of Mohammerah, who was nominally a vassal of the Shah of Persia but in reality a dependent of Great Britain, to allow his lands to be irrigated by a German company.   It cannot be doubted that if these several schemes had matured, Germany would promptly have sent war-ships to the gulf to protect her interests, and that the range of Anglo-German rivalry, already sufficiently large, might have been extended to the Indian Ocean.   As soon as the Germans and the Turks renounced any political ambitions in the gulf, Great Britain, as will presently be seen, withdrew her opposition to the Baghdad railway; but to imagine that she would abdicate a position obtained at such great sacrifices merely at the behest of another Power—and this the Germans expected her to do—illustrates admirably the fact already referred to, that the Germans do not understand the fine art of politics.[1]

In spite, however, of the British opposition, the Baghdad company was able to sign a second convention with the Ottoman Government in June, 1908, which provided for the construction of the four sections beyond Eregli and would bring the line within one section of Mossul. The work was actually carried as far as Burgulu, only to be stopped by the Young Turk revolution and financial difficulties. But Anglo-German differences were not allayed by the suspension of the Baghdad enterprise, and were further envenomed by the Young Turk revolution.

On 24 July, 1908, the absolute power of the Sultan Abdul Hamid II was overturned by a revolution engineered by the officers of the army, who saw that the policy of the Sultan was conducting Turkey toward a general collapse

[1] Dr. Paul Rohrbach ascribes to British policy the twofold purpose of constructing a railway from Damascus to Baghdad, and thence to the gulf along the Tigris (the German line was to follow the Euphrates), and of transferring the Caliphate either to a British puppet ruler of Egypt or to one of the Arabian sheikhs under British influence. The first idea is an old one, having been much ventilated in the middle of the nineteenth century and being in all probability responsible for the acquisition of Cyprus in 1878. Then the matter was dropped until Sir William Willcocks, the famous irrigation expert, began the reclamation of the valley of the Euphrates. In 1909–11 the Homs-Baghdad railway was projected by French and British financiers, with the approval of their governments. They proposed that the Baghdad should be diverted from its original route and follow the Tigris, and that the Anglo-French line should join it at Deir or Anna. Thus the Homs-Baghdad line was to be not the rival but the complement of the Baghdad railway. The Anglo-French promoters, however, could not come to terms with the Germans, and the question never became a matter of practical politics. As to the Caliphate, Dr. Rohrbach ascribes too much importance to the institution, and ought to know that a caliph under the control or influence of a Christian Power would not be acceptable to the Mohammedan world.

that must end in a partition among the Great Powers. In the march of events Anglo-German rivalry played a part which must now be examined.

The intolerable misgovernment of Macedonia at the hands of Abdul Hamid produced a general insurrection in the summer of 1902, and still another in 1903. Austria and Russia, the Powers most directly interested, drew up a programme of reforms which was accepted by the Sultan, but which was not applied, for Abdul Hamid was sure of the support of Germany. It became increasingly likely that the Near Eastern question would be reopened forcibly by the Balkan states, and that a general conflagration might ensue.[1]

True, therefore, to the policy adopted after the Boer War, and in strict conformity with her own interests, Great Britain in 1903 came forward as the advocate of an international régime in Macedonia. She desired the maintenance of the Ottoman Empire as the surest means of protecting her vital interests in the Mediterranean and the Persian Gulf; at the same time it was essential that the lot of the subject peoples should be so improved that constant rebellion would not shake and destroy the entire edifice. Her policy, accordingly, was to rehabilitate the European concert and through it to exert a pressure on the Sultan which he could not resist. On paper considerable success was achieved. Civil, military, and financial agents of the Powers were appointed to assist the Ottoman authorities in Macedonia, and a three-per-cent increase in the Turkish customs was allowed in order that funds might be available for the work of reform. As the next step it was proposed to place the judiciary under international control, and the details of this reform had been prepared

---

[1] On the question of reforms: Victor Bérard, *La Révolution turque* (1909), parts 3 and 4; René Pinon, *L'Europe et l'Empire ottoman*, chaps. 3–6. The extensive *Blue* and *Yellow Books* of the British and French Governments are carefully digested.

by the Powers of the Triple *Entente* when the revolution
of July, 1908, occurred.

Nevertheless, this sweeping programme had effected
little change in the condition of Macedonia, for the agents
of the Powers were not possessed of the authority to *act*—
they could merely advise and report. For this half-measure
of internationalization Germany must be held responsible.
She did not oppose, in principle, the doctrine advocated
by the other Powers, but she adopted an attitude essentially conservative. In brief, she opposed any diminution
of the Sultan's authority in his own dominions, and until
his authority could be controlled no reform was possible.
Her policy was at least consistent. If she abandoned Adbul
Hamid in his time of trouble, she could not hope for a continuance of those economic and political concessions which
were rapidly making the Ottoman Empire a preserve of
her influence and commerce; in particular, the Baghdad
railway depended upon the good will and favor of the Porte,
and a real internationalization of Ottoman affairs would
introduce other influences which would undermine the
prestige that she had acquired by the hard work of many
years. Moreover, autonomy, such as England proposed
for Macedonia, would be the prelude to independence, if
Turkish history furnished any basis for prophecy. Germany, with her hard-and-fast ideas of government, could
not understand how a loosening of the central power would
contribute to the security and strength of the Ottoman
Empire; she much preferred the autocratic and central-
ized system of Abdul Hamid, which corresponded to her
own institutions. Turkey was fast becoming a German
protectorate; when that process was completed Germany
could then undertake a thorough reorganization of its government and finances, and such a reformed Turkey would
make Germany the dominant Power in the Near and
Middle East. Lastly, the Anglo-Russian convention of

1907 had an important bearing on the situation. That
agreement, by its virtual partition of Persia, dealt German
influence a severe blow in the latter country. It also foreshadowed Anglo-Russian co-operation in the affairs of
Turkey, in a sense not palatable to Germany.[1] All the
more, therefore, was she constrained to stand by Abdul
Hamid in his resistance to the repeated representations of
England and Russia, who were regularly accused of plotting
his destruction.

The Young Turk revolution was undoubtedly precipitated by the meeting of Edward VII and Nicholas II at
Reval, in June, 1908. Among the topics discussed was the
Anglo-Russian programme of judicial reform in Macedonia,
which was, indeed, given its final shape, and the two Powers
were expected to exert great pressure in presenting it to
the Porte. German writers go so far as to say that the
reforms were a blind and were devised to provide an
excuse for declaring war on Turkey, whose partition had
been carefully arranged by the King and the Tsar.[2] This
is most unlikely, and no proof has ever been presented of
such a conspiracy; but the Young Turks were alarmed,
and believed that the acceptance of the reform programme
would put their country in the grip of the Powers. Their
prompt action took Europe by surprise and, not least of
all, their proclamation of the old constitution of 1876,
which, by setting up a full-fledged constitutional system,
went much farther in the direction of reform than the
Powers had proposed in their most zealous moments.

[1] "From the moment England and Russia arrived at an understanding the fate
of Turkey in Europe was in jeopardy, and any ambitions which Germany had in
Turkey were doomed to sterility." (Sidney Whitman, *Turkish Memories*, 1914,
p. 277.) Mr. Whitman remarks that German influence in Turkey was not popular
with the masses, who regarded the concessionaires as usurers and as the harbingers
of German political control; nor did the Turkish character respond to the systematic
training of the German officers who were sent to reorganize the army.

[2] *E. g.*, Dr. Rohrbach, "L'Evolution de l'Allemagne comme puissance mondiale,"
Revue Politique Internationale, July, 1914, p. 30.

The latter, for their part, were so pleased to be quit of the business of reform that they withdrew the agents which they had hitherto maintained in the Balkans for advising the Turkish authorities—with what disastrous results the Balkan wars of 1912–13 presently revealed.

Englishmen hailed the overthrow of Abdul Hamid with enthusiasm, not only because a hateful tyranny was supplanted by constitutional government, but because German ascendency in Turkish politics was destroyed, at least for the moment. The British ambassador in Constantinople was lionized in the streets; King Edward telegraphed his felicitations to Kiamil Pasha, a life-long Anglophile, who became grand vizier; and for a time it seemed as if Great Britain would resume her ancient position, maintained until the days of Abdul Hamid, of chief friend and protector of Turkey. And there can be no doubt that if Turkey had fulfilled the promises of the first glorious days of the revolution, when all races and religions fraternized for joy over the disappearance of the Hamidian despotism; if the new government had persevered in the policy of equality, toleration, and the rule of law enshrined in the revived constitution; and if international complications had not arisen—then, British influence might have regained a permanent ascendency and have directed the reforming movement to a successful issue.

But Germany was not disposed to surrender her position without a struggle. When Abdul Hamid, in April, 1909, attempted to overthrow the Young Turk Committee of Union and Progress, it was Germany who urged them to march on Constantinople with the army of Salonika, it was Germany who outlined the plan of campaign and financed the expedition.[1] Abdul Hamid deposed, the military element of the Committee took charge of the govern-

[1] Sir William Ramsay, *The Revolution in Constantinople and Turkey* (1909), pp. 42–44.

mont, and they were mainly men who had received their
education in the German army. Determined to reform
the Turkish army, they naturally turned to Germany for
assistance, which was readily granted in the shape of Baron
von der Goltz, who returned to his old functions in Constantinople. As soldiers they looked askance upon concessions to subject nationalities which might in any way
weaken the military resources of the state, and they soon
returned to the centralizing system of Abdul Hamid; as
financiers they found the bourses of London and Paris
closed to them because the reorganized Turkish army was
suspected of being at the disposal of Germany in case of
a European war.

Baron Marschall von Bieberstein, the German ambassador to the Porte, also made the most of the international
situation. Scarcely was the July revolution over when
Austria proceeded to annex Bosnia and Herzegovina, and
Bulgaria proclaimed her independence. These affronts to
Turkey came from Germany's ally and her friend, and
they were carried through only by the aid of Germany.
None the less German diplomacy persuaded the two cul-
prits to pay damages to the amount of 179,000,000 francs,
which were sorely needed by the Turkish Government;
and it helped to prevent the Cretan question from being
raised. It was easy for so experienced a diplomatist as
Baron von Marschall to point out that Great Britain, the
supposed friend of the new régime, had done nothing to
help it, in spite of many professions, and that she was the
most formidable opponent of Pan-Islamism, with which
the Young Turks, largely freethinkers, were already co-
quetting. If Turkey wished to avoid future international
difficulties, she must reorganize her army and provide
railways for its service: in each case German advice and
assistance could be had for the asking.

So it came about that the influence of England was

speedily shattered, and Germany became as ardent a sup-
porter of the Young Turks as she had been of the Hamidian
system which they had overturned. Henceforth the Committee ignored the criticisms of the British press upon their
ruthless policy, and went serenely to their doom, trusting
in the diplomacy and strength of Germany—after the manner of Abdul Hamid, and with similar results. For just as
in 1908 the old Sultan was left to the mercy of the Young
Turks, so in 1912 Germany did not raise her finger to stay
the Balkan states from the campaign which cost Turkey
her European provinces. Yet, in spite of these bitter experiences, the Turks allowed themselves in the autumn of
1914 to be dragged into war with England by the intrigues
of Germany !

In the early days of October, 1908, Austria-Hungary
announced that she would annex the provinces of Bosnia
and Herzegovina, which she had "occupied and administered" since the Congress of Berlin thirty years before,
and Bulgaria proclaimed her independence, thereby repu-
diating the suzerainty of Turkey laid upon her by the same
Congress. Neither act involved any real change in the
Balkan situation, except to dispose of any hopes which
the Young Turks might have cherished of recovering the
provinces in question; and had the European Powers been
consulted, they would doubtless have consented to the
procedure of the Dual Monarchy and the principality of
Bulgaria. As it was, the Powers were taken by surprise,
and were entitled to protest that the treaty of Berlin could
not be amended without the consent of the signatory
Powers. Out of this situation there arose a crisis which
had an important bearing on the relations of England and
Germany.

The conversion of the Bosnian occupation into a permanent annexation had been a project of Austrian diplomacy
for many years, but Count Goluchowski, foreign minister

from 1895 to 1906, was loyal to the Austro-Russian agreement of 1897 for preserving the *status quo* in the Balkans. His successor, Baron von Aerenthal, was a man of different caliber. Secretive, ambitious, and nimble-witted, he inaugurated a forward policy which, in the hands of Count Berchtold, culminated in the Great War of 1914. Aerenthal resented the rôle of "brilliant second"[1] to Berlin, which the Ballplatz had played ever since the conclusion of the Austro-German alliance, and planned to score a victory of his own, which could be won only in the Balkans. He regarded the liberalizing and reforming policy of Lord Lansdowne and Sir Edward Grey in Macedonia with disgust, and affected to believe that British influence in the Near East was negligible. He therefore endeavored to reconstitute the old Three Emperors' League, with the difference that its centre was to be Vienna and not Berlin. Russia was to be bribed by the opening of the Straits, and France also might be bought off by a free hand in Morocco, provided she would consent to finance the Baghdad railway. Then the *Drang nach Osten* could be resumed in earnest.

Unfortunately for the Austrian statesman, M. Isvolsky, the Russian foreign minister, had other plans, to wit, a reconciliation with England, and the Anglo-Russian convention was signed on 31 August, 1907. Aerenthal now prepared to break with Russia, and did so with characteristic duplicity. In September–October, 1907, he drafted with M. Isvolsky the judicial reform scheme for Macedonia (an English project, which he detested!), and then, by promising not to support it, secured from the Porte in January, 1908, a concession for a railway through the sanjak of Novi-Bazar and western Macedonia to Salonika. As the proposed line had been condemned by the Austrian

---

[1] This was the left-handed compliment addressed to Count Goluchowski by the German Emperor in a telegram after the Algeciras Conference.

general staff and, being longer than the existing route through Belgrade, was useless from a commercial point of view, it was believed that Aerenthal's purpose was so to discredit his Russian colleague that his resignation would follow, and then the Anglo-Russian *entente* would collapse. This did not happen: on the contrary, Russia promptly secured from the Porte the promise of a railway from Nish, Serbia, across Albania to the Adriatic, and M. Isvolsky and Sir Edward Grey proceeded to draft their own programme of reforms, which, as noted above, was the immediate occasion of the Turkish revolution. Thus Aerenthal's diplomacy had secured no positive advantage; in addition, it merited the censure of Sir Edward Grey, that an international project had been utilized by Austria to further her private interests.[1] It is not surprising, therefore, that in the crisis produced by the annexation of Bosnia, Sir Edward Grey did not see eye to eye with Baron von Aerenthal, and that he was disposed to support the contentions of Russia.

The Russian Government had accepted the annexation of Bosnia, in principle, in June, 1908, and again in September, after the Turkish revolution made such a transformation desirable.[2] But M. Isvolsky had stipulated for advance notice of such action: the matter would have to be approved by a European conference, and Russia could then claim her compensation—the opening of the Straits. Nevertheless Aerenthal contented himself with sending M. Isvolsky a private letter two days before the annexation was proclaimed, and the Russian foreign minister felt that he had been tricked. So did the British Government.

[1] House of Commons, 25 February, 1908. (4 *Hansard* clxxxiv. cc. 1700–01.)

[2] An impartial view of the controversy is presented by René Pinon, *L'Europe et la jeune Turquie* (1911), chaps. 4, 5; the Russian and Austrian versions by two articles in the *Fortnightly Review*, September, November, 1909; the British position in H. W. Steed, *The Hapsburg Monarchy* (1913), chapter on "Foreign Policy." The fullest account of the negotiations is given in A. Viallate, *La Vie politique dans les deux mondes*, 1908–9, pp. 156–187.

For when King Edward paid his annual visit to the Emperor Francis Joseph in August not a word was said about the contemplated action of Austria-Hungary. This was doubtless Aerenthal's revenge for the Anglo-Russian agreement of the year before, which he had tried to forestall; but his conduct did not smooth the way for a prompt recognition of the *fait accompli* in Bosnia.

M. Isvolsky and Sir Edward Grey at once agreed to demand the summoning of a European conference, in which they were supported by France. Their position was thoroughly sound, for to admit the Austrian right to tear up a solemn treaty at her convenience was to consign the public law of Europe to the scrap-basket. They went farther —they claimed compensation for Serbia. For that little state saw its cherished ambitions rudely and decisively crushed by the annexation. As long as the provinces in question were even nominally parts of the Ottoman Empire, there was the chance that some day, when Francis Joseph should die, they might be incorporated in a Greater Serbia, which was perhaps the only permanent solution of the Southern Slav problem. To this end an extensive propaganda had been carried on for years in Bosnia-Herzegovina, and with no little success: all such hopes now seemed permanently extinguished. The Serbian Government, therefore, formally protested against the annexation, began to mobilize its army, and assumed a warlike attitude. It counted upon the assistance of Russia, both on account of Russia's particular interest in Serbia and because of the enthusiasm aroused in all walks of Russian life by the appeal of a Slav nation. M. Isvolsky can scarcely be blamed for accepting the Serbian contention and for trying to extricate Russia from a difficult situation which was not of her choosing.

Yet it must be admitted that the Serbian case was open to question. Politically, the situation recalled the Austro-

Sardinian complications of fifty years before. Serbia aspired to unite under her rule those Slavs of the Dual Monarchy who were of the Serb race, even though a majority of the Serbo-Croatian race already lived in Austria-Hungary. In 1859 the kingdom of Sardinia stood forward as the champion of Italian unity against Austrian oppression, and readily conquered the sympathies of Europe and America. In 1908 Serbia could point to the discontent of the Southern Slavs of the Dual Monarchy, whose treatment of them had been disgusting, as an adequate reason for refusing to recognize the annexation of Bosnia, which was considered the forerunner of the conquest of Serbia. None the less, the Serbian claim rested on no treaty, no promise, no sanction of international law. True, the Austrian action was a violation of international law; but the pressure of other Powers might persuade her to allow that action to be formally approved by the signatories of the Berlin treaty, and thus legalized.

But by supporting the Serbian demands for compensation, a purely *political* consideration, the British Government weakened its *legal* right to demand the observance of the violated treaty. Sir Edward Grey might argue that as Austria had broken the law she must be punished, but after all that law prescribed no scale of punishments for its infraction. Doubtless, if Sir Edward had been willing to concede the opening of the Straits, which M. Isvolsky requested and to which Austria was practically pledged, the Serbian controversy would not have arisen, or would have been speedily adjusted, for Russia would have achieved the great goal of her policy. As it was, in default of the greater promise, England made the lesser concession, and with the diplomatic support of England, France, and Russia, the Serbian Government held out against Austria for six months, to the great derangement of the latter's finances and economic life.

The story of those six months need not be told here. Suffice it to say that in March, 1909, the Russian Govern- ment decided not to go to war, and consented to the an- nexation of the provinces to Austria-Hungary. British support of Serbian claims, promised only "so long as they should be seconded by Russia," was also withdrawn, and Sir Fairfax Cartwright, the British ambassador at Vienna, exerted himself to find a satisfactory formula to which Serbia might subscribe. Inasmuch as her declaration of 31 March, 1909, was the basis of the Austrian ultimatum of 23 July, 1914, it is well to give the full text:

"Serbia recognizes that the *fait accompli* regarding Bosnia has not affected her rights, and consequently she will conform to the decisions that the Powers may take in conformity with the treaty of Berlin. In deference to the advice of the Great Powers Serbia undertakes to renounce from now onward the attitude of protest and opposition which she has adopted with regard to the annex- ation since last autumn. She undertakes, moreover, to modify the direction of her policy with regard to Austria-Hungary and to live in future on good, neighborly terms with the latter."

The humiliation of the little kingdom was complete; but it saved its dignity by presenting the note to the *Powers*, and not to Austria, a fact which clearly emphasized the international character of the Balkan problem.

In this fashion the peace of Europe was, for the moment, preserved, but in the end at an excessive cost. Austria had indeed scored a distinct diplomatic success. In the fulness of time, however, the wheel came full circle. The defiance of the public law of Europe was profoundly re- sented in Italy, where it was regarded as the first step toward that Austrian advance along the Adriatic which Italy was determined never to permit.[1] Hence the Italian

[1] Italy, with Russian help, secured the retrocession to Turkey of the sanjak of Novi-Bazar and the release of Montenegro from those limitations of sovereignty over her territorial waters imposed by Article XXIX of the treaty of Berlin.

overtures to Russia, which led to a cordial meeting between the Tsar and Victor Emmanuel III at Racconigi, in October, 1909, thus indicating Italy's distrust of the Triple Alliance. And when the opportunity came Italy went to Tripoli, thus shattering the alliance, because her new colony was at the mercy of the French and British fleets in the Mediterranean. When the Turkish resistance proved stubborn, she encouraged, if she did not abet, the formation of the Balkan League, which practically extinguished the Turkish power in Europe. Out of that conflagration arose the new Serbia which provoked Austria to bring on the present war. Thus for the sake of an unreal triumph, the Dual Monarchy was compelled, after five years, to stake its very existence in a conflict which must raise for —let us hope—a last settlement those problems which it desired to postpone indefinitely.

In the second place, Europe was left divided into two diplomatic camps pursuing conflicting policies and deeply suspicious of each other. For this state of affairs Germany and England were chiefly responsible, for by intervening in disputes not of primary concern to themselves, each gave countenance to the charge of the other that ulterior motives and deep-laid plots had prompted its intervention. To Germany Sir Edward Grey's support of Serbia was explicable only on the ground that England was practically an ally of Russia. Germany therefore acted vigorously in support of her ally. But by so doing she bound Austria so closely to herself that the consolidation of the *Entente*, against which Germany was constantly protesting, became more necessary than ever as a protection against the Austro-German combination.

Baron von Aerenthal did not take the advice of Berlin upon the annexation of Bosnia; he boldly proclaimed it, and then notified his ally. For the moment the German Government was indignant, because the stroke threatened

to injure German interests in Turkey. But Prince Bülow
at once decided to stand by Austria, who would not be able
to resist the pressure of Great Britain, France, and Russia
on behalf of a conference, and on 13 October notified Sir
Edward Grey that "Germany could not, any more than
Austria-Hungary, allow the discussion of the annexation
by the conference." [1] For the rest, she endeavored to
keep out of the discussion, except that she helped effect
the Austro-Turkish accord which enabled Aerenthal to
maintain his intransigent attitude toward Serbia. Then
on 21 February, 1909, when the French and British Governments proposed that the Powers should take joint
action at Vienna and Belgrade—for Austrian and Russian
mobilizations had made the situation very tense—Berlin
flatly refused and demanded that pressure be exerted at
Belgrade to compel an acceptance of Austria's terms.
This was rejected by Russia, and the danger of war increased. But about 21 March, M. Isvolsky prepared to
capitulate. Suddenly, on the 23d, the German ambassador in St. Petersburg was instructed to make representations in favor of Austria, who was neither aware of the
proceedings nor needed such assistance. The published
statement declared that Count Pourtalès had merely offered some "friendly advice" (*avis amical*), but in May,
1910, on the occasion of his visit to Vienna, the German
Emperor boasted that he had supported his ally "in shining armor," and M. Isvolsky always described the incident,
to those entitled to inquire, as *une mise-en-demeure péremp-
toire*, which marks a serious stage in diplomatic negotiations.[2] M. Isvolsky may have preferred yielding to German pressure rather than Austrian stubbornness, but the
German action created a profoundly disagreeable impression on Russian public opinion, and in considering the events
of July, 1914, when German policy followed the prece-

[1] Reichstag, 29 March, 1909.   [2] Steed, *The Hapsburg Monarchy*, p. 262.

dents of 1908–9 with considerable exactness, it is well to remember that the Russian Government could not be expected to undergo such a humiliation a second time.

Germany's diplomatic support of Austria-Hungary was, of course, as justifiable as the assistance given Russia by Great Britain. But Prince Bülow's explanation of his policy reads as follows:

"The German sword had been thrown into the scale of European decision, directly in support of our Austro-Hungarian ally, indirectly for the preservation of European peace, and above all for the sake of German credit and the maintenance of our position in the world. It would now be made manifest whether Germany really had been checkmated by the policy of isolation and whether the Powers that had been drawn into the circle of anti-German policy would find it consistent with their vital interests in Europe to take up a hostile attitude toward the German Empire and its allies. The course of the Bosnian crisis, in point of fact, made an end of the policy of isolation. . . . The policy of isolation, which seemed likely to endanger our safety, was directed against the international trade and the sea power of Germany. By means of our strength as a Continental Power, we tore the web which encompassed us." [1]

The German sword had been thrown into the scale . . . for the sake of German credit : this does not sound like peaceful or disinterested diplomacy anxious to resolve a difficult question that might unchain a general war. Rather, it is the policy of the mailed fist, which succeeded because no one was prepared to resist it. As to the isolation of which Prince Bülow complains, it is sufficient to quote his own remarks in the Reichstag in December, 1908. Adverting to an interview with M. Isvolsky at the beginning of the crisis, he said:

"M. Isvolsky and I were agreed that Russian policy could have no point against Germany, and *vice versa;* in addition, that the

[1] *Imperial Germany*, pp. 62–63, 65.

old friendly relations must be maintained.   The Russian minister, on that occasion, renewed the assurance that there existed no understanding between Russia and England, either public or secret, which could be directed against German interests."

If, as the prince has argued at length in his *Imperial Germany*, Germany's undertakings in the field of world diplomacy depended on her position as a Continental Power, and that was secured by "the hard facts of the Triple Alliance," [1] why should Germany protest against an agreement of the other three Powers?   Great Britain, for her part, never objected to the Triple Alliance, and Sir Edward Grey condemned the allegation that any British differences with Austria had been provoked by hostility to Germany.[2]

On the other hand, British policy during the crisis was not very happily inspired.   Mr. Asquith declared that its attitude was "entirely disinterested," [3] and, according to Sir Edward Grey, "the knowledge that Italy and Germany were working for peace removed all risk of friction with them." [4]   As M. Isvolsky had declared from the first that there would be no war,[5] the danger of an explosion came from the intransigeance of Serbia, and, apparently to forestall such a calamity, Sir Edward Grey promised British diplomatic support to the Serbian claims for compensation. That, as has been seen, prolonged the crisis, and almost brought on the war it was intended to avoid.   Also, it enabled Germany to put forward her theory of a policy of isolation, because England certainly had no direct interest in Serbia.   But instead of crediting Sir Edward with a Machiavellian scheme to injure Germany, it is much simpler and more in keeping with his straightforward character to say that he misjudged the situation and made

[1] P. 66.
[2] House of Commons, 29 March, 1909. (5 *Hansard* iii, cc. 57–58.)
[3] Guild Hall, London, 9 November, 1908.
[4] Coldstream, 22 January, 1909.
[5] Interview in the *Temps* (Paris), 8 October, 1908.

a mistake; as, in fact, he practically confessed when he
refused to express any opinion on the merits of the Austro-
Serbian controversy of July, 1914, and valiantly endeavored to find a solution by means of the European concert.[1]
Great Britain subsequently re-established cordial relations
with Austria, but Germans clung to the idea that the opposition of views in 1908–9 had been dictated by the considered
(or ill-considered) prejudice of the British foreign office
against themselves, and the good effects of King Edward's
visit to Berlin in February, 1909, before the crisis was adjusted, were undone by the British naval programme for
1909–10.

Thus the Bosnian crisis illustrates admirably the remark
of the French writer, quoted on the first page of this book,
who described Anglo-German rivalry as "the essential
fact which dominates the whole policy of our time, which
thrusts itself into all events to embitter and warp them,
and which is to be found at the bottom of all the political
crises by whose succession Europe is periodically agitated."
England and Germany, theoretically, had only a secondary
interest in the controversy about two provinces of the
Ottoman Empire. A mistake on the part of England en-
ables Germany to intervene as a principal; she boasts that
she has dealt a death-blow to the policy of the former;
England resents the accusation that her policy has been
directed against Germany, and strengthens her navy; this
Germany regards as sure proof of England's unremitting
hostility; and finally each country is convinced that the
crisis arose through the machinations of the other, which
must be thwarted by more diplomacy or more armaments,
either of which is bound to increase the suspicions already
cherished on the other side of the North Sea!

In the opinion of the writer, Germany has made out a

[1] Cf. Great Britain and the European Crisis (1914), no. 5, Sir Edward Grey to Sir
M. de Bunsen, 24 July, 1914.

poor case for her intervention "in shining armor," and
Baron von Aerenthal was not grateful for her assistance.
Not only did it deprive him of the credit for the annexation, to which he was entitled; it showed Germany's unwillingness to let Austrian diplomacy pursue its own course
and her determination to assert her own power at all costs.
Until the end of his life Aerenthal had to combat the intrigues of the German ambassador at Vienna, whose influence steadily increased until, with his connivance, if
not under his direction, the fatal ultimatum to Serbia was
drafted in July, 1914. Not until the archives are opened
will the truth be fully known, but it is perfectly clear that
the seed of distrust which produced the catastrophe of
1914 was sown in the crisis of 1908–9, and that the policies
of the three eastern empires were determined in 1914 very
largely by their recollections of what had happened five
years before.

For several years after the Bosnian crisis Near Eastern
politics reflected the diplomatic schism of Europe. In appearance normal relations were restored by an Austro-
Serbian treaty of commerce (31 March, 1909) and a re-
sumption of regular intorcourse between Austria and Russia
(March, 1910). Actually there was little cordiality. The
Powers of the *Entente* labored to bring about a union of the
Balkan states which might raise an effective barrier to
Teutonic influence. To offset this, Germany and Austria
gave their unreserved support to the Young Turk government at Constantinople, and in the summer of 1910 there
were well-defined rumors of a Turco-Rumanian alliance
directed against Bulgaria. About the same time Turkey
applied to the French Government for permission to raise
a loan of 150,000,000 francs on the Paris bourse; this was
refused because the Turks would not give guarantees that
the money would not be used against the political interests
of France and Russia. For similar reasons the British

foreign office persuaded Sir Ernest Cassel, the great London financier, not to float the loan. German banks then raised the money, but on conditions decidedly more onerous than those offered in Paris and London; the money was spent on the Turkish army then being reorganized by a German mission, and this was held to justify the refusal of the *Entente* to participate in the loan.

Germany also succeeded in selling two old battleships to Turkey (August, 1910), a transaction not popular in England because these gaps in the German navy were filled by *Dreadnoughts*. As it turned out, the Turkish Government subsequently ordered two *Dreadnoughts* in England, and these were taken over by the British authorities at the beginning of the Great War. The incident did not, therefore, affect the superiority of the British navy, although the resentment of the Turks at the seizure of the ships seems to have aided the Young Turks in joining Germany against Great Britain. It may also be noted that, as an offset to the German control of the Turkish army, the reorganization of the navy was intrusted to British officers and that the customs were placed under the direction of Sir Richard Crawford, who managed them, to the great profit of the Porte until Turkey joined the European War.

This chapter may conclude with a statement of the progress of the Baghdad railway. The Young Turks, as noted above, very soon discarded all notions of liberty and equality, and embarked upon a policy of centralization and "Turkification." That brought its reward in the shape of constant rebellions, from Albania to Arabia. So it became imperative to establish railway communication with the disturbed regions, and the Baghdad negotiations were resumed. A series of new conventions was signed in the spring of 1911, but not before German diplomacy had obtained the support of Russia to the project, which had hitherto been unpopular in St. Petersburg.

The Anglo-Russian convention of 31 August, 1907, practically closed Persia to German influence, except in the central zone that was supposed to be excluded from British or Russian designs.   In the face of the virtual Russian protectorate over northern Persia, the German school at Teheran lost its importance, and German bankers could not for the future hope to participate in the frequent loans to the bankrupt Persian Government.   Germany at first tried to upset the new arrangements by inciting the Turks to occupy Persian territory in the province of Azerbaijan, to which they had some sort of claim, and by lending some support to the constitutional movement directed against the worthless Shah.   But he was amenable to Russian gold, the constitutionalists were incapable, and the British Government raised no objection to a Russian occupation of northern Persia, because it was threatening to interfere in the south in the interests of British trade.   In other words, the partition of Persia was an accomplished fact, carried out partly from the selfish ambitions of Russia and England, partly as a protection against the *Drang nach Osten*.   In order that the Baghdad railway might not be blocked indefinitely, Germany determined to come to terms with Russia and England, who were not opposed to the line if their own interests were adequately protected.

Accordingly, in November, 1910, the German Emperor received the Tsar at Potsdam, and a bargain was struck. Germany withdrew her opposition to Russian railway schemes in northern Persia, where she recognized the political, strategic, and economic interests of Russia, and Russia accepted the Baghdad railway, on condition that no branch lines were built into Armenia and Kurdistan—a common-sense agreement, for neither Power could prevent the construction of the other's railway.   The Russian and German systems were then to be linked up by a spur from Baghdad to Khanikin on the Persian frontier, which would enable

Germany to share in the trade of northern Persia, where Russia promised to maintain the open door. At the time, this Russo-German accord created an unfavorable impression. The Turks complained that they had been ignored. France feared that Germany was trying to weaken the Dual Alliance. English publicists alleged that Russia had abandoned the Triple *Entente*, and that German policy would have a free hand against British interests in the Persian Gulf; some looked askance upon the proposals for a trans-Persian railway which once more began to be mooted in connection with the probable completion of the Baghdad line. The German press, it may be remarked, paid glowing tributes to Russia on account of what was momentarily regarded as a blow to France and England, which countries were then the chief target of German diplomacy. No talk then of "the Slav peril"!

As a matter of fact, none of these apprehensions seem to have been justified. The railway situation in the Near and Middle East had reached an *impasse*, from which an escape could be found only by mutual concessions. The Potsdam negotiations, which were definitely recorded in a Russo-German convention of 19 August, 1911, may be regarded as the first step toward an equitable solution of the whole difficulty. They were followed by the agreement between the Turkish Government and the Baghdad railway company, the terms of which can now be understood.[1]

By the first of the three conventions, signed in March, 1911, the construction of the line from Halif to Baghdad was provided for, the section over the Taurus being temporarily abandoned. The company renounced any claim to share in the increased revenues expected from the raising of

---

[1] Victor Bérard, "Offres allemandes," "La Choix de Londres," *Revue de Paris,* 1 and 15 April, 1911; R. Said-Ruete, "Anglo-German Relations in the Near East," *England and Germany* (1912), pp. 66–71, a pro-English statement by a former officer in the German army.

the customs from eleven to fifteen per cent, and contented itself with the revenues already allocated for the Anatolian section of the line; this was, of course, a distinct concession to the British point of view. The second convention leased to the company the railway already running from Alexandretta, on the Mediterranean, to Osmanye, and permitted it to exploit Alexandretta as a commercial port; this gave the company an excellent harbor in the eastern Mediterranean. Finally, the company surrendered its right to construct the section from Baghdad to Bassorah, for which a new international company, under Turkish control, was to be formed; the Germans retaining only the right to as large a share of the capital as was accorded to any other Power. This, again, was a virtual acceptance of the British contention that British interests were not protected in the original concession. There remained the section from Bassorah to the gulf, which depended upon a satisfactory arrangement with Great Britain as regards the Sheikh of Koweit. Hakki Pasha, a former grand vizier, therefore repaired to London and opened negotiations with Sir Edward Grey. The discussions dragged on at inordinate length, and were interrupted by the Agadir crisis of 1911 and the Balkan Wars of 1912–13; but an agreement was finally reached, and was about to be published when the Great War and Turkey's participation therein translated the question from the field of diplomacy to the arbitrament of force. The details of the agreement, so far as they are known, will be more appropriately noticed in the chapter entitled "The Eve of the War."

From the above narrative of events the following conclusions appear to be warranted: (1) The policies pursued by England and Germany with respect to Turkey were the expression of their national needs and ambitions, and the conflict of these policies gave additional stimulus to

the rivalry bred by the race for naval supremacy. (2)
The Triple *Entente*, evolved out of the Dual Alliance by
British diplomacy as a protection against Germany, acquired real vitality under the pressure exerted by Germany
in the interest of her Near Eastern policy, because that
policy, if pushed to its logical conclusion, would severely
prejudice the position of the several *Entente* Powers. Thus
the Near Eastern question, instead of being dealt with by
the European concert as the lessons of history required,
became a shuttlecock in the game being played by two rival
groups of Powers, whose differences were so great that they
neglected the opportunity afforded by the Balkan Wars of
1912–13 to make a permanent settlement; with the inevitable result that the new situation was unsatisfactory to all
of them and was the immediate occasion of the Great
War. (3) Great Britain did not object to the economic
enterprises of Germany in the Ottoman Empire except
when they promised to make that Empire a political sat-
ellite of Germany, but she was willing to withdraw her
opposition in return for tangible concessions which secured
her own interests. (4) Great Britain feared the political
designs of Germany in the Near East, partly because they
threatened to undermine the position and prestige gained
through generations of successful commerce and diplomacy;
partly because they seemed intimately connected with
other phases of German policy which had to do with the
balance of power and the affairs of western Europe. This
last consideration brings us to the Morocco crisis of 1911.

CHAPTER XI

AGADIR AND ITS AFTERMATH

ON 1 July, 1911, the German gunboat *Panther* cast anchor in the harbor of Agadir on the Atlantic coast of Morocco. This incident produced the most serious crisis in Anglo-German relations before the actual outbreak of war three years later, and very nearly provoked war at the time. To the world at large, and probably to the European governments, the news of the German action came as a bolt from the blue, although such precipitancy was endemic in German diplomacy; but events were to show that if the Wilhelmstrasse reckoned on presenting Europe with a *fait accompli*, it had, as usual, calculated badly, and that neither France nor England could be cajoled or threatened. In the reaction which followed the peaceful solution of the difficulty, England got the credit for blocking the designs of Germany, although the real blame belonged to the stupid procedure of the German foreign office. This in turn led to much searching of heart in England, and for a brief period a reconciliation seemed possible, only to be shattered by the Great War. Hence the importance of the crisis.

In the early summer of 1911 Anglo-German relations, if not cordial, had lost much of the animosity engendered by the Bosnian troubles of 1908 and the naval scare of 1909. The German Emperor had been well received when he attended the obsequies of his uncle Edward VII, and again on the occasion of the dedication of the national monument to Queen Victoria in May, 1911. On 13 March of the same year Sir Edward Grey had remarked upon the friendly

relations obtaining with all the Powers;[1] on 6 February
Mr. Asquith had declared that British friendships were not
exclusive, and had no hostile tendency or ramifications.[2]
For a year negotiations had been in progress for a limitation
of naval armaments, and the British Government had "as-
sented to the German view that some wider agreement of a
political nature should be a condition precedent to a naval
arrangement."[3] In Germany the death of Edward VII,
who passed for the inspirer of the *Einkreisungspolitik*,
caused a feeling of relief, for King George was not regarded as a diplomatist;[4] at any rate, the crop of pamphlets
in denunciation of British policy, which had been of large
volume from 1904 to 1910, fell off considerably. Above all,
perhaps, the struggle over the Parliament Bill, then at its
height, seemed to render England a negligible quantity
in international affairs. The first of a series of strikes
among the transport workers had also begun. In India
and Egypt the native unrest was still evident, and Canada
was absorbed by the reciprocity treaty with the United
States. That Great Britain should intervene decisively
in a European quarrel was as surprising to German public
opinion and to the German Government as the forcing of
that quarrel was to the British public.

The Act of Algeciras, it will be remembered, conferred
upon France and Spain the task of organizing an international police force in those ports of Morocco which were
open to European commerce. Inaugurated in November,
1906, this reform was distasteful to the Moorish population, who rightly feared the loss of their national independence, and numerous outbreaks followed, in which

---

[1] 5 *Hansard* xxii, c. 1983.   [2] 5 *Hansard* xxi, c. 65.

[3] Sir Edward Cook, *How Britain Strove for Peace*, p. 26.

[4] "With the death of King Edward VII the English policy of isolation, which
he introduced with much adroit statesmanship against Germany, has broken down."
(Bernhardi, *Germany and the Next War*, p. 33.)

several Frenchmen were killed. Finding a naval demonstration ineffective, the French Government occupied first
Udja, in the northeast, just over the Algerian frontier, and
then Casablanca and its environs, the Shawia, on the Atlantic coast.   This in turn led to a rebellion against Sultan
Abdel Assiz, headed by his brother Mulai Hafid, who finally
succeeded in usurping the throne and in getting himself
recognized as Sultan by the Powers, this last at the instigation of Germany (May, 1907–December, 1908).

The French had observed an impartial neutrality between the warring brothers, but when the civil strife was
over they pressed upon Mulai Hafid both a programme of
reforms and their own bill of expenses for the occupation
of Casablanca. M. Pichon, the French foreign minister,
frequently denied that France was aiming to upset the
Act of Algeciras and to establish a protectorate *de jure* or
de facto; [1] nevertheless his application of the act was bound
to make French influence predominant in Morocco and to
reduce the Sultan to a condition of vassalage. Mulai
Hafid saw this clearly enough. Moreover, unlike the
brother whom he had deposed, he was not receptive to
European ideas, and he had risen to power by the help of
the anti-foreign party.   So it was not until 4 March, 1910,
that he signed the treaty presented to him by the French
minister, by which he recognized certain westward exten-
sions of the Algerian frontier and accepted the French
offer to provide funds for liquidating his debts.   The French
were also to remain in occupation of Udja and the Shawia
pending the creation of a Moroccan constabulary that
should be trained by a French military mission; and they
were to be indemnified for the Casablanca expedition by
a yearly payment for seventy-five years.   This convention
did not destroy the sovereignty of the Sultan, but it was
scarcely in keeping with the letter of the Algeciras Act.

[1] Chamber of Deputies, 13 November, 1907.

On the other hand, that act, representing an attempt to reconcile two incompatible theories,[1] was clearly in need of revision, and—what is of vital importance—had been practically set aside by a Franco-German agreement entered into at the behest of Germany, the Power originally responsible for the act.

German opinion, it was noted above, had regarded the proceedings at Algeciras as a *pis aller*. When the French began their armed intervention in the spring of 1907 the press of the fatherland was not long in manifesting its discontent, and the following year it took up the cause of Mulai Hafid with enthusiasm, advocating his recognition by the imperial government as a means of checking the growing influence of France. The new Sultan, for his part, confidently expected German assistance in his struggle for independence; and with no little reason, if the incident of Casablanca were any index of German policy.

At the end of September, 1908, some deserters from the Foreign Legion, some of whom were German subjects, were forcibly taken from the hands of a German consular official at Casablanca as he was embarking them on a German steamer en route to Europe. As he had provided *all* the fugitives, including the non-Germans, with safe-conducts, the French Government could not admit his diplomatic immunity from molestation, and feared that the incident had been provoked for an ulterior purpose. Germany was, indeed, willing to arbitrate the matter, but on conditions intolerable to France. In October and November the tension between Paris and Berlin was so grave that Great Britain and Russia promised support to France. The Bosnian crisis was also in full swing, and all kinds of rumors filled the air, especially when certain military precautions were taken. As Germany had pretended rather ostentatiously to disinterest herself in the Bosnian ques-

[1] *Cf.* Chap. IX, "The Triple Entente," pp. 236–238.

tion, she seemed disposed to reopen the Morocco controversy afresh. This would, of course, be Mulai Hafid's
opportunity.

Suddenly the Wilhelmstrasse yielded, accepted the
French contentions as to the details of the arbitration, and
presently reversed its traditional attitude. The German
ambassador in Paris proposed to settle the Morocco issue
on a new basis, the offer was accepted, and on 9 February,
1909, while King Edward VII was the guest of the German
Emperor in Berlin, the agreement was signed in that city.
The German Government frankly recognized "the special
political interests of France" in Morocco, and declared
itself "resolved not to impede those interests"; in return,
the French Government, "firmly attached to the maintenance of the independence and integrity of the Shereefian
Empire," was "resolved to safeguard the principle of economic equality, and consequently not to obstruct German
commercial and industrial interests in that country."
Both governments, "being equally anxious to facilitate the
execution of the Algeciras Act," agreed not to "pursue or
encourage any measure of a nature to create in their favor
or in that of any Power an economic privilege," and "to
associate their nationals in affairs for which the latter may
obtain a concession."

Thus Germany, the supposed champion of an internationalized Morocco, went behind the Powers and made a
special agreement with France, conceding the vital point
—the political interests of France—that could not be reconciled with the Act of Algeciras, to which lip-homage was
once more rendered. The bargain was not understood at
the time. Frenchmen assumed that they now possessed a
free hand in dealing with the Sultan, and indeed Germany
did not seek to hamper the French political programme.
It might well seem that Germany, convinced by the resolute stand of France in the Casablanca matter that she

could gain little by a policy of bluster, had experienced a change of heart, and would henceforth be content with the satisfaction of a steadily increasing commerce in the Shereefian Empire. Imbued with this idea, the French proceeded in leisurely fashion to secure from Mulai Hafid the convention of March, 1910, which was intended as the entering wedge of their political control. For them, therefore, the German intervention of July, 1911, came not only as a rude awakening, but in the light of a broken promise.

From the German point of view, however, the essential feature of the February agreement was the reciprocal pledge of the two governments *to associate their nationals in affairs for which the latter might obtain a concession.*[1] In a communication of 2 June, 1909, the imperial government proposed that, in order to avoid "sterile and injurious competition," all concessions in Morocco should be reserved to certain French and German groups of financiers and captains of industry who enjoyed the confidence of their respective governments, third parties being admitted only at the expense of the French group. In other words, France and Germany would establish an economic *condominium* and secure a virtual monopoly, in spite of the open door supposedly guaranteed by Article CVII of the Act of Algeciras! Germany was now suggesting the very procedure the possible application of which by France alone had been one of her bases of action in 1905–6. If one remembers also that in German eyes commerce and politics were inseparable, one may well ask whether the political ascendency of France, theoretically recognized by Germany, would not have been found illusory and meaningless. Not until the Morocco question was finally solved by the

---

[1] The Moroccan question from 1909 to 1911 is fully discussed by André Tardieu, *Le Mystère d'Agadir* (1912); *cf.* also, Félicien Challaye, three articles in *Revue de Paris*, 15 January, 1912, 1 February, 1912, 1 February, 1913.

agreements of November, 1911, was it realized that Germany had set a trap into which France walked most unsuspectingly. "Only a few perspicacious observers saw in it a first successful move on the part of Germany to fulfil, by a roundabout but effective method, her fixed purpose of destroying the *entente* between France and England, and the economic subjection of both peoples."[1] The commercial and industrial conquest of Morocco by Germany would nullify the political influence of France, to secure which had been the object of the *entente cordiale:* if the German economic designs were not successful, the Wilhelmstrasse could then reopen the whole question, on the ground that the convention of 1909 had remained a dead letter. In the light of events, this interpretation of German policy appears more reasonable than the view which ascribed to it the desire to be reconciled with France or the immediate exigencies of the Near Eastern question.[2]

No sooner was the German proposal of 2 June, 1909, received than the Quai d'Orsay perceived the danger that other Powers would object to the Franco-German monopoly; yet it was impossible to repudiate the agreement. In his reply M. Pichon insisted that British and Spanish groups should be admitted to any concessions, but he agreed that all enterprises should be reserved to the groups officially supported by the two governments, and nothing was said about the other signatories of the Act of Algeciras. An entire homogeneity of view was never established between the two foreign offices, so that only a miracle could have produced a satisfactory result, even if the principle of the scheme had been far sounder than it really was.

It is not necessary here to set forth the details of the three enterprises promoted by international finance in the

[1] Fullerton, *Problems of Power*, p. 244.
[2] This was the view taken by André Tardieu in *Le Prince de Bülow*, written in 1909. He did not then understand the true purpose of the convention of 1909, one of whose advocates he long was.

eighteen months preceding the *coup* of Agadir. The *Union des Mines marocaines*, a company formed to exploit the mineral resources of Morocco, failed because the German Government was unable to effect a compromise between two rival German groups, one of which, the Mannesmann Brothers, claimed to have received from the Sultan a concession prior to that granted to the *Union*. In the case of the *Société marocaine de Travaux publics*, which proposed to undertake all public works for the whole country, the blame for its collapse rested with the French Government, which, by refusing to guarantee the loans of Morocco with the credit of France, prevented the raising of funds which could be put into public utilities.

The third matter had an important bearing on the crisis of 1911. In 1910 the French authorities decided upon the construction of two railways in Morocco—one in the Udja region, the other out of Casablanca. They alleged military necessity, and the German Government raised no objection. But it demanded "compensation" for German industry, which could not participate in the construction of a military railway, and stipulated that French companies should be forbidden to compete with the *Société de Travaux publics*. At this point Sir Edward Grey intervened to protest that the British Government could not recognize any such economic *condominium*, and that it would support the claims of any English companies put forward under the Act of Algeciras. M. Pichon had relinquished the foreign office with the fall of the Briand ministry (27 February, 1911). M. Cruppi, the new incumbent, with the approval of the Monis cabinet, decided not to proceed further with the question, and this gave the German Government an opening. M. Jules Cambon, the ambassador in Berlin, began to send warnings that "if we give Germany reason to believe that we are going back on our word and shirking our responsibility with her in Morocco, as confirmed by our agreement of 9 February, we shall be creating for ourselves endless trouble." [1]   The situation was still further complicated by a new German request that Germans should be employed on the railways after they were built—a request so impossible for the French to grant that Germany must have been seeking a quarrel; all the more categorically and repeatedly did M. Cambon urge an agreement. But in vain.   M. Cruppi would not accept the German thesis, and the projects were abandoned.   From this time the ill humor of the Wilhelmstrasse became more apparent from day to day.   The *Panther*, as it were, began to load its guns.

It will not be contended that the Franco-German agreement of 1909 had secured for Germany that economic position in Morocco which had been anticipated, although her commerce had developed handsomely in the interval, or that the French Government had gone out of its way to facilitate the German designs.   Even if the Germans had tried to impose unacceptable conditions on their rivals, they might complain that all their energy had only led to the payment of two claims against the Moroccan Government for certain public works constructed by German firms before the agreement of 1909.   They were further chagrined by the failure of another enterprise similar to those attempted in Morocco.

In July, 1909, M. Pichon determined to apply the principle of joint exploitation to other Franco-German difficulties.   For some years the frontier between the French Congo and the German Cameroons had been the theatre of incessant wrangling between the French company of Ngoko-Sangha and the *Südkamerungesellschaft;* on one occasion actual fighting took place.   The difficulties of the

---

[1] This and other quotations from the French *Yellow Book* on Morocco are taken either from Tardieu, *Le Mystère d'Agadir*, or Georges Bourdon, *The German Enigma*.

situation were not diminished by the activities of English merchants or the protests of French and English humanitarian societies against the harsh treatment of the natives. M. Pichon thought to solve the problem by inviting the rival French and German companies to form a *consortium*, by which he hoped to stop the encroachments upon French territory systematically practised by the Germans. After eighteen months of negotiation the agreement was signed in Paris, in the presence of M. Pichon and the German ambassador. In the French Parliament, however, to which the contract was referred for approval, great opposition was manifested by the personal opponents of M. Briand, the prime minister, and the strong party opposed to the existing régime in the French Congo. The *consortium* was therefore negatived, and the Briand-Pichon ministry resigned. In such circumstances the new government could not proceed farther with the scheme, but that fact did not appease the natural indignation of the German ambassador, who remarked that France must display good will in some business arrangement with the Germans. Whatever the merits or demerits of the Ngoko-Sangha enterprise, its rejection, though having no bearing on the convention of February, 1909, added fuel to the flame of discontent evoked by the failure of the schemes based on that convention.

While affairs were in this parlous state, the French Government announced that the lives of Europeans in Fez were endangered by a revolution in the Shereefian Empire, and that a French column would proceed to the relief of the city. In the two years that had elapsed since Germany recognized the predominant political interests of France in Morocco, the government of the Republic had done little toward consolidating its position. The convention with the Sultan, of March, 1910, intended as the entering wedge, had not been followed by any active measures. In particulai, the Sultan had not been supplied with the funds urgently required to equip an adequate army and police force, and no railways had been built. Only the taxes had been increased, and a French supervision of the customs established. In January, 1911, the discontent came to a head in the revolt of some tribesmen near Rabat, and the murder of a French officer. Soon a brother of Mulai Hafid set himself up as rival Sultan, and began to march on Fez. Mulai Hafid thereupon appealed to the French for assistance. The French consul in Fez reported that the rebels were quite out of hand, the Sultan being unable to raise a force to meet them, and that if Fez were taken European lives would be sacrificed. Accordingly, a French force was despatched from Casablanca. It met with no opposition, and entered Fez on 21 May, where all was found quiet. No objection having been raised by either Great Britain or Germany to this expedition, the French declared their intention of withdrawing when the country had been pacified: actually their occupation of Fez precipitated the despatch of the *Panther* to Agadir.

The full history of the march to Fez is not yet available. Writers like M. André Tardieu represent it as the logical, if extreme, conclusion of the convention of February, 1909, as the step absolutely necessary for the establishment of French political ascendency. Their criticisms are directed against the vacillating policy of the French Government, which allowed two years to slip by without repressing the anarchy of Morocco; in their eyes the expedition would not have been necessary had France pursued an active Moroccan policy. The opponents of a French Morocco— Mr. E. D. Morel,[1] the Socialist press of Paris, and German publicists generally—declare that the French deliberately

---

[1] *Morocco in Diplomacy* (1912). For a brief answer to his book, see Philippe Millet, "The Truth about the Franco-German Crisis of 1911," *Nineteenth Century*, June, 1912.

neglected to take up a firm attitude toward Moroccan affairs in order that they might one day discover an excuse for a military occupation. The Europeans in Fez were in no danger, the need of intervention existed only in the imagination of the forward colonial party and the unscrupulous financiers who would profit from French political control. The expedition was intended as the death-warrant of the Act of Algeciras, and was recklessly embarked upon without considering the possibility of tension with Germany, who was bound to resent such an infringement of the international status of Morocco.

The German Government adopted the latter view. No sooner did the news of the troubles in Morocco begin to reach Europe than the German press sought to minimize them. It denied that the Europeans in Fez were in any danger, accusing the French Government of withholding reassuring despatches, and the chancellor himself told M. Jules Cambon that the reports of the German consul gave no cause for alarm. When informed of the intended expedition to Fez, Herr von Kiderlen-Waechter, the foreign secretary, said to M. Cambon: "If you go to Fez, you will not depart. It raises the whole question of Morocco." And a week later: "If the Act of Algeciras goes by the board, we shall reserve our liberty of action." The chancellor was equally explicit. The French were going beyond their rights. "I see," he said, "that this question is fraught with very grave difficulties, which makes me fear for the future." He did not object to the expedition, but he let it be understood that Germany was not to be ignored in the development of affairs.

Thus France had full and ample warning of the approaching storm. From the German point of view, the agreement of 1909 had broken down, while the French were about to establish their influence in Morocco once for all (the chancellor told M. Cambon that even if the

French evacuated Fez they would have to go back within a year, and he did not expect them to retire at all). Therefore Germany was entitled to reopen the whole question. Undoubtedly. But the logical basis of her claims was the convention of 1909, not the Act of Algeciras, which she had endeavored to set aside in her own interest. She could not have it both ways. She could not ignore the stipulations of Algeciras, and then, when her policy had borne no fruit, complain that France had violated them. On paper the Act of Algeciras was still the public law of Europe as regards Morocco, but every chancery knew that it had ceased to exist and that, as Mr. Asquith said later in the House of Commons, "a new situation had arisen." As a matter of fact, although Germany appealed to the Act of Algeciras in sending the *Panther* to Agadir, her action soon made it clear that she regarded the act with no more loyalty then than in the two years preceding. If Germany attached such importance to it, why did she not protest against the Spanish operations in the Riff in 1909 and their occupation of Larache and El-Kasar on the heels of the march to Fez? Granted that the French had practically nullified the agreement of Algeciras, and that Great Britain connived at this proceeding, Germany was equally guilty. It is quite clear, therefore, that the crisis of 1911 was not produced by the French violation of an international agreement, but that the issue was what the Germans call a *Machtfrage*—a question of force—in the solution of which not law but expediency must prevail.

When M. Cruppi realized, from the reiterated warnings of the ambassador in Berlin, that Germany was determined to make capital out of the expedition to Fez, he cast about for a sop of one kind or another. Efforts to reopen the abortive railway negotiations, support of a long-considered Homs-Baghdad railway, a proposal (subsequently withdrawn) for a Congo-Cameroon railway, offers to adjust certain customs difficulties of which German exporters had long complained—anything, in short, except the real issue— Morocco. *That* France was most unwilling to discuss, yet that was unmistakably the German goal. From the beginning of April the German press, irrespective of party, supported the thesis that a partition of Morocco was imminent; that Germany must have her share. Agadir was mentioned by the *Berliner Tageblatt*. Herr von Kiderlen spoke to M. Cambon of Mogador. On 12 June, at the Grunewald races, the ambassador was invited to the imperial box; there he encountered the Crown Prince, who referred to Morocco as "*un joli morceau*," adding, "Give us our share and all will be well." Clearly, then, it was wise "to go to Kissingen and see Kiderlen," as the chancellor advised.

The interview at Kissingen between M. Cambon and Herr von Kiderlen—who had retired thither partly for his annual cure, partly to escape the unwelcome overtures of M. Cruppi—occurred on 22 June, 1911. It partook not a little of high comedy. The ambassador wished to "penetrate the intentions of Germany"; if, as he feared, she was intent on a partition of Morocco, then "France must pay her," for, as he told the secretary, France would never discuss a partition of Morocco. Yet he was unwilling to admit this. He therefore tried to narrow the discussion to the convention of 1909, which Herr von Kiderlen promptly dismissed as a vain effort at "plastering up" (*replâtrage*). Brought to bay, the ambassador suggested "looking elsewhere"; but he hastened to add that this was a "new idea," and he would have to consult people in Paris, whither he was bound. "Bring back something with you," concluded Kiderlen. The ambassador was satisfied that Germany intended to reopen the whole question, but he made no definite offer of "compensations." Before he could "take something back" to Berlin, the Monis cabinet gave

place to that of M Caillaux, and M. de Selves became
foreign minister.   Also, on 1 July, the German ambassador
announced the arrival of the *Panther* at Agadir.

The French bluff had failed.   The Republic might have
taken its stand on the Act of Algeciras, and have given
guarantees that the occupation of Fez would be temporary;
it did pretend to do so, but it did not convince Germany
that a protectorate was not the ultimate goal of its policy.
In the known temper of the Wilhelmstrasse, it would have
been wiser to open negotiations as soon as the expedition
to Fez was launched, and to learn what price Germany
demanded.   As it was, by waiting until the *Panther* appeared on the scene, the French Government added materially to the difficulties of an amicable settlement, for it
had to negotiate under pressure, and it had to "pay"
dearly for the withdrawal of the insignificant man-of-war.
At the same time, the cavalier action of Germany prejudiced the rest of Europe against her.   A sorry business,
from first to last.

A new situation, then, had arisen in Morocco.   The
vital point in the controversy which followed was the intention of Germany.   Was she bent on a partition of the
Shereefian Empire in which she should have a part?   Was
she merely seeking "compensation" from France in return for a French protectorate?   Or did she still cherish the
design of destroying the Triple *Entente*, which was the
essential preliminary of a campaign against England?
Did she propose to "square her account with France," as
General von Bernhardi advised a little later?   Upon the
answer to these questions depends any judgment of British
policy in its relation to Germany.   Unfortunately the evidence is not such as to warrant any positive conclusion,
but such evidence as there is suggests that Germany did
not desire a simple transaction of payment for a French

protectorate in Morocco. Yet that was the ultimate goal of French policy, however much concealed by the Act of Algeciras and the hesitations of the five years following. And by the agreement of 8 April, 1904, Great Britain was pledged to support France in the execution of her policy. The engagement may have been unwise or immoral; it existed, and in all probability the German Government was aware of it. A crisis was inevitable.

On 1 July, at midday, the German ambassadors presented to the Powers the following communication:

"Some German firms established in the south of Morocco, notably at Agadir and in the vicinity, have been alarmed by a certain ferment which has shown itself among the local tribes, due it seems to the recent occurrences in other parts of the country. These firms have applied to the imperial government for protection for the lives of their employees and their property. At their request the imperial government has decided to send a war-ship to the port of Agadir, to lend help and assistance, in case of need, to its subjects and employees, as well as to protect the important German interests in the territory in question. As soon as the state of affairs in Morocco has resumed its former quiet aspect the ship charged with this protective mission will leave the port of Agadir."

This demonstration was as legitimate as the French expedition to Fez, or the Spanish occupation of Larache and El-Kasar. It was not a valid objection, raised in some quarters, that under the Act of Algeciras Agadir was a closed port, for, as the German ambassadors said in several capitals, the Act of Algeciras had lost all force. Expediency must prevail, and Germany was the sole judge of her own interests.

But why should Agadir be selected for a display of force which was sure to arouse suspicions? *To lend help and assistance, in case of need, to German subjects and employees,* said the official notification. It is pretty clearly established that there were no Germans in Agadir, and that there was no unrest in the region   To protect the important German interests in the territory in question. What interests? None existed at the moment: the words must refer to the future, a significant deduction. Nor would a closed port have been chosen without some definite purpose. The best answer is supplied by the statement of the editor of the *Rhenisch-Westfälische Zeitung* on 19 January, 1912, in a suit for libel against the *Grenzboten*.

"Herr Class, the president of the Pan-German League, is prepared to state upon oath before this court that the secretary of state for foreign affairs, Herr von Kiderlen-Waechter, writing to him from Kissingen, requested Herr Class to meet him at the Hotel Pfalzer Hof in Mannheim. During the interview, which lasted several hours, Herr von Kiderlen-Waechter stated: 'The Pan-German demand for Morocco is absolutely justified. You can rely upon it that the government will stick to Morocco. M. Cambon is wriggling before me like a worm. The German Government is in a splendid position. You can rely upon me, and you will be very pleased with our Morocco policy. I am as good a Pan-German as you are.'

"On 1 July Herr Class called at the German foreign office and, failing to find Herr von Kiderlen-Waechter, was received by Herr Zimmermann, the under-secretary. Herr Zimmermann told him: 'You come at a historic hour. To-day the *Panther* appears before Agadir and at this very moment (12 o'clock midday). The foreign cabinets are being informed of its mission. The German Government has sent two *agents provocateurs* to Agadir, and these have done their duty very well. German firms have been induced to make complaints and to call upon the government in Berlin for protection. It is the government's intention to seize the district, and it will not give it up again. The German people absolutely require a settlement colony. Please prevent, wherever in the press you have influence, the raising of claims for compensation elsewhere. Possibly France will offer us the Congo. However, the German Government does not want compensation elsewhere, but a part of Morocco.' " [1]

[1] Quoted by J. Ellis Barker, "Anglo-German Relations and Sir Edward Grey," *Fortnightly Review*, March, 1912.

The authenticity of these interviews was never denied. And it is significant that shortly afterward Herr Class published his brochure *West-Marokko Deutsch!*, in which he demanded for Germany western Morocco from above Rabat to Cape Juby. M. Georges Bourdon, who interviewed Herr von Kiderlen at length in the summer of 1912, says that he "wished for Agadir, and he wished it in the teeth of everything."[1]   The British Government, as will be noted presently, suspected this to be the German design, and early manifested its uneasiness. Yet it was not until 24 July that the ambassador in London gave Sir Edward Grey the positive assurance that no acquisition of territory in Morocco was intended. In the absence of such ambitions, why this delay in reassuring Great Britain? Does it not look as if the German Government, having learned that Great Britain would oppose a German acquisition in Morocco, was counting the cost, and finally decided to capitulate? The course of the negotiations with France confirms this view. There is, accordingly, good reason for believing that at the opening of the crisis Germany aimed at a partition of Morocco, and was prepared to claim its share. If the German press reflected the sentiments of the foreign office, there can be no doubt of it.

On the other hand, the German ambassador told M. de Selves, the French foreign minister, on 7 July that Germany had no territorial aspirations in Morocco and would be content with compensation in the Congo. M. de Selves subsequently stated to a commission of the French Senate that from the first the German Government had said: "Take Morocco, establish therein your protectorate." On this basis—a French protectorate in return for cessions in the Congo—an agreement was soon reached in principle between the Quai d'Orsay and the Wilhelmstrasse. Why, then, any question of Morocco? First, because in the nego-

[1] *The German Enigma*, p. 18.

tiations which followed, the Germans showed every disposition to limit the scope of the French protectorate, and to seek for themselves especial economic privileges. Second, the price asked by Germany was originally so large that France would pay it only under duress. As presented to M. Jules Cambon on 15 July, the German terms included the whole of the French Congo from the river Sangha to the sea, Germany offering, as a sop, to cede Togoland; later France was requested to transfer her right of preemption to the Belgian Congo to Germany. In other words, France was to surrender a large territory in exchange for an ill-defined position in Morocco. France rejected the German scheme of compensation. Might not the negotiations fail? If so, the question would be thrown back upon Morocco. The French certainly feared that this might be the case—that it was even the German design. And, unfortunately for them and for Europe, M. de Selves, while an excellent administrative official (he had been prefect of the Seine), was inexperienced in the ways of diplomacy, and seemed unable to make the negotiations take positive form. Throughout the month of July, therefore, complete uncertainty reigned as to the result of the negotiations. It was this which prompted the intervention of Great Britain.

In notifying the British Government of the despatch of the *Panther* Count Wolff-Metternich, the German ambassador in London, had let it be understood that Germany desired a direct negotiation with France, which Sir Edward Grey took to mean "a definite solution of the Moroccan question." [1] On 3 July Count Metternich was informed that, in the view of the British Government,

[1] The narrative which follows is based on the speeches of Herr von Kiderlen-Waechter to the budget committee of the Reichstag, 17 November, 1911, and of Sir Edward Grey in the House of Commons, 27 November, 1911. The context will indicate from which speech the various quotations are taken.

"the situation was serious and important," and on the following day, after a meeting of the cabinet:

"Our attitude could not be a disinterested one with regard to Morocco. We must take into consideration our treaty obligations to France and our own interests in Morocco. We were of opinion that a new situation had been created by the despatch of a German ship to Agadir. Future developments might affect British interests more directly than they had hitherto been affected, and therefore we could not recognize any new arrangements that might be come to without us."

The position here taken was explained by Sir Edward Grey, speaking in Parliament on 27 November, 1911, in these words:

"I think in the German mind it has sometimes been assumed that our agreement made with France in 1904 entirely disinterested us with regard to Morocco, and, if Germany wished to make a new settlement with regard to Morocco, it was going out of our way and intrusive for us—having given, by our agreement of 1904, a free hand to France in Morocco as far as we are concerned—to interfere with any other Power wishing to make her own arrangements. . . .

"It is quite true we disinterested ourselves in Morocco politically, but we did it on conditions laid down both strategic and economic. What were the reasons of our being disinterested in Morocco? We have no jealousy of other Powers. It is obvious, if the Moroccan question was to be reopened, and a new settlement made, unless we were consulted, unless we knew what was going on, unless we were in some way parties to the settlement, the strategic and economic conditions stipulated for between ourselves, France, and Spain in 1904 might be upset."

This attitude was entirely defensive, for Sir Edward, after consulting the cabinet, declined to fall in with a French proposal that French and British cruisers should be sent to Agadir as company for the *Panther*. In Parliament (6 July), however, Mr. Asquith announced that "a new

situation had arisen" which was engaging the "serious attention" of the government.[1]

A silence of eight days ensued. "On 12 July the British
ambassador in Berlin had occasion to see the German foreign secretary on some minor matters, and took the opportunity to say that there had been at one time mention of
a conversation *à trois* between Germany, France, and Spain,
the inference being that we were to be excluded from it.
The German foreign secretary told our ambassador to inform us that there had never been any such idea." According to the German version, "the ambassador received
a reply on the same day, as an official statement of the
German Government, that such an intention had never
existed." "Except for this negative communication"
Great Britain "had no further information from the German Government of their views."

Sir Edward Grey evidently meant that this "negative
communication" did not exclude a conversation *à deux*
between Germany and France, which was not impossible
in view of the tension between France and Spain resulting from the Spanish occupation of Larache and El-Kasar.
None the less, he made no effort to sound the German
Government further until 21 July. His reasons for intervening on that date can best be told in his own words:

"It appeared in the press, and indeed it was the case, that the
German Government had made demands with regard to the French
Congo of an extent to which it was obvious to everybody who
thought of it that neither the French Government nor the French
Chamber could agree. If Germany was going to negotiate with
France an agreement by which Germany received from France
something in the French Congo and left France in Morocco, as she
was under our agreement of 1904, then, of course, we were prepared
to stand aside and not to intrude. If, however, Germany, starting
negotiations with France on that basis, made demands, not for a
portion but for the greater part of the French Congo, or anything

[1] 5 *Hansard* xxvii, c. 1341.

of that kind, it was quite clear that France must refuse those demands, the negotiations would be thrown back on some other basis, and the question of the possible partition would arise again. That is why I became anxious. I therefore asked the German ambassador to come to see me again."

The French had refused the German demands. Suppose a deadlock were the result, and in such a case a conference, which it was Sir Edward's intention to propose, was not found practicable.

"Then you would have had this situation: You would have had France, Germany, and Spain in occupation of parts of Morocco; a German ship at Agadir, because, of course, the German ship could not leave Agadir with negotiations unsettled; you would have had, at any rate at the beginning, a partition of Morocco without agreement between the three parties, France, Germany, and Spain, who were in occupation of different parts of Morocco; you would have had us no party to the negotiations at that time; and you would have had on record the statement made publicly by the prime minister and the statement made to the German Government on 4 July, that we could not recognize any settlement come to unless we were consulted. You had at any rate the prospect, if negotiations broke down, of a very strained diplomatic situation."

In other words, Great Britain was not sure of the intentions of Germany.

"The German foreign secretary . . . has stated that the intention of taking a part of Morocco had never existed in Germany, as he stated distinctly at the time to a well-known Pan-German. Unfortunately, the gentleman in question did not believe it. If, after we had made the cabinet statement to the German ambassador on 4 July, that intention had been confided to us as definitely as that, I think a good deal of misunderstanding might have been avoided."

This language explains in clear-cut fashion why Sir Edward Grey had hitherto not sought a definite statement as to German policy, as he was later criticised for not doing.

If France and Germany could reach a friendly agreement, England had no title to interfere, for her interests in Morocco were secured under the convention of April, 1904. But if Germany were aiming to impose on France conditions which in themselves, or as a result thereof, would practically nullify the *entente cordiale*—and it is abundantly clear that Sir Edward Grey was haunted by this fear—then both her interest and her obligation to France required Great Britain to intervene. In subsequent discussions of the crisis, Sir Edward was blamed for not requiring France to live up to the Act of Algeciras, but such criticism ignores the express German declaration that the act no longer applied to the situation. The question, in short, was: Should England stand aside and allow Germany to extort from France such concessions as her superior military strength would permit her to dictate? Was the *entente* a mere settlement of ancient quarrels, or was it a co-operation of France and England to resist excessive pressure from a third Power?

Lord Lansdowne had concluded the *entente* in 1904 with the former end in view: the force of circumstances had caused it to approach what was practically a defensive alliance. If Germany was a peace-loving Power, intent only on its own rights, then British intervention in the dispute with France was a gratuitous affront and could be explained only by the desire to block the expansion of Germany at every turn. But if the main thesis of this book is sound, if Germany was a kind of Dick Turpin (the phrase was the *Times*'),[1] then a far-sighted statesmanship could give only one answer to the problem before Sir Edward Grey. Britain must take her place by France so long as the latter was willing to negotiate a reasonable settlement with Germany. But her policy was in no way aggressive: she insisted only that France must act as a free

[1] 22 July, 1911.

agent, and that if the settlement affected British interests England must be consulted. History may record
that Sir Edward Grey committed an error of judgment,
that he should have allowed Germany a free hand and, by
helping her secure a "place in the sun"—at the expense
of another Power—have laid the foundations of an understanding with Britain's great rival. But, as he remarked:
"One does not make new friendships worth having by
deserting the old ones." He could not foresee the future, he
had to be guided by the events of the past ten years, and
he could not await the indefinite development of an obscure
situation.

In his interview on 21 July Sir Edward Grey reminded
Count Wolff-Metternich that Great Britain was "taking
in the Moroccan question the interest which had been indicated by the statement of the 4th." Developing his
fears as to a collapse of the negotiations between Germany
and France, he pointed out that "the Germans were in the
closed port of Agadir; that, according to native rumors,
they were landing and negotiating with the tribe, so that
for all we knew they might be acquiring concessions there,
and that it might even be that the German flag had been
hoisted at Agadir, which was the most suitable port on
that coast for a naval base. . . . The longer the Germans
remained at Agadir, the greater the risk of their developing a state of affairs which would make it more difficult
for them to withdraw and more necessary for us to take
some steps to protect British interests." He wished to
say this now, "in the hope that the negotiations with France
would succeed," for, if he did not, "it would cause resentment later on if the German Government had been led to
suppose . . . that England did not take an interest in the
matter."

"The German ambassador was not in a position to give
any information"—this nearly three weeks after Sir Edward

Grey had indicated his uneasiness. The equivocal nature of Count Wolff-Metternich's reply can be gauged from the German version of the interview.

"He could not admit that the demands [upon France] were unacceptable, as otherwise Germany would not have put them forward. Sir Edward Grey had stated, though not officially, that as British interests were involved, the time had now come for negotiations *à trois* and he had based this pretension on the idea that Germany might eventually establish a naval base in Agadir and cut off the hinterland. These were suppositions of which the ambassador had no knowledge, and on mere suppositions no claim could be founded. Should, however, British interests have been injured by the German proceedings, perhaps the minister would be so good as to name them. As he was not in a position to do so, it would be more correct to wait until he could show that an English interest or right was affected. The ambassador repeated that Germany had not the slightest intention of injuring English rights or interests. He could not admit that this had been done by the despatch of a war-ship to Agadir. He had communicated to the minister the object and intention of this act when he made his first statement to him on the subject, namely, the protection of the interests of German subjects by the presence of a war-ship until peace and quiet were restored. Hitherto it had been a generally recognized principle that a European nation is justified in personally undertaking the protection of its interests in a semibarbaric country which does not belong to a third party. No third Power was bound by the Anglo-French convention of 1904. Since this convention Germany was bound only by the Algeciras Act and one treaty with France of 1909. Both the act and convention assumed as a condition for everything else the independence of the Sultan and the integrity of Morocco. After the lasting occupation of the Shawia and after the recent French expedition of conquest in a great part of Morocco, no one could seriously maintain that the territory had not been violated and that its Sultan was still independent. Germany had made no complaint on this score, as had been stated in the first conversation. Owing to the course events had taken, however, the moment had arrived when Germany was compelled to come to an understanding with France on the Moroccan question. Germany had now undertaken this step. If, as Sir Edward Grey assumed, German proposals in other directions were considered unacceptable, this merely showed that France appeared to attach less importance than might have been expected to a free exercise of those pretensions of hers in Morocco which had not obtained international recognition.

"A glance at the map would show that a North African colonial Empire, extending from the Tripolitan frontier to the Senegambia, together with supremacy in Morocco, was no small thing. England had obtained compensation from France in Egypt, which was no small thing; Germany, however, had obtained nothing. If France desired that Germany, like England—but always subject to the protection of our commercial interests—step into the background in Morocco, she must offer some compensation approximately equivalent in value to the great goal she had in view. If not, Germany would know how to safeguard her independent position in Morocco. The minister appeared to attach great importance to the fact that Germany had despatched a war-ship to a closed port of Morocco, and that this port should have been Agadir, the appearance at which of a French war-ship last autumn had led us to address an inquiry to the French Government. To this the ambassador had to observe that last autumn the French expedition of conquest (*Eroberungszug*) had not yet been decided upon. He could not conceal from the minister that he seemed to be applying two standards—one standard for France and another for Germany. According to his conception, a situation had arisen by the despatch of a German war-ship to Agadir, which, looked at from the standpoint of English interests, demanded an explanation. If he attached so much importance to the inviolability of Moroccan territory, he should apply first and foremost to France for explanations. The occupation of the Shawia territory, the fact that a French army was spreading itself over the interior of Morocco meant, undoubtedly, a more active intervention in Moroccan affairs than the German action, so far as it went."

The ambassador's inability or unwillingness to appreciate the frankness of Sir Edward Grey, always a barrier to confidence between the two men, is evident. He gave a reasoned statement of Germany's grounds for reopening the Moroccan question, to which Sir Edward Grey raised no objection, and which was, indeed, sound enough; but he did not answer the questions put to him by the British

foreign secretary, and his attitude was far from conciliatory. Sir Edward's reply, according to the German
version, was sufficiently explicit.

"The minister [Grey] replied that he would in no wise stand in
the way of an extension of German colonial possessions in the heart
of Africa; he could not, however, shut his eyes to the fact that
English interests might be most seriously affected by the Moroccan
question itself. He had, therefore, honestly hoped for an understanding between France and Germany. It was only in the un-
wished-for possibility of the failure to arrive at such an understanding that he was compelled forthwith to make it clear that the
démarche in Agadir would lead to an exchange of views between
Germany and England. He considered that the situation would
become less acute if an exchange of views took place before fresh
events occurred at Agadir, which would compel England to take
up a definite attitude in regard thereto. He had always hoped
for an understanding between Germany and France on Moroccan
questions, and had, therefore, also welcomed the agreement of
1909."

The justice of the British position was recognized by
the German Government itself. Realizing, if tardily, that
Great Britain would not sanction a German establishment
in Agadir, Herr von Kiderlen, immediately on receipt of
Count Wolff-Metternich's report of the interview, telegraphed the desired assurances.

"Not a man had as yet been landed. . . . Germany had never
thought of procuring a naval harbor on the coast of Morocco, nor
would ever think of such a thing. She also had no design on Moroccan territory, though she had to insist that France should either
observe strictly the Algeciras Act, or, if she thought she could not
do so, come to an understanding with Germany."

This information was conveyed to Sir Edward Grey on
24 July, but Sir Edward was refused permission to inform Parliament that not a man had been landed, pending instructions from Berlin to the ambassador. Some

critics of Sir Edward Grey's policy have argued that he
ought not to have objected to a German naval base at
Agadir.   Only the expenditure of much money could have
made it a suitable base, and the result would have been to
divide the naval energies of Germany.   All depends on
the view taken of the German navy, and as that question
has already been discussed, no repetition here seems necessary of the reasons why England was justified in opposing
an extension of German naval power to the western Atlantic and the Mediterranean.   In all probability the tension between England and Germany over the matter would
have been ended by the German communication of 24
July but for the speech delivered by Mr. Lloyd George,
the chancellor of the exchequer, on 21 July.

British public opinion had followed the Agadir crisis
from the beginning with great anxiety, for the very reasons
given later by Sir Edward Grey to Parliament.   On 20
July the *Times* published an account of the German terms,
although the negotiations were supposed to be carried on
in secret.   The worst was at once feared, the *Times* adopting an intransigent tone which Sir Edward Grey was careful to avoid in his interview with the German ambassador.
The foreign secretary felt that some public statement was
desirable, and Mr. Lloyd George, who was scheduled to
speak before the Bankers' Association on 21 July, was commissioned by Mr. Asquith and Sir Edward Grey to give
assurances that British interests would be guarded, for it
was known that Germany desired a direct transaction with
France.   To a conference of financiers, Mr. Lloyd George
not unnaturally spoke of the blessings of peace, but he
added:

"But I am also bound to say this—that I believe it is essential
in the highest interests, not merely of this country but of the world,
that Britain should at all hazards maintain her place and her prestige amongst the Great Powers of the world.   Her potent influence

has been many a time in the past, and may yet be in the future, invaluable to the cause of human liberty. It has more than once in the past redeemed Continental nations, who are sometimes too apt to forget that service, from overwhelming disaster and even from international extinction. I would make great sacrifices to preserve peace. I conceive that nothing would justify a disturbance of international good will except questions of the gravest national moment. But if a situation were to be forced upon us in which peace could only be preserved by the surrender of the great and beneficent position Britain has won by centuries of heroism and achievement—by allowing Britain to be treated, where her interests are vitally affected, as if she were of no account in the cabinet of nations—then I say emphatically that peace at that price would be a humiliation intolerable for a great country like ours to endure. National honor is no party question. The security of our great international trade is no party question; the peace of the world is much more likely to be secured if all nations realize fairly what the conditions of peace must be. And it is because I have the conviction that nations are beginning to understand each other better, to appreciate one another's point of view more thoroughly, to be more ready to discuss calmly and dispassionately their differences, that I feel assured that nothing will happen between now and next year which will render it difficult for the chancellor of the exchequer in this place to respond to the toast proposed—of the continued prosperity of the public peace."

According to Sir Edward Grey, the speech was made "in quite general terms." The chancellor of the exchequer "claimed no pre-eminence, no predominance, for England in international affairs. It contained no menace, such as the saying of 'Hands off!' to any one anywhere. It did not say that there was any particular demand or claim on the part of Germany that was inconsistent with British interests. Its purport and its point was that where British interests were affected we must not be treated as if we were of no account. If the time ever comes when this cannot be said by a minister speaking in the position the chancellor of the exchequer was in then, we shall have ceased to exist as a great nation." Nevertheless, the remarks of Mr. Lloyd George were everywhere construed as a warning *ad hoc* to Germany, and were responsible for a more serious tension between England and Germany than had existed hitherto. There was, apparently, no truth in certain rumors then current that the speech was intended as a protest against Germany's having left a British despatch unanswered for more than two weeks, for, according to Sir Edward Grey himself, he had addressed no despatches to Germany, and Herr von Kiderlen explicitly denied that such a breach had occurred. But it was regrettable that, at a moment when the German Government had been officially asked for a statement of its policy, but before a reply could be received, a new element should have been introduced into the discussion. The comment of the German Government was quite pertinent.

"If the English Government," Herr von Kiderlen instructed Count Wolff-Metternich to say to Sir Edward Grey, "had intended to complicate the political situation and to bring about a violent explosion, it could certainly have chosen no better means than the speech of the chancellor of the exchequer, which took into so little account for us the dignity and position of a Great Power which was claimed by him for England." The speech "had given rise to violent attacks against Germany on the part of a large portion of the English press and the whole of the French press. It might remain an open question as to how far the British minister had intended to produce this effect. The British Government could not, in any case, fail to perceive that this effect of a speech delivered by one of its ministers was bound to produce a bad impression in Germany."

Sir Edward Grey's sincere desire to promote a Franco-German understanding cannot be doubted, but the Lloyd George speech was a blunder.

For on 25 July the German ambassador made to Sir Edward Grey a communication "exceedingly stiff in tone," to

the effect that, "in view of the speech of the chancellor of
the exchequer," the German Government could not consent
that the assurances as to Morocco, given the day before,
should be used in Parliament. Sir Edward replied that,
"as the speech of the chancellor of the exchequer seemed to
[him] to give no cause for complaint, the fact that it had
created surprise in Germany was in itself a justification of
the speech, for it could not have created surprise unless
there had been some tendency to think that England might
be disregarded." Thus the real issue—Agadir, which had
been adjusted—was converted into an affair of prestige, a
most dangerous stage at any time, and particularly so in
view of the inflamed state of public sentiment on both sides
of the North Sea.

Herr von Kiderlen : It was not possible for us to comply with the
request made in the meantime by the British minister that we
should authorize him to make use in Parliament of our notification
that we had no designs on Moroccan territory. This would have
made it appear as if the explanation had been given as a result
of Mr. Lloyd George's speech.

Sir Edward Grey : The German Government had said that it
was not consistent with their dignity, after the speech of the chancellor of the exchequer, to give explanations as to what was taking
place at Agadir. I said to the ambassador that the tone of their
communication made it inconsistent with our dignity to give explanations as to the speech of the chancellor of the exchequer.

The two days from 25 July to 27 July were very difficult,
although Sir Edward Grey had reiterated his desire for a
Franco-German settlement. For Sir Edward "sounded
the German Government as to whether a proposal for a
conference would be acceptable if negotiations reached a
deadlock, and the reply . . . , though not absolutely conclusive, pointed to the fact that a proposal for a conference
might not be acceptable." For this reason, doubtless, the
British Government stopped shore leave from the fleet,

which was ordered to Portsmouth, and took other military precautions. The responsibility for this dangerous situation rested with both governments, as the narrative of events clearly establishes, for if Germany had shown herself unduly reticent, Great Britain had taken too little account of German susceptibility. The Germans probably expected the constitutional crisis to keep England quiet; the English were too anxious to present a united front in the face of an international difficulty.

Suddenly the atmosphere cleared, supposedly because Germany perceived that Great Britain would support France at all costs. On 27 July Count Wolff-Metternich made another communication, which Sir Edward Grey described as "exceedingly friendly." The German Government, appealing to the "minister's great loyalty," requested him to state in Parliament that the German *pourparlers* with France did not touch British interests. Owing to the pledge of secrecy, no details could be vouchsafed, even to Sir Edward Grey, but the territories to be exchanged were exclusively German and French—that is, Morocco was not involved. "Adverse criticisms from the English side must obviously render the negotiations more difficult. On the other hand, a public statement that England would be pleased to see a successful conclusion of the Franco-German *pourparlers* would have a most beneficial influence on an auspicious result for which Germany most earnestly hopes." The ambassador and the secretary easily agreed that "the new German communication might be taken as a new point of departure, and that [they] need not go back on things which might lead to mutual recrimination."

On the afternoon of the same day Mr. Asquith made the following statement in Parliament:

"Conversations are proceeding between France and Germany; we are not a party to those conversations; the subject-matter of them may not affect British interests. On that point, until we know the ultimate result, we cannot express a final opinion. But it is our desire that those conversations should issue in a settlement honorable and satisfactory to both the parties and of which His Majesty's Government can cordially say that it in no way prejudices British interests. We believe that to be possible. We earnestly and sincerely desire to see it accomplished. The question of Morocco itself bristles with difficulties, but outside Morocco, in other parts of West Africa, we should not think of attempting to interfere with territorial arrangements considered reasonable by those who are more directly interested. Any statements that we have interfered to prejudice negotiations between France and Germany are mischievous inventions without the faintest foundation in fact. But we have thought it right from the beginning to make quite clear that, failing such a settlement as I have indicated, we must become an active party in discussion of the situation. That would be our right as a signatory of the treaty of Algeciras; it might be our obligation under the terms of our agreement of 1904 with France; it might be our duty in defense of British interests directly affected by further developments." [1]

This statement was well received in Germany, and, according to Sir Edward Grey, "from that date onward there were no further difficulties between the German Government and ourselves about the Morocco negotiations."

Those negotiations may be briefly summarized. On 2 August, after several changes of front on both sides, it was agreed that France, without surrendering any of the coastline, should afford Germany access to both the Congo and the Ubangi Rivers. But no progress was made. On 13 August the French Government was alarmed by the report that the German general staff was studying a plan to land troops in Morocco, and on the 16th the French foreign minister and the German ambassador in Paris were agreed that the situation was "grave." Two days later the negotiations were suspended in Berlin, Herr von Kiderlen going off to see the Emperor, M. Jules Cambon returning to

---

[1] 5 *Hansard* xxviii, cc. 1827–28.

Paris for further instructions.   The rupture was probably
not unconnected with the strike of the railway servants
in England, for as soon as the strike was settled a more
hopeful view of the situation was taken.   It is certain
that the intervention of the British Government in the
railway dispute (15–23 August) was prompted largely by
the fear of renewed international complications, due to the
revival by Herr von Kiderlen of certain pretensions with
respect to Morocco.

M. Jules Cambon returned to Berlin at the end of August,
and on 4 September reopened his "conversations" with the
German foreign secretary.   He was instructed first of all
to secure a definite agreement on the subject of Morocco;
then, and then only, was he to treat of compensation in
the Congo.   The only serious difficulty arose in the second
week, when Herr von Kiderlen proposed to revive the economic *condominium* embodied in the convention of 1909,
which, with certain political privileges to be accorded to
Germans, would have seriously hampered the protectorate
that Germany had accepted in theory.   Saturday, 9 September, witnessed a great crash on the Berlin bourse.
Various rumors began to circulate, and the situation was
not without danger.

It is known that coal was shipped across England in
large quantities for the use of the navy.   Later it was alleged that the German fleet, then in Norwegian waters,
was watched by British destroyers, and that the British
fleet, at Cromarty Firth, was cleared for action.   Still
another story was that an Anglo-French military co-operation had been worked out, and that the admiralty had
refused to guarantee the transport of the British expeditionary force because the battle squadrons were not
concentrated.[1]   It was also at this time, perhaps, that the
German Government gave a preliminary warning to men

---

[1] *Annual Register*, 1911, *passim*.

and officers of the reserve;[1] certainly the press of the
United States was filled with reports ot the readiness of
the German armies for any eventuality. But, in the absence of authentic information, it would be dangerous to
say that a rupture was imminent. Fortunately, good
sense prevailed. On 4 October the two negotiators initialed the convention which gave France a protectorate
de facto in Morocco, although the term protectorate was
not used; in return, she pledged herself most explicitly
to observe the principle of the open door in letter and in
spirit. With the assistance of Great Britain, the goal of
French colonial policy had been won at last.

The Congo negotiations lasted from 15 October to 2
November. They resulted in the curious solution by
which Germany received two prongs of French territory
that brought the Cameroons in touch with the Congo and
the Ubangi at Bonga and Mongumba respectively, surrendering in exchange part of the Duck's Beak in the Chad
region. The outbreak of the Tripolitan War between Italy and Turkey hastened the agreement, for Germany required all her energy to conserve her position in Turkey,
now the victim of attack from Germany's ally. The only
difficulty arose over the German demand that France
transfer to Germany her right of pre-emption to the Belgian Congo, but with the assistance of Russia a formula
was found by which any change in the status of the Congo
was reserved to the decision of the Powers signatory to
the Berlin African Act of 1885. Sir Edward Grey stated
that Great Britain did not interfere in these negotiations,
and it may safely be said that no one was more pleased
by the signature of the Moroccan and Congo conventions
on 4 November, 1911.

The settlement was a great triumph for France, which
was all the more notable for the fact that since 1870 her

---

[1] M. Jules Cambon to M. Pichon, 6 May, 1913, no. 3 in French *Yellow Book* (1914).

relations with Germany had usually found her in the position of suppliant. Now, as a result of the unqualified
manifestations of national unity and determination and
with the assistance of British diplomacy, the Republic
had debated with Germany as an equal. More than that,
it had driven an exceedingly profitable bargain. By surrendering certain lands in the heart of Africa, the loss of
which might be resented for reasons of sentiment, it had
secured control of the most desirable region of the globe
not already in the possession of a European nation. The
price paid to Germany for a definitive solution of the Moroccan question was not excessive; it was scarcely greater
than the concessions made to England, Italy, and Spain.
France, then, had scored, and scored heavily.

Nowhere was this better understood than in Germany.
When the treaties of 4 November were made public, a
chorus of indignation swept over the fatherland. A few
leagues of marsh land in Africa were a poor compensation
for a prolonged international crisis, the renunciation of all
ambitions in Morocco, and the open hostility of England.
The discontent was aggravated by the resignation of the
colonial secretary, Herr von Lindequist, who declined to
defend the treaties before the Reichstag, and by the lack
of precise information as to the course of events. But one
thing seemed certain: the intervention of England, proved
by the Lloyd George speech, had compelled Germany to
grant France better terms than she deserved. Probably
few could have quoted or had ever read the exact words
of Mr. Lloyd George; but, as was reported to Sir Edward
Grey, "what was objected to was not the speech itself,
but the fact that it had been made at a moment when
France and Germany were coming to terms and that it
upset the negotiations." All over Germany, even in circles
hitherto friendly to England, a bitter feeling of hostility
began to manifest itself, and the task of the chancellor,

when he rose in the Reichstag on 9 November to justify the treaties, was, indeed, a difficult one.

The position taken by Dr. von Bethmann-Hollweg was entirely accurate. He pointed out that Germany had obtained "a considerable increase of its colonial domain" without giving up anything in Morocco that had not already been surrendered; that "an important dispute with France had been settled peacefully." Declaring that by substituting "Germany" for "England" right through the Lloyd George speech, a German statesman might have made that speech with equal propriety, he denied that as a result of Mr. Lloyd George's utterance, Germany had "retreated before England." His only criticism was that "a great portion of the English press interpreted the speech in a chauvinistic sense, and in a manner spiteful toward Germany, and that this interpretation was not repudiated from the English side." But the British Government had not taken part in the negotiations with France, an agreement with France had been reached, and, "on the basis of this agreement, not only better relations with France can be built up in the future, but it will also be possible to clean the slate in regard to our relations with England." Let bygones be bygones, was the chancellor's thought; on this basis a *rapprochement* between the three great nations of western Europe was not impossible.

This appeal was coldly received by the Reichstag, whose sentiments were thus expressed by Herr von Heydebrandt, the Conservative leader:

"Like a flash in the night all this had shown the German people where the enemy is. We know now, when we wish to expand in the world, when we wish to have our place in the sun, who it is that lays claim to world-wide domination. . . . We shall secure peace not by concessions, but with the German sword."

This harangue, bitterly anti-English from start to finish, and applauded by the Crown Prince, who was a spectator

in the gallery, merited the censure bestowed upon it by
the chancellor the following day. But the tide of Anglophobia continued to ebb. On 17 November Herr von
Kiderlen-Waechter gave a confidential report of the negotiations with England, which was soon made public, and
for the first time people learned how serious the situation
had been in the summer. The German complaint was that
Great Britain had stood in the way of German expansion,
and by its diplomatic support encouraged the French to
revive their dying hopes of a war of revenge to recover
the lost provinces. For what other reason could Britain
have interfered in a dispute which concerned solely France
and Germany?

So far as Morocco was concerned, the German charge
was perfectly true. England did intervene to keep the
Germans out of Morocco, and the vehemence of their resentment indicates how keenly they aspired to a share of
Morocco. And the renaissance of French national sentiment, so conspicuous in the last few years and directed
solely against Germany, owed not a little to the *entente
cordiale*. Yet the Germans never admitted, and probably
they never will, that the policy of their own government
was primarily responsible for transforming a simple settlement of colonial disputes between England and France
into an informal alliance for mutual protection. Nevertheless the Kaiser's speech at Tangier in 1905, and the
despatch of the *Panther* to Agadir in 1911 were at the bottom of Anglo-French co-operation, which would have been
avoided by a less brutal and more consistent diplomacy.

For Morocco was lost to Germany as much by her inconsistency as by her rattling of the sabre. 1904: acceptance
of the Anglo-French convention; 1905: promise to the
Sultan that he should remain free and independent; 1906:
admission, in the Act of Algeciras, that France and Spain
should enjoy a privileged position in Morocco; 1909: complete abandonment of the Act of Algeciras; Franco-German

economic exploitation; 1911, 1 July: determination to effect a partition of Morocco; 24 July: denial of such intention; September: efforts to restrict French protectorate, and revival of old German demands. Is it any wonder that, pursuing a policy everything by shorts and nothing long Germany was able to make no headway against the diplomacy of France, bent on establishing French influence in Morocco, and the resolution of England to stand by France as the agreement of 1904 postulated? Germany might have raised no objection to a French absorption of Morocco in return for compensation elsewhere; she might have insisted on a share for herself; or she might have clung to the theory of an internationalized Morocco. She tried, at one time or another, to do all three, and the incalculable character of her policy justly laid her open to the charge of cherishing some deep-laid plan not necessarily involving Morocco at all.

That plan, apparently, was to destroy the *entente cordiale*, and then to force upon France a collaboration in Germany's schemes for economic and political expansion in Africa, the Near East, and China. As the vassal of Germany, France would be free from attack and could abandon the Russian alliance. Then Germany would be master of Europe, and could throw down the gauntlet to England at her convenience. Incidentally, the wealth of France could be invested in the building of more *Dreadnoughts* for the German navy. Perhaps Germany had not thought out the details just specified, and there are no documents to prove them; but such would have been the result had Germany won the diplomatic bout of 1911. For that reason Morocco assumed an extreme importance in the eyes of both France and Great Britain; for that reason they subordinated all other considerations to the maintenance of the *entente;* for that reason Germans were, from their point of view, righteously angry against England, without whose assistance the French must have been defeated. Thus, when Germany ascertained, as she did on 21 July, that the *entente* would stand the strain to which she had subjected it, she perceived that she must modify her tone and her demands, and she did so. From first to last the Moroccan question can be understood only if it is viewed in its largest aspect. The details are important for determining the justice of French or German claims, but the real issue was whether Germany was to lord it over France, and thereby break both the Dual Alliance and the Triple *Entente*. Statesmen and ministers could not put it so baldly, but they understood the situation none the less clearly, and after Dr. von Bethmann-Hollweg and Herr von Kiderlen-Waechter had expounded their views to Germans, it was imperative for Sir Edward Grey to justify himself to English opinion, which had been somewhat impressed by the German revelations and was becoming restive.

Had they followed the German example, Englishmen would have visited most of their wrath upon the foreign secretary of the government with which their own had been in conflict, and the conduct of Herr von Kiderlen was by no means ignored. But the most bitter criticisms were reserved for Sir Edward Grey, who did not then enjoy the prestige he subsequently acquired as the peacemaker of Europe.[1] It was unfortunate for him that at the moment the Russians should have been busy getting rid of Mr. Morgan Shuster as treasurer-general of Persia, for British opinion would have welcomed a strong stand by Sir Edward Grey against the Russian pretensions. Indignant at his refusal, publicists and politicians began to complain of his violent prejudice against Germany, which alone could have

[1] The case against Sir Edward Grey is presented by G. H. Perris, *Our Foreign Policy and Sir Edward Grey's Failure* (1912); Diplomaticus, "Sir Edward Grey's Stewardship," *Fortnightly Review*, December, 1911; Sidney Low, "An Anglo-French Alliance," *ibid.*

dictated his interference in the Morocco controversy. He had taken office in December, 1905; in the course of six years he had not improved but aggravated Anglo-German relations. In helping France to tear up the Act of Algeciras, he had almost led England into war with Germany. France had made an agreement with Germany in 1909, another in 1911; Russia had gone to Potsdam in 1910; England alone had not held out the hand of friendship. Rather she had been drawn into the net of Continental politics, with the burden of increased military and naval expenses, with all the obligations of an alliance and none of its advantages. The case against Sir Edward Grey seemed to be complete, and his resignation was demanded by those Radicals who, opposed to further expenditure on armaments, desired an understanding with Germany at any cost.

There was also a considerable feeling that British foreign policy was too much the preserve of a few officials at the foreign office and the more important members of the diplomatic service.[1] Parliament exercised no control over policy, treaties being presented to it as accomplished facts and not for ratification, as was the democratic practice. This criticism seemed well taken when the secret clauses of the Anglo-French convention of 1904, the real basis of the British support of France in the Morocco controversy, were published by a Paris newspaper several days before Sir Edward Grey's speech. Parliament knew nothing of negotiations, either pending or intended, and could not easily force the publication of documents if the foreign office demurred. Sir Edward himself spoke but seldom in Parliament or on the platform, so that little was known of the man or his policy, except by results, which were not considered satisfactory. Thus a strong-willed foreign

[1] The demands of the Radicals are presented by the committee of the House of Commons, "Our Foreign Policy and Its Reform," *Contemporary Review*, April, 1912.

secretary might give a direction to British policy which Parliament would not approve, and it was alleged that Sir Edward Grey had displayed a hostility to Germany out of all proportion to the feeling of Parliament and the wishes of Englishmen.

The speech of 27 November, 1911,[1] delivered nominally to the House of Commons—in reality to the world—was a memorable effort. In lucid English and with great detail, Sir Edward Grey explained his attitude toward the Morocco controversy, and described his interviews with the German ambassador; his account, supplementing rather than contradicting the version of the German Government, forms the basis of the narrative set forth earlier in this chapter.

More important was the attitude toward the future. The main points were: first, that the British Government had no secret agreements with any Powers;[2] second, that no member of the Triple *Entente* would pursue "a provocative or aggressive policy toward Germany"; and third, that Britain could not pursue a policy of splendid isolation without being felt "a public nuisance," against whom all other Powers would be building war-ships. With respect to Germany, he repeated publicly the assurance given privately to Count Wolff-Metternich, that England would not stand in the way of a legitimate German expansion:

"If there are to be big territorial changes in Africa, brought about, of course, by the good will of and negotiation with other Powers, then we are not an ambitious competing party; and being not an ambitious competing party ourselves, if Germany has friendly arrangements to negotiate with other foreign countries with regard to Africa, we are not anxious to stand in her way any more than in theirs."

[1] 5 *Hansard* xxxii, cc. 43–65.
[2] On 6 December, 1911, and again on 24 March, 1913, Mr. Asquith stated explicitly in Parliament that the British Government was bound by no military engagements which would compel it to go to war without the consent of Parliament. (5 *Hansard* xxxii, c. 1400.)

Ho recognized that the German chancellor, in his recent speeches, had been "studiously careful to avoid saying anything that might offend British public opinion," and welcomed the fact that "the German understanding with France as to Morocco had also cleaned the slate in respect of German relations with England." He did not conceal the difficulties of an Anglo-German understanding:

"Do not let us imagine that we can force the pace at this moment in improving the relations with Germany. We cannot compel suddenly, after the friction of the last few months, a favorable breeze of public opinion either in Germany or here. At present the breeze is anything but favorable . . . but what we want is not to cease to steer a favorable course, and to steer it straight ahead, whenever we can."

But Germany must do her part. If her policy was not aggressive, then he was sure that "in two or three years the talk about a great European war will have passed away, and there will have been a growth of good will, not only between Germany and England, but between those countries and the friends of both." These noble words have been mocked by the events of 1914, but at the time they gave grounds for hope that the great calamity of which Sir Edward Grey spoke would be spared Europe and the world. We shall see that he did his best to fulfil his own prophecy.

In the course of the debate which followed, Mr. Asquith confirmed what Sir Edward Grey had said.

"We do not want," said the prime minister, "to stand in the way of any Power that wishes to find a place in the sun. We have no sort of quarrel with any of the Great Powers of the world. The first of all British interests remains, as it has always done, the peace of the world, and to the attainment of that great object diplomacy and our policy will still with single-mindedness be directed." [1]

[1] 5 *Hansard* xxxii, c. 110.

To complete the account, the remarks of the German chancellor in the Reichstag on 5 December may be appended:

"English ministers and other speakers in the House of Commons have expressed a desire for the betterment of Anglo-German relations. For myself, I am in accord with that wish, but I remember that the same wish has been expressed repeatedly by both sides for a number of years. Nevertheless, we have obtained experience through what has occurred. My phrase, 'a clean slate,' has been taken up in England, but the slate of the recent past has been written on with a hard pencil, leaving permanent scratches, which cannot be written over in the future if suspicion holds the pencil.

"The English foreign minister rightfully sees that Germany's growing strength covers no aggressive plans. We wish sincerely not only for peace and friendship, but for the actual betterment of relations tending to keep the peace. This is our wish—only, so far as England is concerned, she needs to demonstrate her desire in a positive manner in her policy."

The most immediate result of the Morocco crisis was an outburst of recrimination on both sides of the North Sea which did not burn itself out for several months. The Germans took exception to the entire policy of Great Britain, considering that the charge of "encirclement" had been thoroughly proved by the events of July, 1911. They were further irritated by Mr. Churchill's description of the German fleet as a "luxury," a remark which was useful to Admiral von Tirpitz in securing the assent of the Reichstag to the navy law of 1912. It was at this time that General Friedrich von Bernhardi's famous book *Germany and the Next War* made its appearance. In England the new navy law provoked the usual criticisms. At the same time sober men and the two governments perceived that Anglo-German relations must become either better or worse—they must be mended or ended.

Early in the year 1912 positive efforts were made in the

direction of an Anglo-German reconciliation. In January Dr. Solf, the German colonial minister, came to London with the object, so it was believed, of discussing the secret treaty made between Great Britain and Germany, in 1898, for a disposition of the Portuguese colonies. Nothing however, was disclosed as to either the treaty or any negotiations that may have been begun. But the English press received the idea sympathetically, because it evinced British good will toward German colonial expansion.

In February, at the request of the German Emperor, Lord Haldane, then lord high chancellor of Great Britain, journeyed to Berlin to discuss Anglo-German relations with the German Government. Such a discussion, desirable in any case, was the more feasible because the Franco-German convention of 4 November, 1911, had materially altered the diplomatic situation. As Lord Morley had remarked in the House of Lords, it would have been intolerable if Great Britain had refused France her share of the profits of the *entente cordiale*, that is, Morocco.[1] But now that the Moroccan question had been liquidated, and the immediate purpose of the *entente* fulfilled, Great Britain was free to resume her liberty of action, and might even disinterest herself in Continental politics, provided always that the friendship with France developed during the diplomatic rough weather of the past eight years was not challenged and provided the peace of Europe was not disturbed. This was the view of British publicists and, so far as one can tell, it was the attitude of the British Government.

If any one British statesman could have effected an Anglo-German understanding, that person was Lord Haldane. Educated in Germany and unusually appreciative of German culture, he was *persona grata* to the court of Berlin, without being any the less a stanch British patriot.

[1] 28 November, 1911. (5 *Hansard* x, 382.)

The navy law of 1912 was under consideration when he arrived in Berlin on 9 February, 1912. In the course of his visit he saw the Emperor and the leading German statesmen. What happened may be gleaned from documents and statements given out since the Great War began.

The German chancellor submitted a draft treaty of six articles to Lord Haldane.[1] Assuring each other "mutually of their desire for peace and friendship," and pledging themselves that they would not, "either of them, make or prepare to make any unprovoked attack upon the other, or join in any combination or design against the other for the purpose of aggression," the two Powers were to agree, in Article III:

"If either of the high contracting parties becomes entangled in war with one or more Powers [in which it cannot be said to be the aggressor], the other party will at least observe toward the Power so entangled benevolent neutrality, and will use its utmost endeavor for the localization of the conflict. [If either of the high contracting parties is forced to go to war by the obvious provocation of a third party, they bind themselves to enter into an exchange of views concerning their attitude.]"

According to the German version,[2] the words placed in brackets were omitted in the first German proposal. Article IV provided that the duty of neutrality would have no obligation in so far as it was not reconcilable with the existing obligations of the contracting parties; and Article V pledged them not to make any new agreements. In the last article, the two governments declared that they would "do all in their power to prevent differences and misunderstandings arising between them and other Powers."

With respect to this "unconditional neutrality agreement," "Lord Haldane put some pertinent questions to the Emperor, the chancellor, and Admiral von Tirpitz. What

[1] Statement by the British foreign office, 31 August, 1915.
[2] *Norddeutsche Allgemeine Zeitung*, 19 July, 1915.

would be the use of entering into a solemn agreement of amity, if Germany was going at the same moment to increase her battle fleet as a precaution against Great Britain, in which case Great Britain would have to increase hers as a precaution against Germany? Would not an agreement for introducing a better spirit into the relations of the two countries be received with world-wide derision if it were to be followed immediately by an increased German shipbuilding programme?"[1] In reply the chancellor seems to have asked

"whether an open agreement with us, which would exclude not only an Anglo-German war, but any European war whatsoever, did not seem to him of more importance than a couple of German *Dreadnoughts*, more or less. Lord Haldane appeared inclined to this view. He asked me, however, whether, if we were assured of security in regard to England, we would not fall upon France and destroy her. I replied that the policy of peace which Germany had pursued for more than forty years ought really to save us from such a question. If we had planned robber-like attacks we could have had the best opportunity during the South African War and the Russo-Japanese War to show our love of war. Germany, which sincerely wished to live in peace with France, would just as little think of attacking another country."[2]

The negotiations were conducted in London. In the opinion of Sir Edward Grey, Articles IV and V of the proposed treaty were "one-sided and unfair," for whereas Germany was permitted to fulfil all obligations arising under the Triple Alliance, Great Britain, which had no alliances except those with Japan and Portugal, would be effectually excluded from taking part in a European war. If Germany were actually attacked by France or Russia, England would stand aside; but the reservation in Article III, "if either party is forced to go to war by the open prov-

[1] Sir Edward Cook, *How Britain Strove for Peace*, pp. 30–31.
[2] Reichstag, 19 August, 1915.

ocation of a third party," had a sinister ring, and in the light of the German declaration of war on Russia in 1914, it is well that England did not bind herself on the German terms. Sir Edward Grey therefore rejected the German offer. But he proposed the following formula:

"England will make no unprovoked attack on Germany and pursue no aggressive policy toward her. Aggression upon Germany is not the subject and forms no part of any treaty, understanding, or combination to which England is now a party, nor will she become a party to anything that has such an object."

Count Wolff-Metternich thought this formula inadequate, and suggested two alternative additional clauses:

"England will therefore observe at least benevolent neutrality should war be forced upon Germany"; or
"England will therefore, as a matter of course, remain neutral if war is forced upon Germany."

The ambassador added that this would not be considered binding unless the British wishes were met with in the naval question; but it subsequently appeared that the German Government would not do more than modify, without giving up, the navy law of 1912. To the end of the negotiations Germany would not agree to any limitations of armaments unless Great Britain would pledge herself to an unconditional neutrality, and this Sir Edward Grey refused to do. Moreover, the chancellor objected to the term "unprovoked attack"; "among civilized Powers it was not the custom to attack other Powers without provocation or to join combinations which were planning such things" (!) Therefore the promise to refrain from such attacks could not form the basis of an agreement.

Sir Edward Grey eventually proposed the following formula:

"The two Powers being mutually desirous of securing peace and friendship between them, England declares that she will neither make nor join in any provoked attack upon Germany. Aggression upon Germany forms no part of any treaty, understanding, or combination to which England is now a party, nor will she become a party to anything which has such an object."

Beyond this England could not go. As Sir Edward explained to Count Wolff-Metternich, "there was no aggressive design in British policy, and France knew perfectly well that if she acted aggressively against Germany no support would be forthcoming from the British Government or be approved by British public opinion." Great Britain could not bind herself in advance to remain neutral whatever might happen, for she could not forget that in recent years Germany had threatened both France and Russia with the use of force.[1] Sir Edward Grey went so far as to say that His Majesty's Government would not make the continuance of the negotiations dependent upon the withdrawal of the new German navy law, but the German Government insisted upon its own terms, and the negotiations presently collapsed. With them ended "the hope of a mutual reduction in the expenditure for armaments by the two countries."

The German version says that Sir Edward Grey based his refusal of an unconditional neutrality agreement on "the fear of otherwise endangering the existing friendly relations of Great Britain with other Powers," but there is no such argument in the British account. On the evidence produced, Mr. Asquith's remarks appear justified:

"[The British formula] was not enough for German statesmen. They wanted us to go farther. They asked us to pledge ourselves absolutely to neutrality in the event of Germany being engaged in war, and this, mind you, at a time when Germany was enormously increasing both her aggressive and defensive resources, and especially on the sea. They asked us—to put it quite plainly—for a free hand, so far as we were concerned, when they selected the

[1] Sir Edward Cook, *How Britain Strove for Peace*, p. 32.

opportunity to overbear, to dominate, the European world. To such a demand but one answer was possible, and that was the answer we gave." [1]

Count Wolff-Metternich admitted to Sir Edward Grey that "the chancellor's wish amounted to a guarantee of absolute neutrality." Is it not fair to conclude that Germany was seeking, in a new and unexpected fashion, to shatter the Triple *Entente?* She had tried to wean France away, and had failed; England might be more amenable, although the *Entente* was the creation of British diplomacy. The British reply to the German offers came, as will be seen, in November, 1912.

In May, 1912, Baron Marschall von Bieberstein, the German ambassador at Constantinople, was transferred to London, for Count Metternich had not succeeded in allaying British apprehensions. English opinion was somewhat suspicious that the famous diplomatist might attempt to dominate the British Government as he had the impressionable officials of the Sublime Porte, and to seduce the British press by the arts of which he was admittedly a master. Such fears were probably groundless, even unworthy of a free people. As it was, the new ambassador died in September, before he had really entered upon his duties. Sir Edward Grey was evidently not alarmed, for on 10 July he qualified Anglo-German relations, hitherto "correct," as "excellent." [2]

Theoretically, the international situation remained unchanged. The *entente cordiale* was not disturbed by the British negotiations with Germany, as Sir Edward Grey repeatedly made perfectly clear.[3] Also the visit of M. Poincaré, the French premier, to St. Petersburg in August,

---

[1] Cardiff, 2 October, 1914.

[2] 5 *Hansard* xl, c. 1995.

[3] Both the British Government and British public opinion looked coldly on the agitation conducted by the *Morning Post* and the *Spectator* in favor of a formal Anglo-French alliance.

with a view to consolidating the Dual Alliance by a naval convention, necessarily brought England and Russia into greater intimacy. And curiously enough the German Government, after many years' protest against the Triple *Entente* as an anti-German combination, suddenly gave it an unexpected recognition. The Tsar and the Emperor William met at Port Baltic on 4 July, and in the official *communiqué* occurred these interesting words:

"The political conversations, which extended to all questions of the day, strengthened on both sides the conviction that it still remains of the highest importance for the interests of the two neighbor Empires and of the general peace to maintain the mutual contact, *based on reciprocal confidence.* There could be no question either of new agreements, because there was no particular occasion for them, or of producing alterations of any kind in the grouping of the European Powers, *the value of which for the maintenance of equilibrium and of peace has already been proved.*"

In this statement Germany confessed her inability to destroy the Triple *Entente* and admitted that it was an arrangement for peace, not an incentive of war; an admission which the Germans seem to have forgotten since their propagandists set out to convince the world that the fatherland was innocent of provoking the Great War. But it would be a great mistake to suppose that by recognizing the Triple *Entente* as a legitimate combination, Germany desired to see it become a permanent institution of European politics. It is impossible to say whether Germany sincerely desired to arrange a permanent understanding with Great Britain, but, if so, she must satisfy the condition laid down by Sir Edward Grey: she must demonstrate that her policy was pacific and well-intentioned. As for England, on the basis of the German declaration, she could negotiate an agreement with Germany in good conscience, and, as a matter of fact, public opinion in England was crystallizing in favor of an understanding, which would have forced the hand of Sir Edward Grey, even if he himself had not been anxious to promote such an arrangement. If circumstances warranted it, Great Britain desired nothing better than to withdraw from the maelstrom of Continental politics and concentrate her energies on the varied problems of her far-flung Empire.

In the movement for better relations with Germany, the Liberal party in England was especially active. In a series of articles in the *Westminster Gazette*,[1] the editor, Mr. J. A. Spender, a close political friend of Sir Edward Grey, described the German as well as the British view of the situation, and urged that Great Britain must not oppose the legitimate ambitions of Germany. In another place he wrote:

"If we had 'left it alone' in recent years; if we had refrained from publishing inelegant extracts from each other's leading articles; . . . if we had left men of good will to work peacefully and gradually for the removal of misunderstandings, and, in the meantime, had silenced our own chorus, might we not by now have been in a better position? . . . After all, the worst has been said, . . . and, having 'liberated our souls,' we can approach each other without malice." [2]

The University of Manchester organized a series of lectures by eminent scholars who treated German problems in a sympathetic spirit; their discourses were published in a small volume entitled *Germany in the Nineteenth Century*. The reviews ceased to be full of anti-German articles, and the *Times*, long the most bitter critic of all things German, paid a respectful tribute to the Emperor William II on the twenty-fifth anniversary of his accession to the throne.[3] In October, 1912, the Labor party in Parliament and the

[1] Republished in pamphlet form under the title *The Foundations of British Policy* (1912).
[2] *England and Germany* (1912), pp. 14–15.   20 June, 1913.

Socialists of the Reichstag published a joint manifesto protesting against the increased naval expenditure and alleging that a war between the two countries would only further the interests of capital. The appointment of Prince Lichnowsky as German ambassador was welcomed in England; for, although he was known as a stanch advocate of the German navy, he was a man of moderate opinions and believed that a reconciliation was possible. He stated frankly that his business in London would be to work for an understanding.[1]   At a conference of the National Liberal Federation in November Sir John Brunner, the president, declared that the naval rivalry was the product of the armor-plate press, that the English and German peoples knew too little of each other, and that the first step to be taken was the exemption of merchant shipping from capture in time of war.[2]   Finally, the moderation of German policy from the outbreak of the Balkan War created an excellent impression in England. It may fairly be said that the country had been converted to the necessity and possibility of an agreement with Germany.

In Germany the attitude, if more reserved, was hopeful. Lord Haldane's visit had been greeted with a flood of anti-English pamphlets,[3] and the press was rather cool. But Herr Eduard Bernstein, the eminent Socialist, in a little brochure, *Das deutsche Volk und die englische Gefahr*, mercilessly flayed both the German Government for its aggressive policy and the German press for its ignorance and its pugnacity. He quoted the conciliatory statements of Mr. Asquith and Sir Edward Grey, and remarked that Germany was well-nigh friendless in the world. "Germany has not so many friends that the hostility of England is a matter to be taken lightly." And the continuation of Anglo-German tension was the greatest possible stimulus

[1] *Times*, 18 October, 1912.   [2] *Times*, 22 November, 1912.
[3] A brief list is given in the *Spectator*, 30 March, 1912.

of French ideas of revenge.   The book might well have
been written by an Englishman.

   In the June and July (1912) issues of his magazine *Nord
und Süd* Dr. Ludwig Stein had the happy idea to collect a large number of opinions from eminent statesmen, business men, and thinkers in both countries; an
English translation was promptly published under the
title *England and Germany*.   The discussion, if it did not
touch upon all the issues, was not only frank, but valuable for its freedom from jingoism, for the sincerity with
which a settlement was advocated.   Dr. Ernst Sieper of
Munich began the publication of a series of monographs
entitled *Die Kultur modernen Englands*, which would provide accurate and impartial information.   On the other
hand, the doctrines of Mr. Norman Angell, as set forth in
The Great Illusion, which found a ready welcome in England, did not rouse a corresponding echo in Germany.
But in general, if there were fewer organized visits of clergy-
men, workmen, and journalists between the two countries,
the number of tourists certainly increased, and in the end
such intercourse was bound to encourage friendliness.

   A promising experiment was the lecture tour undertaken by Sir Harry Johnston, the eminent African explorer
and administrator, who was favorably known in Germany
for his advocacy of the Baghdad railway and his support
of the German pretension to ascendency in the Near East.
Indeed, no English writer had presented the German case
for expansion more fairly than Sir Harry Johnston; he
was also in close touch with official circles throughout the
British Empire.   No one was better fitted to expound
British foreign policy to Germans.   So in 1912, with the
good will of the foreign office, he travelled through Germany and discussed international problems before all
kinds of audiences.   In south Germany particularly he
met with a cordial reception, and his suggestion that Fran-

co-German enmity might be buried by the retrocession of
Metz and French-speaking Lorraine was respectfully received. The Prussian spirit was more intractable, but on
the whole the results of his visit were encouraging.[1] The
substance of his remarks may be found in a book entitled
Common Sense in Foreign Policy, which, in spite of its somewhat arbitrary suggestions for transfers of territories, well
deserves to be studied in connection with the treaties
which will end the Great War.

Finally, there must be some reference to a remarkable
little book published anonymously in Germany during the
year 1913, *Deutsche Weltpolitik und kein Krieg!* In brief,
it is an eloquent answer to General von Bernhardi, and
a plea for the revival of Bismarck's Continental policy.
The idea of a "preventive war" arouses the bitter derision
of the author, and he is not impressed by the need of a
place in the sun. If Germany must expand, let it be in
Africa, not in the Near East, where the hostility of Russia
will ultimately prove fatal. He accepts completely Sir
Edward Grey's promise not to stand in the way, and declines to believe in the implacable hostility of England.
He laughs to scorn the idea that German interests require
Germany to support an Austrian expansionist policy in the
Balkans, for such a policy will benefit the Slavs, not the
Germans. It is Germany's business to see that Austria and
Russia do not come to blows, and to cultivate the friendship
of England, whose geographical position gives her a latent
control of German commerce and whose power must not
be underestimated. England, the author argues, wishes to
withdraw from Continental politics, and leave the Triple
and Dual Alliances confronting each other. Then she can
assume the position of a mediator between them, as she
did in the days of Salisbury; she can become the leader of
the European concert, which is the great hope of Europe.

---

[1] The writer is indebted to Sir Harry Johnston for this account of his tour.

Sir Edward Grey's achievements during the Balkan Wars are warmly praised as an index of future possibilities. Finally, it is pointed out—quite prophetically—that if Germany goes to war in support of Austrian ambitions, "we shall once again be regarded as the disturber of the public peace, who, in the endeavor to carve out a sphere of influence in Asiatic Turkey, has conjured up a universal conflagration";[1] which means that England will at once join with France and Russia for the annihilation of Germany. One would like to know who is the author of this book, and what he thinks of the war which he did not succeed in averting.

Thus, within a year after the crisis of 1911, sober-minded persons in both Germany and England had come to talk seriously of an understanding, and to discuss its terms. The relations of the two governments were more cordial than they had been for many years; in the Balkan Wars they were to become even friendly. The next chapter will give even greater point to the tragedy of August, 1914.

[1] P. 76.

CHAPTER XII

THE EVE OF THE WAR

THE European war of 1914 was the direct result of the Balkan conflagration of 1912-13. For thirty-five years the Ottoman Empire had been a potent cause of international rivalry, for its ultimate collapse was confidently expected, and the inability of the Great Powers to devise a satisfactory partition had operated as an incentive to ambitious and mischievous diplomacy. For a brief interval the Young Turk revolution promised to relieve Europe of its insoluble problem. Such anticipations, however, were not realized, partly because the Young Turks soon became the instruments of German designs, partly because their handling of the Balkan situation revived the unrest latent among the Christian populations. For the latter resented the policy of Turkification adopted by Constantinople in the supposed interest of military efficiency and, suppressing their racial animosities, began to make common cause against the Young Turk régime (February, 1912). It became apparent that only an effective measure of decentralization would prevent the reopening of the Macedonian question, and this was not forthcoming. In August, 1912, therefore, Count Berchtold suggested an exchange of views between the Powers.

If intended to stem chauvinistic tendencies, its effect was to render war inevitable. For in the spring of the year, the four Balkan kingdoms,—Bulgaria, Greece, Serbia, and Montenegro,—weary of the constant disturbances in Macedonia, formed an alliance to drive the Turk out of

358

Europe and seize his territories for themselves. But the successful application of such reforms as Count Berchtold was supposed to favor would deprive them of their expected booty. They therefore hastened to provoke the Turks, and in October declared war, in spite of some feeble efforts by European diplomacy to keep the peace.

The dramatic campaign which followed aroused the most intense emotions in a Europe which dared not interfere. Within six weeks the Ottoman Empire in Europe had ceased to exist, except for three beleaguered cities,—Adrianople, Scutari, and Janina,—which were gradually reduced by superior armies. The ambitions of the Balkan allies and the procrastinations of Turkey delayed the treaty of peace until 30 May, 1913, when the Sultan formally surrendered all the territory west of a line drawn from Enos on the Ægean to Midia on the Black Sea. This treaty, as the *Times* fittingly remarked, "closed a great chapter in the history of the world," and was "an event so momentous in possible results that it stood beyond the reach of imagination and of judgment." [1] At the same time, it belied several of the most cherished maxims of contemporary politics.

In the first place, because the Turk had for centuries enjoyed an enviable reputation for fighting, and because the Balkan nationalities were considered the tools of the Great Powers, it was taken for granted that the liquidation of the Macedonian problem would be effected by the European concert at the conclusion of a general war. Again, any solution hitherto predicted had involved territorial aggrandizement for certain Great Powers. Finally, the question of Constantinople and the Straits had always seemed an integral part of the whole Near Eastern problem. Yet the Balkan states waged a campaign against the Turks with little interference from nations mightily armed for

[1] 30 May, 1913.

that purpose; no Great Power was enriched; and the Sultan remained the lord of Constantinople.

To this happy result, as it then seemed, the restraint of all the Powers contributed; but the most potent factor in the preservation of peace between the Powers was unquestionably the moderating influence of Sir Edward Grey, who very early in the development of the situation perceived the danger of isolated action by one or more Powers. It was everywhere understood that the victories of the Balkan League were a blow to Germany's position in Europe, and had the Triple *Entente* been desirous of unchaining a war against Germany and Austria the opportunity then offered would not have been neglected. Instead, Sir Edward Grey revived the European concert through a conference of ambassadors in London, and with their assistance skilfully adjusted the conflicting claims of those Powers directly interested in the Balkans. In this task he received great assistance from Germany, which seemed to confirm the impression already abroad, that an Anglo-German *rapprochement* was actually taking shape. Indeed, both Herr von Kiderlen, before his death (December, 1912), and Herr von Jagow, his successor, publicly testified to the unexpected intimacy and friendliness which had developed between London and Berlin; and Sir Edward Grey spoke in the same vein. Thus, not only was the peace of Europe preserved, but the greatest danger to its disturbance, Anglo-German rivalry, had been diminished by the confidence that both England and Germany had worked for peace.

If the Balkan League, resting on the valor of a million veteran soldiers, could have been preserved intact, it would have been impossible for either Austria or Russia to precipitate a general war in pursuit of a Balkan policy. With this contingency eliminated, with England and Germany on the road to reconciliation, the peace of Europe might

have endured indefinitely. Unfortunately, the members
of the Balkan League quarrelled among themselves. To
some extent the revival of ancient jealousies that had been
laid aside for the struggle with Turkey was responsible for
the fratricidal war of July, 1913. But the real cause was
the meddling of the Powers directly interested.

The Ballplatz had allowed the war against Turkey to
proceed on the assumption that the hated Serbians would
be promptly trounced. Instead, they marched everywhere
to victory and occupied western Macedonia; in revenge
Austria supported the extravagant claims of Bulgaria in
the division of the spoils. Russia, of course, backed up the
pretensions of Serbia. The London conference of ambassadors declined to interfere, and Bulgaria, trusting in
the support of Vienna, appealed to the sword. She was
defeated, because Greece and Rumania joined Serbia, and
Turkey attacked her in the rear. But the treaty of Bucharest, signed 10 August, 1913, which deprived Bulgaria
of most of her gains, did not settle the Balkan question;
rather it left Bulgaria sullen and discontented, and it regis-
tered a second defeat for the Dual Monarchy, which was
now confronted by an enlarged Serbia, in alliance with
Greece and on cordial terms with Rumania. Unless the
labors of a generation were to be thrown away Vienna
must destroy this new Balkan alliance as it had the original
league. That is to say, the new Serbia must be crushed
by force of arms, and since the speech of Signor Giolitti,
in the Italian Parliament,[1] we know that Austria would
have gone to war in August, 1913, had not Italy, her ally,
refused to countenance an aggression upon Serbia.

In the west also Austria had interfered with sinister
results. When, on 28 November, 1912, a Serbian army
occupied Durazzo on the Adriatic coast, Count Berchtold
demanded its withdrawal, and in April, 1913, he required

[1] 5 December, 1914.

the Montenegrins to evacuate Scutari, which they had
conquered after a long siege. Not only did this policy
compel Serbia to seek compensation in Macedonia at the
expense of Bulgaria and thus make certain the Serbo-
Bulgarian quarrel; of far greater moment was it that the
issue was fairly joined between Austria and Russia, the
latter of whom seemed disposed to take up the cudgels
for her *protégés*. Austria mobilized 900,000 men in order
to carry through her policy, and brought Europe to the
verge of war, which was averted only by the patience of
Russia and the mediation of Great Britain. In passing,
it should be noted that Sir Edward Grey repeatedly accepted the Austrian view, even going so far as to send
British cruisers to help overawe the Montenegrins in the
matter of Scutari; which was scarcely the act of a man
committed to an anti-German or anti-Austrian interpretation of all events, as we are asked to believe. The net
result of the tension was the creation of an independent
Albania, but Austria paid dearly for her success—the open
hostility of Russia and the certainty that Italy would
never consent to an Austrian control of the new state.

The unsatisfactory nature of the Balkan settlements was
generally admitted, but men consoled themselves with the
thought that a European war had been avoided, and with
the hope that when the question was reopened diplomacy
would once more rise to the occasion. The genuineness
of this feeling was attested by the universal meed of praise
accorded to Sir Edward Grey, who seemed to have acquired
an ascendency in the councils of Europe that no statesman
had enjoyed since the days of Bismarck. His speech in
the House of Commons on 12 August, 1913, reviewing the
work of the concert and expressing his fervent belief in
its efficacy, was received with applause in all the European capitals, and nothing seemed more unlikely than that
within a year he would have to confess the bankruptcy

of European statesmanship and the failure of his own
policy.

The success of the concert, however, depended upon the
continuance of existing conditions—that is, upon a Triple
Alliance balanced by a Triple *Entente*—and, from the German point of view, the balance had been upset to the disadvantage of the Triple Alliance, especially in the Balkans.
The new Serbia blocked the march of the Austrian "white
coats" to Salonika, and the defeat of the Turks seriously
diminished the support which they had been expected to
furnish against the *Entente*. In case of war Austria would
be forced to leave a large covering force on her southern
frontier as a protection against Serbian hostility, which
in turn would compel Germany to use against Russia troops
that she would need for her campaign in France. The
Triple Alliance, although formally renewed in December,
1912, was a broken reed,[1] for by her expedition to Tripoli
Italy had given hostages to fortune, and her jealousy of
Austrian designs in Albania would almost preclude sincere
co-operation in an Austro-German enterprise. Thus, at
the hands of the Balkan states, Germany had suffered a
potential defeat, and it was these military considerations
which prompted her military law of 1913. By this measure
she made a supreme effort to preserve the ascendency she
had enjoyed since 1871; but when France, Russia, and
Belgium had followed her example, and added to their
military establishments, no real advantage had been gained,
except that Germany, with her superior organization,
promptly gave effect to her new programme while her
rivals were maturing their plans—and was accordingly
tempted to strike before it was too late.

Diplomatically, the situation was changing rapidly.

---

[1] This was notoriously the opinion of General von Bernhardi, and was confirmed
not only by the events of 1914 but by the refusal of Italy to take active measures
against Serbia in August, 1913.

First in point of time and foremost in importance was the agreement between England and France. On *11* November, 1912, when the Austro-Serbian dispute over Albania was taking on the character of an Austro-Russian quarrel and was threatening the peace of Europe, Sir Edward Grey and M. Paul Cambon, the French ambassador in London, by an exchange of letters, agreed that

"if either government had grave reason to expect an unprovoked attack by a third Power, or something which threatened the general peace, it should immediately discuss with the other whether both governments should act together to prevent aggression and to preserve peace, and, if so, what measures they would be prepared to take in common. If these measures involved action, the plans of the general staffs would at once be taken into consideration and the governments would then decide what effect should be given to them." [1]

No flight of imagination could construe this agreement as more than a defensive alliance, even if positive proof were not furnished by the pacific policy of both England and France throughout the Balkan crisis. But Germany was not pleased. "From a trustworthy source" the Wilhelmstrasse secured copies of the letters in March, 1913, as well as information respecting the arrangements for Franco-British naval co-operation under which the French fleet was concentrated in the Mediterranean. "England has by this agreement and the existing military arrangements already given herself up beyond salvation to the French *revanche* idea," declared the informant of the German Government, which, since it has published his despatch,[2] must have accepted his interpretation.

After the treaty of Bucharest there was a succession

[1] Sir Edward Grey, House of Commons, 3 August, 1914 (5 *Hansard* lxv, *c.* 1813); also in *Great Britain and the European Crisis*, no. 105.

[2] Documents published by the *Norddeutsche Allgemeine Zeitung*, 17 October, 1914, no. 1.

of incidents distasteful to Germany. A visit of President Poincaré to Spain in the autumn of 1913 indicated that the Franco-Spanish jealousies generated by the Moroccan troubles had evaporated, and that Spain was now ranged with the *Entente* Powers; hence France would be free to withdraw her troops from the Spanish frontier in case of war. In May, 1914, an agreement was reached between Great Britain and Italy respecting Italian ambitions in Asia Minor, which would further cement the traditional friendship between those countries. Then, in June, the Tsar paid a visit to the King of Rumania, the first hospitality of this kind ever arranged. Described by the Rumanian foreign minister as "an event of the greatest importance," [1] it was understood to foreshadow the marriage of the Grand Duchess Olga of Russia to Prince Carol, the heir presumptive of the Rumanian throne. In striking fashion the Bucharest Government had announced the abandonment of that pro-Austrian policy consistently maintained since the Congress of Berlin. Bulgaria remained the sole outpost of Teutonic influence in the Balkans.

In May King George and his consort visited Paris, where they were splendidly received. The official *communiqué* anent the conversations between Sir Edward Grey and the French foreign minister said:

"While placing on record the results of the policy pursued by the two governments together with the imperial Russian Government, Sir Edward Grey and M. Doumergue are completely agreed upon the necessity that the three Powers should continue their constant efforts for the maintenance of the balance of power and of peace."

According to the documents published by the *Norddeutsche Allgemeine Zeitung*, on 17 October, 1914, the visit was regarded by German diplomatists as the preliminary to

[1] *Times*, 15 June, 1914.

"transforming the Triple *Entente* into an alliance of the type of the Triple Alliance," and as another of "the numerous proofs of British diplomacy's entire lack of power to resist the influence of the *Entente*";[1] although it passes the wit of man to discover why an agreement comparable to the much-vaunted Triple Alliance should be of such concern to Germany, unless, of course, the latter alliance was intended for an offensive policy.

The German story, as developed in the same documents, is that during Sir Edward Grey's visit in Paris, M. Isvolsky, the Russian ambassador, proposed an Anglo-Russian naval convention; that the British minister "received this suggestion in a sympathetic manner" and "warmly recommended" it to the British cabinet, which accepted his views; and that the negotiations were promptly begun in London between the admiralty and the Russian naval attaché, whose instructions were published as part of the evidence. Early in July Herr von Bethmann-Hollweg, the German chancellor, "caused it to be intimated to the English Government that its secret negotiations with Russia over a marine treaty were known to" him, and "directed earnest attention to the dangers for the peace of the world which lay in this English policy."[2] Was this a warning for England to keep clear of the storm that was about to break?

Questioned in the House of Commons about this convention, rumors of which were freely circulating, Sir Edward Grey denied that the British Government had concluded any agreement which would hamper the decision of Parliament on the outbreak of war as to British participation therein.[3] The German diplomatist who reported this to Berlin complained that Sir Edward had not answered the question put to him, and that his answer did not pre-

---

[1] No. 5.   [2] Reichstag, 2 December, 1914.
[3] 11 June, 1914. (5 *Hansard* lxiii, c. 458.)

clude such a convention. But the same gentleman quoted "a person of the minister's immediate entourage" to the effect that "no naval agreement had been concluded with Russia, nor was any going to be concluded." He also quoted an equally explicit statement of the *Westminster Gazette*, which "left nothing to be desired," and which was supposed to be inspired by Sir Edward Grey himself.[1] In July, when President Poincaré visited St. Petersburg, M. Sazonof, the Russian foreign minister, assured the German ambassador that such a naval convention existed only "in the mind of the *Berliner Tageblatt* and in the moon."[2] For the present it would be rash to dogmatize, but, on the evidence produced by the Germans, no one will be convinced that an Anglo-Russian naval convention was under way. It is possible that consultations were being pursued between the British and Russian naval experts similar to those engaged in by the general staffs of the French and British armies since the year 1906. But it is improbable that Great Britain had bound herself to Russia: not only did her attitude during the momentous days of July, 1914, consistently belie such a theory, but she had practically consummated an agreement with Germany which marked the triumph of the policy of adjustment adopted after the Boer War. This does not mean that Great Britain was ready to sacrifice the *Entente* on the altar of German friendship, or that she would cease to support the balance of power. If, however, Germany accepted the bargain as evidence of British good will and made no effort to disturb the peace of Europe, then the British Government, having settled its various disputes with all the Great Powers, would naturally withdraw from purely Continental politics and would be able in good faith to act as the "honest broker" between the two alliances.

[1] *Norddeutsche Allgemeine Zeitung*, nos. 7, 8.   [2] *Ibid.*, no. 11.

The Anglo-German *rapprochement* had been made possible by the pacific conduct of Germany during the Balkan crisis. The great obstacle hitherto had been the utter lack of confidence on the part of England in the German professions of peaceful ambitions, and her suspicions of the German navy. The recurring difficulties over Morocco and the circumstances in which the German fleet was built, justified these apprehensions. But when Admiral von Tirpitz accepted, even conditionally, the sixteen-to-ten ratio for the construction of *Dreadnoughts;* when Germany co-operated with England to localize the Balkan Wars, and when public opinion on both sides of the North Sea seemed sincerely to desire the end of the long quarrel, then it was possible to negotiate a settlement of such issues as had in the past, or might in the future, give rise to difficulties. The agreement was not made by Great Britain from fear of Germany, for such a feeling would have dictated the conversion of the Triple *Entente* into an alliance, and, indeed, the persistent refusal of British statesmen to adopt the latter policy is the most conclusive proof of their willingness to cultivate the friendship of Germany. It is well to remember that at any time during the ten years preceding the Great War, England could have had the alliance of France and Russia by adopting the Continental military system. She declined all such offers because such a policy would have fatally compromised her relations with Germany, and have laid on her shoulders the responsibility for a war of revenge undertaken by France or a war of prestige begun by Russia. For ten years England kept a middle course. In the summer of 1914 she appeared to have reaped her reward in the shape of the long-desired understanding with Germany.

German statesmen are entitled to their share of the credit for this achievement, which augured so well for the peace of the world. During the negotiations of July, 1914,

Herr von Bethmann-Hollweg assured the British ambassador in Berlin that "ever since he had been chancellor the object of his policy had been to bring about an understanding with England";[1] he said the same thing in the Reichstag on 2 December, 1914. Certainly he was regarded with less distrust in England than Prince Bülow, who was supposed to be distinctly anti-English. More important still was the attitude of Prince Lichnowsky, who succeeded Baron Marschall von Bieberstein in the London embassy. He seemed to have taken sincerely and seriously the mission of reconciliation with which his coming had been heralded. He and his wife revived the social traditions of the embassy, which had faded away under the long régime of Count Metternich, and easily conquered the affections of London society. The ambassador spoke frequently to commercial and financial organizations; he always emphasized the identity of British and German economic interests, and argued that war would be disastrous to the prosperity of the fatherland.[2] Leaving the past alone, he talked only of the future, in a spirit of good will and encouragement. With Sir Edward Grey he was *persona grata*.

Thus the road was opened to an understanding, in spite of what Prince Lichnowsky called "the seemingly irreconcilable forces at work in both countries to prevent it." On 4 February, 1914, Herr von Jagow told a committee of the Reichstag that Anglo-German relations were "very good" (*recht gut*). According to Sir Edward Grey, they had "sensibly improved" since the Balkan troubles.[3] For some months before the war negotiations were known to be in progress, with respect to which Herr von Beth-

[1] *Great Britain and the European Crisis*, no. 85. Sir Edward Goschen to Sir Edward Grey, 29 July, 1914.

[2] *New York Times*, 1 February, 1914.

[3] *Great Britain and the European Crisis*, no. 101. Sir Edward Grey to Sir Edward Goschen, 30 July, 1914.

mann-Hollweg expressed the hope that they would "bring
the relations of the two countries permanently back into
the quiet paths which for a time they had threatened to
leave." [1]   At the least they were expected to inspire the
two governments with mutual confidence, which might
be the forerunner of a wider political agreement. By the
early summer of 1914 the agreement had been initialed, as
well as an accord between England and Turkey. Publication was withheld pending the conclusion of a complementary arrangement between Germany and Turkey, but
for all practical purposes the bargain had been sealed
when the Austrian ultimatum to Serbia ushered in the
final crisis.

None of the three interested governments has revealed
the precise terms of the three-cornered agreement. Its
general scope, however, can be established from several
sources. According to the statement of Sir Edward Grey
in the House of Commons on 29 June, 1914, Great Britain
withdrew her claim to participate in the construction of
the Baghdad-Bassorah section of the Baghdad railway;
in return the section from Bassorah was not to be built
without British approval. British trade was to enjoy the
same privileges as Germany's on all sections of the line,
as a guarantee of which two Englishmen were admitted to
the board of directors. The navigation of the Tigris was
recognized as a substantial British interest. Great Britain admitted the suzerainty of Turkey over the Sheikh of
Koweit, on condition that his autonomy was not interfered with, and that the *status quo* in the Persian Gulf,
that is, the predominance of British interests, was accepted. In return the British Government agreed to the
increase of the Turkish customs to fifteen per cent.[2]   Dr.
Paul Rohrbach gives a slightly different account: "Extensive recognition was given to the German point of view in

[1] Reichstag, 9 December, 1913.   [2] 5 *Hansard* lxiv, cc. 116-120.

the Baghdad railway question, but also in the matters connected with it—the exploitation of the Mesopotamian oil-
fields and the navigation of the Tigris." [1] Each party
gave up some of its previous contentions, yet managed to
retain what was essential to itself. In any case, the agreement removed the most serious dispute then outstanding
between England and Germany. It also showed, as argued
in an earlier chapter, that England's objection to the Baghdad railway lay not in the line itself, but in certain details
which could be adjusted by mutual concessions.

Less is known about the African clauses of the Anglo-
German agreement. Dr. Rohrbach contents himself with
the remark that "English policy showed itself surpris-
ingly accommodating." Sir Edward Grey did not refer to
the subject. But on 31 December, 1913, the *New York
Times* published despatches from its Berlin and London
correspondents to the effect that England and Germany
had agreed to purchase and divide the Portuguese colonies in Africa. There could be no question of pressure
on Portugal, for by the treaty of alliance between that
country and Great Britain—which was first concluded
in the fourteenth century, and in its present form was
renewed at the outset of the Boer War—the possessions
of Portugal were guaranteed by the full strength of the
British Empire. But of recent years the Government of
Portugal, whether monarchical or republican, has been in
such financial straits that it could not develop its vast
overseas dominions and might very well wish to dispose
of them for a good price. The London correspondent of
the *New York Times* stated that the Portuguese authorities were only waiting for public opinion to show itself receptive to a sale. The Berlin version, however, was that
neither England nor Germany desired to "interfere with
the sovereignty of Portugal," but desired merely to mark

[1] *Grössere Deutschland*, 11 August, 1914; *Zum Weltvolk hindurch!* (1914), p. 47.

out "trading spheres" for itself. In any case, Angola, which was contiguous with German Southwest Africa, would become a German protectorate; England would take the part of Mozambique south of the Zambesi River, for the port of Delagoa Bay was the natural outlet for the Rand mines. The region north of the Zambesi would be added to German East Africa, which might also be increased, according to the *Frankfurter Zeitung*, by the Kagera River district of Uganda.[1] This division would be in keeping with the secret Anglo-German treaty of partition arranged in 1898, when the late Joseph Chamberlain was anxious for the good will of Germany.

Certain railway enterprises were also contemplated. Germany obtained the right to build a line across Angola to a point in Rhodesia where it would join the Cape to Cairo railway. This latter project had always been opposed by Germany, who saw that it would block her own designs for a Central African Empire stretching from ocean to ocean, but the *Frankfurter Zeitung* expressed the opinion that the continuation of the Rhodesian railway northward through the country west of Lake Tanganyika (the Belgian Congo) would not be injurious to the German railway east of Tanganyika. So far as is known, the question of the Congo was not involved in the negotiations, although German ambitions in that direction were clearly revealed by the Morocco treaty of 1911 with France and were actually admitted in a conversation between Herr von Jagow and M. Jules Cambon in March, 1914, in which the German foreign secretary "developed the opinion that only the Great Powers were in a position to colonize."[2]

It is quite impossible to say how far the Anglo-German agreement would have satisfied German public opinion. Would the complaint have been made that England re-

[1] 25 February, 1914.
[2] Second Belgian *Grey Book*, no. 2.

ceived quite as much as she gave? Writing in June, 1913,
Dr. Rohrbach boldly set up the thesis that "Germany
could not content herself with the rôle of registering increases of England's power, and must take up the very
self-evident position that the principle of compensation
should be given a certain retroactive force." [1] In other
words, England must recompense Germany for the enormous extension of the British Empire in the last quarter
of the nineteenth century, beginning with the occupation
of Egypt. Professor Hans Delbrück took practically the
same view in March, 1912, as noted in another chapter.
If such doctrines were cherished by official Germany, then
no peace was possible between England and Germany.
For these conditions could be satisfied only if England was
willing to surrender part of her own Empire or to give
Germany *carte blanche* to take what she liked from weaker
Powers—France, Portugal, Belgium, Holland. To this
England would never consent. And it is surely significant
that, when making his bid for British neutrality on the
eve of the war, Herr von Bethmann-Hollweg refused to
guarantee the integrity of the French colonies; just as in
his Reichstag speech of 2 December, 1914, he complained
that England would not permit "the free development of
Germany's powers." On these grounds there is much to
be said for the view current in England after the war began
that Germany's purpose in making the agreement was to
throw dust in England's eyes, to persuade her that German
policy was peaceful, and to lull her into a false sense of
security.

Nevertheless, whatever Germany's motives may have
been, the fact remained that in July, 1914, Anglo-German
relations were more cordial than they had been at any time
since the Boer War. England had tried by her action to
prove that she was not opposed to German expansion;

[1] *Preussische Jahrbücher*, July, 1913; *Zum Weltvolk hindurch !*, pp. 15–16.

Germany had been willing to negotiate an agreement with England on the basis of give and take. When the Archduke Francis Ferdinand was assassinated at Serajevo, on 28 June, talk of an Anglo-German war had been relegated to the limbo of those prophecies which twenty years before had represented an Anglo-French or an Anglo-Russian war as the inevitable outcome of irreconcilable ambitions. In his interesting book, *The War of Steel and Gold*, Mr. H. N. Brailsford ridiculed the idea that any Power—least of all Germany—would unchain a general war, and roundly belabored British statesmen for ever assuming that she would do so. To all outward appearances England and Germany had "cleaned the slate."

The collapse of this auspicious beginning is the most tragic feature of the war. There were only two outstanding questions in Europe: the Near East and Alsace-Lorraine. The definitive solution of the former was not imperative at the moment. For, besides the Anglo-German-Turkish arrangement, other agreements were under way between Germany, France, Russia, Italy, and Turkey, which would have divided the Ottoman Empire into economic spheres of interest, each reserved for a particular Power. The outlook for Armenian reforms, under international auspices, was hopeful. The Turk, in short, was to be given a final chance, and, if he failed, the Great Powers might solve his problem peacefully by keeping the territories they were now staking off for purposes of exploitation.

As regards the other question, were London reconciled with Berlin, it might play the mediator between Paris and Berlin. Frenchmen certainly had not forgotten Alsace-Lorraine, but they were tired of militarism, and they had shot their last bolt in the revival of three years' service. If the Republic could have been guaranteed against attack, perhaps by the retrocession of Metz; if Germany could have brought herself to concede genuine self-government to the disputed provinces, one cannot help thinking that in time France would have abandoned the Russian alliance. Certainly her peasants and bourgeoisie could invest as profitably in German commercial enterprises as in Russian state bonds. In spite of all the difficulties—and they were many—a peace league of France, Germany, and England was not more unthinkable than was a few years ago the reconciliation of England with France and Russia, or the more recent *rapprochement* between England and Germany. In such a case good will is everything, and in each of the three countries forces were at work to break down the age-old barriers of hatred and suspicion. Not in a day would the task have been accomplished, but could the peace of Europe have been preserved ten years longer, the democracies of France, Germany, and England, one likes to believe, would not have been unresponsive to the idea which their more enlightened leaders had already put before them.

An outsider would consider it a clever stroke on the part of Germany to have allayed the suspicions of England at a time when Russo-German relations were becoming strained. Curiously enough, the German Government did not take this view at all. In describing the situation of Germany at the outbreak of the war, Herr von Bethmann-Hollweg said in the Reichstag on 2 December, 1914, that "the circle was closed," and that Germany therefore "assumed the consequences arising out of this whole state of affairs"—language which can only mean that Germany was determined to shatter the *Entente* at all costs. "A people of the greatness and capacity of the Germans," said the chancellor, "will not allow itself to be smothered in its free and peaceful development." The root of the evil was that the *Entente* had been designed by England to serve the principle of the balance of power. "Therein lay the aggressive character of the Triple *Entente* as compared with the purely defensive tendencies of the Triple Alliance; therein lay the germ of a powerful explosion."

In the course of his speech Herr von Bethmann-Holl-weg baldly admitted that the aim of his policy had been to break up the *Entente* by means of separate agreements with the different members. There was the Morocco treaty with France, and "some agreements with Russia had been arrived at"; but the French *revanche* idea and the Russian alliance with France, together with the Pan-Slavic aspirations, "rendered impossible any agreement that would have excluded the danger of war in the case of political crises."

England, however, had repeatedly declared that her hands were free. The chancellor believed that "the growing power of Germany and the increasing risk of war" would persuade England to make "a friendly compromise with Germany." His hopes seemed to have been realized in part. "By dint of long, hard work an understanding was reached as to various contested questions of economic interests respecting the Near East and Africa," by which "the number of possible political friction-points was to be reduced." But, all the time, "England was increasingly intent upon making its relations with Russia and France steadily closer. . . . She was, indeed, ready to reach understandings with Germany concerning separate questions, but the chief and first principle of the English policy was the same—the free development of Germany's powers must be held in check by the balance of power. That is the boundary line for friendly relations with Germany. And its purpose is: to strengthen the Triple *Entente* to the uttermost."

It is, of course, perfectly true that Great Britain is fighting to preserve the balance of power. But is not the chancellor's charge an admission that Germany is aiming at world dominion? Moreover, when he claimed that

England had engineered the *Entente* to serve the balance of power, he forgot that in the documents published by the *Norddeutsche Allgemeine Zeitung* England was represented as the dupe of France and Russia. Once again, Germany cannot have it both ways. England could not engineer the *Entente* and at the same time be the dupe of her partners. Nor can Germany, with complete freedom of action, make an agreement with England, and then, when it leads to unexpected results, blame England that it did not go far enough. As has been pointed out in previous pages of this book, *Inconsistency, thy name is Germany!*

The Anglo-German understanding was a by-product of the Balkan revolution; so also was the bitterness which characterized Russo-German relations in the last six months of peace. Hitherto, as joint abetters of the partition of Poland, Russia and Germany had considered their interests identical in restraining the schemes of the Poles to recover their independence. They also regarded themselves as the bulwarks of monarchical absolutism against the tide of democratic progress, so much so, in fact, that during the Russian revolution the authorities of Berlin afforded every facility to the Russian Government for tracking down and capturing Russian revolutionaries in Germany.

Likewise, in the domain of high policy, co-operation was long the order of the day. At the time of the Crimean War Prussia steadfastly resisted the urgings of France and England to join them, and was rewarded by Russian neutrality in the wars of 1866 and 1870 against Austria and France, without which the Prussian triumphs would have been impossible. Bismarck, regarding the friendship of Russia as the keystone of his policy, always "kept the wire open to St. Petersburg"; and if William II abandoned this policy as being "too complicated," he managed to preserve excellent personal relations with the Tsar by supporting

Russian designs in the Far East. As recently as 1910, it will be remembered, Russia accepted the German proposals for the Baghdad railway and was enthusiastically praised in the German press for what appeared to be an abandonment of France and Great Britain, which countries were then the chief antagonists of German diplomacy.

Russo-German intimacy was shattered by two circumstances. In the first place, Russian opinion gradually became convinced that the road to Constantinople lay through Berlin.[1] Bismarck's conduct at the Congress of Berlin, where he supported England and Austria in demanding the revision of the treaty of San Stefano, dictated as it was by the Russians at the gates of Constantinople, caused profound resentment throughout the Tsardom, and was never forgotten. Thanks to this, the Russian Government had no little difficulty in restraining the popular demand for war in 1908–9, when Germany supported Austria-Hungary in the annexation of Bosnia, and again in 1912–13, in the creation of an independent Albania. Moreover, for twenty years Germany had done her best to regenerate Turkey, with the purpose of checking the Russian advance, and to keep Russia in leading strings, in order that Austria might have a free hand in the Balkans. The liberal elements in Russia regarded Prussia as the chief prop of the Tsar's autocratic system, and Berlin was credited with making threats which prevented justice being done to Russian Poland. The commercial treaty dictated by Germany during the Japanese War was rather unfavorable to Russia, and Germany was expected to insist upon its renewal. In short, all the evils from which Russia was suffering—political, economic, social—were ascribed to the malign influence of Germany, whose culture had been unpopular

[1] Professor Mitrofanof, of the University of St. Petersburg, in *Preussische Jahrbücher*, June, 1914. This letter to Professor Hans Delbrück and his reply are invaluable for the study of Russo-German relations.

with the mass of Russians since the very day when Peter the Great first tried to foist it upon his barbarous subjects.

On the other hand, Germany had been suspicious of Russia ever since the Anglo-Russian convention of 1907, for that agreement, along with a Russo-Japanese understanding, gave Russian policy a free hand in the Near East, without fear of irritation from Manchuria or Persia. German publicists convinced themselves that Russia was at last preparing in earnest for the subversion of Turkey, and that Germany would not receive her share. The difficulties that arose over the Bosnian crisis have been discussed at length in an earlier chapter; we have also seen how the Balkan revolution upset the existing situation, entirely to the disadvantage of the Dual Monarchy—whose Balkan policy Germany had made her own, in spite of Bismarck's warning—and therefore of Germany. It was also problematical how long Turkey could survive the operation performed by the Balkan states. In German eyes the danger was increased when the Russian Government protested, in January, 1914, against the appointment of General Liman von Sanders as reorganizer of the Turkish army.

Russian opinion had been decidedly irritated by the German chancellor's prediction, made anent the German army bill of 1913, of an approaching struggle between *Germanentum* and *Slaventum*. When, therefore, on 2 March, 1914, the *Kölnischer Zeitung*, imitating its fanfare of a year before, to the effect that France was "the disturber of the peace," now declared that Russia would have struck at Germany during the Balkan Wars if she had been strong enough, the Russian press was allowed to reply in kind. With remarkable unanimity the organs of all parties declared that Russia would proceed with her military plans regardless of German remonstrances, and that Russian diplomacy would not submit to further humiliations. The government gave ample warning. It hinted that a practise mobilization would be carried out in the autumn of 1914, and actually mobilized one corps on the Austrian frontier. Then, on 23 May, M. Sazonof re-affirmed in the Duma the policy of the Balkans for the Balkan peoples. Finally, in the same month, the Duma passed a bill which levied duties on rye, peas, and beans imported through the western frontier, thereby dealing a hard blow at German agriculturists; for the cultivation of rye had assumed large proportions in Prussia, where it was amply protected, and the surplus output had been sold almost entirely in Russia. Russo-German friendship had, in brief, become a legend.

The German press now began to discuss freely the de-sirability of a "preventive" war with the Russian colossus. There seems to have been a general conviction that Russia was seeking an opportunity to attack Germany.[1] It was universally believed that the Balkan League of 1912 had been created by Russia for a flank attack on Austria; that only an accident had diverted it against Turkey; and that it was being reformed with Rumania in the place of Bul-garia. It was alleged that France had returned to the three years' service at the demand of Russia, and that Germany's huge military increases in 1913 were called forth as a reply. It was known that the last Russian loan in Paris, amounting to 2,500,000,000 francs, would be ap-plied to the construction of strategic railways in Poland, to the purchase of new equipment, and to a considerable increase of the army. The *Kölnischer Zeitung* calculated that the entire scheme of army reorganization would be worked out by 1917: then the Russian attack would begin. Was it not better to anticipate while Germany was ready and her opponent was not?

[1] Paul Rohrbach, *Zum Weltvolk hindurch !*, pp. 24–33; *Der Krieg und die deutsche Politik* (1914), pp. 54–69.

No doubt there was a military party in Russia.   The
desire to retrieve the humiliations of the Manchurian campaign was strong among the higher officers, and there was
an indisposition to admit the much-vaunted superiority
of the German military machine.   Also, the official world,
troubled at the spectre of revolution which was again
raising its head, was not unwilling to provide a diversion
by a war against the national enemy.   But there is no
evidence to show that the direction of Russian policy was
not in the hands of the Tsar and M. Sazonof, the responsible
foreign minister, both of whom were convinced supporters
of peace.   Nor has there been developed in Russia that
cultivation of the martial spirit, that constant appeal to
the doctrine of force which is the essence of militarism.
Militarism, some one has remarked, is a state of mind, a
particular view of life which tests all things and all men
by the standards of power and subordinates to its own ends
all the finer instincts.   As means to its ends it demands
order, discipline, efficiency—all foreign to the Russian character; it is the negation of Russian life, as for that matter
the Germans have boasted when they compared their own
army to the huge, seemingly unwieldy mass of the Tsar's
subjects.

A Russo-German war *may* have been inevitable, for the
ambitions of the two countries were as conflicting as national policies well can be.   But so were once the designs
of England and France, England and Russia, England and
Germany, and *rapprochements* had been effected.   And,
even if it be assumed that Russia would one day have
called Germany to account in order that she might reach
the ultimate goal of her policy, it must be admitted that
Russian policy has never been directly oriented against
Germany, whereas in the years 1907–14 German diplomacy
went out of its way whenever possible to administer doses
of disagreeable medicine to its eastern rival.   Of course

neither side was entirely free from blame, but, historically
considered, the major responsibility for the Russo-German
rupture must be assigned to Germany, primarily because
here as elsewhere she insisted on having her way and demanded instant obedience from Russia, which no self-
respecting nation could render.   It is but another illustration of German loose thinking, when we are desired to
believe that because Russia might have loosed the dogs of
war in 1917, she is, in consequence, responsible for their having got loose in 1914.   The real question is: which Power
worked for peace in the last days of July, 1914, Germany
or Russia?

The time is probably far off when a definitive account
can be given of the events of 1913–14 in their proper perspective and true inwardness.   Scarcely any documents
relating to that period have been published by the belligerent governments, and the information at present available must be culled from the press, the occasional speeches
of statesmen, and the mass of ephemeral literature evoked
by a great crisis.   But gradually evidence of one kind or
another is accumulating to show that the Teutonic Powers
were preparing for war long before the murder of the Archduke Francis Ferdinand at Serajevo.   Granted that this
testimony proceeds entirely from the Allied countries, or
from sources favorable to their cause, it is noteworthy that,
in all the strenuous propaganda conducted by Germany
and her agents, no effort has been made to disprove the
evidence against her.   The historical student will not accept the scattered charges here assembled as conclusive
proof of a German conspiracy to provoke a war, but he
can set up a case which Germany cannot demolish by the
asseveration, *Es ist nicht wahr*.[1]   In the absence of official

[1] This method—the reiteration of the phrase, "It is not true," was adopted in the
manifesto of the ninety-three German intellectuals issued shortly after the beginning of the war.

information, he is entitled to formulate opinions on the basis of such circumstantial stories as may be told.

The case against Austria-Hungary may be examined first. How the unexpected results of the Balkan Wars prompted her to invoke the *casus fœderis* of the Triple Alliance in August, 1913, and how she failed to secure the approval of Italy, is known from the revelations of Signor Giolitti, already noted. In April, 1914, Count Tisza, the Hungarian premier, published an article in the *Jgazmondo* of Budapest, in which he cautioned Russia to keep her hands off the Balkans if she wished to maintain friendly relations with the Dual Monarchy.[1] In the same month, according to the Bucharest correspondent of the *Morning Post*, "the Marquis Pallavicini, the Austro-Hungarian ambassador at Constantinople, made a stay of three days at Bucharest, during which he sounded various political personages whether Rumania would follow Austria and Germany in the event of the former declaring war, the Marquis affirming that Austria would be obliged to proceed to this extremity."[2] A pretext would easily have been found, for Serbia had just concluded a concordat with the Vatican which challenged the traditional claim of Austria to protect Catholics in the western Balkans. And it has been asserted that when the German Emperor visited the Archduke Francis Ferdinand at Konopischt, two weeks before the tragedy of Serajevo, the latter secured from his guest the promise of Germany's assistance for an aggressive policy in the south.[3] Certain it is that the idea of "direct action" had become increasingly popular with the German and Magyar elements of the Monarchy since Count Berchtold had failed to obtain any positive advantages from the collapse of Turkey in Europe. His own character did not inspire confidence in his conservatism, and the chief of the

[1] *New York Times*, 26 April, 1914. [2] *Ibid.*, 7 December, 1914.
[3] Politicus, *Fortnightly Review*, September, 1914, p. 450.

general staff, General Conrad von Hötzendorf, was notoriously reckless and belligerent.   At no time, in short, since the disposition of other peoples and others' lands became the chief industry of the European chanceries had the Dual Monarchy shown such willingness to embark on a career of adventure and aggression.

As to Germany, the most striking evidence is afforded by the French *Yellow Book*.   In a secret report on the strengthening of the German army, dated 19 March, 1913, and "received from a reliable source" by the French minister of war on 2 April, occur these words:

"We must accustom the people to think that an offensive war on our part is a necessity, in order to combat the provocations of our adversaries.   We must act with prudence, so as not to arouse suspicion, and to avoid crises which might injure our economic existence.   We must so manage matters that under the heavy weight of powerful armaments, considerable sacrifices, and strained political relations, an outbreak should be considered as a relief, because after it would come decades of peace and prosperity, as after 1870. We must prepare for war from the financial point of view; there is much to be done in this direction.   We must not arouse the distrust of our financiers, but there are many things which cannot bo oonooalod."

The writer of the report then emphasizes the necessity of creating diversions for Germany's enemies in their colonial possessions, and continues:

"Risings provoked in time of war by political agents need to be carefully prepared and by material means.   They must break out simultaneously with the destruction of the means of communication; they must have a controlling head to be found among the influential leaders, religious or political.   The Egyptian school is particularly suited to this purpose; more and more it serves as a bond between the intellectuals of the Mohammedan world." [1]

Even more illuminating is the report of a conversation between the German Emperor and the King of the Belgians,

[1] No. 2, part 2.

in November, 1913. What actually passed between the two monarchs is not divulged, but it is not difficult to imagine the purport:

"The person addressed by the Emperor," wrote the French ambassador in Berlin, "had thought up till then, as did all the world, that William II, whose personal influence had been exerted on many critical occasions in support of peace, was still of the same state of mind. He found him this time completely changed. The German Emperor is no longer the champion of peace against the warlike tendencies of certain parties in Germany. William II has come to think that war with France is inevitable, and that it must come sooner or later. . . .

"During the course of the conversation the Emperor, moreover, seemed overstrained and irritable. As William II advances in years, family traditions, the reactionary tendencies of the court, and especially the impatience of the soldiers obtain a greater empire over his mind. Perhaps he feels some slight jealousy of the popularity acquired by his son, who flatters the passions of the Pan-Germans, and who does not regard the position occupied by the Empire in the world as commensurate with its power. . . .

"Whatever may have been the object of the conversation related to me, the revelation is none the less of extreme gravity. . . . It would be well to take account of this new factor, namely, that the Emperor is becoming used to an order of ideas which were formerly repugnant to him, and that to borrow from him a phrase which he likes to use, 'we must keep our powder dry.'"[1]

General utterances of this kind, however, are scarcely sufficient to establish the thesis that a war was in immediate preparation. Much more to the point is the succession of curious incidents which filled the first six months of 1914. In January the Krupps endeavored to take up £2,000,000 worth of new shares offered by the Poutiloff Arms Factory of St. Petersburg, which executes orders for the Russian Government; this transaction would have transferred the control to the German company. As the concern possessed the secrets of the French artillery, which

[1] No. 6.

the Russian army had adopted, the change of ownership might have had far-reaching effects, and was, in fact, prevented by the government.

In March the British admiralty announced that instead of the usual annual manœuvres a practise mobilization of the entire fleet would be carried out. It is believed that this measure was taken as a precaution against the event of war; according to one account Mr. Churchill was warned by an ambassador of one of the Triple Alliance Powers at a Continental court that stirring days were ahead.[1]

The month of June witnessed the forced sale on the London stock exchange of large quantities of German securities. Though not understood at the moment, it was later interpreted as an effort to throw British credit out of gear, and at the same time to increase the amount of gold in Germany.

A curious letter, written on 20 July, 1914, was published in the *Petit Parisien* on 10 January, 1915. The writer, a Dr. Magnan, Director of the French School of Advanced Research, spent the spring and early summer in the Rhine provinces studying the German treatment of typhoid. He learned that lists had been made of "typhoid bearers"— persons who might distribute germs among large numbers of men; these persons were to be deported to central Germany "immediately on the outbreak of war." Luxemburg was asked to furnish similar lists but refused. Dr. Magnan also saw work on six new strategic railways between Treves and Karthaus being feverishly concluded, and in Luxemburg was told that war was imminent.

On 14 June secret instructions, subsequently intercepted, were addressed to the commander of the German cruiser *Eber*, then in dock at Cape Town. They "revealed a com-

[1] *Nation* (New York), 27 August, 1914, p. 245. (London correspondence of 11 August.)

plete system for coaling the German navy on the outbreak of war through secret service agents in Cape Town, New York, and Chicago," the commander being given the names of shippers and bankers with whom he could deal confidentially.[1]

On 1 August the German liner *Cap Trafalgar* arrived at Buenos Aires, bringing extra guns, which were transferred by night to other German ships in port. In the same city Germans were said to display letters from their government ordering them to hold themselves in readiness. Both the liner and the letters must have left Germany not later than 1 July.[2]

Of great interest is the letter published by *El Liberal* of Madrid on 7 September, 1914. It is a series of questions said to have been addressed on 8 July by the German consul in Palma, Majorca (in the Balearic Isles) to the president of the works committee of the port, who, instead of forwarding the letter to the naval authorities, answered the inquiry directly. Among the points on which information was desired were: the amount of Welsh coal available, size of quays and docks, depth of port, number of tugs available, and many other details.[3] This document derives its interest from the presence of the German cruisers *Goeben* and *Breslau* in the Mediterranean at the opening of hostilities. If they could seize the islands as a naval base, the main German fleet, then off the coast of Norway, could sweep around the north of Scotland into the Atlantic, and then, bursting into the Mediterranean, prevent the French from transporting troops from Africa—a scheme apparently abandoned when the British fleet was not dispersed after its mobilization.

The cumulative effect of these various facts, stories, or allegations—whatever one may choose to call them—cer-

[1] *Times* (weekly edition), 9 October, 1914. [2] *Ibid.*, 7 August, 1914.
[3] *New York Times*, 8 September, 1914.

tainly favors the view that the murders of Serajevo merely furnished the excuse for an aggressive move definitely and carefully planned for the summer of 1914.

That season promised well for the success of a war suddenly sprung and rapidly conducted. On 13 July a startling indictment of the deficient organization and equipment of the French army was made by M. Charles Humbert in a report to the Senate. The forts on the frontier were alleged to be poorly constructed; guns lacked ammunition; there was a bad shortage of boots. The French artillery was falling behind that of Germany, in numbers at least; in heavy guns especially did the Germans have a distinct superiority. The essential truth of these charges was proved in the early days of the war, and the Germans, with their elaborate spy system, may well have known of this state of affairs. Furthermore, France seemed absorbed by the Caillaux trial. The political situation was obscure, owing to the confusion of parties resulting from the recent general election and the kaleidoscopic ministerial changes. Toward the end of the month the President of the Republic and the prime minister proceeded on a visit to Russia, and did not return until the crisis was well developed.

In Russia revolution seemed to have raised its head again. The forcible suppression of earlier strikes, the persecution of the labor press, the frequent dissolution of trade-unions, taken with the hard conditions of living, had provoked general unrest. Rioting began in St. Petersburg at the time of President Poincaré's visit; the tram and railway services were soon disorganized, and for a while the days of 1905 seemed to have returned. German and Austrian inspiration of this outbreak has been charged, but nothing definite has leaked out. German diplomacy may have hoped by this means to paralyze the Russian army temporarily, or it may have argued that the Tsar's Government would be the more inclined to try the arbitrament of war as a solution of domestic difficulties. In either case Germany had nothing to lose by the intrigue.

Across the North Sea the very stars in their courses seemed to be fighting for the German cause. In far-away Vancouver the deportation of some would-be Hindu immigrants by the Canadian authorities had provided the London Government with a thorny problem that showed no disposition to solve itself on the traditional basis of compromise. In the middle of July the *Times* military correspondent had adverted to the deficit of recruits for the regular army since 1907, averaging nearly 5,000 a year. It was notorious that the territorials were far below the stipulated establishment. Spies were also said to have predicted a strike of the transport workers when mobilization was proclaimed.[1]

But, above all, there was Ireland. Now, if ever, would the old adage be remembered: "England's danger is Ireland's opportunity." King George himself had said that the danger of civil war was present to all responsible and sober-minded people. Gun-running in Ulster and an incipient mutiny of the army officers had gone so far without punishment that in the third week of July riots had occurred in Dublin, and the whole island was one vast powder magazine, only awaiting the spark of ignition. Baron von Kuhlmann, the councillor of the London embassy, who was more trusted by his government than the ambassador himself, is believed to have reported to Berlin that effective action could not be taken by a government in such straits as the Asquith ministry; his intimate relations with Lord Morley, Mr. John Burns, and Mr. Ramsay Macdonald may have persuaded him that Great Britain would not intervene in a European war.

[1] *New York Times*, 23 October, 1914.

It is commonly asserted that Germany laid her plans on this last assumption, and the theory is plausible. A Liberal government was in power, was rated as favoring peace at any price, and had recently been cultivating good relations with Germany. The pro-German party was vigorous and respected. The colonial agreement about to be published had disarmed old suspicions of German ambitions. The pacifists were aghast at the naval estimates. If only the bribe were high enough, England would stand aside, for the nation of shopkeepers had lost the martial spirit and looked sordidly to its commerce and its pleasures.

Doubtless the German Government hoped to keep England neutral until it had settled its account with France and then dealt the Russians a sharp blow sufficient to render them harmless for a time. But it is inconceivable that the Emperor and his advisers seriously expected England to stand aside permanently. They knew Sir Edward Grey as the firm friend of France and the ardent advocate of the balance of power; the chancellor later admitted that he had never hoped to break down the British obsession of a Europe in equilibrium.[1] If the past history of England meant anything, it postulated intervention sooner or later against a Power about to dominate Europe. The German fleet had not been constructed for nothing; the decision to make war had not been postponed to no purpose until the summer of 1914, when the deepening of the Kiel Canal, just finished, permitted the use of the fleet in either the Baltic or the North Sea. During the negotiations the Wilhelmstrasse was repeatedly warned that in certain conditions Great Britain would be drawn into the conflict, in spite of which the declaration of war was launched against Russia. Above all, there was Belgium, whose neutrality the general staff was determined to violate. Now, since the fourteenth century England has con-

[1] Reichstag, 2 December, 1914.

sistently opposed the absorption of the Low Countries by a strong Power; this was the issue in her struggle with Louis XIV, and she entered the lists against the French Revolution precisely because the First Republic was bent on extending its frontier to the Rhine. At the Congress of Vienna in 1815, on the occasion of the Belgian revolution of 1830, in the War of 1870, she had manifested the same inflexible determination to keep Belgium a free and independent state. So in 1914. The truth is, so inevitable was the intervention of England if Belgium was molested that Germany must actually have desired to see England drawn in—or else her statesmen and diplomatists were the sorriest or most incapable that ever directed the destinies of a great nation.

After all, why should Germany fear English intervention? The "contemptible little army" that might be sent over to help the French was an inconsequential muster of hirelings and would probably arrive too late to be of service. Civil war in Ireland would paralyze action on a grand scale. The colonies would revolt, to the accompaniment of open sedition in Egypt and India. There would be the usual attempt to "muddle through," but against German efficiency it would be of no avail. The colossus with feet of clay would fall like its namesake at Rhodes, and on the wreck of the British Empire victorious Germany would dictate the terms of peace which would make her the mistress of the world.

When General Botha returned to Cape Town, in July, 1915, after his conquest of German Southwest Africa, he made a speech which bears out these contentions:

"One of the most interesting discoveries in German Southwest Africa was a map showing the redistribution of the world after the 'Peace of Rome, 1916.' It placed the whole of Africa south of the equator as a greater German Empire. There was a small portion segregated as a Boer reserve.

"This and other indications of the same character showed the German designs upon the Union of South Africa, and what faith could be placed in their word? It was established that Maritz [the leader of the unsuccessful rebellion] had sent a delegate to German Southwest Africa in 1913 and had received an encouraging reply. Before the war broke out the rebellion was brewing, and in these circumstances Maritz sent a delegate to inquire how far the rebels would be able to obtain assistance in artillery, arms, and ammunition, and how far the independence of South Africa would be guaranteed."

Then, according to information which General Botha received, correspondence took place between the governor of German Southwest Africa and the Kaiser. The Kaiser's answer was as follows:

"'I will not only acknowledge the independence of South Africa, but will even guarantee it, provided the rebellion is started immediately.'"[1]

If one remembers how delicate the international situation was in 1913, during the Balkan crisis, one cannot help wondering whether behind the support given by Germany to Sir Edward Grey's mediation there did not lurk a secret design to precipitate the war then if France, Russia, or England, separately or together, should make a false step. The story of the South African intrigue is the most damaging evidence yet produced against Germany.

So Germany's hour of destiny had come. Never again could she hope for so favorable an opportunity. Her army was at the highest absolute and relative efficiency; her war-chest was full; she believed herself invincible; and her people could be expected to respond magnificently to the call. The long years of preparation and education had not been in vain. "Your Majesty can have no conception," said General von Moltke to the King of the Belgians, in the

[1] *Times* (weekly edition), 30 July, 1915.

presence of the Emperor, "of the irresistible enthusiasm with which the whole German people will be carried away when the day of war comes." [1] It merely remained so to shuffle the cards that the fatherland might appear the victim of an unprovoked aggression. As it happened the gods could not have provided a better opportunity for this exercise of kingcraft than the catastrophe of Serajevo.

[1] French *Yellow Book*, no. 6.

CHAPTER XIII

THE CRISIS OF 1914[1]

ON 28 June, 1914, the Archduke Francis Ferdinand, the heir to the Austrian throne, and his wife, the Duchess of Hohenberg, were assassinated at Serajevo, in the province of Bosnia. The assassins were subjects of the Dual Monarchy, but it was charged by the Austrian Government that they had procured their arms from the Serbian state arsenal at Kragujevacz and had received other assistance from Serbian government officials. They were, in fact, members of the Narodna Odbrana, the Serbian secret society which was carrying on an active propaganda in Bosnia and Herzegovina, with the object of detaching those provinces from the Hapsburg dominions and effecting their incorporation in the Kingdom of Serbia.— Gavril Princip and Nedeljko Gabrinovitch, the actual murderers, assuredly had no thought of producing a world wide war: they were impressionable students imbued with intense hatred for the Austrian régime, and would seem to have been the obedient tools of men higher up in the Narodna Odbrana, more especially one Milan Ciganovitch, of the Serbian state

[1] This chapter and the two following have been written almost entirely from the documents published by the belligerent governments, which have been collected by the British Government in a single volume, under the title *Collected Diplomatic Documents Relating to the Outbreak of the European War* (1915). The documents are referred to by nationality and number, as "British, no. 101." The German *White Book* is quoted from the *Collected Diplomatic Documents*; also certain other documents published after the original *Papers* and *Books*. The British *White Paper* ("Correspondence Respecting the European Crisis") was republished as a *Blue Book* ("Great Britain and the European Crisis"), to which was prefixed an "Introductory Narrative of Events," of great interest. Unfortunately this "Narrative" was not included in the *Collected Documents*: reference must therefore be made to the *Blue Book* itself, and as the pagination differs in the various editions, only to the sections of the "Narrative."

394

railways, and Major Voija Tankositch, who secured the six bombs and six pistols used by Princip and his associates, instructed them in the use of these weapons, and arranged for the secret crossing of the Serbo-Bosnian frontier. It was the alleged complicity of these men which enabled the Austrian Government to charge that the Narodna Odbrana was "entirely dominated by the Belgrade foreign office," and that its policy of agitation, together with the enlistment of volunteers "for the coming war with the Austro-Hungarian Monarchy," represented the ambitions of the Serbian Government, which had also "permitted its press to disseminate hatred against the Dual Monarchy." [1]

In its broad outlines this indictment was undoubtedly true. The Serbian people and their government ardently desired the disintegration of Austria-Hungary in order that their ideal might be realized of a Greater Serbia coterminous with the boundaries of the Serb race. To this ambition, which aimed not only at her dismemberment but would also cut her off from the sea, Austria-Hungary, a Great Power with a long history and a traditional policy of territorial expansion, was bound to oppose the resistance of all her forces. For at least a decade the fight had been waged on both sides with all the ferocity and cunning ever associated with Balkan politics, and the assassination of the archduke was merely the culminating incident. It is not yet possible to form an impartial opinion of the controversy. Serbia's throne was blood-stained, and her people the most backward in the Balkans except, of course, the Albanians; their record in the past was not such as to inspire excessive confidence in their liberating mission. Since their triumphs over Turkey and Bulgaria they had become somewhat conceited and demanding. On the other hand, the whole trouble was due very largely to the treatment meted out to their Slav subjects by Austria and Hun-

---

[1] Austrian, no. 19 (the dossier of evidence against Serbia).

gary alike, which had been a perversion of justice, a denial of the most solemn legal obligations. Nor, as was brought out in the famous Agram and Friedjung trials, had the Ballplatz hesitated to manufacture documents for the purpose of incriminating the Serbian Government in plots which did not exist. Clearly, therefore, Austria, no more than Serbia, came into the "court of civilization" with clean hands.

There was a solution of the difficulty: the incorporation of the Kingdom of Serbia in the Hapsburg Monarchy, and the complete reorganization of that monarchy on the basis of trialism or federalism—that is, all the Southern Slav provinces would be formed into a single kingdom, analogous to the Empire of Austria and the Kingdom of Hungary, or there might be established local self-government for each of the provinces—Slav, Magyar, or German—under the supreme authority of a single parliament. Such a solution would effect the unity of the Serb race, and would at the same time preserve to the monarchy its outlet on the Adriatic. But it would come within the realm of practical politics at the present time only if both Russia and Serbia were reduced to military impotency; and even then its feasibility may well be doubted, for the hatred of the Serbs for all things Austrian is now too deep to be reconciled by belated concessions.

The assassination of the archduke was not without its grim irony. Francis Ferdinand was one of the few Hapsburg statesmen who perceived the necessity of a new policy toward the Slav peoples of the Monarchy. His precise views were unknown, for he talked little, but he passed for a federalist, and he was certainly a true friend of the Slavs. Yet, as the embodiment of Hapsburg policy, he was disliked by them and was murdered by one of them. But because of his Slavophile leanings his death would seem to have caused profound satisfaction in German and

Magyar circles, and it solved one pressing problem. When he married the Countess Sophie Chotek, he had been compelled to renounce for her children all claims to the Austrian throne; in Hungary, however, their rights were fully admitted. A confused succession thus loomed in the future. But with the disappearance of Francis Ferdinand the Archduke Charles Francis Joseph became the undisputed heir to all the Hapsburg lands. It has been charged that the political enemies of the archduke, though warned of the plot against him, deliberately neglected to take proper precautions at Serajevo, as he himself complained when the first attempt to assassinate him failed.

The importance of the Serajevo tragedy was immediately recognized in every corner of Europe, and the verdict may be given in the words of Sir Edward Grey:

"No crime," says the "Introductory Narrative of Events," prefixed to the British *Blue Book*, "has ever aroused deeper or more general horror throughout Europe; none has ever been less justified. Sympathy for Austria was universal. Both the governments and the public opinion of Europe were ready to support her in any measures, however severe, which she might think it necessary to take for the punishment of the murderer and his accomplices." [1]

The only question was whether she would observe the restraint incumbent upon a Great Power in dealing with a small and weak nation, no matter how great the provocation. As the Serbian minister in Vienna pointed out, Austria had to choose one of the following courses: "Either to regard the Serajevo outrage as a national misfortune and a crime which ought to be dealt with in accordance with the evidence obtained, in which case Serbia's co-operation in the work would be requested in order to prevent the perpetrators escaping the extreme penalty; or to treat the Serajevo outrage as a Pan-Serbian, South-Slav and Pan-

[1] Sec. 1, par. 2.

Slav conspiracy, with every manifestation of the hatred, hitherto repressed, against Slavdom." [1]

Austria chose the latter alternative, thereby dispensing with her rights, under international law, to demand the assistance of a neighboring state in the apprehension of criminals, and frankly placing the question on the plane of political expediency. It may be admitted that her position was difficult. The Serbian Government claims to have warned the Austrian authorities that Ciganovitch was a dangerous person, and to have received the reply that he was under Austrian protection. It repeatedly declared its willingness to conduct an investigation of the murder, and, in reply to Austrian complaints that no such investigation had been undertaken, asserted, on 19 July, that "not once did the Austro-Hungarian Government apply to the Serbian Government for their assistance in the matter." [2] The studiously correct attitude of Belgrade afforded no pretext for that decisive action which the Monarchy desired, for the Vienna foreign office did not establish, before or since the war began, the complicity of the Serbian Government in the crime of Serajevo. The elaborate dossier of evidence published in the Austrian *Red Book* proves only—what nobody denied—that the political ambitions of Serbia were subversive of Austria's integrity. And it is inherently improbable that the Serbian Government was privy to the conspiracy hatched by Princip and his associates.

Serbia had not recovered from the Balkan Wars. Her army was depleted; the stock of munitions and uniforms had not been replenished; the finances were heavily burdened; the territory acquired in Macedonia had not been organized. To the west the new Albanian kingdom was

---

[1] Serbian, no. 17.
[2] *Great Britain and the European Crisis*, "Narrative," sec. 2, par. 3; Serbian, no. 30.

a source of constant trouble. With the Government of Vienna delicate negotiations were in progress for the transfer to Serbia of that part of the Oriental railway within her frontiers. Every consideration demanded for Serbia a period of recuperation, and her statesmen may surely be credited with enough wisdom to see that any untoward incident directed against Austria must, in the temper of Austro-Serbian relations, lead to reprisals that were likely to be disastrous to Serbia.

For these very reasons, however—the impossibility of convicting the Serbian Government and the very weakness of the little kingdom—Austria was constrained to bring a general indictment against the Serbian nation, although Baron Macchio, one of the under-secretaries at the Ballplatz, had said to the Serbian minister that Austria did "not accuse the Serbian Government and the Serbian nation but the various agitators." [1] After all, the opportunity to place Austro-Serbian relations on a new basis was too precious to lose; and in fairness one will not blame Austrian statesmen for making the most of a situation which was not of their invention. They were right, from their point of view, in proceeding to measures which would relieve them once for all of trouble with their southern neighbor; nor was any Power disposed to interpret in a narrow sense the measures which might be decided upon.

At the same time Austria had a duty complementary to her "right," and that duty was to consider the interests of Europe. Indeed, she affected to do so, for she argued that Belgrade was the focus of European disturbance and that the peace of Europe would be infinitely more secure if the Serbian propaganda was exterminated at its source; hence the statement of Count Mensdorff, the Austrian ambassador in London, that "before the Balkan War Serbia had always been regarded as being in the Austrian sphere

[1] Serbian, no. 12.

of influence." [1] But no diplomatist seriously imagined that Austria could undertake a political action against Serbia without bringing Russia into the field and reopening the whole Balkan question. For more than a hundred years the international character of this question had been unreservedly admitted by all the Great Powers, and Austria herself had been the consistent champion of that idea. For no reason whatsoever could she expect to be permitted to dictate a solution imposed by herself alone, any more than she could expect Russia to disinterest herself in the fate of a Slav people. These things were commonplaces in European diplomacy. "They were the facts of the European situation, the products of years of development, tested and retested during the last decade. Patient work might change them, but the product of years could not be pushed aside in a day." [2]

Yet, in spite of this, which was as apparent to Count Berchtold as to Sir Edward Grey, the Austrian minister embarked upon a policy which, as he himself admitted, "might develop into a collision with Russia." [3] This willingness to provoke a quarrel with Russia is the chief item in the bill against Austria and the most convincing reason for believing that she desired to settle her account with Russia. Otherwise, why should she present to the Serbian Government an ultimatum the rejection of which was desired [4] and which was bound to arouse Russian public opinion to irresistible indignation? It is quite beside the point, as it seems to the writer, to argue, as did both the Austrian and German Governments, that the affair was no concern of Russia, that she had no right to interfere, that Serbia must be left to her fate, etc. The fatal flaws in such reasoning are: first, the admission by both those

[1] British, no. 91.
[2] *Great Britain and the European Crisis*, " Narrative," sec. 2, par. 5.
[3] Austrian, no. 26.   [4] British, no. 20, 161; French, no. 27.

governments that they expected Russia to take a hand; and second, the ultimate, if belated, acceptance by Count Berchtold of the Russian claim to interfere. The comment of Sir Edward Grey is pertinent: "There was nothing doubtful in the general international situation, no incalculable element which Austria could not take into full consideration. Whatever she did, she would know accurately the consequences of her action." [1]   Austria had a case against Serbia, and the other Powers were ready to help her obtain satisfaction; she declined their assistance, and held to her own course until too late, when it was absolutely certain that an international conflagration would ensue. When a state decides upon a line of policy, and resolves to enforce that policy to the last detail, regardless of any obstacles which may arise, even at the point of the sword, it cannot absolve itself from responsibility by saying that the obstacles had no business to be in the way. That is the manner, however, in which Austria-Hungary "took the road pointed out by honor and duty." [2]

A word as to the thesis developed in the "Introduction" to the Austrian *Red Book:*

"There can be no doubt that the small Serbian state would never have ventured, with an animosity which was scarcely concealed, to work for the separation from the great neighboring Monarchy of the territories which were inhabited by Southern Slavs, if she had not been sure of the secret approval and protection of Russia, and if she had not been able to depend on the powerful Pan-Slavist tendency in the Empire of the Tsar forcing the Russian Government, if necessary, to come to the aid of the Kingdom in its struggle for the realization of the Great-Serbian projects."

The charge is in great measure true, but it is not the whole truth. The Great-Serbian agitation had been very strong during the crisis of 1875-8, but Russia then con-

[1] *Great Britain and the European Crisis,* "Narrative," sec. 2, par. 5.
[2] Austrian *Red Book,* "Introduction," last sentence.

sented to the Austrian occupation of Bosnia and Herzegovina. Nothing was heard of it for the next twenty-five
years. What led to its recrudescence after 1903? Partly
Russian inspiration, no doubt, but Austrian policy toward
Serbia, which aimed to keep that kingdom in economic
and political subjection to the Dual Monarchy, was also
to blame. In fact, the Serbs turned to Russia for help,
because life under the Austrian protectorate was intolerable. At the same time they received no particular assistance from the great Slav empire until Count Aerenthal
broke the Austro-Russian agreement to maintain the *status
quo* and began a policy of adventure. Granted that Russia
has done everything in her power to thwart the ambitions
of Austria in the Balkans and has abetted the Serbs at
every turn, it seems clear, from the historical point of view,
that the latter has herself to blame, and that she was driven
to make war on Serbia because she saw no other way to
revenge herself for the mistakes of the past.

Exactly one month after the archduke's death the Dual
Monarchy declared war on Serbia, and the events of that
interval merit a close scrutiny. In the first place, the
press of both Austria-Hungary and Serbia indulged in a
wild orgy of mutual vituperation, full reports of which
were duly sent to each government by its representatives
in the other country. Twenty-six samples of Serbian opinion are collected in the Austrian *Red Book;*[1] the Serbian
Government took refuge behind the legal freedom of the
press, but asserted that it had issued warnings and that
the papers quoted in Austria were neither representative
nor "the organs of any party or corporation."[2] But it is
probable that, as was reported to Count Berchtold, the
news of the archduke's death was received throughout
Serbia "with evident satisfaction"; that it "evoked before
the Serbian people visions of the impending disintegration

[1] No. 19, appendix 9.   [2] Serbian, no. 20.

of the Hapsburg Empire"; and that the electoral campaign was "waged under the watchword of battle against Austria-Hungary." [1] The fact that London, Paris, and St. Petersburg emphatically urged calmness upon Belgrade indicates their uneasiness lest the inflamed public opinion of Serbia might aggravate an already difficult situation.[2]

In Vienna and Budapest discretion was thrown to the winds. The press, with two exceptions, clamored for the condign punishment of Serbia, and fed its readers on the most exaggerated specimens of Serbian journalism. The reports of the Serbian minister testify to a campaign carefully organized to excite the passions and patriotism of the polyglot inhabitants of the Dual Monarchy. The climax was reached when the *Militärische Rundschau* threw off the mask, saying:

"If we do not decide for war, that war in which we shall have to engage at the latest in two or three years will be begun in far less propitious circumstances. At this moment the initiative rests with us; Russia is not ready; moral factors as well as right are on our side." [3]

Nor was the excitement confined to the press. "The crime of Serajevo," wrote the French ambassador on 2 July, "arouses the most acute resentment in Austrian military circles, and among all those who are not content to allow Serbia to maintain in the Balkans the position which she has acquired." [4] According to the Serbian minister, "high Catholic circles" were also advocating strong measures. The old Emperor was believed to be against war, but his power to stem the flood was doubted, for "official German circles" were reported "especially ill disposed." [5]

The German press was also active. As early as 4 July the *Hamburger Fremdenblatt* spoke of an attack on Serbia

---

[1] Austrian, nos. 1, 3, 5, 6.   [2] Serbian, nos. 10, 13, 14; British, no. 30.
[3] French, no. 12.   [4] French, no. 8.   [5] Serbian, nos. 17, 22.

as a settled thing, and added that if Russia interfered "there cannot be a particle of doubt that the German ambassador in St. Petersburg would notify the Tsar that Germany would consider it a *Bündnisfall*." The *Germania* of Berlin accused "the whole Serbian nation"; the *Tageblatt* (which Herr von Jagow later described as "pestilential") immediately raised the Serajevo crime to the dignity of an international matter.[1]

"Unfortunately, though the attitude of public opinion in Austria, and to a less degree in Germany, was plain, the intentions of the Austrian Government remained almost equally obscure." [2]   All the *Books* agree as to the impenetrable mystery surrounding the Ballplatz in the first three weeks of July. No intimation of the impending storm was conveyed even to the Duke of Avarna, the ambassador of the allied Italian kingdom, much less to the British, French, and Russian ambassadors.[3]   The last, "in consequence of the reassuring explanations made to him at the ministry of foreign affairs," left Vienna on 21 July for his own country.[4]   "On 11 July the Serbian minister at Vienna had no reason to anticipate a threatening communication from the Austrian Government, and as late as 22 July, the day before the Austrian ultimatum was delivered at Belgrade, the minister-president of Hungary stated in Parliament that the situation did not warrant the opinion that a serious turn of events was necessary or even probable." [5]   The French ambassador called at the Ballplatz at the very moment when the ultimatum was being presented, and was told nothing of it.[6]

Counsels of moderation were not lacking. The French ambassador was "instructed to use all his influence with

---

[1] *Nation* (New York), 30 July, 1914, p. 121.
[2] *Great Britain and the European Crisis*, "Narrative," sec. 2, par. 3.
[3] British, no. 161; Serbian, no. 52.   [4] French, no. 18.
[5] *Great Britain and the European Crisis*, "Narrative," sec. 2, par. 3.
[6] Serbian, no. 52.

Count Berchtold" in that direction.[1] From St. Petersburg came the warning that Austria must not attempt a
search by her own officials on Serbian soil for the insti-
gators of the Serajevo outrage.[2] Sir Edward Grey promised
Prince Lichnowsky to preach conciliation at St. Petersburg,
but he "assumed that the Austrian Government would
not do anything until they had first disclosed to the public
their case against Serbia, founded presumably upon what
they had discovered at the trial."[3] But "both the British
and the German Governments knew that peace might be
disturbed."[4]

We now know that the Austrian attitude was a blind.
The story has been told once for all by the German Government.

"It was clear to Austria," says its *White Book*, "that it was not
compatible with the dignity and the spirit of self-preservation of
the Monarchy to view idly any longer this agitation across the
border. The imperial and royal government appraised [*sic*] Germany of this conception and asked for our opinion. With all our
heart we were able to agree with our ally's estimate of the situation,
and assure him that any action considered necessary to end the
movement in Serbia directed against the conservation of the Monarchy would meet with our approval. . . . We permitted Austria a
completely free hand in her action toward Serbia, but have not
participated in her preparations."[5]

On the basis of the published evidence, it is not open to
doubt that, as the British Government has charged, it
was "the deliberate intention" of Germany and Austria
"to take both Serbia and Europe by surprise."[6] Not
until 20 July did M. Dumaine, the French ambassador in
Vienna, secure a *résumé* of the projected note "from a
person specially well-informed as to official news."[7] Sir

[1] French, no. 17.   [2] French, no. 10.   [3] British, no. 1.
[4] *Great Britain and the European Crisis*, "Narrative," sec. 2, par. 2.
[5] *Collected Diplomatic Documents*, p. 406.
[6] *Ibid.*, p. vi.   [7] French, no. 14.

Edward Grey received "a forecast of what was about to happen" from Sir Maurice de Bunsen, the British ambassador, on 16 July,[1] but he felt constrained to ask Prince Lichnowsky on the 20th "if he had any news of what was going on in Vienna with regard to Serbia." [2]   Meanwhile, the Austrian Government had mobilized eight army corps in Hungary, with which to begin military operations,[3] and the pessimism on the bourses of Berlin and Vienna indicated pretty clearly the trend of events.

It is probably true, as Herr von Jagow repeatedly asserted,[4] that in a technical sense the German Government had no precise or official knowledge of the Austrian note beforehand. If so, its responsibility is only the greater, for Austria would scarcely have dared present such a communication of its own initiative. M. Jules Cambon justifiably expressed "surprise at seeing [the foreign secretary] undertake to support claims, of whose limit and scope he was ignorant," [5] and the British chargé was equally astonished "at the blank check given by Germany to Austria." [6]

But not all official Germany was ignorant, for the president of the Bavarian council was acquainted with the terms of the note.[7] Sir Maurice de Bunsen later reported that he had "private information that the German ambassador (in Vienna) knew the text of the Austrian ultimatum to Serbia before it was despatched and telegraphed it to the German Emperor." [8]   That he "was kept informed of the note even in its minutest details" and "co-operated in drafting it" was the Serbian minister's account.[9]   Herr von Tschirscky himself avowed that "Germany knew very well what she was about," [10] thereby practically convicting

---

[1] British, no. 161.   [2] British, no. 1.   [3] French, no. 18.
[4] French, nos. 15, 30, etc.; British, nos. 18, 25, etc.; *White Book*, p. 406; Russian, no. 18.
[5] French, no. 30.   [6] French, no. 41.   [7] French, no. 21.
[8] British, no. 95.   [9] Serbian, no. 52.   [10] British, no. 32.

his government of bad faith. For, unless the Berlin foreign office knew what was going on, how could the German chancellor, on the very day that the ultimatum was presented, inform the German ambassadors in the *Entente* capitals that "the action as well as the demands of the Austro-Hungarian Government can be viewed only as justifiable"?[1] Why should Prince Lichnowsky have expressed to Sir Edward Grey, as early as 20 July, the opinion that the situation was "very uncomfortable"?[2] Why otherwise should "the preliminary notices for mobilization, the object of which is to place Germany in a kind of 'attention' attitude in times of tension, have been sent out to those classes which would receive them in similar circumstances"?[3] Such conduct is not that of a government anxious to keep the peace and ready to negotiate in a delicate matter, but the resolute expression of a policy which can have only one end—war.

Austria-Hungary, then, was under no restraints in whatever policy she might elect to pursue. The driving force in her calculations was the desire to exalt her prestige.

"If we neglect to clear up our relations with Serbia, we shall lay ourselves open to blame for increased difficulties and disadvantages in a future conflict which is bound to come. In the view of an official representative of the Austro-Hungarian Government, who is observing events on the spot, the realization is inevitable that we cannot afford to permit any further diminution of our prestige."[4]

So wrote Baron von Giesl, the minister at Belgrade, on 21 July. So also the secretary-general of the Italian foreign office, who remarked upon "the conviction of the Austro-Hungarian Government that it was absolutely necessary for their prestige, after the many disillusions which the

[1] German, no. 1; British, no. 9; French, no. 28; Russian, no. 18.
[2] British, no. 1.   [3] French, no. 15.   [4] Austrian, no. 6.

turn of events in the Balkans had occasioned, to score a definite success." [1]   Hence the necessity of surprise tactics.

On only one matter does there seem to have been any divergence of opinion between the Teutonic allies—the probable conduct of Russia.   Granted that "Count Berchtold and the diplomatists desired at the most localized operations against Serbia," [2] neither he nor the Austrian military party was under any illusion as to the likelihood of Russian intervention: they fully expected it, and were simply anxious to face it under conditions advantageous to themselves.   For a moment, indeed, after the Russian mobilization there was a show of yielding, but Count Berchtold was well aware that Germany would make the Russian mobilization a *casus belli*,[3] and that Austria would receive the first blows of the Russian attack.   The forward march once begun, there could be no drawing back.

In the German *White Book* there is this admission:

"We were perfectly aware that a possible warlike attitude of Austria-Hungary against Serbia might bring Russia upon the field, and that it might therefore involve us in a war, in accordance with our duty as allies." [4]

At the same time, several of the German representatives abroad let it be known that they expected Russia to stand aside.   Herr von Tschirscky, at Vienna, expressed the "confident belief" that "Russia would keep quiet during the chastisement of Serbia" [5]—but Sir Maurice de Bunsen thought he "desired war from the first." [6]   Count Pourtalès, at St. Petersburg, told the Serbian minister that the Austro-Serbian dispute "did not concern any one else." [7] According to Sir Edward Goschen, many people in Berlin shared the opinion that "Russia neither wanted nor was

[1] British, no. 38.   [2] French, no. 14.   [3] Austrian, no. 28.
[4] *Collected Diplomatic Documents*, p. 406.
[5] British, no. 32.   [6] British, no. 141.   [7] Serbian, no. 36.

in a position to make war." [1]   In the French *Yellow Book*, also, there are several reflections of the same idea.   After all, the point is a minor one.   Germany's conduct from first to last was that of a Power that was prepared to use her entire strength to gain her ends; she knew that Russia would not yield except to a show of force, and when Russia did not yield she instantly declared war.   The Russian position was specified with such precision, immediately after the presentation of the Austrian note, that German underestimates, if genuine to begin with, must have been based on a doubt not as to her policy but as to her courage.   All things considered, it is difficult to avoid the conclusion that, as M. Sazonof said, "Austria's action was in reality directed against Russia," [2] and, since Germany, on her own admissions, stood resolutely behind her ally, that her policy was also from the first intended to provoke Russia.   If Germany did not wish war, she willed peace on impossible terms—the complete humiliation of Russia and the submission of the Balkans to Austria-Hungary; after which she could proceed at leisure to that attack on France which she was surely meditating.

Thus the ground had been carefully prepared by both Austria and Germany.   Sir Edward Grey made a last effort to bring Austria to reason.   Informed by Count Mensdorff of the character of the ultimatum on the day of its delivery, he "could not help dwelling on the awful consequences of the situation."   He spoke quite plainly of the prospect of war involving Austria, France, Russia, and Germany, and of the "complete collapse of European credit and industry."   He also remarked that "it required two to keep the peace." [3]   In other words, the British Government dissociated itself from the view taken in Berlin the day before, that "the question at issue was one for settlement between Serbia and Austria alone, and that

[1] British, no. 71.   [2] British, no. 17.   [3] British, no. 3.

there should be no interference from outside in the discussions between those two countries." [1] The warning passed unheeded. At 6 P. M. of the same day Baron von Giesl presented to the Serbian Government an ultimatum, of which Sir Edward Grey said that he "had never before seen one state address to another independent state a document of so formidable a character." [2]

The ultimatum[3] began by quoting the Serbian declaration of 31 March, 1909, in which Serbia had promised to "modify the direction of her policy with regard to Austria-Hungary and to live on good, neighborly terms with the latter." This promise, said the Austro-Hungarian Government, had not been fulfilled: on the contrary, the Serbian Government had connived at "a subversive movement," that aimed to detach certain provinces from the Dual Monarchy. It had "permitted the criminal machinations of various societies and associations directed against the Monarchy"; had "tolerated unrestrained language on the part of the press, the glorification of the perpetrators of outrages, and the participation of officers and functionaries in subversive agitation"; it had "permitted an unwholesome propaganda in public instruction—in short, all manifestations of a nature to incite the Serbian population to hatred of the Monarchy and contempt of its institutions." It was held responsible for the crime of Serajevo, concerning which the findings of the Austrian investigation were communicated in a brief summary.

For these reasons the Serbian Government was required to publish in its *Official Journal* of 26 July, 1914, a declaration in a prescribed form, by which it condemned all propaganda against Austria-Hungary, expressed its regret that public officials should have been involved in such

---

[1] British, no. 2.   [2] British, no. 5.
[3] Austrian, no. 7; German *White Book*, pp. 414–417; Serbian, no. 32; British, no. 4; French, no. 24; Russian, no. 2; Belgian, no. 1.

propaganda, and promised henceforth to punish all persons guilty of such machinations. This declaration was also to be communicated to the army as an order of the day. Moreover, the Serbian Government had to undertake:

1. To suppress any publication directed against Austria-Hungary.

2. To dissolve the Narodna Odbrana, and to prevent the formation of similar societies in the future.

3. To eliminate from the public schools all persons and all methods of instruction calculated to foment the propaganda.

4. To remove all army officers and civil functionaries whom Austria should indicate as being guilty of propaganda against the Monarchy.

5. To accept the collaboration of Austrian representatives in the suppression of the subversive movement.

6. To take judicial proceedings against accessories to the Serajevo plot on Serbian territory; "delegates of the Austro-Hungarian Government will take part in the investigation relating thereto."

7. To arrest Major Voija Tankositch and Milan Ciganovitch.

8. To prevent the illicit traffic in arms, and to dismiss and punish severely those officials who had assisted the Serajevo conspirators to cross the frontier.

9. To explain the hostile utterances of Serbian officials, at home and abroad, concerning the crime of Serajevo.

10. To notify the Austro-Hungarian Government of the execution of the above measures.

Forty-eight hours were allowed for a reply.

On the following day, 24 July, the ultimatum was communicated to the Great Powers for their information, together with an explanation of the Austrian attitude and the statement that a dossier of evidence was held at the disposal of the various governments.[1]   As Count Berchtold believed that "Great Britain might bo most easily led to form an impartial judgment on the step we are taking at Belgrade,"[2] it is well to record the opinion of Sir Edward Grey.   Admitting that "Austria was under provocation," for "she had to complain of a dangerous popular movement against her government," he said that "the merits of the dispute between Austria and Serbia were not the concern of His Majesty's Government": he would consider the matter "simply and solely from the point of view of the peace of Europe," and he was "very apprehensive of the view Russia would take of the situation."[3]   The attitude of St. Petersburg was, indeed, for the moment, all-important, for the Prince Regent of Serbia had promptly telegraphed to the Tsar, "praying his Majesty to be pleased to interest himself in the fate of the Kingdom of Serbia."[4]

In the thirty-one hours at its disposal[5] before the ultimatum would expire, the Russian Government gave overwhelming proof of its pacific and reasonable attitude. First, not only did it not reply to the Prince Regent's telegram, but it urged Belgrade to make all concessions possible which were compatible with the dignity of Serbia.[6] Second, it requested Vienna to extend the time limit of the ultimatum, in order that the Powers might have the opportunity to study the demands and advise Serbia;[7] and it desired the British, French, Italian, and German Governments to support this request at Vienna.[8]   Third, M. Sazonof, evidently not convinced by the assurances of

---

[1] Austrian, no. 8; British, no. 5; French, no. 25; Russian, no. 3.
[2] Austrian, no. 9.
[3] *Great Britain and the European Crisis*, sec. 3, par. 3; British, no. 5.
[4] Serbian, no. 37; Russian, no. 6.
[5] The text of the ultimatum was not communicated to the Russians for seventeen hours after its presentation at Belgrade. (Russian, no. 77.)
[6] British, no. 22.   [7] Russian, no. 4; French, no. 38.
[8] Russian, no. 5; French, no. 39; British, no. 13.

Count Berchtold to Prince Kudachef, the Russian chargé at Vienna,[1] held long interviews with Count Szapary and Count Pourtalès, the Austrian and German ambassadors at St. Petersburg. He listened to their explanations, but insisted that the question was international; Austria, he said, "had certainly created a serious situation," and Russia "could not accept it with indifference."[2] And this warning was followed up by a public announcement:

"Recent events and the despatch of an ultimatum to Serbia by Austria-Hungary are causing the Russian Government the greatest anxiety. The government is closely following the course of the dispute between the two countries, to which Russia cannot remain indifferent."[3]

At the same time, there was nothing intransigent in this attitude. For, fourth, as M. Sazonof said to the British ambassador:

"If Serbia should appeal to the Powers, Russia would be quite ready to stand aside and leave the question in the hands of England, France, Germany, and Italy. It was possible, in his opinion, that Serbia might propose to submit the question to arbitration."[4]

Finally, the Russian foreign minister begged Great Britain to "proclaim her solidarity with Russia and France": she would sooner or later be dragged into war if it did break out, and should have rendered war more likely if she did not, from the outset, make common cause with France and Russia.[5]

[1] Austrian, no. 18; German, no. 3; British, no. 7.
[2] Austrian, nos. 14, 16; German, no. 4.
[3] Russian, no. 10; Austrian, no. 15.
[4] British, no. 17. On 29 July the Tsar, in a telegram to the Emperor William, said: "It would be right to give over the Austro-Serbian problem to The Hague tribunal." (*Collected Diplomatic Documents*, p. 542.) No further reference to this proposal appears in the published correspondence. The German press subsequently characterized it as "unimportant."
[5] British, no. 6.

It must always redound to the credit of Russia that she took her position promptly, openly, fearlessly, and that she maintained it consistently to the end. "She made no parade of pacific intentions; she played on no weaknesses; she counted on no doubtful factors; she took refuge neither in silence nor in catchwords. She stated openly the circumstances under which war would become inevitable. But she gave every chance to international action; she shunned no discussion; she was ready to accept any compromise provided only that the Austrian troops paused on the Serbian frontier. She steered her policy throughout by the light of the guiding fact that the Austro-Serbian conflict could not be localized even by her own abstention, for that conflict was not a simple attack on Serbia, but a recommitment of the whole Balkan question. Her action during the whole crisis is entitled to the respect which is due to honesty and openness in international relations." [1]

In the same interval Great Britain took four steps looking to the preservation of peace. Before learning of M. Sazonof's *démarche*, Sir Edward Grey requested of Count Mensdorff an extension of the time limit,[2] and the next day he instructed Sir Maurice de Bunsen to support the formal representations addressed to Vienna by Russia.[3] Next, he advised Serbia to avoid an absolute refusal of the Austrian demands and to reply favorably to as many points as the time limit allowed.[4] In both of these steps he was supported by France. Third, he at once appealed to Germany. He said to Prince Lichnowsky that, "in view of the extraordinarily stiff character of the Austrian note, the shortness of the time allowed, and the wide scope of the demands upon Serbia," he felt "quite helpless" to exercise moderating influence at St. Petersburg; but he proposed that "the four Powers—Germany, Italy, France, and Eng-

---

[1] *Collected Diplomatic Documents*, p. xiv.
[2] British, no. 5.
[3] British, no. 26; French, no. 49; Russian, no. 16.
[4] British, no. 12.

land—should work together, simultaneously at Vienna and St. Petersburg, in favor of moderation in the event of the relations between Austria and Russia becoming threatening." In any case, "it would be very desirable to get Austria not to precipitate military action."[1] Finally, being informed by Count Mensdorff that the Austrian note should be considered not as an ultimatum but as "a *démarche* with a time limit," by which it was understood that military operations would not immediately follow a diplomatic rupture,[2] Sir Edward Grey promptly telegraphed this information to Paris and St. Petersburg, as "it made the immediate situation rather less acute."[3]

Since Russia had already requested the international action which Sir Edward Grey proposed, since his suggestion was cordially received by France and Italy,[4] only Germany's acceptance was needed, for no one doubted the ability of the Wilhelmstrasse to restrain Austria if it wished to do so. Now, on 24 July, the German Government had addressed a note to London, Paris, and St. Petersburg, in which it justified the attitude of its ally, and characterized the demands upon Serbia as "equitable and moderate." The note concluded:

"The imperial government wants to emphasize its opinion that in the present case there is only question of a matter to be settled exclusively between Austria-Hungary and Serbia, and that the Great Powers ought seriously to endeavor to reserve it to those two immediately concerned. The imperial government desires urgently the localization of the conflict because every interference of another Power would, owing to the different treaty obligations, be followed by incalculable consequences."[5]

The last sentence might almost be construed as a threat; at the very least it intimated that Germany was not in-

---

[1] British, no. 11; Russian, no. 22.   [2] Austrian, no. 17.   [3] British, no. 14.
[4] *Great Britain and the European Crisis*, sec. 4, par. 4.
[5] British, no. 9; French, no. 28; German, no. 1.

clined to exert pressure on her ally to alleviate the tension already evident. Consequently, although Herr von Jagow told Sir Horace Rumbold, the British chargé at Berlin, that "he was quite ready to fall in with the suggestion as to the four Powers working in favor of moderation at Vienna and St. Petersburg," [1] and Prince Lichnowsky believed that "Austria might be able with dignity to accept" mediation between herself and Russia,[2] the German foreign secretary contented himself with merely "passing on" Sir Edward Grey's suggestion for an extension of time limit, incidentally remarking that Count Berchtold was absent from Vienna and that it would be too late.[3] And he seems to have put off receiving M. Broniewsky, the Russian chargé, who desired German support for M. Sazonof's proposal, until it was too late.[4] Thus Germany's conduct during the first two days of the crisis was not such as to inspire confidence in either her disinterestedness or her intentions.

At Vienna there was a complete refusal to make any concessions. Count Berchtold departed for Ischl, where the Emperor Francis Joseph was staying, perhaps to avoid the representations which were to be expected from the other Powers. Prince Kudachef had, therefore, to address him by public telegrams *en route*, and to repeat verbally to Baron Macchio his government's request for an extension of time.[5] From both Austrian officials he received an absolute refusal, on the familiar ground that the issue concerned only Austria and Serbia and that "action had been forced upon Austria by the developments of a situation which compelled her to defend her most vital interests." [6] Owing to the delay in receiving their instructions, the French and British ambassadors were not able to support the Russian *démarche*.[7] They could only report to

---

[1] British, no. 18.   [2] British, no. 25; French, no. 37.
[3] British, no. 18; French, no. 43; Russian, no. 14.
[4] French, no. 42.   [5] Russian, no. 11; French, no. 45.
[6] Austrian, nos. 20, 21; Russian, no. 12.   [7] French, no. 50.

their governments that the "language of the press leaves the impression that the surrender of Serbia is neither expected nor really desired."[1]

A few hours before the expiration of the time limit Sir Edward Grey received from Belgrade a forecast of the Serbian reply, which indicated an almost complete surrender to the Austrian demands.[2] He immediately communicated it to Prince Lichnowsky, and expressed the hope that "the German Government would feel able to influence the Austrian Government to take a favorable view of it."[3] Once again Herr von Jagow was content to "pass on" a British suggestion:[4] the efficacy of this proceeding may be gauged from the fact that Herr von Tschirscky, whose duty it was to convey Berlin's opinions to the Ballplatz, described the Serbian concessions to his British colleague as "all a sham."[5]

The Serbian reply was handed to the Austrian minister at 5.58 P. M. on 25 July.[6] He left Belgrade on the regular train at 6.30.[7] In those thirty-two minutes, some of which were required for getting from the legation to the station and into the train, Baron von Giesl could scarcely have done more than read the Serbian note and break off diplomatic relations. He certainly could not have formulated in his mind the elaborate and technical reasons which the Austrian Government subsequently adduced as its grounds for considering the Serbian reply unsatisfactory. There is no better reason for believing that the ultimatum of 23 July was intended, not to secure the punishment of the criminals of Serajevo, but to effect the humiliation of Serbia and to deal a resounding blow at the new settlement of the Balkans, to which, as we have seen, the blundering diplomacy of Austria had very largely contributed.

[1] British, no. 31.   [2] British, no. 21.   [3] British, no. 27.
[4] British, no. 34.   [5] British, no. 32.
[6] Austrian, no. 24.   Serbian, no. 41, gives 5.45 as the hour of the reply.
[7] British, no. 23; Austrian, no. 22.

International courtesy demanded that Baron von Giesl explain to the Serbian Government the reasons for his rejection of its reply; there is no record that such an explanation was given, even if time had permitted. However, as Baron Macchio remarked to Prince Kudachef, "one's interests sometimes exempted one from being courteous." [1]

The Serbian Government, which had already mobilized its army, withdrew to Nish the same evening, and was followed by the diplomatic corps. Henceforth, unless international action could be started, either by Russia or the other Powers, war between Austria and Serbia was inevitable. The question of the next three days, 25–28 July, was, therefore: Could Austria be kept quiet pending some agreement with Russia?

During those three days four distinct efforts were made to effect some adjustment of the Austro-Serbian dispute which would obviate the necessity of Russian intervention. Three of these were inspired by Russia. First, M. Sazonof telegraphed to Rome that "Italy might play a part of the first importance in favor of preserving peace, by bringing the necessary influence to bear upon Austria, and by adopting a definitely unfavorable attitude toward the dispute on ground that it could not be localized." [2] Nothing more is heard of this in any of the *Books*, but in his speech to the Italian Parliament, on 2 June, 1915, Signor Salandra stated that on 25 July, 1914, he warned the then German ambassador, Herr von Flotow, that Italy would not stand with Austria if the latter found herself at war with Russia on account of her aggressive action at Belgrade. On the same day, when he appealed to Italy, M. Sazonof advised Serbia to ask for the mediation of England.[3] This also disappears from view, but, curiously enough, Austria herself subsequently invoked the same mediation.

Much more important was the action of Sir Edward

[1] French, no. 45.   [2] Russian, no. 23.   [3] French, no. 53.

Grey. On 26 July he converted into an official proposal the idea already ventilated to Prince Lichnowsky. He invited the French, German, and Italian Governments to instruct their ambassadors in London to meet with him "in conference immediately for the purpose of discovering an issue which would prevent complications."[1] He further suggested that Vienna, Belgrade, and St. Petersburg should be requested to "suspend all active military operations pending results of the conference"; and the following day, when informed by Prince Lichnowsky that the German Government accepted mediation between Austria and Russia "in principle," he proposed that the "Serbian reply should at least be treated as a basis for discussion and pause."[2]

Meanwhile the Russian foreign minister had come forward with a new scheme. In an interview with the Austrian ambassador he proposed that Count Szapary "should be authorized to enter into a private exchange of views in order to redraft certain articles of the Austrian note of 23 July,"[3] which proposal was formally made to Vienna by M. Schebeko, who had returned hurriedly to his post, on the following day (27 July).[4] M. Sazonof admitted to Count Szapary that the intention of Austria to put a stop to a dangerous agitation was legitimate, but he objected to the procedure. "Take back your ultimatum," he concluded, "modify its form, and I will guarantee you the result."[5] Since he objected to only three of the ten Austrian demands, his offer can scarcely be regarded as unreasonable.

From this plethora of suggestions and proposals one must surely have been acceptable, had there been a general will to peace and a sincere desire to avoid war. As it was,

[1] British, no. 36. [2] British, no. 46.
[3] Russian, no. 25; Austrian, no. 31; German, no. 5; British, no. 45.
[4] Russian, no. 41; British, no. 56. [5] French, no. 54.

the French and Italian Governments immediately accepted
Sir Edward Grey's proposal for a conference of ambassadors;[1] and M. Sazonof, though preferring "direct explanations with the Vienna cabinet," was "ready to accept
the British proposal, or any other proposal of a kind that
would bring about a favorable solution of the conflict."[2]
In the same spirit the Tsar replied to the telegram of the
Prince Regent of Serbia:

"My government is using its utmost endeavor to smooth away
the present difficulties. I have no doubt that Your Highness and
the royal Serbian Government wish to render that task easy by
neglecting no step which might lead to a settlement. . . . So long
as the slightest hope exists of avoiding bloodshed, all our efforts
must be directed to that end."[3]

Obviously, therefore, "the key of the situation was to be
found at Berlin,"[4] for it was everywhere understood that
Austria would not listen to any advice but that of her ally.

The conduct of the German Government during these
three days was nothing if not equivocal. From the *White
Book* we know that it had given Austria "a free hand"
and the promise of all necessary support. Yet it could
not then avow this to the other Powers, beyond stating
that the Austro-Serbian dispute must be localized. In
other words, it had to gain time in order that the Austrian
measures against Serbia might be set on foot without interference. Such is certainly the impression left from a
study of Berlin's attitude from 25 to 28 July.

To begin with, the Berlin press refrained from publishing the text of the Serbian reply, doubtless "because of the
calming effect it would have on German readers."[5] Next,
the Wilhelmstrasse endeavored to set up a distinction

[1] British, nos. 49, 51, 52; French, nos. 61, 70.
[2] British, no. 53; Russian, no. 32.   [3] Russian, no. 40; Serbian, no. 43.
[4] Russian, no. 43; British, no. 54.   [5] Russian, no. 46.

between the Austro-Serbian dispute and the Austro-Russian tension produced by that dispute.[1] Theoretically, of course, the distinction is sound; but it was not raised in the crisis of 1912–13 and it is made ridiculous by the admission in the *White Book* that "a possible warlike attitude of Austria-Hungary against Serbia might bring Russia upon the field."[2] Nevertheless, on this ground Herr von Jagow rejected the proposed conference, which "would practically amount to a court of arbitration" between Austria and Serbia. Sir Edward Goschen rightly replied that Sir Edward Grey's "idea had nothing to do with arbitration, but meant that representatives of the four nations should discuss and suggest means for avoiding a dangerous situation."[3] Both he and M. Jules Cambon, however, had to be content with Herr von Jagow's statement that "he was ready to join England and France in a common effort," the form of which would have to be found by the cabinets.[4] This tallied with Prince Lichnowsky's acceptance of mediation "in principle," but it offered nothing definite, and it did not stop the march of events, which was the *sine qua non* of a peaceful settlement. To gain time for the operations of diplomacy was imperative; Herr von Jagow's attitude made it well-nigh impossible for diplomacy to act before it was too late.

In fairness, no one will wish to press this point against the German foreign secretary, for the ways of diplomacy are often devious. But did he carry out in good faith the rôle of mediator between Vienna and St. Petersburg, of which the chancellor was making such a parade?[5] For the third time he "passes on" a British proposal to Vienna, this time the suggestion that the Serbian reply should be taken as a basis of discussion:[6] with the usual result—that

---

[1] German *White Book*, p. 409; German, no. 13.
[2] German *White Book*, p. 406.   [3] British, no. 43; French, no. 73.
[4] French, no. 74.   [5] German, nos. 14, 15.
[6] German *White Book*, p. 409; British, no. 67; Austrian, no. 43.

it was too late to stay the hand of the impetuous ally.[1] At St. Petersburg, however, there is no trace of such timidity. On 26 July Count Pourtalès is instructed to make the following declaration:

"Preparatory military measures by Russia will force us to counter-measures which must consist in mobilizing the army. But mobilization means war. . . . We are of the opinion that Russia can afford to assume an attitude of waiting."[2]

In addition the military attaché tells the Russian minister of war that mobilization against Austria would be in itself "very menacing."[3] The basis of these threats is a report that Kovno has been declared in a state of war, the belief of the military attaché that mobilization has been ordered for Kiev and Warsaw, and the "impression that complete preparations for mobilization against Austria are being made":[4] to indulge in open threats on such flimsy excuses is, to say the least, not very pacific, and is quite likely to make the situation more rather than less strained. German mediation between Austria and Russia is to take the form of pressure on Russia to prevent any interference with Austria, who is to go ahead with impunity!

On a par with this were the efforts to deprive Russia of the diplomatic support of her associates in the Triple *Entente*. Herr von Bethmann-Hollweg requested Sir Edward Grey "to act at St. Petersburg with all possible emphasis" to keep Russia from mobilization and interference.[5] At Paris Herr von Schoen twice besought the Quai d'Orsay to "exercise its influence at St. Petersburg in favor of

---

[1] Austrian, no. 44: "The imperial and royal government . . . is no longer in a position to adopt an attitude toward the Serbian reply in the sense of the British suggestion, since at the time of the *démarche* made by Germany a state of war between the monarchy and Serbia had already arisen, and the Serbian reply has accordingly already been outstripped by events." *Cf.* also Austrian, no. 38; British, no. 76.

[2] German *White Book*, p. 408.   [3] German, no. 11; Austrian, no. 28.
[4] German, nos. 6, 7, 8.   [5] German, no. 10.

peace," and proposed to communicate a statement to the press to the effect that France and Germany were acting together "in a spirit of peaceful co-operation." [1] The French not unnaturally regarded these *démarches* as a plan to compromise them with their ally and to create an impression of Franco-German solidarity "which might have been misinterpreted." In both capitals the German ambassadors were informed that France and England could not make representations at St. Petersburg unless Germany would do the same at Vienna: the danger lay in precipitate action by Austria, whereas Russia had shown herself conciliatory and pacific. The logic was irrefutable, but neither Herr von Schoen nor Prince Lichnowsky would promise that Germany would preach moderation at Vienna.

How little disposed Germany was to do her share of conciliation is best seen from the fate of a proposal made by M. Jules Cambon. On 27 July he suggested that Great Britain, Germany, Italy, and France should advise Vienna "to abstain from all action which might aggravate the existing situation." Herr von Jagow "refused point-blank to accept this suggestion, in spite of the entreaties of the ambassador, who emphasized, as a good feature of the suggestion, the mixed grouping of the Powers, thanks to which the opposition between the Alliance and the *Entente*—a matter of which Jagow himself had often complained— was avoided." [2] For all the German talk about mediation, are we allowed to see the substance?

The idea of a conference having been rejected and no other form of international action being under consideration, the only hope of a peaceful solution of the crisis lay in direct conversations between Russia and Austria on the basis of the Serbian reply. Now M. Sazonof had proposed

---

[1] German, no. 10*a*; French, nos. 56, 57, 62; Russian, nos. 34, 35.
[2] Russian, no. 39.

this discussion at the suggestion of Count Pourtalès, the German ambassador at St. Petersburg.[1] But when the Russian chargé in Berlin desired Herr von Jagow to support the proposal at Vienna the latter replied that "he could not advise Austria to give way."[2] No wonder that M. Sazonof telegraphed to London that "this attitude of the German Government is most alarming" and that "the Berlin cabinet, who could have prevented the whole of this crisis from developing, appear to be exerting no influence on their ally."[3] Once again the actual conduct of Germany, as opposed to her professions, fails to disclose even the shadow of mediation. On 28 July the German chancellor telegraphed to St. Petersburg:

"We continue in our endeavor to induce Vienna to elucidate in St. Petersburg the object and scope of the Austrian action in Serbia in a manner both convincing and satisfactory to Russia."

But it was not explanations which Russia wanted; she insisted that Austria refrain from "action in Serbia," and to that demand the chancellor can only reply with astonishing naïveté: "The declaration of war which has meanwhile ensued alters nothing in this matter"![4] Mediation which does not restrain an ally from making war had better be called "benevolent neutrality."

Sure of Germany's support, Austria would make no concessions. The Serbian reply was published on 28 July, but in such a way as to make it an indictment of Serbia. For in a running commentary the Austrian Government elaborated at great length the reasons, often concerning a matter of phraseology, why it could not regard the reply as satisfactory. In an official *communiqué* of the press bureau, it was charged that Serbia recognized her reply to be "insufficient" because it proposed to submit one of

[1] British, no. 78.
[2] Russian, no. 38.
[3] Russian, no. 43; British, no. 54.
[4] German, no. 14.

the Austrian demands to arbitration![1] To the Russian ambassador Count Berchtold represented the mobilization of Serbia, before the reply was given, as "a hostile act"; he also said that "there was a deep feeling of general excitement which had already mastered public opinion." It was not surprising, therefore, that Count Berchtold declined M. Schebeko's proposal that Count Szapary should be instructed to discuss the Serbian reply with the Russian foreign minister.[2] He also refused to entertain Sir Maurice de Bunsen's representations in favor of Sir Edward Grey's project of a conference of ambassadors.[3] To both ambassadors he explained that their actions were belated, for the Monarchy had already declared war on Serbia, and that that war was "just and inevitable"; and he paid no attention to their warnings that by her action Austria was endangering the peace of Europe. The Austrian action, however, was at least consistent. War had been determined upon; the assistance of Germany was promised; a fortunate accident had provided a plausible case. Therefore nothing must be allowed to prevent that "energetic action" which had been announced to the chanceries, and nothing was allowed to prevent it. We may disapprove of the policy adopted; we may doubt whether the aims of that policy were those communicated to the other governments; but we must recognize that there was no assumption of a pacific attitude in order to conceal other intentions, which is such a formidable item in the case against German diplomacy.

With the Austrian declaration of war, which was conveyed to Serbia in the form of an open telegram from Count Berchtold to the Serbian foreign office,[4] the crisis entered on a new phase. Russian intervention now be-

---

[1] French, no. 75 (2).　　　　　[2] Russian, no. 45; Austrian, no. 40.
[3] Austrian, no. 41; British, no. 62; French, no. 83.
[4] Austrian, no. 37; Serbian, no. 46.

came a certainty unless the Austrian troops could be stopped before they crossed the frontier. But before narrating the events that led up to the declaration of war upon Russia by Germany it will be advisable to examine the Austrian ultimatum to Serbia and the Serbian reply thereto, together with the assurances of Austria that she cherished no designs against the territorial integrity of Serbia. For if the ultimatum was justified and the Serbian reply was really inadequate, then assuredly Russia had no title to intervene and is in very truth responsible for the Great War.

Of the ten demands practically all involved some diminution of the sovereignty of Serbia, although numbers 6–8 may be, to some extent, regarded as police measures incumbent upon any law-abiding government and not without justification in the circumstances of the Serajevo outrage. Number 1 involved a change in both the law and the constitution of Serbia; the second part of number 6 was contrary to the constitution. With every allowance for the necessity of Austria to put a stop to the great Serbian agitation, it is evident that her demands were such as an independent state would be expected to grant only after a complete military defeat. Furthermore, the despatches of the French and British ambassadors in Vienna leave no doubt that the rejection of the Austrian ultimatum was both expected and desired. Prince Lichnowsky's remark to Sir Edward Grey is also illuminating:

"Speaking privately, his excellency suggested that a negative reply must in no case be returned by Serbia; a reply favorable on some points must be sent at once, so that an excuse against immediate action might be afforded to Austria." [1]

But most conclusive of all are the admissions of Herr von Jagow, who "confessed privately that he thought the note

[1] British, no. 11.

left much to be desired as a diplomatic document." He admitted that "the Serbian Government could not swallow certain of the Austro-Hungarian demands," that the Austrians "wished to give the Serbians a lesson, and that they meant to take military action."[1] In spite of this the German Government was officially of the opinion that the Austrian demands were "moderate and equitable!" Equitable, perhaps, because they promised to make a general war inevitable! Nor must the extremely short interval allowed for the reply, forty-eight hours, be overlooked. To the Austrian contention that a short time limit was needed to avoid Serbian procrastination, it is sufficient to reply, with Sir Edward Grey, that a time limit could be introduced later.[2]

By general consent the Serbian reply went very much farther toward an accommodation than was anywhere expected—was, in short, an almost complete acceptance of the Austrian programme. The Belgrade Government denied the charge that it had abetted the anti-Austrian propaganda, in violation of the declaration of 31 March, 1909, but agreed to publish the desired declaration in the *Official Journal* condemning such propaganda. It promised to amend its press laws and the constitution; to suppress the Narodna Odbrana; to purge its schools of the propaganda; to remove those of its servants who might be proved guilty of propaganda at the request of the Austrian Government; to accept such collaboration of Austrian officials "as agrees with the principle of international law, with criminal procedure, and with good, neighborly relations"; to open an inquiry against the criminals of Serajevo; to arrest Ciganovitch (Tankositch had already been arrested); to reform the administration of the frontier service; to give explanations of such utterances of officials as should be brought to its attention; and to give due notice

---

[1] British, no. 18.   [2] British, no. 5.

of the execution of the above-promised measures. It declined to accept the participation of Austrian officials in the judicial inquiry, but it offered to refer the entire dispute to the arbitration of The Hague or the Great Powers which took part in drawing up the declaration of 31 March, 1909.[1]

The governments and the public opinion of the countries of the *Entente* and the press of the United States regarded this reply not only as a remarkable concession to an astonishing demand but also as a satisfactory settlement, or at least as the basis of a settlement. According to the Russian chargé in Paris, the Austrian ambassador in that capital, when informed of the Serbian reply, "did not conceal his surprise that it had failed to satisfy Giesl."[2] Herr von Jagow, who put off reading it for several days, finally admitted that it constituted "a basis for possible negotiation."[3] Obviously, therefore, its reasoned and summary rejection by the Austrian Government calls for close inspection. The Austrian criticisms[4] give the appearance of having been composed with the view of justifying the *fait accompli* of Baron von Giesl; still, they must be examined impartially.

The main objection seems to be contained in the following passage:

"Our grievance is that the Serbian Government has omitted to suppress the agitation directed against the territorial integrity of the Dual Monarchy, notwithstanding the obligations it entered into under the terms of the note of 31 March, 1909. . . . The contention of the royal Serbian Government that utterances of the press and the activities of associations are of a private character and are beyond the control of the state, is plainly at variance with the institutions of modern states, even of those which have the

[1] Serbian, no. 39; Austrian, no. 25; German *White Book*, pp. 417–423; Russian, no. 13; British, no. 39; French, no. 49; Belgian, no. 4.
[2] Russian, no. 27.   [3] French, no. 92.
[4] Austrian, no. 34; German *White Book*, pp. 417–423.

most liberal regulations in this respect; these regulations, designed to safeguard public polity and right, impose state supervision upon both press and associations. Moreover, the Serbian institutions themselves provide for such supervision."

It is not the first time that Austrian statesmen have put forward this argument. The student of Italian history will recall that when Cavour was arousing the sentiment of Italians against the Austrian régime by means of the Sardinian press, Buol, the Austrian foreign minister, demanded the suppression of the offending papers and received much the same answer as was given to Count Berchtold. History has passed judgment on that controversy. In the present cases there emerges the fundamental difference between Teutonic and English or American conceptions of the press. Shall public opinion be made to order, or shall it reflect the will and wishes of a free people? A nation and a government may be offended by what is said of them in the press of another country—Englishmen and Germans complained bitterly of the tone of each other's newspapers, but it is not recorded that either government made such outpourings a cause for war. Austria was entitled to warn the Serbian Government that it would be held responsible for any attempts to carry out the territorial aspirations involved in the Great-Serbian propaganda, but in the absence of any overt act (and let it be remembered that the complicity of the Serbian Government in the murders of Serajevo has not been established) she had no claim to exact punishment for a possible future offense. And when we read, in the criticism of the Serbian reply to demand number 1, that the passage of a new press law would be "immaterial," and that an amendment to the constitution "of no use," we are persuaded that the object of the Austrian policy was simply to stifle the intellectual and political life of Serbia.

With respect to the declaration to be published in the

Official Journal, the Austrian Government complained that by inserting the words "according to the communication of the Austro-Hungarian Government," Serbia was disavowing the existence of propaganda in the past and keeping its hands free for the future. The point seems a mere quibble, for the Serbian Government actually disavowed and repudiated "all idea of interfering or attempting to interfere with the destinies of the inhabitants of any part whatsoever of Austria-Hungary," and promised to prosecute all propagandists.

For the rest, some flaw was found with the reply to nine of the ten demands. As regards number 7, it was stated that Ciganovitch's arrest had been prevented by the chief of the Belgrade police: this is a fair complaint, if true. But a dispassionate reading of the ultimatum, the reply, and the Austrian comments will not convince one that the reply was conceived in a spirit of deceitfulness and evasion, as the Austrian Government alleged. Granted that there were points of difference, it was surely open to the Austrian Government to indicate those points to Serbia, to Europe, or to The Hague, and to give Serbia a chance to amend her reply if the decision went against her. The refusal of the Ballplatz to allow any such reference cannot be explained away by phrases about "the most peace-loving Power in the world" (Count Szapary) and the "well-known pacific character of the Emperor, as well as his own" (Count Berchtold).[1]

Count Mensdorff admitted to Sir Edward Grey that "on paper the Serbian reply might seem to be satisfactory; but the Serbians had refused the one thing—the co-operation of Austrian officials and police—which would be a real guarantee that in practise the Serbians would not carry on their subversive campaign against Austria."[2] Demands numbers 5 and 6 required Serbia to accept the

---

[1] Austrian, no. 14; British, no. 62.   [2] British, no. 48.

"collaboration" of Austrian officials in suppressing the propaganda, to open a judicial inquiry (*enquête judiciaire*) as to the plot at Serajevo, and to allow Austrian delegates to take part in the investigations (*recherches*). Serbia replied that she did not understand what was meant by the first, and must reject the third because it was contrary to the constitution. The Austrian comment was that the Serbian attitude was "unintelligible," and that "if the Serbian Government misunderstood this point, it must do so deliberately, for the distinction between *enquête judiciaire* and simple *recherches* must be perfectly familiar to it." Now it is curious that statesmen as experienced as the British, French, and Russian foreign ministers were at once alarmed by these Austrian demands;[1] and more curious still is it that Count Berchtold deemed it wise to inform M. Sazonof "in confidence" that the Austrian collaboration would involve the establishment in Belgrade of a private *bureau de sûreté* analogous to Russian secret police establishments in Paris.[2] If the matter was so patent, why this secret communication to Russia? And why was the information given too late to influence the Serbian reply? Moreover, France, as the ally of Russia, might make certain concessions in matters of police which Serbia, as the enemy of Austria, could not tolerate. As to the confusion between *enquête judiciaire* and *recherches*, the Serbian Government may have been guilty of misrepresentation, although there is no proof of this; but the objection to the appearance of Austrian officials in Serbia is not removed by the Austrian explanations. Since, however, Serbia was willing to admit such collaboration as was consonant with international law, the Austrian criticisms cannot be accepted as showing good cause for the rejection of the Serbian reply. The German *White Book* remarks that the

[1] Austrian, nos. 11, 14; British, no. 5; French, no. 25.
[2] Austrian, no. 27.

reply was "entirely a play for time." [1]   Precisely: in order
that diplomacy might effect a peaceful settlement honorable to both parties.   But that was, apparently, the last
thing that Austria wanted.

When Austria rejected the Serbian reply, a war with
Serbia became inevitable, failing international action.
But, in the expectation of Russian interference, Austrian
and German statesmen began to pour forth assurances that
Austria would not disturb the territorial integrity of the
little Slav kingdom.   The idea runs through all the communications emanating from Vienna and Berlin, and is put
forward as a sufficient reason why Russia should stand
aside in an Austro-Serbian conflict.   At first sight, Count
Berchtold's remark to Prince Kudachef, "I pointed out
that we did not aim at any increase of territory, but only
at the maintenance of what we possess," [2] seems conclusive
evidence of good faith.   But presently qualifications are
introduced.   The British and Russian Governments were
informed that Serbia "will have to make good the military
expenses" incurred by Austria in enforcing her demands.[3]
Sir Rennell Rodd telegraphed from Rome "reliable information that Austria intends to seize the Salonika railway," which runs through Serbia.[4]   The British chargé at
Constantinople gathered from a remark let fall by the
Austrian ambassador that "the designs of Austria may
extend considerably beyond the sanjak and a punitive occupation of Serbian territory." [5]

Of course, the essential point was that Austria might
not annex any Serbian territory and at the same time reduce Serbia to a state of vassalage.   "This," as M. Sazonof
pointed out, "would upset the equilibrium in the Balkans,
and this was how Russian interests became involved." [6]

[1] *Collected Diplomatic Documents*, p. 423.   [2] Austrian, no. 18.
[3] Austrian, nos. 17, 20.   [4] British, no. 19.
[5] British, no. 82.   [6] Austrian, no. 47.

Yet the Austrian Government did not, until its negotiations with Russia had been overtaken by the Russo-German quarrel over mobilization, offer any guarantees on the subject of Serbian independence and sovereignty. On the contrary, the German ambassador in Paris, though stating that "Austria would respect the integrity of Serbia," "gave no assurance" that "her independence would also be respected."[1]   Similarly Count Pourtalès, according to the German *White Book*, declared on 29 July that "there would be time at the peace conference to return to the matter of forbearance toward the sovereignty of Serbia."[2] It is entirely improbable that if Austria had been allowed to proceed without interference against Serbia, she would have done no more than compel Serbia to accept her note of 23 July *in toto*, even if that itself would not have seriously compromised the independence of Serbia.   In spite of the fact that an annexation of Serbia would have increased the Slav population of the Monarchy, and have made more difficult the maintenance of German and Magyar ascendency in the Monarchy, it is against the logic of Austrian history and the expansionist spirit of the age to believe that Hapsburg statesmen could have been content with a demonstration of their power and have left Serbia to her own devices.   To secure the payment of the indemnity which Count Berchtold spoke of would have required the occupation of Serbian territory for an indefinite period; nor is it open to doubt, in the light of the past, that a harsh commercial treaty would have been forced upon a helpless Serbia.

M. Sazonof exposed the root of the difficulty when he pointed out, as he did several times,[3] that the Serbian declaration of 31 March, 1909, to which Austria appealed to justify her ultimatum, had been drafted by the Great

[1] British, no. 59.
[3] British, no. 17; Austrian, no. 16.

[2] German *White Book*, p. 409.

Powers.   If Serbia had failed to observe the promise made
at that time, then it was the duty of those Powers to see
to it that she did mend her ways and "live in good, neighborly relations" with Austria.   But for Austria to undertake single-handed to impose her solution of the problem
was to cut away the whole framework which European
diplomacy had erected around the Balkan question by
the laborious effort of more than a century.   If Russia
and the other Powers had refused to admit the necessity
of some satisfaction to Austria, she would have been justified in going ahead alone; but, in the face of the repeated
assurances of M. Sazonof that Serbia would meet all the
reasonable demands of Austria, the extraordinarily sub-
missive tone of the Serbian reply, and the strenuous endeavors of Sir Edward Grey to discover a *modus vivendi*,
little or no sympathy can be accorded to a policy which
we cannot doubt was devised to prevent a settlement,
to take Europe unawares, and to forestall any international action.   Whether viewed in the light of history or
from the angle of diplomatic procedure, the conduct of
Austria and the connivance of Germany must be held responsible for the situation which, from 28 July, 1914,
made Russian intervention a matter of course and caused
Russia and Austria to begin the mobilization of their
armies.

CHAPTER XIV

ARMAGEDDON

WHEN the news of the Austrian declaration of war reached St. Petersburg, which, as it happened, preceded a telegram from M. Schebeko to the effect that Count Berchtold had declined the Russian proposal for direct conversations, M. Sazonof took prompt action. To London he telegraphed:

"The Austrian declaration of war clearly puts an end to the idea of direct communications between Austria and Russia. Action by London cabinet in order to set on foot mediation with a view to suspension of military operations of Austria against Serbia is now most urgent." [1]

At the same time he informed the German Government that on the next day (29 July) Russia would order the mobilization of the military conscriptions of Odessa, Kief, Moscow, and Kazan—that is, of the thirteen army corps intended to operate against Austria.[2] He insisted upon "the absence in Russia of any aggressive intention against Germany," but the announcement was intended as a clear warning that Russia could not be ignored. Count Berchtold at once construed the mobilization as "a threat against Austria-Hungary," and "urgently" requested the German Government to inform Russia that "these measures would be answered by the most extensive military counter-measures, not only by the Monarchy but by the German Empire"; he preferred that Germany should take this step alone, but Austria was also "ready." [3] From this

[1] Russian, no. 48.   [2] British, no. 70 (1).   [3] Austrian, no. 42.

time on military considerations assume an increasing importance, and the effort of diplomacy becomes daily more
difficult.

On Wednesday, 29 July, the Russian foreign minister,
foreseeing, perhaps, what Count Szapary called "the military competition which now threatened to ensue on account
of false news," endeavored to reassure the German and
Austrian ambassadors. He told Count Szapary that the
Russian troops were not intended to attack Austria, and
"would stand to arms only in case Russian interests in the
Balkans should be in danger": Count Szapary intimated,
for the first time, that Austria "had no idea of touching
the sovereignty of Serbia." [1] To Count Pourtalès M.
Sazonof denied that the Russian military preparations
could be taken as aggressive measures against Austria,
"their explanation being the mobilization of the greater
part of the Austro-Hungarian army." He proposed that
parallel conversations should be conducted between Austria and Russia, and in a conference of the four Powers not
directly interested; he thought that "it should not be difficult to find a compromise . . . provided that Austria
showed some good will and that all the Powers used their
entire influence in the direction of conciliation." Count
Pourtalès, however, "could merely undertake to report
the conversation, and took the position that, after Russia
had decided upon the baneful step of mobilization, every
exchange of ideas appeared now extremely difficult, if not
impossible." [2] It is worth noting that whereas the Austrian ambassador had yielded a little, the attitude of his
German colleague indicated a certain stiffness that boded
ill for the delicate negotiations ahead.

M. Sazonof was evidently alarmed by the development
of the situation, for he renewed the request for British

[1] Austrian, no. 47.
[2] Russian, no. 49; British, no. 93 (2); German *White Book*, p. 409.

mediation which he had made the day before. He telegraphed to Count Benckendorff, the Russian ambassador
in London:

"From now on nothing remains for us to do but to rely entirely
on the British Government to take the initiative in any steps
which it may consider advisable." [1]

As a further inducement, he told Sir George Buchanan,
the British ambassador in St. Petersburg, that "he would
agree to anything arranged by the four Powers provided it
was acceptable to Serbia." [2]   And, indeed, it was only
through the mediation of Sir Edward Grey that the preservation of peace seemed possible.

For Count Berchtold had informed Berlin that unless
the Russian partial mobilization measures were stopped
without delay, a general mobilization of the Austro-Hungarian forces would follow at once. He added that "in
their military operations against Serbia they would not
allow themselves to be diverted from their path," [3] a fact
which was duly reported to their respective governments
by the British, Russian, French, and Italian ambassadors
in Vienna.[4]   More ominous still were the complaints which
Herr von Bethmann-Hollweg and Herr von Jagow at
Berlin, and Count Pourtalès at St. Petersburg, began to
make of the Russian mobilization,[5] for this, they asserted,
would put it out of their power to preach moderation at
Vienna. Hitherto the argument had been that pressure
could not be exerted because it would encourage Austria
to present Europe with a *fait accompli;* but now, in the
presence of the *fait accompli*, mediation would be difficult
because of the Russian mobilization, which the very *fait*
had produced! However, by this time the reader has
learned not to expect consistency in German diplomacy.

---

[1] Russian, no. 50; British, no. 93 (3).   [2] British, no. 78; French, no. 86.
[3] Austrian, no. 48.   [4] British, no. 79; French, no. 93.
[5] British, nos. 71, 76, 78; Russian, no. 51.

Nevertheless, as if to pile Pelion on Ossa, the Wilhelmstrasse, which was regretting its inability to preach conciliation at Vienna, would actually seem to have been giving Austria the advice to come to an agreement with Russia. The chancellor assured Sir Edward Grey, through Sir Edward Goschen, that "he was doing his very best both at Vienna and St. Petersburg to get the two governments to discuss the situation directly with each other, and in a friendly way." [1]   This was on July 28.   The following day the chancellor said that he had asked Austria specifically to state her intentions, as this would facilitate her conversations with Russia.[2]   On the same day Herr von Jagow told M. Jules Cambon that he had asked Vienna to resume direct conversations with St. Petersburg, and he answered in the affirmative the ambassador's question whether "he did not think that common action could be exercised by the four Powers by means of their ambassadors." [3]   At Paris Herr von Schoen declared that his government was "still continuing its efforts" at Vienna,[4] and M. Isvolsky reported the opinion of the French foreign minister that "Germany now inclines toward mediatory action both at St. Petersburg and at Vienna." [5]   Finally, the first telegram of the Emperor William II to the Tsar, dated 28 July, 10.45 P. M., promised the "entire influence" of the Emperor "to induce Austria-Hungary to obtain a frank and satisfactory understanding with Russia." [6]   It seems probable, therefore, although there is only one despatch in the German *White Book* (exhibit 14) to corroborate the statement, that for about twenty-four hours after the Austrian declaration of war Berlin did, as the *White Book* claims, "advise Vienna to show every possible advance compatible with the dignity of the Monarchy." [7]

[1] British, no. 71.   [2] British, no. 75.   [3] French, no. 92.
[4] French, no. 94.   [5] Russian, no. 53.   [6] German, no. 20 (1).
[7] *Collected Diplomatic Documents*, p. 409.

In these circumstances the chances for mediation in some form or another seemed decidedly favorable. Nor was there any lack of suggestion. Sir Edward Goschen, M. Jules Cambon, M. Viviani, the French premier, and the Marquis di San Giuliano, then Italian foreign minister, urged Sir Edward Grey to let Herr von Jagow propose the form which mediation should take, for he had accepted the idea "in principle." [1] So, at four o'clock on the afternoon of 29 July, Sir Edward Grey telegraphed to Berlin an account of his interview with Prince Lichnowsky:

"The German Government had said that they were favorable in principle to mediation between Russia and Austria if necessary. They seemed to think the particular method of conference—consultation or discussion, or even conversations à quatre in London—too formal a method. I urged that the German Government should suggest any method by which the influence of the four Powers could be used together to prevent war between Austria and Russia. France agreed, Italy agreed. The whole idea of mediation or mediating influence was ready to be put into operation by any method that Germany could suggest if mine were not acceptable. In fact, mediation was ready to come into operation by any method that Germany thought possible, if only Germany would 'press the button' in the interests of peace." [2]

This despatch is one of the most important in the entire correspondence of the belligerent governments, for it proves conclusively that France, Italy, Great Britain, and Russia (M. Sazonof had appealed for mediation) were willing to give Germany the lead in any move by which the existing difficulties might be resolved. The problem was not more serious than that created by the Balkan revolution eighteen months before; no military operations, as distinct from military preparations, had been begun; there was needed only good will; but no time could be lost.

This telegram was answered by one of even greater im-

[1] British, nos. 60, 80; French, nos. 81, 97.
[2] British, no. 84; French, no. 98; Russian, no. 54.

portance, in which Sir Edward Goschen described an interview with the German chancellor. Under the presidency of the Emperor, who had returned to Berlin on 27 July, a council of the highest authorities of the Empire was held at Potsdam on the night of the 29th. It is not known what happened on that fateful occasion, but the events of the next twelve hours suggest that the decision to make war was practically taken. Otherwise the return of the chancellor to Berlin that night, his haste in seeing the British ambassador, and the tenor of his remarks are inexplicable.

"He said," reported Sir Edward Goschen, "that should Austria be attacked by Russia a European conflagration might, he feared, become inevitable, owing to Germany's obligations as Austria's ally, in spite of his continued efforts to maintain peace. He then proceeded to make the following strong bid for British neutrality. He said that it was clear, so far as he was able to judge the main principle which governed British policy, that Great Britain would never stand by and allow France to be crushed in any conflict there might be. That, however, was not the object at which Germany aimed. Provided that neutrality of Great Britain were certain, every assurance would be given to the British Government that the imperial government, aimed at no territorial acquisitions at the expense of France should they prove victorious in any war that might ensue.

"I questioned his excellency about the French colonies, and he said that he was unable to give a similar undertaking in that respect. As regards Holland, however, his excellency said that, so long as Germany's adversaries respected the integrity and neutrality of the Netherlands, Germany was ready to give His Majesty's Government an assurance that she would do likewise. It depended upon the action of France what operations Germany might be forced to enter upon in Belgium, but when the war was over Belgian integrity would be respected if she had not sided against Germany." [1]

That Germany should thus cynically avow to Great Britain her resolution to make war, at a moment when other Powers

[1] British, no. 85.

were straining to secure a peaceful settlement, is not only
the crowning proof of the ineptness of her diplomacy, but
an adequate commentary on her professions that she strove
valiantly for peace to the end of the controversy. From
this time on the efforts she made for peace took the form of
threats which she can scarcely have expected to be heeded.

The explanation of the chancellor's appeal to Sir Edward
Goschen is found in the *démarche* of Count Pourtalès at
St. Petersburg, which is itself highly significant. On the
afternoon of 29 July, or about twenty-four hours after the
Russian Government had informed Berlin of its intention
to mobilize against Austria, he declared to M. Sazonof
that if Russia did not stop her military preparations Germany would mobilize her army. If it is recalled that three
days before Count Pourtalès had announced that "mobilization meant war," and also that Herr von Jagow had
promised both the British and the French ambassadors
that Germany would not respond to a Russian mobilization against Austria alone, it is clear that Germany was
not only breaking faith but threatening Russia with war.
The ambassador's communication was practically an ultimatum without the name, and was so understood by M.
Sazonof, who telegraphed as follows to the Russian ambassadors in the great capitals:

"We only began these preparations in consequence of the mobilization already undertaken by Austria, and owing to her evident
unwillingness to accept any means of arriving at a peaceful settlement of her dispute with Serbia. As we cannot comply with the
wishes of Germany, we have no alternative but to hasten on our
own military preparations and to assume that war is inevitable." [1]

As a matter of fact, the mobilization against Austria had
not yet been ordered at the time of Count Pourtalès's interview, for the French ambassador informed his government

[1] Russian, no. 58

that "the tone in which Count Pourtalès delivered his communication has decided the Russian Government this very night to order the mobilization of the thirteen army corps which are to operate against Austria."[1] The German ambassador may have assumed that the intention to mobilize, which the Russian Government did not conceal, was identical with the order to mobilize; but inasmuch as the whole German case against Russia rests upon the Russian mobilization, it was surely his business to ascertain whether *mobilization was a fact* before making threats which would certainly precipitate mobilization. Of course, it is alleged in the German *White Book* that while the Russian minister of war had given his "word of honor" that "nowhere had there been a mobilization up to three o'clock in the afternoon" of 29 July, actually extensive measures were under way.[2] Then why did not Count Pourtalès complain to M. Sazonof of this "attempt to mislead" Germany? It may therefore be reasonably asserted that the *démarche* of Count Pourtalès was unprovoked and uncalled for; it can be explained only on the assumption that Germany wanted war, for if persisted in it would make the Russian mobilization inevitable and, according to the German conception of international relations, that meant war. It is suggestive that no mention of this incident, or of the one immediately following it, occurs in the *White Book*. Why? Obviously because it is destructive of the German thesis that Russia "spoiled everything" by her premature mobilization, for it would have provided Russia with the best of all reasons for mobilizing.

As it happened, the German Government decided not to proceed *à outrance* for the moment. Its attitude remained the same, as may be seen from the Emperor's telegram dated 30 July, 1 A. M.[3] But it may have per-

---

[1] French, no. 100.   [2] *Collected Diplomatic Documents*, p. 410.
[3] German, no. 23.

ceived the weakness of the case it was setting up; or it
may have had its zeal tempered by the warning conveyed
by Sir Edward Grey to Prince Lichnowsky, that Germany
must not count upon England's standing aside in all circumstances.[1] At all events, Count Pourtalès visited M.
Sazonof again at 2 A. M. on 30 July, and instead of formally requiring the cessation of Russian mobilization, which
was the logical step after his communication of the afternoon before, asked upon what conditions Russia would
consent to demobilize.   After the usual statement by Count
Pourtalès that Austria would not infringe upon the territorial integrity of Serbia, and the familiar complaint from
M. Sazonof that Germany was refusing to intervene at
Vienna in order to gain time for the Austrian advance into
Serbia, the Russian foreign minister dictated the following
formula to the German ambassador:

> "If Austria, recognizing that her dispute with Serbia has assumed
> the character of a question of European interest, declares herself
> ready to eliminate from her ultimatum the clauses which are dam-
> aging to the sovereignty of Serbia, Russia undertakes to stop all
> military preparations." [2]

According to Sir George Buchanan, Count Pourtalès "completely broke down on seeing that war was inevitable,"
and M. Paléologue, the French ambassador, stated that
"Count Pourtalès promised to support this proposal with
his government," although, in point of fact, it involved
absolutely no change in the attitude which the Russian
Government had consistently upheld from the very beginning of the crisis.   The sincerity of M. Sazonof in making
this proposal is seen from his remark to M. Paléologue,
that in the course of the night "the general staff had suspended all measures of military precaution, so that there

[1] British, nos. 89, 102.
[2] Russian, no. 60; British, no. 97; French, no. 103.

should be no misunderstanding," [1] the reference, of course, being to the mobilization against Austria, which had been ordered on the evening of 29 July. The reception of the Russian formula merits the most careful study, because it represented the last effort to preserve peace and for a brief space promised to be successful.

Count Berchtold at once showed himself more conciliatory than at any time since the beginning of the crisis. In an interview with the Russian ambassador he explained that his refusal to allow Count Szapary to continue the conversation was due to a misunderstanding; he did not say that he would allow the ambassador in St. Petersburg to discuss the Austrian ultimatum and the Serbian reply, but he was willing to "discuss what settlement would be compatible with the dignity and prestige for which both empires had equal concern." He also gave positive assurances that Austria would not infringe the sovereignty of Serbia, and he did not manifest any alarm over the Russian military measures, to which Austria would have to reply as a measure of precaution. The *Entente* ambassadors in Vienna were encouraged by the friendly tone of the interview, which took place on 30 July.[2] The next day Count Berchtold practically abandoned the position he had hitherto maintained, for he telegraphed to London that "we are quite prepared to entertain the proposal of Sir Edward Grey to negotiate between us and Serbia." [3] Even though he posited the conditions that "our military action against Serbia should continue to take its course," and that the Russian mobilization should be brought to a standstill, "in which case we will also at once cancel the defensive military counter-measures in Galicia," the offer approximated the Russian formula sufficiently to warrant negotiations.

[1] French, no. 102.   [2] Austrian, no. 50; British, no. 96; French, no. 104.
[3] Austrian, no. 51.

How very different was the attitude of Berlin! The Russian ambassador was informed by Herr von Jagow that "he considered it impossible for Austria to accept our proposal." [1] The French ambassador, recalling the promise that "Germany would only consider herself obliged to mobilize if Russia mobilized on her German frontiers," was told that "the words . . . did not constitute a firm engagement." [2] Herr von Jagow justified this repudiation on the ground that the heads of the army were clamoring for mobilization, "for every day was a loss to the strength of the German army." As a matter of fact, the military party had got the upper hand at the council on 29 July, as evidenced by the fact that at 1 P. M. on the 30th the *Lokal Anzeiger* published a special edition announcing the mobilization of the German army.[3] The news turned out to be premature, but the newspaper would not have acted thus without official inspiration. The next day the chancellor "was so taken up with the news of the Russian measures along the frontier that he received without comment" Sir Edward Grey's reply to the bid for British neutrality; he also said to Sir Edward Goschen that "it was quite possible that in a very short time, to-day perhaps, the German Government would take some serious step." [4] As this conversation occurred *before* Berlin learned of the Russian general mobilization, it is obvious that Germany was preparing to take the situation into her own hands, in imitation of her procedure of March, 1909.

The position of Sir Edward Grey was now difficult in the extreme. The German Government "had not had time to send an answer" to his proposal that it should indicate the form mediation should take, and Herr von Jagow practically evaded it by stating that he would communicate directly with Austria.[5] The chancellor's bid for

[1] Russian, no. 63; French, no. 107.
[2] French, no. 109.
[3] French, no. 105; Russian, nos. 61, 62.
[4] British, nos. 108, 109.
[5] British, no. 107; French, no. 109.

British neutrality and the *démarche* of Count Pourtalès at St. Petersburg evidently convinced Sir Edward that Germany was bent on war. Hence his stinging reply to the chancellor's "infamous proposals" and his negotiations with M. Paul Cambon, the French ambassador in London.

The reply to the chancellor reveals at once the intense indignation of Sir Edward Grey and his capacity of restrained expression.

"His Majesty's Government," he wrote, "cannot for a moment entertain the chancellor's proposal that they should bind themselves to neutrality on such terms.

"What he asks us, in effect, is to engage to stand by while French colonies are taken and France is beaten, so long as Germany does not take French territory as distinct from the colonies.

"From the material point of view such a proposal is unacceptable, for France, without further territory in Europe being taken from her, could be so crushed as to lose her position as a Great Power, and become subordinate to German policy.

"Altogether apart from that, it would be a disgrace to us to make this bargain with Germany at the expense of France, a disgrace from which the good name of this country would never recover.

"The chancellor also, in effect, asks us to bargain away whatever obligation or interest we have as regards the neutrality of Belgium. We could not entertain that bargain either. . . .

"We must preserve our full freedom to act as circumstances may seem to us to require in any such unfavorable and regrettable development of the present crisis as the chancellor contemplates." [1]

On the same day (30 July) Sir Edward discussed with the French ambassador the question whether the agreement made in November, 1912, would not now come into operation, that is, whether the French and British Governments should not discuss what they would do if the peace of Europe was threatened. The ambassador did not press for a promise that Great Britain would intervene, but for

[1] British, no. 101.

a statement of intentions under certain circumstances, in this case an aggression by Germany on France. Sir Edward Grey promised to consult the cabinet the next morning and to see the ambassador in the afternoon.[1] In other words, so alarmed were England and France two days before the German declaration of war on Russia that they were making preparations to meet all eventualities.

That is one side of the picture. On the other hand, Sir Edward Grey did not cease from his endeavors to keep the peace. On 29 July he had suggested to Prince Lichnowsky that Austria might be persuaded to stop her military action with the occupation of Belgrade.[2] The Wilhelmstrasse seemed to approve of the suggestion, and promised to support it at Vienna: Sir Edward accordingly, on 30 July, communicated it to St. Petersburg, with the hope that on this basis "Russia would consent to discussion and suspension of further military preparations, provided other Powers did the same."[3] He also pointed out that "if the Russian Government object to the Austrians mobilizing eight army corps, this is not too great a number against 400,000 Serbians."[4]

The German Government was informed of this overture through the regular diplomatic channel, and also by a telegram from King George to Prince Henry of Prussia, which contained the additional information that England was asking France to postpone her military preparations.[5] The length to which Sir Edward Grey was willing to go can be measured from his two memorable offers of 30 and 31 July:

"If the peace of Europe can be preserved, and the present crisis safely passed, my own endeavor will be to promote some arrangement to which Germany could be a party, by which she could be

[1] British, no. 105.   [2] British, no. 88.   [3] British, no. 103.   [4] British, no. 110.
[5] Second German *White Book* (published in *Norddeutsche Allgemeine Zeitung*, 20 August, 1914), no. 2, in *Collected Diplomatic Documents*, p. 539

assured that no aggressive or hostile policy would be pursued against her or her allies by France, Russia, and ourselves, jointly or separately. I have desired this and worked for it, as far as I could, through the last Balkan crisis, and, Germany having a corresponding object, our relations sensibly improved. The idea has hitherto been too utopian to form the subject of definite proposals, but if the present crisis, so much more acute than Europe has gone through for generations, be safely passed, I am hopeful that the relief and reaction which will follow may make possible some more definite *rapprochement* between the Powers than has been possible hitherto."[1]

This proposal came at the end of Sir Edward Grey's refusal to barter away British neutrality, and it envisaged a Europe organized for peace on the basis of a reduction of armaments by all the Powers. Statesmanship has never risen higher, and this vision of Sir Edward Grey may yet be realized. But in July, 1914, the German chancellor received the proposal "without comment"![2]

More specific and more practical was the second offer:

"I said to the German ambassador this morning (31 July) that if Germany could get any reasonable proposal put forward which made it clear that Germany and Austria were striving to preserve European peace, and that Russia and France would be unreasonable if they rejected it, I would support it at St. Petersburg and Paris, *and go the length of saying that if Russia and France would not accept it His Majesty's Government would have nothing more to do with the consequences;* but otherwise, I told [the] German ambassador that if France became involved we should be drawn in."[3]

Here was the opportunity that Germany had been seeking for many years: to shatter the *Entente* and lay the foundations of an alliance with England. For England to make such an offer was to strain almost to the breaking-point her most cherished friendships and obligations; it was her supreme effort for peace. Yet there is no record in the diplomatic correspondence that the German Government gave

[1] British, no. 101.　　[2] British, no. 109.　　[3] British, no. 111.

the least consideration to this invitation or hesitated a moment in the course upon which it had embarked: Herr von Jagow said "it was impossible for the imperial government to consider any proposal until they had received an answer from Russia to their communication" demanding demobilization of the Russian army.[1]

The mobilization of both the Russian and the Austrian armies was ordered on 31 July. Nevertheless the situation, as between those two countries, seemed to be clearing on that and the following day. Immediately upon receiving Sir Edward Grey's proposal for a discussion on the basis of the Austrian occupation of Belgrade, M. Sazonof combined it with his own suggestion, and produced the following formula:

> "If Austria consents to stay the march of her troops on Serbian territory, and if, recognizing that the Austro-Serbian conflict has assumed the character of a question of European interest, she admits that the Great Powers may examine the satisfaction which Serbia can afford to the Austro-Hungarian Government, without injury to her sovereign rights as a state and to her independence, Russia agrees to preserve her waiting attitude." [2]

Austrian troops had already bombarded Belgrade when this offer was forwarded to Vienna and Berlin. Nevertheless, the Tsar telegraphed to the German Emperor:

> "It is far from us to want war. As long as the negotiations between Austria and Serbia [sic] continue, my troops will undertake no provocative action. I give you my solemn word thereon." [3]

Finally, the Russian ambassador in Vienna declared that "Russia would be satisfied even now with assurance respecting Serbian integrity and independence," [4] and that "his government would take a much broader view than

---

[1] British, no. 121.   [2] Russian, no. 67; British, no. 120; French, no. 113.
[3] German *White Book*, p. 411. "Serbia" is obviously a misprint for "Russia," as Austro-Serbian relations were broken off on 25 July.
[4] British, no. 141.

was generally supposed of the demands of the Monarchy." [1]
It is surely fair to say that the Russian Government went
to the extreme limit of conciliation.

Austria, for her part, realizing from the Russian mobili-
zation that her policy of bluff had failed, gave every appearance of yielding. She did not airily brush aside
M. Sazonof's formula, as she had done his earlier proposals.
The ambassador in Paris, Count Scézsen, declared that
Austria would respect the integrity and independence of
Serbia; that she would not occupy the sanjak of Novi-
Bazar; and she would answer Serbia, or any Power speaking
in the name of Serbia, any questions as to the conditions
of a settlement.[2]   In London, "Count Mensdorff begged
the Russian ambassador to do his best to remove the
wholly erroneous impression in St. Petersburg that the
'door had been banged' by Austria-Hungary on all further
conversations." [3]   Finally, "Count Szapary at last conceded the main point at issue by announcing to M. Sazonof
that Austria would consent to submit to mediation the
points in the note to Serbia which seemed incompatible
with the maintenance of Serbian independence." [4]   The
Russian foreign minister accepted this on condition that
Austria refrain from the actual invasion of Serbia, and proposed that the mediation should be prepared in London.[5]
It would be too much to say that Austria and Russia had
come to terms, but they were certainly in a fair way to
do so, and neither Power showed the slightest disposition
to begin hostilities.

Suddenly Germany intervened, just as she had in March,
1909, when the Austro-Russian quarrel over the annexation of Bosnia was approaching a settlement, and, to borrow Herr von Jagow's complaint about Russian mobiliza-

[1] French, no. 104.   [2] French, no. 120; **Russian, no. 73**
[3] British, no. 137.   [4] British, no. 161
[5] Austrian, no. 56; British, nos. 120, 139.

tion, "spoiled everything." Her precipitate action was the more remarkable because she was insisting that her mediation at Vienna was responsible for the altered attitude of Austria.[1] The explanation given in the *White Book* runs as follows:

"During the interval from 29 July to 31 July, whilst these endeavors of ours for mediation were being continued with increasing energy, supported by English diplomacy, there appeared renewed and cumulative news concerning Russian measures of mobilization. Accumulation of troops on the East Prussian frontier and the declaration of the state of war over all important parts of the Russian west frontier allowed us no further doubt that the Russian mobilization was in full swing against us, while simultaneously all such measures were denied to our representative in St. Petersburg on word of honor." [2]

Now the curious thing is that not a single despatch corroborative of this charge is printed in the *White Book*, nor is there mention of any remonstrances by either the German foreign secretary or the German ambassador in St. Petersburg. Not until 2 P. M. on 31 July does the German Emperor protest to the Tsar against "serious preparations for war going on on my eastern frontier."[3] The *White Book* produces four telegrams as proof of Russian mobilization before 29 July: why is it silent as regards the next two days? The Russian mobilization may have been in full swing against Germany before the order for general mobilization (31 July), but the historian cannot accept the fact as conclusive on Germany's *ipse dixit*.

The news of the Russian general mobilization became known in the German capital sometime in the afternoon of 31 July. *Kriegsgefahrzustand* was at once proclaimed, and

German *White Book*, pp. 410–411; despatch of the German chancellor to the German ambassador in Vienna, 30 July, 1914, published in the *Westminster Gazette*, 1 August; King George to the Emperor Nicholas, 1 August, *Collected Diplomatic Documents*, p. 536; British, nos. 98, 112.

[2] *Collected Diplomatic Documents*, p. 411.   [3] German *White Book*, p. 412.

two ultimatums were launched. The one to Russia, presented in St. Petersburg at midnight, stated that "if within twelve hours—that is by midnight [*sic*] on Saturday—Russia had not begun to demobilize, not only against Germany but also against Austria, the German Government would be compelled to give the order for mobilization." To M. Sazonof's inquiry whether this meant war, "the ambassador replied in the negative, but added that they were very near it." [1] For the moment we may postpone the consideration of the equity of this demand and continue the narrative of events. The ultimatum to France, presented at 7 P. M., recited that Germany had taken "no measures toward mobilization," but that she would be forced to do so if Russia did not demobilize within twelve hours. Since "mobilization inevitably implies war," the French Government was asked to reply in eighteen hours "whether it intended to remain neutral in a Russo-German war." [2]

Only a miracle could now avoid war. Yet the Tsar did not expect war: so he stated in his telegram of 1 August to King George. [3] Consequently, although the German ultimatum expired at noon, at 2 P. M. he telegraphed to the German Emperor:

"I comprehend that you are forced to mobilize, but I should like to have from you the same guarantee which I have given you, viz., that these measures do not mean war, and that we shall continue to negotiate for the welfare of our two countries and the universal peace which is so dear to our hearts." [4]

The French Government, for its part, tactfully kept its troops ten kilometres behind the German frontier, [5] and Sir

---

[1] Russian, no. 70; German, no. 24. The British and French ambassadors complained to Herr von Jagow that Germany had made the matter more difficult by requiring to demobilize against Austria as well as herself. (British, no. 121; French, no. 116.)

[2] German, no. 25; French, no. 117; British, no. 117.

[3] *Collected Diplomatic Documents*, p. 537.   [4] German *White Book*, p. 413.

[5] British, nos. 134, 136, 140; French, no. 136.

Edward Grey informed Berlin that "His Majesty's Government are carefully abstaining from any act which may precipitate matters." [1]

The British Government may also be credited with the last efforts to preserve peace. Sir Edward Grey advised Berlin that "things ought not to be hopeless so long as Austria and Russia are ready to converse," and communicated the amended Russian formula.[2] Then, on the basis of a report that the German ambassador had suggested that Germany might remain neutral in an Austro-Russian war if Great Britain secured the neutrality of France, Sir Edward made overtures to Prince Lichnowsky toward that end, only to learn that the ambassador's proposal was that Great Britain and France should remain neutral while Germany went to war with Russia.[3]

Steps were also taken to restrain Russia. King George sent to the Tsar a long statement of the German Government, to the effect that its mediation had been upset by the Russian mobilization, and that war was imminent. The King made "a personal appeal" to his cousin "to remove the misapprehension which he felt must have occurred, and to leave still open grounds for negotiation and possible peace." [4] Sir Edward Grey telegraphed that "if, in the consideration of the acceptance of mediation by Austria, Russia can agree to stop mobilization, it appears still to be possible to preserve peace." [5] Now, since the Tsar, in his reply to King George's telegram, said that he "would gladly have accepted your proposals had not the German ambassador this afternoon presented a note to my government declaring war," [6] it seems probable that Russia was quite willing to negotiate for a general demobilization, and

[1] British, no. 131.
[2] British, no. 131.
[3] Sir Edward Grey, House of Commons, 28 August, 1914. (5 *Hansard* lxvi, c. 264.)
[4] *Collected Diplomatic Documents*, p. 536.
[5] British, no. 135.
[6] *Collected Diplomatic Documents*, p. 537.

that, as Sir Maurice de Bunsen sorrowfully said, "a few days' delay might in all probability have saved Europe from one of the greatest calamities in history," [1] provided, of course, that Germany was not determined at all costs to pick a quarrel.

All was in vain. At 12.52 P. M., on Saturday, 1 August, or fifty-two minutes after the expiry of the ultimatum, the German ambassador in St. Petersburg was instructed to declare that, as Russia had refused to comply with the German demand for demobilization, "and having shown by this refusal that her action was directed against Germany, . . . His Majesty the Emperor, in the name of the German Empire, accepts the challenge and considers himself in a state of war with Russia." [2] According to Baron Beyens, the Belgian minister in Berlin, Herr von Jagow and Herr Zimmermann, the under-secretary of the foreign office, besought the Emperor to await a reply from Russia, which might have been delayed by the military preparations, and not to order the mobilization of the German army.[3] His Majesty, however, followed up the declaration of war by an imperious telegram,[4] and at 5 P. M. ordered the mobilization of the German army and navy. Count Pourtalès presented the declaration of war to M. Sazonof at 7.10 P. M.

"However," says the *White Book*, "before a confirmation of the execution of this order had been received, . . . Russian troops crossed our frontier and marched into German territory. Thus Russia began the war against us." [5] No proof is adduced, except a statement in the Austrian *Red Book* that "the Russian troops have crossed the German frontier at Schwidden." [6] Nor were the British and Austrian ambassadors in Berlin informed of this

---

[1] British, no. 161. [2] German, no. 26; Russian, no. 76.
[3] "La Semain tragique," *Revue des Deux Mondes*, 1 June, 1915.
[4] German *White Book*, p. 413. [5] *Ibid.*, p. 413. [6] Austrian, no. 57.

breach of international usage until the next day.[1] But granted that the violation of frontier took place: "to put it forward, as does the German and Austrian correspondence, as the actual ground for the commencement of hostilities is to assume the imposition that the fate of nations is subject to the reported action of a roving patrol."[2]

It is now necessary to examine the German contention that because Russia mobilized her army while Germany was mediating between Russia and Austria, the security of Germany was thereby menaced and a declaration of war forced upon the Emperor. On general principles, it is quite impossible to admit such a theory, for every sovereign state has the right to dispose of its armed forces within its own frontiers as it sees fit. If a neighboring state conceives itself endangered by military movements over the frontier, it can mobilize its own army, but it cannot make such movements a *casus belli* without putting itself in the wrong; the obvious action is to make the other side declare war. Unfortunately, German "open mobilization was the last stage. It was not a military preparation; it was in itself an offensive movement. On that order the German armies did not merely concentrate; they marched."[3] The German thesis is disproved by two circumstances. First, to all the overtures made by the British Government to the German for a limitation of armaments, the reply invariably was that every state must remain master of its military powers. Germany cannot claim such rights for herself and deny them to Russia. She could mobilize her own army; she might refuse to exert pressure on Austria; she could give notice that any attack on Austria would be met by a German declaration of war; but by no criterion of international conduct was she entitled to go beyond that. Second, on the eve of the crisis, the British fleet

[1] British, no. 144; Austrian, no. 57.
[2] *Collected Diplomatic Documents*, p. xi. [3] *Ibid.*, p. xiv.

was mobilized for manœuvres, and when the crisis opened was not disbanded. Why did not Germany insist upon its demobilization as a condition precedent to British participation in the negotiations? Its own fleet, then in Norwegian waters, was surely in as much danger from a British attack as was the East Prussian frontier on 31 July–1 August. Suppose that Great Britain, France, or Russia had made formal complaint to Berlin of the preparatory military measures which they believed Germany to be taking; is it open to doubt what the German answer would have been?

The German case against Russia rests partly upon the alleged priority of the Russian mobilization. Now, it is difficult to say "who began it." In the various *Books* there are some forty despatches relating to mobilization in its various stages. If accepted at their face value, they show that the British, French, German, Austrian, and Russian Governments were taking precautionary measures from the early days of the crisis. Some of the reports may be false, but until the records of the general staffs are available the chaff cannot be separated from the wheat, and meanwhile the student can only speculate upon the psychological effects produced upon the several foreign offices as news of military preparations by a probable enemy comes in. If Germany asks us to accept her testimony about Russian secret preparations, she must permit us to note what the French and Russian despatches say about her own activities. In other words, the German charge that Russia "betrayed" Germany by denying the existence of preparations that were in reality being carried on can be met by the counter-charge that Germany "betrayed" France and Russia.

The one serious question, therefore, is: Was the Russian mobilization premature? For it is to be remembered that, although Austria began by denying the legitimacy of Rus-

sian intervention, she ended by conceding it, since she agreed
to discuss with Russia the substance of her ultimatum to
Serbia. Russia mobilized her four southern conscriptions
on the morrow of the Austrian declaration of war against
Serbia. Ought she to have waited until the Austrian troops
actually invaded Serbia? A negative answer seems justified by the fact that Count Berchtold, after a brief inclination to regard the move as a "threat," soon showed himself ready, for the first time since the crisis began, to make
concessions which would obviate the necessity for an armed
intervention by Russia.

The general mobilization affords a more difficult problem.
The Germans contend that the Russian order could not
have been caused by the Austrian mobilization, and that
it was given before Austria had replied to the proposal
embodied in M. Sazonof's first formula.[1] As to the first,
there is the definite statement of the Russian Government
in its public announcement and the statement of the Tsar
to King George, that the mobilization was induced by Austria's previous mobilization. Is it possible to test the accuracy of these statements? The one precise piece of information is that given by the French ambassador in Vienna,
according to whom the Austrian mobilization was declared
at 1 A. M. on 31 July,[2] the decree for which was apparently prepared as early as 28 July.[3] For the Russian mobilization three general statements are available. Count
Szapary says that it was ordered "early to-day"—31
July.[4] What does "early to-day" mean? The German
White Book says it occurred "*am Vormittag*," [5] which would
seem to mean in the latter part of the morning. The
Emperor, telegraphing to the Tsar at 2 P. M., does not
mention it.[6] Finally, in his telegram to King George of

---

[1] Dr. Karl Helfferich, "The Dual Alliance *versus* the Triple Entente," *New York Times*, 14 March, 1915.
[2] French, no. 115.   [3] Russian, no. 47.   [4] Austrian, no. 52.
[5] *Collected Diplomatic Documents*, p. 412.   [6] German *White Book*, p. 411.

31 July, the Emperor says: "I have just heard from the chancellor that Intelligence had just reached him that Nicholas this evening has ordered the mobilization of his entire army and fleet." [1]   The probability certainly is that the Russian mobilization was ordered *after* that of Austria. The Russian *Orange Book* and the Austrian *Red Book* are both strangely silent upon the subject, so it may be that each government ordered its mobilization independently of any knowledge of the other's intentions; but the published evidence seems to absolve Russia of having anticipated the Austrian mobilization.

It does appear to be true that Russia ordered her mobilization before Austria had vouchsafed a reply to either Sir Edward Grey's proposal that she should open a discussion with Russia as soon as she had occupied Belgrade, or to M. Sazonof's own formula.   And, inasmuch as Russia was aware, from the communication of Count Pourtalès, that Germany would immediately imitate the Russian mobilization and that mobilization meant war, it is evident that Russia must have counted the consequences when she ordered the general mobilization.   Had she waited another twenty-four hours before mobilizing, an agreement might have been reached with Austria which would have obviated the necessity of mobilization.   So far as mobilization was the cause of the war, Russia must bear some share of the responsibility.

At the same time, quite apart from the fact that mobilization does not afford a sufficient ground *per se* for declaring war, Russia was in a difficult position.   She had every reason to believe that Austria would make no concessions. Belgrade had been bombarded on 30 July, and the mobilization of the whole Austrian army had been ordered, according to the Russian version of events.   M. Sazonof also claimed to have information concerning German prepara-

---

[1] Second German *White Book*, no. 3.

tions against Russia.[1] In these circumstances there is
much to be said for the plea made to King George by the
Tsar:

"That I was justified in ordering a general mobilization is proved
by Germany's sudden declaration of war, which was quite unexpected by me, as I have given most categorical assurances to the
Emperor William that my troops would not move so long as mediation negotiations continued." [2]

All things considered, we may admit that it would have
been wiser for Russia not to have mobilized when she did;
but we must remember that her provocation was very
great, that she had throughout the crisis displayed admirable restraint, and that it was her complete mobilization
which actually forced from Austria the promise to discuss
with Russia the substance of her ultimatum.

Furthermore, if Russia can be criticised for a premature,
if intelligible, mobilization, Austria is open to the same
charge. Count Berchtold was fully aware of the *démarche*
of Count Pourtalès, and had himself requested Germany to
notify Russia that Russian mobilization would call for
counter-measures by Germany.[3] Now, it stood on the
cards that an Austrian mobilization would immediately
be followed by that of Russia; this was, indeed, a com-
monplace of diplomacy, and Count Berchtold can scarcely
have sanctioned the Austrian mobilization without a full
appreciation of its effect upon Russia, upon Germany,
and in the end upon Europe. It is this consideration which
raises the most serious doubt whether the Austrian concessions on 31 July and 1 August were sincere, were not, in
fact, intended as plays for time or as manœuvres to place
Russia in the wrong. For, although she agreed to discuss
the substance of her ultimatum with Russia, she did not

[1] British, no. 97; Russian, no. 68; French, no. 102.
[2] *Collected Diplomatic Documents*, p. 537.   [3] Austrian, nos. 28, 42.

promise to stop her march on Belgrade, and did not stop it. Nevertheless, the situation as between Austria and Russia was not irretrievable until Germany took umbrage at the Russian mobilization and proceeded to force the pace.

As a matter of fact, this lengthy analysis of the German case against Russia is scarcely needed to demonstrate its utter hollowness. If Germany had proceeded to invade Russia upon her declaration of war, one could understand the argument of Herr von Jagow that Germany "had the speed and Russia had the numbers, and the safety of the German Empire forbade that Germany should allow Russia time to bring up masses of troops from all parts of her wide dominions." [1] But Germany did not attack Russia: she waited for the Russian army to invade East Prussia, and hurled her own legions against France even before she had declared war on the Republic! One cannot avoid the suspicion that the German attitude toward Russia was assumed with the view to providing an opportunity for an invasion of France, whose conduct throughout the crisis was eminently correct and conciliatory.

The German ultimatum to France expired at 1 P. M. on 1 August. At 11 A. M. Herr von Schoen visited the Quai d'Orsay, and was informed that "the French Government failed to comprehend the reason which prompted his communication of the previous evening." M. Viviani referred to the hopeful prospect of an Austro-Russian agreement, and "laid stress on the serious responsibility which the imperial government would assume if, in circumstances such as these, it took an initiative which was not justified and of a kind which would irremediably compromise peace." [2] At 1.05 P. M. Herr von Schoen telegraphed to Berlin that "upon his repeated definite inquiry whether France would remain neutral in the event of a Russo-Ger-

[1] British, no. 138.   [2] British, no. 126; French, no. 125.

man war, the prime minister declared that France would do what her interests dictated." [1] At 3.40 the mobilization of the French army and navy was ordered.

"On the morning of the next day," says the German *White Book*, "France opened hostilities." [2] In the Reichstag, on 4 August, Herr von Bethmann-Hollweg said that "aviators dropped bombs, and cavalry patrols and French infantry detachments appeared on the territory of the Empire." The charges are particularized in the French *Yellow Book :*

"Eighty French officers in Prussian uniform attempted to cross the German frontier in twelve motor-cars at Walbeck, to the west of Geldern."

"Several of the aviators openly violated the neutrality of Belgium by flying over the territory of that country; one attempted to destroy buildings near Wesel; others were seen in the district of the Eifel, one threw bombs on the railway near Carlsruhe and Nuremberg." [3]

The French premier "formally challenged these inaccurate allegations," [4] and the government stated that it had given explicit orders that its troops should remain ten kilometres behind the frontier. Such denials are scarcely conclusive. But two French professors, MM. Durkheim and Denis, of the University of Paris, had the happy idea to ascertain whether German newspapers had given a detailed account of the alleged occurrences. Their account of their researches is as follows:

"We consulted five of the principal newspapers (*Vorwärts, Arbeiter Zeitung* of Vienna, *Frankfurter Zeitung, Kölnische Zeitung, Münchner Neuste Nachrichten*) from the end of July to 5 August. First of all we noticed that the aviator who is said to have flown over Carlsruhe is not mentioned. As for the others, the account of them is as vague as it is in the official note. These incidents, given as the cause of determining war, take up one line, two or

[1] German, no. 27.
[3] French, nos. 146, 147.
[2] *Collected Diplomatic Documents*, p. 413.
[4] French, no. 148.

three at the most. *The bombs never left any trace.* One of the aeroplanes, that at Wesel, is said to have been brought down; nothing is said of the aviator and what became of him, nor is there anything about the aeroplane itself. In a word, the Germans took care to draw attention to their arrival in Germany and then never spoke of them again. They were never seen to return to their starting-point.

"But we have still more convincing evidence. We have been able to procure a Nuremberg newspaper, the *Frankischer Kurrier.* On 2 August, the day the bombs are supposed to have been thrown, not a word is said about the incident. Nuremberg received the news on the 3d by a telegram from Berlin identical to that published by the other newspapers. Again, the *Kölnische Zeitung* of the 3d, in its morning edition, published a telegram from Munich which read as follows: 'The Bavarian minister of war is doubtful as to the exactness of the news announcing that aviators had been seen above the lines Nuremberg-Kitzingen and Nuremberg-Ansbach, and that they had thrown bombs on the railway.' " [1]

More interesting is the fact that although the alleged violations of the frontier occurred on 2 August, the German Government did not declare war on France for thirty-six hours, at 6.45 P. M., on 3 August.[2] On the morning of the 2d the ambassador in London telegraphed that England would not guarantee the neutrality of France.[3] If the French attacks were to be made the official cause of war, why was the declaration delayed so long? The Germans have hardly made out a convincing case.

It may also be observed that Germany did not regard the mobilization of the French army as a *casus belli*, although the danger to Germany was very much greater on this side than on the Russian. And yet the neutrality of Belgium was violated because it was necessary for Germany to prevent the French from getting their attack started first! In the midst of such inconsistencies one finds additional reason for believing that the German attitude toward the

[1] *Who Wanted War ?* (1915), p. 50, note 1.
[3] Second German *White Book*, no. 9.
[2] French, no. 147.

Russian mobilization was only an excuse for launching an attack on France.

The French, on their side, alleged that the German troops violated the French frontier at Ciry, Longwy, Delle, Joncherey, and Baron, on 2 August.[1] The chancellor's statement in the Reichstag on 4 August, that only one of these violations, which he did not specify, had been committed, is worth as much or as little as the French premier's similar denial of French aggressions. But it is curious to find, in the German account of the negotiations with England for the neutrality of France, this statement of the Emperor William to King George, in a telegram of 1 August: "The troops on my frontier are at this moment being kept back by telegraph and by telephone *from crossing the French frontier.*"[2] Evidently it was the German intention to invade France on that date, when the German ambassador was still in France and had not asked for his passports. This admission and the detail with which the French supported their charges afford reasonable ground for believing that the Germans were across the French frontier thirty-six hours before the declaration of war, conduct which is quite on a par with the policy that based a declaration of war on the alleged zeal of a few aviators.

There is, however, one charge against France made by the Germans which must be examined with great care. In his extremely acute analysis of the *Books* published by the *Entente* Powers, Dr. Karl Helfferich, secretary of the German treasury, contends that "the Franco-Russian treaty of alliance did not pledge France to an unconditional accompaniment of Russia in war," and that France, by prematurely promising to stand by Russia, was unable to exert pressure at St. Petersburg in the interests of peace, and strengthened the hand of the Russian war party.[3]

[1] French, nos. 136, 139.   [2] Second German *White Book*, no. 6.
[3] *New York Times*, 14 March, 1915.

Inasmuch as the German *White Book* is generally re-garded as perhaps the most damning evidence against its authors, Germany is quite justified in trying to prove the guilt of the *Entente* Powers by their own documents. Dr. Helfferich first cites the interview on 24 July between M. Sazonof, Sir George Buchanan, and M. Paléologue, at which the French ambassador declared that "France would fulfil all the obligations imposed by her alliance with Rus-sia, if necessity arose, besides supporting Russia strongly in any diplomatic negotiations." Sir George Buchanan reported to Sir Edward Grey his opinion that, "even if England declines to join them, France and Russia are de-termined to make a strong stand," the extent of which might be gauged by the remark of M. Sazonof that "Rus-sian mobilization would at any rate have to be carried out." [1] This declaration of French policy, according to Dr. Helfferich, so tied the hands of Paris that it would not listen to the repeated requests of Herr von Schoen to use its moderating influence at St. Petersburg.

The decisive step, however, was not taken until 29 July, when the French premier confirmed to the Russian ambas-sador "the French Government's firm determination to act in concert with Russia," [2] to which M. Sazonof replied that "in the existing circumstances that declaration is specially valuable to us." [3] The following day M. Viviani telegraphed to London and St. Petersburg that "France is resolved to fulfil all the obligations of her alliance." [4] Finally, French diplomacy exerted itself to the uttermost, and most unscrupulously,[5] to secure a pledge of English

[1] British, no. 6.
[2] Russian, no. 55.
[3] Russian, no. 58.
[4] French, no. 101.
[5] In the original edition of the British *White Paper*, no. 105 (3), which purports to be a report from Paris of German military preparations, is dated "31 July," although it is enclosed in a British despatch to Paris of 30 July! It also contains the words "yesterday, Friday," yet Friday was 31 July. Is the document a forgery, as the Germans contend? No explanation has ever been vouchsafed. In subse-quent editions of the *White Paper* the date and the words quoted have been omitted,

assistance. From 29 July France believed herself sure of
English support, and made her promise to Russia. Therefore, argues Dr. Helfferich, the aggression during the crisis
came from France and Russia, and it was due to France
that Russia embarked on her policy of mobilization, which
made war inevitable.

"Left to depend upon herself alone, Russia would have risked
the war with Austria-Hungary and Germany only in an extreme
case in the defense of national vital interests, but never as a result
of weighing the probable result. Only the assurance of the active
co-operation of other Great Powers made possible the determination
of the leading circles of Russia for war."

Nevertheless, in spite of the sequence of events as established by Dr. Helfferich, his conclusions do not necessarily follow. First of all, his point about the Franco-
Russian alliance does not seem well taken. He assumes
that Germany will loyally support her ally Austria, yet
questions the justice of France standing by her ally Russia.
As to the statement that France was not bound under all
circumstances to fight for Russia, by which is meant, presumably, that the alliance was defensive, the same thing
may be predicated of Germany. Her alliance with Austria
was also defensive: none the less she considered herself
bound to declare war on Russia, in defense of her ally,
before the latter was herself at war with Russia. It would
have been highly desirable if Germany and France could
have left the dispute to be settled between the two prin-
cipals, but since they did not Germany cannot deny to
France the same privilege to support her ally which she
claimed for herself.

In the second place, there is nothing in the whole correspondence to show that the attitude of Russia was stiffened

and the French *Yellow Book* dates a similar document (no. 106) 30 July. British,
nos. 99, 117, 119, 124, 134, 136; French, nos. 106, 114, 127, indicate how anxious
France was for the promise of English support.

as a result of French policy. The Russian Government took its position at the very outset of the crisis and, as we have already observed, maintained it consistently to the end. Dr. Helfferich would have us believe that the Russian mobilization would not have occurred without the assurance of French assistance. As a matter of fact, the Russian mobilization was determined upon, that is, if it was necessary to enforce Russia's claim to share in the settlement of the Austro-Serbian question, on 25 July,[1] or four days before France promised her assistance. Then, in spite of Dr. Helfferich's argument to the contrary, the actual order for mobilization does seem to have been given as a consequence of the Austrian mobilization. Nor is it fair to say that France did nothing for peace. She did not play a prominent part in the diplomacy of the twelve days—23 July–4 August—but she supported all the proposals of Sir Edward Grey, which is more than can be said of Germany, and she requested her ally to avoid "every military measure that could offer Germany the pretext for general mobilization."[2] After all, the Germans themselves have recognized the perfect propriety of France's conduct. In the German note to the *Entente* Powers of 24 July we read: "The imperial government desires urgently the localization of the conflict, because every interference of another Power would, *owing to the different treaty obligations*, be followed by incalculable consequences."[3]

If Germany had waited for Russia to attack her or Austria, and had then been attacked by France, she could convince the world that she was the victim of unprovoked aggression. But when she declared war on Russia, and then on France, while the latter carefully refrained from coming to the assistance of its ally, it is absurd for Ger-

---

[1] Telegram of the Emperor Nicholas to the Emperor William, 30 July, German, no. 23a.
[2] French, no. 101   [3] German, no. 1; British, no. 9; French, no. 28

many to argue that the war would not have come if France had not promised to assist Russia. No amount of special pleading can explain away the fact that negotiations were proceeding between Austria and Russia when Germany intervened violently and fatally. Furthermore, if Germany had sincerely desired to keep the peace with France, as Herr von Schoen kept saying at the Quai d'Orsay, she would have concentrated in Alsace-Lorraine—for France had promised to respect the neutrality of Belgium—an army sufficient to beat back a French attack, and have waged her own war immediately against Russia who, it was alleged, had caused all the trouble by threatening Germany's ally.

CHAPTER XV

THE ANGLO–GERMAN RUPTURE

IT is at last possible to discuss the reasons why Great Britain declared war on Germany. The various phases of the rivalry between the two nations have been analyzed: the struggle for the control of the seas in time of war; the competition for the markets of the world; problems of colonial expansion; mutual suspicion generated in the political sphere by the reaction of the three factors just mentioned; and the profound differences in the national temperaments, institutions, and ideals. A conflict was, perhaps, inevitable. At the same time, it has been seen that the naval rivalry was in process of adjustment; that Great Britain was not jealous of the commercial progress of Germany; that the colonial ambitions of Germany had been recognized by the Anglo-German agreement arrived at on the very eve of the war, As a result of this general relaxation of tension the relations between the two countries in July, 1914, were more friendly than they had been at any time since the retirement of Bismarck. The Triple *Entente* still remained as an obstacle to German aggression; but Great Britain had made it very plain, not merely in words but by her action, that she was in no way disposed to support France and Russia in an aggressive policy against Germany, and that if Germany was determined to live in peace on the basis of a fair field and no favors she would find no more earnest coadjutor and friend than England and the British Empire. On both sides there seemed to be developing a willingness to forget the quarrels of the past and to work toward a general understanding which would effectually guarantee the peace of the world.

When the crisis of 1914 was sprung, Sir Edward Grey had, therefore, every reason to suppose that any efforts to preserve peace which he might make would receive the cordial approval and support of Germany, more especially as such co-operation had been vouchsafed in the crisis of 1912–13. Instead, he had seen Germany refuse to exert pressure on her ally, decline to join in some form of international action, and declare war on Russia. As many French and English publicists who passed for jingoes had predicted, the Bismarckian spirit, without its cleverness, still guided German diplomacy; the Teutonic legions had been sent forth almost without warning, and the neutrality of Belgium was soon discovered to be a paper guarantee. Sir Edward Grey's correspondence bears many a trace of disappointment that he was unable to secure from Germany a favorable response to his repeated overtures, and he is reported to have said, after his speech to the House of Commons on 3 August: "This is the saddest day of my life." But such reflections did not solve the awful problem whether Great Britain should participate in the war. The mere fact that she was not drawn in automatically proves that she was not committed to France and Russia by secret agreements or military conventions and Sir Edward Grey stated to Parliament on 3 August that he "did not know the terms of the Franco-Russian alliance." Clearly, then, the British Government was a free agent in any decision which it might recommend Parliament to take.

Four possible policies presented themselves for its choice: First, the British Government might take the position that the war was simply an enlargement of the Austro-Serbian dispute, that "direct British interests in Serbia were nil," and that its "idea had always been to avoid being drawn into a war over a Balkan question." [1] And

[1] British, nos. 6, 87.

as late as 31 July Sir Edward Grey informed Sir Francis Bertie, the British ambassador in Paris, that "nobody here feels that in this dispute, so far as it has yet gone, British treaties or obligations are involved." [1] The adoption of this position would have required England at once to proclaim her unconditional neutrality. This was a possible policy, but in the light of British history it was not a very probable or promising one.

Second, England might have decided to cut the Gordian knot by following up the cue of Anglo-German reconciliation made possible by the agreement of 1914, and, abandoning her friends of the *Entente*, have contracted a formal alliance with Germany. The German chancellor had such a development in mind when he made his famous bid for British neutrality; and he must have meant the same thing when he declared in the Reichstag on 2 December, 1914, that "the cabinet of London could have made the war impossible if it had told St. Petersburg unequivocally that England had no intention of permitting a Continental war of the Great Powers to grow out of the Austro-Serbian conflict." For, of course, the *Entente* would have been shattered by such a policy, and England would have been thrown into the arms of Germany. The very idea of an Anglo-German alliance is hard to grasp, in view of the past relations of the two countries. But Sir Edward Grey must have reckoned with it when he said that "if Germany could get any reasonable proposal put forward which made it clear that Germany and Austria were striving to preserve European peace, and that Russia and France would be unreasonable if they rejected it, . . . His Majesty's Government would have nothing more to do with the consequences." [2] This offer, more than any other incident of the crisis, must prove the disinterestedness and sincerity of Sir Edward Grey's diplomacy, and he is not to blame if

[1] British, no. 116.   [2] British, no. 111.

Germany did not seize the opportunity to place Anglo-German relations on a sound basis.

Third, Sir Edward Grey might, as he was repeatedly urged by French and Russian statesmen to do, have immediately declared the solidarity of Great Britain with France and Russia. This step was advocated on the ground that Germany would not provoke a general war if she were convinced that Great Britain would be found in the ranks of her enemies. It may be that such a declaration would have stayed the hand of the German military party, but it is extremely doubtful. Not only were the Germans supremely contemptuous of Britain's fighting capacities, but their government was repeatedly warned, by the remarks of Sir Edward Grey to Prince Lichnowsky, that if the war became general Great Britain would be drawn in. Sir Edward even went so far as to say that "the German Government do not expect our neutrality." [1] It should be noted, however, that the Marquis di San Giuliano thought "it would have a great effect" if Germany believed that "Great Britain would act with Russia and France." [2]

The Germans have tried to prove that, as a matter of fact, England did practically declare her solidarity with France and Russia, and that this was responsible for the French promise to stand by Russia and the unyielding attitude of M. Sazonof. On 29 July Sir Edward Grey said to Prince Lichnowsky "something that was on his mind."

"The situation was very grave. While it was restricted to the issues at present actually involved we had no thought of interfering in it. But if Germany became involved in it, and then France, the issue might be so great that it would involve all European interests; and I did not wish him to be misled by the friendly tone of our conversation—which I hoped would continue—into thinking that we should stand aside." [3]

[1] British, no. 116.   [2] British, no. 80.   [3] British, no. 89.

The ambassador "took no exception" to this, and Herr von Jagow admitted to Sir Edward Goschen that he had heard it "with regret, but not exactly with surprise." [1] But Sir Edward Grey had already informed the French ambassador that he intended to convey this warning to Prince Lichnowsky.[2] It was this, says Dr. Helfferich, that enabled France to promise her assistance to Russia and thus compromise the situation. Proof of the altered state of affairs is adduced in the letter from the Belgian chargé in St. Petersburg to his government which was intercepted in Germany after the war began.

"England," wrote M. de l'Escaille on 30 July, "at the start let it be understood that she did not want to be dragged into a conflict. Sir George Buchanan said so openly. To-day every one in St. Petersburg is convinced—has even the assurance—that England will support France. This encouragement has had a powerful effect, and has contributed not a little to giving the war party the upper hand." [3]

It is possible that some comfort was derived in St. Petersburg from the attitude of Sir Edward Grey, and it is difficult to see why he informed M. Paul Cambon of what he intended to say to the German ambassador; all the more so because his policy was apparently shaped by the feeling that uncertainty as to the intentions of Great Britain was the best guarantee of peace. If the *Entente* practically became an alliance on 29 July, then the German attitude deserves more sympathy than has hitherto been accorded it. But such does not seem to have been the case, in spite of M. de l'Escaille. If Sir Edward Grey had considered himself morally bound to stand by France, he would scarcely have made the two memorable offers to Germany of 30 and 31 July, which have already been adverted to several

[1] British, no. 98.   [2] British, no. 87.
[3] *Norddeutsche Allgemeine Zeitung*, 11 September, 1914; published in American newspapers, 4 October, 1914.

times. Nor would he have been at such pains to convince M. Paul Cambon that the British attitude would be determined by public opinion, and that public opinion would not necessarily support British intervention.[1] But there is still better proof that England's help was not considered as a matter of course. On 31 July M. Poincaré, the President of France, addressed an autograph letter to King George, begging the British Government to take some step which would demonstrate the solidarity of the *Entente*; to which the King replied in a vague and non-committal fashion.[2] On 1 August M. Viviani wrote to London:

"I am persuaded that in case war were to break out, British opinion would see clearly from which side aggression comes, and that it would realize the strong reasons which we have given to Sir Edward Grey for asking for armed intervention on the part of England in the interest of the future of the European balance of power." [3]

This is not the language of assurance, but of entreaty. On the same day Sir Edward Grey, while refusing to state to Prince Lichnowsky the terms on which Great Britain would remain neutral, said: "Our hands are still free, and we are considering what our attitude will be." [4] On 2 August the cabinet discussed the terms of neutrality,[5] and the promise of naval assistance which was given to France on 3 August was made conditional on the approval of Parliament. Finally, the Tsar's telegram to King George of 1 August concluded with the hope that "your country will not fail to support France and Russia." [6] On the basis of these facts, as opposed to the opinion of a subordinate diplomatist in St. Petersburg and the somewhat forced ar-

[1] British, nos. 87, 105, 116, 119, 148; French, nos. 110, 126.
[2] *Collected Diplomatic Documents*, pp. 542–544.
[3] French, no. 127.   [4] British, no. 123.
[5] Sir Edward Grey, House of Commons, 27 August, 1914. (5 *Hansard* lxvi, c. 124.)
[6] *Collected Diplomatic Documents*, p. 537.

gument of Dr. Helfferich, it is reasonable to believe that
Great Britain was not committed to France and Russia
before the outbreak of war, and that, as Prince Lichnowsky
reported Sir Edward Grey to have said on 1 August,
"there was not the slightest intention to proceed in a hostile manner against Germany" [1] merely because she was
Germany.

Suppose Great Britain had declared her solidarity with
France and Russia. If Russia were bent on war, the
promise of British assistance would make it inevitable.
Sir Edward Grey evidently believed Russia to be pacific,
but he could take no chances. Next, such a declaration
would have infuriated Germany and in all probability have
whetted her appetite for war; if, by good fortune, peace
had been preserved, the whole movement toward an Anglo-
German understanding which had been nursed with such
tender care would have come to an untimely end, and
Great Britain would have been faced with still another increase of the German fleet. In fact, had Sir Edward Grey
accepted the argument of solidarity, he would have stulti-
fied himself, for his consistent policy had been to resist
all temptations toward a formal alliance with France and
Russia, however much he might support them in opposing
the aggressions of Germany and Austria. In the existing
situation, Sir George Buchanan was entirely right when
he said that "England could play the rôle of mediator at
Berlin and Vienna to better purpose as a friend who, if
her counsel of moderation were disregarded, might one day
be converted into an ally, than if she were to declare herself Russia's ally at once." [2]

Thus the true policy of Great Britain, and the one which
she actually pursued, was to co-operate in all measures

[1] Telegrams published in *Norddeutsche Allgemeine Zeitung*, 6 September, 1914.
no. 2 (*Collected Diplomatic Documents*, p. 541).
[2] British, no. 17.

which might preserve the peace of Europe; to suggest such
measures herself; to use her influence with France and
Russia in favor of moderation; and to secure the help of
Germany in calming the adventuresome spirit of Austria.
At the same time, Great Britain had no intention of abandoning France and Russia if they were the victims of an
unprovoked attack, and she therefore repeatedly warned
Germany that, while she desired above all things to
work with her for peace, yet Great Britain would be
drawn in if war came about by the action of Germany.
Nevertheless, she kept her hands free and did not make
any decision to intervene until 2 August, that is, until
Germany had declared war on Russia and had violated
the neutrality of Luxemburg as the first step in her invasion
of France.   It remains to describe the steps by which Great
Britain abandoned her waiting attitude and became the
ally of France and Russia.

On the morning of 30 July it was quite evident, thanks
to the German bid for British neutrality and the communications of Count Pourtalès to the Russian foreign
minister, that the storm was about to break, and that its
extent would not be limited to eastern Europe.   In such
circumstances, the neutrality of Belgium assumed a vital
importance, not merely because of its bearing on the immediate diplomatic situation but on its own merits.   A short
statement, therefore, seems desirable, in spite of all that
has been said and written about the matter since the beginning of the war.
     The neutrality of Belgium was not born of any particular
consideration for the people of that country, but was essentially a political expedient.   From time immemorial the
Low Countries had been the cockpit of Europe, the decisive
battle-ground of innumerable wars since the sixteenth century.   Furthermore, the possession of this territory, which

gave outlets on both the Channel and the North Sea, was considered the key to European domination, as the careers of Philip II of Spain, Louis XIV, and Napoleon showed only too well.   The French, in particular, had displayed a relentless cupidity, and when the Revolution declared war on the Old Europe, in 1792, their first step was to occupy the southern provinces and, later on, Holland.   When the Congress of Vienna met, after the fall of Napoleon, to find some solution of the problems provoked by his meteoric career, nothing aroused more interest than the necessity of hemming France in on all sides by states strong enough to resist a renewed aggression on her part when she should have recovered from the exhaustion of her struggle with the rest of Europe.   At the demand of Great Britain a Kingdom of the Netherlands was created, consisting of the old Dutch Republic and the Netherlands proper, which had hitherto belonged to Spain or Austria.   But that union proved utterly unworkable, for the excellent reason that between the Dutch of the north and the Belgians of the south there was not one interest in common.   In religion, language, political ideals, economic interests, social organization, and traditions, the two peoples were as distinct as Frenchmen and Germans; so that union was as unreal in the nineteenth century as it was in the sixteenth, when William the Silent vainly tried to organize the seventeen provinces for resistance to Spain.   Inasmuch as the constitution granted in 1815 by the Dutch King William entirely favored his own people, the only recourse of the southerners was to carry through a revolution, which they did in 1830, proclaiming their independence and appealing to the Powers for recognition.

Their conduct was a deliberate violation of the settlements of 1815, upon which Europe had bestowed so much care.   None the less, France and England responded favorably to the Belgian appeal, which was resisted by the three eastern monarchies, Prussia, Austria, and Russia. The difficulty was that Belgium would not be strong enough to withstand a French attack, and that the new French King, Louis Philippe, who owed his throne to a revolution, might be tempted to undertake a war for the sake of prestige. Prussia did not relish the prospect of an attack on the lower Rhine; England was as unwilling as ever for any part of the Low Countries to pass into the hands of a strong Continental Power. It was therefore agreed that the new European state should be "neutral in perpetuity."[1] The idea of the statesmen who thus divided the Low Countries into two independent states was that, "if it was made impossible for a Great Power to invade them, war would become increasingly difficult and dangerous."[2] Consecrated by two international treaties (1831, 1839) signed by all the Powers and recognized by two generations of statesmen, the neutrality of Belgium was observed for eighty-three years, during which period only one war harassed western Europe, in striking contrast to the frequent conflicts of the seventeenth and eighteenth centuries. In the apt phrase of Sir Edward Grey, Belgian neutrality had become "the main rivet" of the peace of Europe. Consequently the argument of Herr von Jagow to Sir Edward Goschen that the Germans "had to advance into France by the quickest and easiest way, so as to be able to get well ahead with their operations and endeavor to strike some decisive blow as early as possible,"[3] falls little short of the ridiculous: "the neutrality of Belgium had not been devised as a pretext for wars, but to prevent the outbreak of wars."[4] In other words, just as Austria sought to impose her particular solution of the international Balkan question, so Germany proposed to ignore the historical

---

[1] Article VII, treaties of 1831 and 1839.
[2] *Great Britain and the European Crisis*, "Narrative," sec. 6, par. 3.
[3] British, no. 160.
[4] *Great Britain and the European Crisis*, "Narrative," sec. 6, par. 4.

background of Belgian neutrality, which had been devised in no small degree for the protection of Prussia herself.

No time need be wasted over the German arguments that by her acquisition of the Congo or that, by leaving her French frontier poorly defended while she strongly fortified her German frontier, Belgium had forfeited her neutrality. The assurances given by Herr von Bethmann-Hollweg to the Belgian Government in 1911, the statement of Herr von Jagow to the budget committee of the Reichstag in 1913,[1] and, above all, the admission of the German chancellor in the Reichstag on 4 August, 1914, that the entry of German troops into Belgium was "a breach of international law," "a wrong," dispose once for all of the contention that Germany had in any way repudiated the signature of Prussia to the treaty of 1839.

Great Britain was also formally committed to observe her signature to the same treaty. In a despatch of 7 April, 1913, recording an interview with the Belgian minister in London, Sir Edward Grey said that "he was sure that this [the Liberal] government would not be the first to violate the neutrality of Belgium, and he did not believe that any British government would be the first to do so, nor would public opinion here ever approve of it." So long as it was not violated by any other Power Great Britain would certainly not send troops into Belgian territory.[2]

This last sentence is particularly important, because it refutes the German interpretation of the documents discovered in Brussels by the Germans after their capture of the city.[3] In the spring of 1906 General Ducarne, of the Belgian general staff, and Lieutenant-Colonel Barnardiston, the British military attaché in Brussels, worked out a

---

[1] Belgian, no. 12.

[2] *Collected Diplomatic Documents*, p. 350.

[3] *Norddeutsche Allgemeine Zeitung*, 25 November, 1914; *Collected Diplomatic Documents*, pp. 354–361.

plan for the co-operation of 100,000 British troops with those of Belgium. The Germans published General Ducarne's report of this plan as evidence that Belgium had sold herself and her neutrality to Great Britain, and that the latter would undertake offensive operations against Germany through Belgium. Unfortunately, the document bears the following marginal note: "The entry of the English into Belgium would take place only after the violation of our neutrality by Germany." In 1912 Lieutenant-Colonel Bridges, in a confidential interview with General Jungbluth, remarked that "the British Government, at the time of the recent events (the Agadir crisis), would have immediately landed troops on Belgian territory, even if Belgium had not asked for help"; to which the general replied that "their consent would be necessary for this." From the document itself it is impossible to determine whether the British attaché was revealing what had been the secret intentions of his government or was voicing a personal opinion; but the Belgian Government has semi-officially stated that there was only "a private conversation between two officers of high rank, which had no reference to any official mission." [1] The documents are not conventions formally signed between the British and Belgian Governments, but are records of conversations; Sir Edward Grey has stated that he never knew of these conversations, and that no reports of them are on file at the British war office, which fully demonstrates their unofficial character. Finally, King Albert of Belgium has said:

"No one in Belgium ever gave the name of Anglo-Belgian conventions to the letter of General Ducarne to the minister of war, detailing the entirely informal conversations with the British military attaché, *but I was so desirous of avoiding even the semblance of anything that might be construed as unneutral that I had the matters*

[1] J. Van den Heuvel, Belgian minister of state, *On the Violation of Belgian Neutrality*, in *Collected Diplomatic Documents*, p. 364.

of which it is now sought to make so much communicated to the German military attaché in Brussels. When the Germans went through our archives, they knew exactly what they would find, and all their present surprise and indignation is assumed." [1]

There is, then, no reason for believing that the conduct of both the British and the Belgian Governments was otherwise than correct: the object of the conversations was to guard against the two governments being taken unawares if the neutrality of Belgium was actually violated by Germany. Now, "the strategic dispositions of Germany, especially as regards railways, have for some years given rise to apprehension that Germany would attack France through Belgium." [2] This fear was, indeed, a matter of common discussion. If the reader will consult the *Fortnightly Review* for February, 1910, and February, 1914, he will find two articles describing in great detail the military railways of Germany on the Belgian frontier, and arguing that the purpose of such lines was to make possible a German advance through Belgium. The *New York Times* of 23 January, 1914, contains a Brussels despatch, under date of 9 January, describing the new line just completed which linked up the Belgian town of Stavelot with the German town of Malmédy. The correspondent commented upon probable lack of both passengers and freight for the railway, which he described as "another strategic line which, in the case of war between England and Germany, or particularly in the case of an Anglo-French and German war, would be of great strategic value to Germany." He continued:

"Germany has thereby accomplished the first and more essential part of her plan for the peaceful penetration of the Ardennes. England has done nothing to stop it; France has done nothing. With-

[1] Interview with H. N. Hall, in American newspapers, 22 March, 1915.
[2] "Memorandum" prepared by the British foreign office, in *Collected Diplomatic Documents*, p. 365.

out their very energetic intervention Belgium is helpless, and so Germany perfects and prolongs her railway system, like her navy, for 'the day' without stay or interference."

In the light of what has been said, the interest of Great Britain in the maintenance of Belgian neutrality is apparent, and, considering the German attitude assumed on 29 July, the one hope of preserving peace lay in the chance that Germany might hesitate if she were convinced that Great Britain would resist by force an attempt to invade France through Belgium. Accordingly, on 31 July Sir Edward Grey addressed the following identic communication to the French and German Governments:

"I still trust that situation is not irretrievable, but in view of prospect of mobilization in Germany, it becomes essential to His Majesty's Government, in view of existing treaties, to ask whether French (German) Government are prepared to engage to respect neutrality of Belgium so long as no other Power violates it." [1]

Informing the Belgian Government of this *démarche*, Sir Edward said:

"I assume that the Belgian Government will maintain to the utmost of their power their neutrality, which I desire and expect other Powers to uphold and observe." [2]

It is impossible to say whether Sir Edward Grey really expected Germany to abide by her treaty obligation, but it was his duty to put this question to her, just as Lord Granville had put it in 1870. The language used by Sir Edward deserves close scrutiny. He asked if the French and the Germans were "prepared to engage to respect the neutrality of Belgium." If the replies were in the affirmative, his next step would doubtless have been, following the precedent of 1870, to submit to France and Germany identic treaties, by which the British Government bound itself,

[1] British, no. 114; Belgian, no. 13; Russian, no. 72.   [2] British, no. 115.

in case one Power violated the neutrality of Belgium, to assist the other Power with all its forces. Of course, it may be argued, and it has been argued, that Sir Edward Grey was, for all practical purposes, well aware of Germany's intention to march across Belgium, and that his question was asked simply to provide him with an excuse for advising Parliament to sanction a British declaration of war against Germany. Is not the question somewhat academic? Those who believe that England was bound, both morally and for her own interests, to support France in a defensive war against Germany will say that Sir Edward Grey was entirely justified in seeking a legal and sound justification for British intervention. If the other theory is held—that Germany was attacked by Russia, and was driven in self-defense to cross Belgium—then British intervention was a gratuitous affront; then the parading of Belgian neutrality was a sham quite worthy of English hypocrisy. As a matter of fact, the following paragraphs will endeavor to show that if Germany had agreed to respect the neutrality of Belgium British participation in the Great War would have been unlikely, as the situation stood on 4 August, 1914.

The French Government replied immediately to the British demand, that they were "resolved to respect the neutrality of Belgium, and it would only be in the event of some other Power violating that neutrality that France might find herself under the necessity, in order to assure defense of her own security, to act otherwise."[1] From Brussels the news came that "Belgium expects and desires that other Powers will observe and uphold her neutrality, which she intends to maintain to the utmost of her power."[2] Sir Edward Goschen, however, telegraphed from Berlin:

"I have seen secretary of state, who informs me that he must consult the Emperor and the chancellor before he could possibly

[1] British, no. 125; French, no. 122.   [2] British, no. 128; Belgian, no. 11.

reply. I gathered from what he said that he thought any reply they might give could not but disclose a certain amount of their plan of campaign in the event of war ensuing, and he was therefore very doubtful whether they would return any answer at all. His excellency, nevertheless, took note of your request." [1]

This reply, or rather refusal to reply, by the German Government made it certain not only that Germany was intending war but that she was preparing to march through Belgium. When military considerations prevent an answer to a diplomatic question, there can be only one interpretation of the state of affairs, and this must be kept in mind when considering the events of Saturday, 1 August.

Even before receiving the German reply Sir Edward Grey knew that the situation was desperate, although he continued his efforts for peace; for the ambassador in Paris had informed him of the German ultimatums to Russia and France.[2] The French Government inquired what would be the attitude of England. A decision must soon be made. Nevertheless, at the cabinet meeting held Saturday morning no action was taken,[3] no doubt because Sir Edward Grey thought he might be able to restrict the conflict to eastern Europe.

It had been reported to him that Prince Lichnowsky had suggested that Germany might remain neutral in an Austro-Russian war if Great Britain remained neutral and secured the neutrality of France, and that in this case Germany would engage not to attack France.[4] Sir Edward Grey asked Prince Lichnowsky about this over the telephone about eleven o'clock Saturday morning. To Sir Edward the essential thing was to secure the neutrality of Germany, as that would insure the immunity of France, but Prince Lichnowsky grasped only the second part of the

---

[1] British, no. 122; French, no. 123; Belgian, no. 14.
[2] British, no. 117.   [3] French, no. 126.
[4] Sir Edward Grey, House of Commons, 28 August, 1914. (5 *Hansard* lxvi, c. 264.)

idea. So he telegraphed for authority to declare that "in the event of France remaining neutral in a German-Russian war, Germany would not attack the French."[1]   The chancellor replied to the ambassador, and the German Emperor telegraphed to King George, that Germany was ready to accept the British proposal "in case England guaranteed with all her forces absolute neutrality of France in Russo-German conflict."[2]   Sir Edward Grey had to explain that Prince Lichnowsky had misunderstood his proposal, and that the German counter-proposal was, so far as he knew, not compatible with the Franco-Russian alliance; that is, the *casus fœderis* must operate equally with France and Germany.[3] Prince Lichnowsky promised to send a second telegram to Berlin to remove the misunderstanding, but apparently did not do so,[4] except to say that "the suggestions of Sir Edward Grey, based on the desire of creating the possibility of lasting neutrality on the part of England, were made without any previous inquiry of France and without knowledge of the [German] mobilization, and have since been given up as quite impracticable."[5]   In just what fashion England could have guaranteed the neutrality of France was not explained by the German Government. In deed, at the very time of making this proposal, Germany was despatching her declaration of war to St. Petersburg (12.52 P. M.).   She cannot have seriously imagined that, if she attacked Russia, France would remain neutral, unless she was prepared to repudiate her alliance and place herself at the mercy of a victorious Germany.   In view of Prince Lichnowsky's first telegram, the German Government may

---

[1] Second German *White Book*, no. 5; telegrams in *Norddeutsche Allgemeine Zeitung*, 6 September, 1914, no. 1. (*Collected Diplomatic Documents*, p. 541.)

[2] Second German *White Book*, nos. 6, 7.

[3] Sir Edward Grey, House of Commons, 28 August, 1914. (5 *Hansard* lxvi, c. 265.)

[4] The German Government denied that such a telegram was received from Prince Lichnowsky. (*Norddeutsche Allgemeine Zeitung*, 6 September, 1914.)

[5] Second German *White Book*, no. 9.

be acquitted of bad faith, but it is scarcely fair to charge, as did the *Norddeutsche Allgemeine Zeitung* in publishing the correspondence, that Great Britain rejected a positive opportunity to secure both its own and French neutrality. The German offer was based on a misconception, and was beyond the realm of practical politics.

On Saturday afternoon Sir Edward Grey had another interview with Prince Lichnowsky. He read to the ambassador this declaration of the cabinet:

"The reply of the German Government with regard to the neutrality of Belgium is a matter of very great regret, because the neutrality of Belgium does affect feeling in this country. If Germany could see her way to give the same positive reply as that which has been given by France, it would materially contribute to relieve anxiety and tension here, while, on the other hand, if there were a violation of the neutrality of Belgium by one combatant while the other respected it, it would be extremely difficult to restrain public feeling in this country." [1]

The ambassador then asked whether, if Germany promised to respect the neutrality of Belgium, Great Britain would engage to remain neutral. Sir Edward would only say that "our attitude would be determined very largely by public opinion, and the neutrality of Belgium would appeal very strongly to public opinion." Finally, pressed by the ambassador to formulate the conditions of British neutrality, including, it was suggested, the integrity of France and her colonies, Sir Edward "felt obliged to refuse definitely any promise to remain neutral on similar terms."

This incident has been very generally misunderstood. At first sight the British Government seems convicted, on its own evidence, of declining to formulate the conditions in which it would stand aside. Therefore, it is argued, England was committed to France and Russia. Nothing is

---

[1] British, no. 123.

farther from the truth. In the first place, Prince Lichnowsky credited Sir Edward Grey with saying that "for the time there was not the slightest intention to proceed in a hostile manner against us," and that "it would be their desire to avoid this if there was any possibility of doing so."[1] Next, as Sir Edward later pointed out, the offers of Prince Lichnowsky were entirely unofficial and quite contrary to the terms proposed officially by the German chancellor; also that so far was the German Government from guaranteeing the neutrality of Belgium that two days later it was asking Great Britain not to make that neutrality one of the conditions of her own neutrality.[2] Third, the circumstances of the moment must be fully considered. Sir Edward Grey knew that Germany had required Russia to demobilize within twelve hours and had asked France what her intentions were; at the same time Austro-Russian conversations were proceeding. The German declaration of war was on its way, but this was not known in London. There was the barest chance that peace might still be kept, but that chance depended upon the uncertainty as to the British attitude. If Great Britain definitely promised to stand aside, the last restraint on Germany would be removed. Sir Edward Grey could not regard the overtures of Prince Lichnowsky as other than a bribe, which was unacceptable, no matter what the terms were. The only sound policy for the British Government was to stand firm against all temptations, whether from Germany or France, and to keep its hands free, and this policy it adopted; for, if Sir Edward Grey would not promise British neutrality to Germany, neither would he promise British assistance to France. The wisdom of this decision became apparent when the news arrived that the German authorities at

[1] Telegrams in *Norddeutsche Allgemeine Zeitung*, 6 September, 1914, no. 2. (*Collected Diplomatic Documents*, p. 541.)

[2] French, no. 144; *cf.* also the appeal to British public opinion, published by the German embassy on 3 August, 1914, and British, no. 157.

Hamburg were detaining British merchant ships.[1] Such measures certainly cast a doubt upon the sincerity with which the German Government was angling for the neutrality of England, and more than justified the waiting attitude of Sir Edward Grey.

From now on events marched rapidly. "Very early" Sunday morning German troops penetrated into the Grand Duchy of Luxemburg by the bridges of Wasserbillig and Remich, in spite of the protests of the Grand Ducal Government.[2] Whether this news turned the scale in the British cabinet—which was still discussing the question of neutrality—in favor of intervention cannot be ascertained. Under the terms of the treaty of 1867, as interpreted by Lord Derby and Lord Clarendon, the British Government was bound to act only if all the guaranteeing Powers agreed to do so. The *Times*, however, demanded immediate action on the ground that Belgium would be the next victim. At all events, after the cabinet, Sir Edward Grey gave the following memorandum to the French ambassador:

"I am authorized to give an assurance that, if the German fleet comes into the Channel or through the North Sea to undertake hostile operations against French coasts or shipping, the British fleet will give all protection in its power.

"This assurance is, of course, subject to the policy of His Majesty's Government receiving the support of Parliament, and must not be taken as binding His Majesty's Government to take any action until the above contingency of action by the German fleet takes place."[3]

Sir Edward Grey also informed M. Paul Cambon that the British Government was considering whether it should make the violation of Belgian neutrality a *casus belli*.

[1] British, no. 130.
[2] British, no. 147; French, no. 131; Belgian, no. 18.
[3] British, no. 148; French, no. 137.

The next day, 3 August, the decision was taken to regard the Belgian question in this light, and this, together with the promise of assistance to France, received the support of both Houses of Parliament, after Sir Edward Grey, in a masterly speech, had explained his policy and the obligations of the government.[1]

The foreign secretary admitted that no legal obligations bound Great Britain to assist France, for the exchange of letters of 22 November, 1912, left the hands of both governments free to take what decision the circumstances of the moment required. But, since the French Government, relying on the friendship of England, had withdrawn its fleet from the Channel and concentrated it in the Mediterranean, the British Government was morally bound, urged Sir Edward Grey, to protect the undefended coasts of France. The question, however, was not so much one of sentiment as of British interests, and it was primarily on the ground of British interests that Parliament was asked to approve the promise of naval assistance. The distinction is all-important. If Sir Edward Grey had limited his argument to the moral duty of England to support France, it is problematical whether he would have carried the House of Commons with him. But when he said that British interests required a certain policy he aroused the patriotism of members and achieved an overwhelming victory. Sordid reasoning, perhaps. But does it not show that as the situation stood on 3 August, 1914, Sir Edward Grey did not consider that British interests demanded the despatch of an expeditionary force to the Continent? He did not hint at this in the course of his speech, except in case Great Britain should be called upon to defend the neutrality of Belgium. This is not to say that ultimately a British army might not have been sent to the assistance of France. But it is useless to discuss possibilities. The

[1] 5 Hansard lxv, cc. 1809-27.

essential fact is that Great Britain, with perfect freedom, did not go beyond the offer of naval assistance in a defined contingency.

Now, just before Sir Edward Grey went to the House of Commons he was informed that Germany was prepared to pledge herself not to attack the coasts of France in return for British neutrality. Sir Edward declared that this offer was "far too narrow an engagement," because it did not guarantee the neutrality of Belgium, although Germany was ready to respect its territorial integrity and independence.[1] If to this offer Germany had been willing to add the neutrality of Belgium, it would have been practically impossible for Great Britain to join France and Russia against Germany. Her own conditions would have been accepted by Germany; she would have had no case before the world; her public opinion would not have sanctioned a war in which British interests were not directly involved, even though the balance of power would have been upset by a German victory over France.

In their book, *Why We Are at War: Great Britain's Case*, the members of the Oxford faculty of modern history say:

"History will doubtless attribute the outbreak of war between ourselves and Germany to the development of the Belgian question, and, we are confident, will judge that, had it not been for the gratuitous attack made on a neutral country by Germany, war with Great Britain would not have ensued on 4 August, 1914." [2]

With this opinion the present writer is in complete agreement. Sir Edward Grey may possibly have desired a general commitment to France; he did not advocate it to Parliament, and his straightforward character and honesty forbid us to believe that he would have concealed a per-

[1] British, no. 157; Herr von Bethmann-Hollweg, Reichstag, 4 August, 1914.
[2] P. 90.

sonal opinion of such magnitude. He relied frankly on public sentiment, and it is generally agreed that, until Belgium appealed for British help against Germany, the sentiment of England was averse to intervention in the terrible struggle.   Once she decided to make war, England would fight for her own interests as well as those of Belgium.   But there is nothing in the published evidence to show that her declaration of war was dictated by a considered hostility to Germany, or that she avoided a single effort which would have enabled her honorably and with a rightful concern for her own national interests to remain at peace.

The rest of the story can be quite briefly told.   As early as 24 July the Belgian Government was considering what action would be required of Belgium "to fulfil the international obligations imposed upon her by treaty in the event of a war breaking out on her frontiers." [1]   On 29 July the army was placed on "a strengthened peace footing," [2] and on the 31st mobilization was ordered, before the British minister had communicated the note from Sir Edward Grey asking Belgium "to do her utmost to maintain her neutrality." [3]   On the same day, however, the German minister was informed that Belgium's military preparations in no way implied an attitude of distrust toward her neighbors,[4] but that she must fulfil her obligations.   Thus before Sir Edward Grey raised the question of her neutrality Belgium was preparing to resist any attempt to infringe it: she did not resist under British pressure, as has been alleged by Germany.   Indeed, on 1 August, as soon as the refusal of Herr von Jagow to answer Sir Edward Grey's question became known in Brussels, the Belgian representatives to the guaranteeing Powers were instructed to inform those Powers that, although Bel-

[1] Belgian, no. 2.   [2] Belgian, no. 8.
[3] Belgian, no. 10.   [4] Belgian, no. 12.

gium confidently expects that her territory "will remain free from attack," nevertheless "all necessary steps to insure respect of Belgian neutrality have been taken by the government." [1] On Sunday, 2 August, M. Davignon, the Belgian foreign minister, and Herr von Below-Saleske, the German minister, were assuring each other of the "perfect correctness" in the relations of their two countries. [2]

At 7 P. M. Herr von Below met M. Davignon again— to present a note proposing friendly neutrality, and allowing twelve hours for a reply.

"Reliable information has been received by the German Government," declared the ultimatum, "to the effect that French forces intend to march on the line of the Meuse by Givet and Namur. This information leaves no doubt as to the intention of France to march through Belgian territory."

Therefore the German Government demanded a free passage for its troops through Belgium, in return for which it guaranteed to maintain the independence of Belgium in full, to evacuate Belgian territory on the conclusion of peace, and to pay an indemnity for any damage caused by the German troops. But, should Belgium oppose the advance of the German troops, she would be treated as an enemy, and "the eventual adjustment of the relations between the two states must be left to the decision of arms." [3] At 1.30 A. M. on 3 August the German minister came again to the foreign office to say that "French dirigibles had thrown bombs, and that a French cavalry patrol had crossed the frontier" into Germany; "these acts, which were contrary to international law, were calculated to lead to the supposition that other acts contrary to international law would be committed by France"! [4]

The German ultimatum "made a deep and painful im-

---

[1] Belgian, nos. 16, 2 (enclosure).   [2] Belgian, no. 19.
[3] Belgian, no. 20.   [4] Belgian, no. 21.

pression upon the Belgian Government," which replied with a considered refusal,[1] and informed the Powers that "Belgium was firmly resolved to repel any attack by all means in her power." [2]   But as no act of hostility was committed by Germany on 3 August, although the ultimatum expired at 7 A. M., the Belgian Government did not appeal to the Powers for assistance.   It contented itself with the despatch of a telegram from King Albert to King George, making "a supreme appeal to the diplomatic intervention of Your Majesty's Government to safeguard the integrity of Belgium." [3]   At 6 A. M., on 4 August the German minister communicated a second note, announcing the intention of his government "to take—if necessary by force of arms—those measures of defense already foreshadowed as indispensable, in view of the menace of France." [4]   But still Belgium waited.   Both Great Britain and France offered their assistance to the harassed little kingdom,[5] but not until the evening of 4 August, until the Belgian frontier had actually been violated at Gemmenich,[6] did the Belgian Government appeal to Great Britain, France, and Russia, "to co-operate as guaranteeing Powers in the defense of her territory." [7]   "We see in this narrative how scrupulously careful the Belgian Government was to avoid the slightest sign of suspicion, the slightest inclination to one of the guaranteeing Powers rather than the other, the slightest confession of mistrust—in short, the smallest movement in any direction, by word or deed, which could furnish the shadow of a pretext for such charges as those which have since actually been made." [8]

With regard to the German allegations that France had violated the neutrality of Belgium, it is sufficient to ob-

---

[1] Belgian, no. 22.   [2] Belgian, no. 23.   [3] Belgian, no. 25.
[4] Belgian, no. 27; British, no. 154; French, no. 154.
[5] British, nos. 151, 155; French, no. 142; Belgian, nos. 24, 28, 37.
[6] Belgian, no. 30; British, no. 158; French, no. 151.
[7] Belgian, no. 40; French, no. 152.   [8] *Collected Diplomatic Documents*, p. xvi.

serve: first, that the German ultimatum speaks only of the intentions of France; second, that Herr von Bethmann-Hollweg, in the Reichstag on 4 August, simply said that "France stood ready for an invasion," although he admitted that "the French Government declared at Brussels that France would respect Belgian neutrality as long as her adversary respected it"; and third, that the French campaign, so far from being launched through Belgium, was actually directed into Alsace and Lorraine. Subsequently, the Germans charged that French officers were sent to the Liège forts, and that the British had accumulated supplies in Maubeuge, before the outbreak of war. No proof of either charge was ever produced, and both were denied by the interested governments. There seems to be no adequate ground for assertions that either England or France had in any manner trespassed upon Belgian soil before their assistance was formally invited by the Belgian Government. With quite exemplary frankness Herr von Jagow brushed aside all such quibbles when Sir Edward Goschen made a final appeal to him "to avoid the terrible consequences which would necessarily ensue."

"Herr von Jagow at once replied that he was sorry to say that his answer must be 'No,' as, in consequence of the German troops having crossed the frontier that morning, *Belgian neutrality had already been violated;* Herr von Jagow again went into the reasons why the imperial government had been obliged to take this step, namely, that they had to advance into France by the quickest and easiest way, so as to be able to get well ahead with their preparations and endeavor to strike some decisive blow as soon as possible. It was a matter of life and death for them, as, if they had gone by the more southern route they could not have hoped, in view of the paucity of roads and the strength of the fortresses, to have got through without formidable opposition entailing great loss of time. This loss of time would have meant time gained by the Russians for bringing up their troops to the German frontier." [1]

[1] British, no. 160.

When King Albert's telegram to King George had been considered and when Sir Edward Goschen reported that there was "no information available" about the detention of British ships at Hamburg,[1] Sir Edward Grey sent an exceedingly stiff note to Berlin. Quoting the text of the Belgian King's appeal, he said:

"His Majesty's Government are also informed that the German Government have delivered to the Belgian Government a note proposing friendly neutrality entailing free passage through Belgian territory, and promising to maintain the independence and integrity of the kingdom and its possessions at the conclusion of peace, threatening in case of a refusal to treat Belgium as an enemy. An answer was requested within twelve hours.

"We also understand that Belgium has categorically refused this as a flagrant violation of the law of nations.

"His Majesty's Government are bound to protest against this violation of a treaty to which Germany is a party in common with themselves, and must request an assurance that the demand made upon Belgium will not be proceeded with, and that her neutrality will be respected by Germany. You should ask for an immediate reply." [2]

In the course of the day the British Government learned of the second German note and the violation of Belgian territory by German troops.[3] Herr von Jagow sought to "dispel any mistrust . . . by repeating most positively [the] formal assurance that, even in the case of armed conflict with Belgium, Germany will, under no pretext whatever, annex Belgian territory," the sincerity of this pledge to be guaranteed by the promise to respect the neutrality of Holland. "It is obvious that we could not profitably annex Belgian territory without making at the same time territorial acquisitions at the expense of Holland." [4] But such a promise, coming as it did from a government which had already broken a much more solemn obligation—a

---

[1] British, no. 150.
[3] British, nos. 154, 158; Belgian, no. 36.
[2] British, no. 153.
[4] British, no. 157.

formal treaty—was obviously worthless, and did not meet the unassailable objection that the neutrality of Belgium had been devised to prevent, not to encourage, war. So Sir Edward Grey despatched his ultimatum:

"We hear that Germany has addressed a note to Belgian minister for foreign affairs stating that German Government will be compelled to carry out—if necessary by force of arms—the measures considered indispensable.

"We are also informed that Belgian territory has been violated at Gemmenich.

"In these circumstances, and in view of the fact that Germany declined to give the same assurance respecting Belgium as France gave last week in reply to our request made simultaneously at Berlin and Paris, we must repeat that request, and ask that a satisfactory reply to it and to my telegram of this morning be received here by twelve o'clock to-night. If not, you are instructed to ask for your passports, and to say that His Majesty's Government feel bound to take all steps in their power to uphold the neutrality of Belgium and the observance of a treaty to which Germany is as much a party as ourselves." [1]

As is well known, Herr von Jagow informed the British ambassador that "to his great regret he could give no other answer than that which he had given earlier in the day." The ambassador then proceeded to visit the chancellor, who said that "just for a word—'neutrality'—word which in war time had so often been disregarded—just for a scrap of paper Great Britain was going to make war on a kindred nation who desired nothing better than to be friends with her." [2] Herr von Bethmann-Hollweg subsequently sought to explain away the fatal words. He had meant that Great Britain was availing herself of Belgian neutrality as a pretext to engage in a war to which she was already committed. The argument, however, will not be accepted by those who accept the thesis advanced in previous paragraphs—that Belgian neutrality was the *actual* and not the

[1] British, no. 159; Belgian, no. 39.   [2] British, no. 160.

assumed cause of the British declaration of war. In any case, the Germans have been too fertile in finding excuses for their acts after they have been condemned by the conscience of the world.

The reflection is inevitably suggested by the German violation of Belgian neutrality that it was designed not merely as a step in the conquest of France, but as an incentive to involve Great Britain in the war. If the history of England holds one hackneyed fact, it is that the island kingdom has always resisted any attempt upon the liberties of the Low Countries. Germany was as aware of this as any one else, and must have counted the consequences. It is possible that Herr von Bethmann-Hollweg and Herr von Jagow hoped to cajole Great Britain into standing aside; but the military party, which was always the centre of the Anglophobe agitation, can have had no illusions. After all, Germany could not achieve her self-imposed destiny until she had destroyed the existing British Empire; so that, if England had bargained away her obligation to defend Belgium, she would one day have had to withstand unaided the attack of a Germany that had achieved an easy victory over France and Russia. That Germany would have been immeasurably more powerful, more aggressive, than the Germany of 1914. Thus England's interest quite as much as England's honor compelled her to take sides in the Great War, and it is no reproach to her that she made the two identical and declared war to preserve both.

There may have been another motive for the invasion of Belgium. For years Germany has looked longingly toward the Congo. The chancellor has said that on 4 August he "already had certain indications, but no absolute proof upon which to base a public accusation, that Belgium long before had abandoned its neutrality in its relations with England." This not only confirms the argument of the last paragraph, but suggests that Germany knew that Belgium would resist her infringement of neutrality. But Herr von Jagow assured Sir Edward Grey that Germany would not annex Belgian territory, meaning, according to the context, Belgian territory in Europe. Yet Belgium assuredly would not go unpunished for resistance to German arms. The penalty might be paid in Africa, by the cession of the Congo. This also would have affected British interests under certain conditions, and was perhaps an additional factor in convincing Sir Edward Grey that England must protest to the bitter end against all pressure upon Belgium in whatever guise it might be invoked.

This is the end of our story. It has not been contended in this book that all the right in the Anglo-German controversy has been on one side and all the wrong on the other. It has been freely admitted that at times the attitude of both the British Government and the British people was not friendly to the aims and aspirations of Germany. But it has been argued that much the greater share of the provocation came from Germany, and that the English position from first to last was essentially defensive. Furthermore, in the two years before the war a determined effort was made by England to heed such complaints of Germany as could be met by reasonable concessions, and with such apparent success that an adjustment of all difficulties seemed possible. In the negotiations preceding the war, however, these hopeful auguries were not fulfilled, and despite the strenuous efforts of Sir Edward Grey Germany allowed the war to come—even precipitated it herself. Thus Germany must bear almost the entire responsibility for the fatal ending of her rivalry with England.

This fact is too apt to be overlooked, now that the world is weary of the great struggle and longs passionately for peace. But for England there can be no bargaining for peace until Belgium is restored to her independence and integrity, until France is secured against future aggression, the rights of small nations vindicated, and the Prussian military machine defeated. It is a formidable programme, and at the moment of writing (September, 1915) the prospect is anything but cheering for the Allies. But to talk of peace now—except in the unimaginable hypothesis that Germany will evacuate Belgium and Poland—is futile, for it would be tantamount to admitting the justice of German aggression. Britain's record in the past is not unstained, and even in this war she has done some things that are not palatable to American tastes. But, compared with the crimson offenses of Germany, her peccadilloes are insignificant. Until Great Britain and Greater Britain are actually beaten to their knees, we shall continue to believe that Germany will be punished for having unchained this terrible war; and we take courage from the glorious past. To the lover of liberty and the opponent of forceful domination, the situation need not seem less hopeless than was the state of affairs about 1811, when the whole of Europe, except England, lay prostrate at the feet of Napoleon. The Napoleonic Empire collapsed with nerve-racking suddenness. We are permitted to hope that British stubbornness, British credit, British valor will yet, with the assistance of its allies, prevail against the forces of militarism and absolutism, and that the German *débacle*, far off as it may be, is as inevitable as the fall of the first French empire.

APPENDIX

SINCE this book was written the German Government has published, under the title *European Politics in the Decade before the War as Described by Belgian Diplomatists*, a series of secret reports made to the Belgian Government in the years 1905-14, by its ministers in London, Paris, and Berlin. Found in Brussels when that city was occupied by the German army, the reports are published with the remark that they "provide a running commentary on European history during the past decade, throwing light which, once shed, could by no means ever be spared, on the causes of the cataclysm through which Europe is now passing." The future historian is assured that the documents "will rank high" among the sources to which he will turn in the writing of a definitive narrative:

"They are not the words of German apologists. They are the words of disinterested expert observers—the considered words, though set down in the very midst of events as they pass. They register the convictions of five professional students of contemporary international history, living in the three chief capitals of Europe and possessing unparalleled access to the facts, with the advantage of being detached and unprejudiced with regard to them."

The despatches are supposed to prove that England enticed France—and later Russia—to oppose Germany, and engineered a campaign for the diplomatic isolation of the great Empire in central Europe. Much is also made of reports from the legation in Paris respecting the revival in France of the idea of *revanche*, for which President Poincaré chiefly, and to a lesser extent M. Delcassé, are held responsible. Russian diplomatists are criticised by the minister in Berlin for their personal ambitions and lack of discipline. In short, it is contended, the documents prove the entire correctness of German policy in the ten years before the war and its eminently peaceful character.

499

"A more complete indictment of English statesmanship," concludes the introduction, "as the enemy of the peace of the world, a deliberate and persistent conspirator against an unoffending neighbor, could not possibly be framed."

As to the renascence of French patriotism, chauvinism if one likes, after the crisis of 1911, no one ever denied it, but surely the conduct of Germany in that year and the subsequent increases of the German army were as much responsible as the fact that M. Poincaré came from Lorraine and neglected no opportunity to remind France of the lost province. The "revelations" about French policy in Morocco and the willingness of Great Britain to assist France in that matter contain nothing that was not known to students of diplomacy; as a matter of fact, the points made by the Belgian ministers have been discussed in Chapters IX and XI of this book.

The criticisms of Russian policy, although they reflect the irritation of the German Government at the Anglo-Russian agreement, which had been considered impossible, refer chiefly to the period of the Balkan Wars. They do not extend beyond the fact that Russia was behind the Balkan League and supported the contentions of Serbia against Austria; but they testify to the pacific intentions of M. Sazonof, and do not mention that on the advice of Russia Serbia receded from her position and acceded to the demands of Austria. The comments of the Belgian minister in Vienna are not published.

The minister in London seems to have been genuinely suspicious of the British attitude toward Germany, but he adduces no new facts. He merely repeats the hackneyed charge that England was jealous of German commercial expansion, laying special emphasis on the activities of the late King Edward VII. But he does not go so far as his colleague in Berlin, who wrote (no. 85) that "everybody in England and France considers the *entente cordiale* as a defensive and offensive alliance against Germany"; on the contrary, Count de Lalaing in one despatch (no. 11) remarked that England was "evidently animated by the desire to avoid a conflict." The criticisms of English policy furnished by the Belgian minister cannot be ignored, but, after

all, he was only an observer, and other observers, probably as
acute as himself, have formed other opinions. It is pertinent
to ask: If the Belgian Government shared his views as to the
danger to Belgium from British or French policy, why did it
permit the conversations between the British and Belgian military authorities concerning the defense of Belgian neutrality?
Is it not likely that, with all due respect to Count de Lalaing
and his colleagues in Paris and Berlin, King Albert's Government regarded the danger as greater from the German than
from the Anglo-French side?

It is, indeed, quite impossible to accept the Belgian testimony
at the value placed upon it by the German foreign office.
There are constantly references, in the despatches from each
capital, to reports which are not published. Whether the Germans found these reports in the Brussels archives and suppressed them is not known, but the historian will insist on seeing them before forming a final opinion on the attitude of any
Belgian minister. Again, there are no reports from Vienna,
Rome, or St. Petersburg, reports which might very well contra-
dict the opinions of the ministers in the other three capitals.
Thirdly, sixty of the one hundred and nineteen despatches
come from the legation in Berlin, forty-nine during the incum-
bency of Baron Greindl, who was notoriously anti-English and
anti-French in his views and descants at length upon the supposed intentions of London and Paris. His successor, Baron
Beyens, was more impartial; incidentally, he remarks in one
place (no. 113) that his view "may be wrong or influenced by
the reading of political writings emanating from German pens."

The reports do not cover all the events of the years 1905–14.
The Baghdad railway is scarcely mentioned; the Turkish revolution not at all. The Austrian railway scheme of 1908 is referred to once casually; the annexation of Bosnia-Herzegovina
in two despatches. The Franco-German convention of February, 1909 about Morocco and its subsequent history is ignored. The truth is, the reports, as they stand, give a very
incomplete view of the multifarious activities of European
diplomacy, and with possibly two exceptions bring to light no
facts which were not known to students of contemporary history.

Finally, the German foreign office is not content to let the documents speak for themselves. Forgetful that its *White Book*, published at the outbreak of the war, failed to carry conviction, because it presented a German interpretation of events supported by occasional telegrams, instead of publishing the diplomatic correspondence *in extenso*, it has prepared an introduction to the present collection. By removing selected passages from their context it is possible to make out a brilliant case against the *Entente* Powers, but sometimes this procedure is dishonest. The introduction prints this question, raised by Baron Beyens on 24 April, 1914:

"We have had the proof that a co-operation of the British army and the despatching of an expeditionary corps to the Continent have been considered by the military authorities of the two governments (England and France).

"Would it be the same to-day, and *should we still have to fear* THE ENTRY OF BRITISH SOLDIERS INTO BELGIUM IN ORDER TO HELP US DEFEND OUR NEUTRALITY BY FIRST COMPROMISING IT?"

But it does not print Baron Beyens's answer to his own question:

"If the question is examined from the German point of view— the only one which I can consider a negative answer is not doubtful" (!)

In general, the introduction never refers to certain statements of the ministers in Paris and Berlin, that the people of France were peace-loving, and that the policy of their government was, on the whole, animated by similar motives, even though it was often subjected to pressure from the small but noisy war party. Thus Baron Guillaume, the minister in Paris, writing on 25 April, 1914, says, *à propos* of Anglo-French relations:

"They have during the last months given undisputable proofs of their efficacy and they were favorable for the maintenance of general peace, while at the same time they were not in the way of other attempts at *rapprochement* which equally furthered the European equilibrium." (No. 114.)

Nor would the reader of the introduction learn that an Anglo-German *détente* was being prepared on the eve of the war, although there is some evidence of it in the despatches themselves. To make matters worse, black letters, and sometimes capitals, are used to emphasize those passages of the documents which are favorable to the German case.

It would be idle to ignore these Belgian reports, for they are almost the only documents covering the years 1905–14 that have come to light; but they are incomplete: they may be quoted against France and England, but they do not establish a case that is irrefutable.

Another collection of documents has also appeared too late for use in the writing of this book. It is the second Belgian *Grey Book*. The first *Grey Book* dealt with the action of the Brussels Government to preserve its neutrality in the struggle which was felt to be impending after the presentation of the Austrian ultimatum to Serbia. In this volume we are allowed to see the impressions made upon the Belgian ministers in the several capitals by the diplomacy of the Great Powers in July–August, 1914. And since the German foreign office, in the collection of despatches reviewed above, was pleased to insist upon the impartiality of the Belgian diplomatists, it is worth while to notice what these gentlemen say about the course of events immediately preceding the Great War.

In general, the ministers in Paris, Berlin, Vienna, and St. Petersburg testify to the absolute loyalty of the *Entente* governments in trying to preserve peace, and to an equally determined refusal on the part of Germany and Austria to give heed to warnings or expostulations. Space permits only a few citations from the correspondence. Count Errembault de Dudzeele at Vienna and Baron Beyens at Berlin agree that Count Berchtold's policy was influenced largely by the desire to recover the prestige which had been shattered by his conduct during the Balkan Wars (nos. 3, 6). They also believe that he would not have proceeded so recklessly without inspiration from Berlin (nos. 8, 9). Baron Beyens is inclined to believe that the German foreign office would have liked to see a peaceful solution of the crisis (nos. 6, 52), but "a superior power intervened to precipitate the march of events." The minister in St. Petersburg quotes the French ambassador in that capital to the effect that Count Pourtalès worked for peace (no. 17). Baron Beyens specifically ascribes the attitude of the German Emperor to "the opinion which prevails in the German general staff that war with France and Russia is unavoidable and near —*an opinion which the Emperor has been induced to share*" (no. 8). The Emperor's hatred of regicide also played its part in bringing about his decision. With respect to the Emperor's exchange of telegrams with the Tsar, Baron Beyens writes on 1 August, 1914 (no. 20):

"The German Government seems to have arranged this scenario in order to lead up to the war, which it seeks to render inevitable, but the responsibility for which it desires to throw upon Russia."

Reference was made on p. 472 to the intercepted despatch of the Belgian chargé in St. Petersburg, according to which Russia was sure of British support as early as 29 July. To the reasons there given for rejecting this interpretation may be added the statement of the Belgian minister, who returned to his post on 31 July (no. 17):

"I have just had a talk with the British ambassador. He tells me that M. Sazonof had tried from the outset to ascertain the intentions of the London Government, but, up till now, in spite of the mobilization of the British fleet, Sir George Buchanan has not yet been instructed to make any communication of this kind to the Pont des Chantres. The instructions of the ambassador are to explain to St. Petersburg that if Russia desires the support of Great Britain, it must carefully avoid even the appearance of any aggressive step in the present crisis."

As regards the conduct of Belgium, three despatches may be noted. On 22 February, 1913, Baron Guillaume, the minister in Paris, explained to the French foreign office that "it was the intention of Belgium to possess an army which should be strong enough to be taken seriously, and which would allow her to fulfil completely her duty of safeguarding her independence of neutrality" (no. 1). This ought to dispose of the German contention that Belgium had sold herself to England by the conversations of 1906 and 1912, even if there were not recorded the categorical declaration of Baron Beyens to Herr Zimmermann, of the German foreign office, that "if France had been ready first and had demanded a passage of us on the same conditions as Germany, we should have made the same reply to her" (no. 52). Baron Beyens also forced from Herr von Jagow the admission: "Germany has nothing with which to reproach Belgium, whose attitude has always been correct." The German foreign secretary finally said that "as a private individual" he recognized the justice of Belgium's position, and that the violation of her neutrality was "the most painful resolution and the most cruel thing [he had] had to do throughout [his] career" (no. 51).

If Germany contends that the Belgian despatches from 1905 to 1914 establish the guilt of the *Entente* Powers, she must also admit that the second *Grey Book* disposes effectually of the thesis that she is not to blame for the outbreak of war on 1 August, 1914.

INDEX

Abbas II, Khedive of Egypt, 273.
Abdel Assiz, Sultan of Morocco, 229, 304.
Abdul Hamid, Sultan of Turkey, 142, 152, 260, 261, 262–263, 272, 278, 279–280, 281, 282, 283, 284.
Abyssinia, Anglo-French-Italian agreement of 1907 *in re*, 240.
Aden, 195.
Admiralty Memorandum (1912), 174.
Adrianople, 359.
Adriatic Sea, 240, 256, 287, 396.
Aerenthal, Baron von, Austrian foreign minister, 1906–1912, 286, 287, 291, 296, 402.
Affaires du Maroc (French *Yellow Books*), 224, 310.
Afghanistan, 5, 18, 21, 32, 241, 272.
Africa, 5, 15, 20–21, 28, 32, 78–79, 84–85, 135–137, 141–142, 144, 147, 239, 263, 272, 336, 343, 356, 371–372, 391–392, 497.
African Act (1885), 336.
Agadir, 302, 309, 312, 314–319, 321, 323, 325–327, 329, 332, 339.
Akaba, 272.
Albania, 256–257, 297, 362–364, 378, 395, 398.
Albert, King of the Belgians, 384–385, 392–393, 479–480, 492, 494, 501.
Albert, Prince Consort of Queen Victoria, 123, 125.
Aleppo, 272.
Alexander, Crown Prince and Prince Regent of Serbia, 412, 418.
Alexander, King of Serbia, 257.
Alexander, Prince, of Battenberg, 134.
Alexander I, of Russia, 120.
Alexandretta, 300.
Alexandria, 19, 178, 198.
Alfonso, King, of Spain, 29, 239.
Algeciras, Act of, 303–304, 306–307, 309, 313–314, 317, 326, 328, 342.
Algeria, 79, 230, 233.
Alsace-Lorraine, 46, 48–49, 118, 120, 128, 136, 139, 356, 374, 467, 493, 500.

Ameer of Afghanistan, 17, 29.
Amran, L. von, *Englands Land-und-See Politik und die Mächte*, 197.
"An Englishman's Home," 185.
Anatolian Railway Company, 266.
André, General, French war minister, 179.
Angell, Norman, 98; *The Great Illusion*, 63, 76, 355.
Anglo-Congolese treaty (1894), 141.
Anglo-Dutch wars, 198, 205.
Anglo-French arbitration treaty (1903), 25, 224; convention (8 April, 1904), 28, 139, 153, 180, 224, 235, 322, 323, 324, 326, 334, 342.
Anglo-German agreement *in re* Turkey and Africa (1914), 195, 367–377, 470; alliance, proposed (1899), 148–150; convention *in re* Africa (1890), 137, 139; convention *in re* China (October, 1900), 147, 150–151; treaty *in re* Portuguese colonies (1898), 85, 144, 346, 372.
Anglo-German-Japanese alliance, proposed (1901), 148.
Anglo-Japanese alliance (1902), 26, 28, 29, 148, 179, 243, 348.
Anglo-Portuguese alliance, 348, 371; treaty (1884), 136.
Anglo-Russian convention (31 August, 1907), 30, 241–242, 281–282, 286, 298, 379.
Anglo-Turkish agreement (1914), 370.
Angola, 372.
Angora, 266.
Angra Pequena, 78, 135, 145.
Anna, 279.
Annual Register, 145, 180, 224, 245, 250.
Arabi Pasha, 19.
Arabia, 253, 258, 262, 271, 275, 297.
Arbeiter Zeitung (Vienna), 461.
Arbitration, 25, 413, 428.
Armenia, 298; massacres, 259–260; reforms, 374.
Army and Navy Gazette, 206.

507

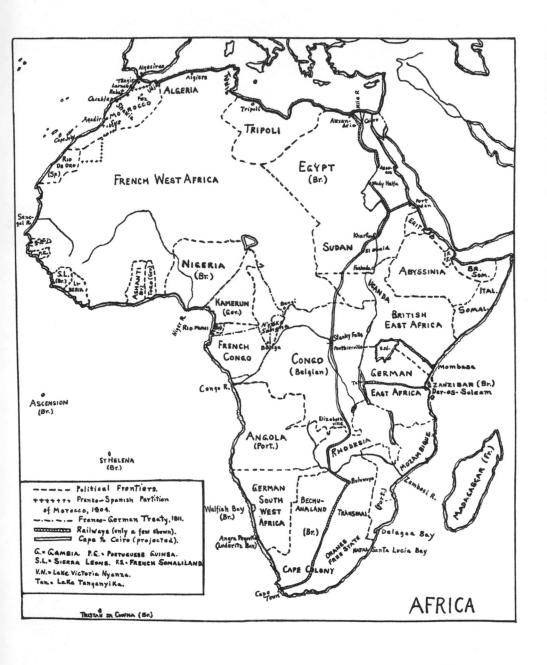

AFRICA

Legend:

- – – – – Political Frontiers.
- ✛✛✛✛✛✛ Franco-Spanish Partition of Morocco, 1904.
- –·–·–·– Franco-German Treaty, 1911.
- ▒▒▒▒▒▒ Railways (only a few shown).
- ━━━━━ Cape to Cairo (projected).

G. = Gambia. P.G. = Portuguese Guinea.
S.L. = Sierra Leone. F.S. = French Somaliland.
V.N. = Lake Victoria Nyanza.
Tan. = Lake Tanganyika.

Map labels:

- Algeciras
- Tangier
- Larache
- Rabat
- Casablanca
- Fez
- Agadir
- Mogador
- MOROCCO
- Cape Juby
- Rio De Oro (Sp.)
- Senegal R.
- S.L. (Br.)
- Liberia
- ALGERIA
- Algiers
- Tripoli
- TRIPOLI
- FRENCH WEST AFRICA
- ASHANTI
- Togo
- NIGERIA (Br.)
- KAMERUN (Ger.)
- Banzi
- N'gok Sanga
- Bonga
- Niger R.
- Rio Muni (Sp.)
- FRENCH CONGO
- Congo R.
- CONGO (Belgian)
- Stanley Falls
- Ponthierville
- Elizabethville
- ANGOLA (Port.)
- ASCENSION (Br.)
- St Helena (Br.)
- EGYPT (Br.)
- Alexandria
- Cairo
- Nile R.
- Assouan
- Wady Halfa
- Port Sudan
- Khartoum
- El Obeid
- Fashoda
- SUDAN
- ERITREA
- ABYSSINIA
- BR. SOM.
- ITAL.
- SOMAL.
- UGANDA
- BRITISH EAST AFRICA
- Mombasa
- V.N.
- GERMAN EAST AFRICA
- Tabora
- ZANZIBAR (Br.)
- Dar-es-Salaam
- Tan.
- RHODESIA
- Bulawayo
- MOZAMBIQUE (Port.)
- Zambesi R.
- MADAGASCAR (Fr.)
- GERMAN SOUTH WEST AFRICA
- Walfish Bay (Br.)
- Angra Pequena (Luderitz Bay)
- BECHUANALAND (Br.)
- TRANSVAAL
- ORANGE FREE STATE
- NATAL
- Delagoa Bay
- Santa Lucia Bay
- CAPE COLONY
- Cape Town
- Tristan da Cunha (Br.)

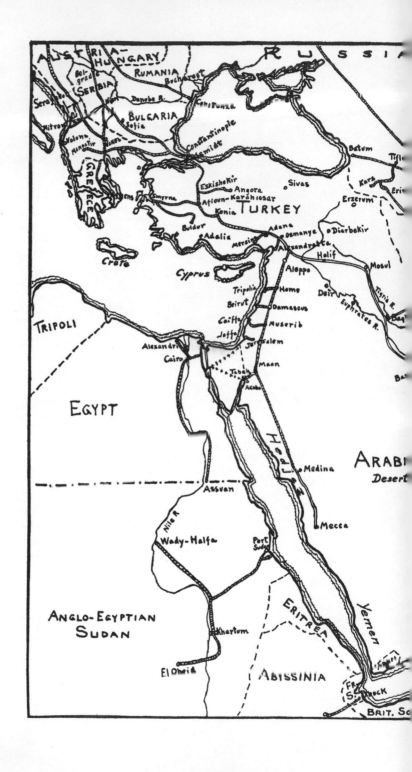

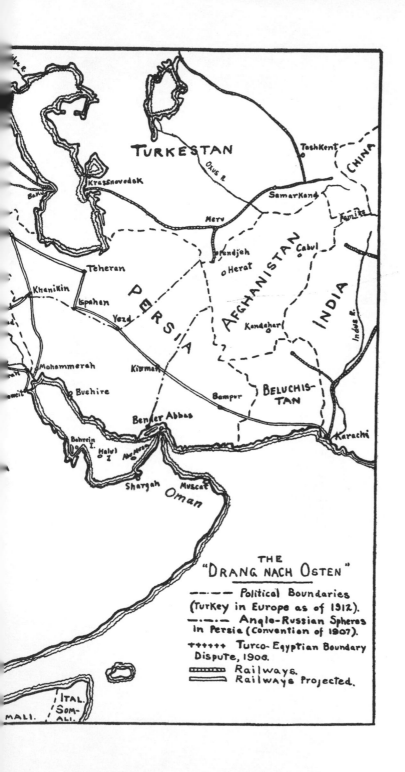

THE
"DRANG NACH OSTEN"

⋅—⋅⋅— Political Boundaries
(Turkey in Europe as of 1912).
—⋅—⋅— Anglo-Russian Spheres
in Persia (Convention of 1907).
+++++ Turco-Egyptian Boundary
Dispute, 1906.
▭▭▭▭ Railways.
▭▭▭▭ Railways Projected.